THE AGE OF MANUFACTURES, 1700–1820

Industry, innovation and work in Britain

SECOND EDITION

Maxine Berg

London and New York

Second edition published 1994
by Routledge
11 New Fetter Lane, London EC4P 4EE

Simultaneously published in the USA and Canada
by Routledge
29 West 35th Street, New York, NY 10001

Reprinted 1996

© 1994 Maxine Berg

Typeset in Garamond by
Florencetype Ltd, Stoodleigh, Devon

Printed and bound in Great Britain by
Biddles of Guildford

Printed on acid free paper

British Library Cataloguing in Publication Data
A catalogue record for this book is available from the British Library

Library of Congress Cataloguing in Publication Data
A catalogue record for this book is available from the Library of Congress

ISBN 0–415–06934–3 (hbk)
ISBN 0–415–06935–1 (pbk)

For the history students at Warwick University;
and for Michael Lebowitz who taught me as an undergraduate

CONTENTS

PLATES

FIGURES

TABLES

PREFACE

The first edition of this book was written nearly ten years ago. In the intervening years there has been a flowering of research on the eighteenth century. While this new edition does not address all of this history, it has in many ways been inspired by it.

The most important new perspectives on the eighteenth-century economy have been offered by N. F. R. Crafts and A. E. Wrigley, who have argued for slow continuous change and the handicap of a large and sluggish industrial sector. My original edition had argued the case for 'the other Industrial Revolution' which included domestic industry and artisan workshops at least as much as the factory system. It argued for an Industrial Revolution which relied on tools, small machines and skilled labour much more than it did on steam engines and automatic processes, and an Industrial Revolution which was created by women and children at least as much as it was by male artisans and factory workers. This new edition affirms this position, but sets it much more explicitly apart from the slow growth formulae of Crafts and Wrigley.

Friends and colleagues working on a range of eighteenth-century subjects have provided new insights and evidence which have reshaped some of my arguments and helped to confirm others. These have included Robert Allen and Jeanette Neeson on agriculture and common right, Pat Hudson on regions, Jan de Vries and Amanda Vickery on consumption, Patrick O'Brien on trade, Joel Mokyr and David Landes on technology, and Pamela Sharpe and Brenda Collins on women's industries. Ruth Pearson has continued to illuminate for me the connections between current new technologies and women's work. Against the background of this research the new edition of *The Age of Manufactures* like the old still provides the only easily accessible overview of manufacturing during the eighteenth century. The history of manufacture is placed within the framework of debates about the Industrial Revolution and of changes in agriculture and international markets. It remains, however, essentially a history of the technologies, forms of work organization and the labour forces of Britain's key industries during the period.

The book has benefited especially from work which Pat Hudson and I did together for our article, 'Rehabilitating the Industrial Revolution', and our many discussions on these topics over the years. I am grateful as well to R. N. Nash and James Thomson who read the book in full, and provided helpful criticisms and suggestions. The Simon Fellowship at Manchester University gave me the time to revise the book, at the same time as pursuing new research.

John Robertson has kept me conscious of how all this fits with broader historical issues, and my three daughters have grown more vociferous in their efforts, still unsuccessful, to banish history and the Industrial Revolution from the kitchen table.

INTRODUCTION

My introduction to the first edition of this book was written in the very different economic climate of the early 1980s, and in the different intellectual climate which then prevailed, where industrial and social revolutions were still considered to be formative of our modern identity.

My book then was about industry and technology; it placed these at the centre of an account of the Industrial Revolution. For over a generation accounts had focused on the 'macroeconomics' of the Industrial Revolution – patterns of economic growth, capital formation, demand, income distribution and economic fluctuations made up the rather dull Anglo-American cuisine of the student diet. Indeed students in numbers studied economic history in Coventry, Birmingham, Leeds, Liverpool and Manchester, and found it increasingly easy to understand their subject without noticing the cities they lived in and without visiting the factories and workplaces which gave these places an industrial identity.

I hoped that my book would make a difference to this. It was meant to bring to light the long and varied experience of organizational and technological change in manufacture going back to the early eighteenth century. My book was about the content of that manufacture, not just its results in the indices of economic growth. The economy I analysed was not one of economic indicators and national accounts. It was made up of the people and processes of industry, their work, their inventions and their communities. It was furthermore a book which brought out of the shadow cast by quantitative history the processes of manufacture and parts of the labour force, especially women, children and the unskilled, which played a central role not reflected in official statistics. The book raised innumerable questions over criteria for 'transition', 'successes' and 'failures', and charted the different technological choices and routes of industrial development. It challenged former apocalyptic metaphors of change and the much-vaunted achievements of factory and large-scale power technologies. It called for new research into a whole range of industries which we still know little about, and enquiry into the social realities behind the changes in productivity at the time. My book was intended, if metaphor be allowed, to recreate a Babette's

1

feast of trades, crafts, new products and industries, of girls, old women and mothers, as well as of proud artisans and casual labourers, of machines, tools and skills.

A new historical framework is now on the agenda, and I have written a new edition of the book to engage with this. First, a new economic climate has emerged from the restructuring of the 1970s and 1980s. The major feature of the 1780s to 1830s was the rise in the place of industry. Where industry's share in national product rose from 23 per cent in 1801 to 34 per cent in 1840, and on to 40 per cent in 1901, in the early 1990s that trend has been sharply reversed. In the course of two decades from 1973 to 1990 manufacturing's share of gross domestic product fell from 30 per cent to 20 per cent. Britain's manufacture of capital and intermediate goods and components all but dropped out of world trade during the 1980s. During the recession of the 1990s the industrial towns of the Midlands and the North are in decline and demoralization. The factories and the workshops neglected by a past generation of students, by governments and by our cultural icons are now only skeletons.

David Lodge wrote about this in *Nice Work*, published in 1988 at the peak of a boom. He described the industrial suburbs of Birmingham, once the Black Country, as

> a district dominated by factories, large and small, old and new. Many are silent, some derelict, their windows starred with smashed glass. Receiverships and closures have ravaged the area in recent years, giving a desolate look to its streets . . . A factory is sustained by the energy of its own functioning, the throb and whine of machinery, the clash of metal, the unceasing motion of the assembly lines, the ebb and flow of workers changing shifts, the hiss of airbrakes and the growl of diesel engines from wagons delivering raw materials at one gate, taking away finished goods at the other. When you put a stop to all that, when the place is silent and empty, all that is left is a large, ramshackle shed – cold, filthy and depressing.[1]

The result of this economic decline and the savage reduction of the country's industrial heartland has been a period of prolonged introspection over the national identity. As Linda Colley has put it, the British 'came to define themselves as a single people not because of any political or cultural consensus at home, but rather in reaction to the Other beyond their shores'.[2] One part of this reaction was in defining themselves as the first industrial nation. That identity as 'first' has long disappeared, now so too has that of 'industrial' nation. The industry has, indeed, become part of the iconography of past glories – long-abandoned industrial sites have been made a part of the national heritage, a new picturesque landscape, a postmodern comment on the pastoral picturesque scenes of the eighteenth century. Those landscapes were not 'natural' as the poets and painters tried to present them, nor the remains of an ancient rural birthright. They were the deindustrialized and poverty-stricken regions of Scotland, Wales, the South-West and other 'marginalized' communities of Britain.[3] Our new industrial picturesque is likewise a celebration of a past at some remove from the industrial unemployment of the present.

A part of that introspection, however, has also been a calling to account of the industrial past. At one level this has been a questioning of the 'sacred cows' of the postwar boom – the heavy capital investment, large-scale industry and regional concentration. The failings of our own heavily capitalized, large-scale factories have been measured against the revival of alternative smaller-scale units elsewhere. And the inflexibilities and industrial conflict of hierarchically organized systems of management have entailed new attempts at network capitalism, just-in-time production systems, franchises, subcontracting and co-operative ventures. Smoke stack capitalism has had its day, its assembly lines and 'ramshackle sheds' abandoned for the airport and motorway flows of 'designer capitalism'.

At another level the historical facts of Britain's industrial identity have been challenged. These facts were not, however, investigated as I had hoped, through the processes of industrial change, the sources of innovation, the potentialities for or inhibitions upon technological creativity which existed within communities and industrial structures. Instead, the application of different statistical techniques to quantitative indicators has brought to these a new precision, however spurious, and brought them to the forefront of analysis, to the exclusion of discussion of the processes and microeconomics of industrial change. Economic historians now emphasize slow continuous change rather than the dramatic break with the past which the term 'Industrial Revolution' once conveyed. The first edition of my book was published just before N. F. R. Crafts's *British Economic Growth*,[4] and, like the challenging articles by Crafts and Harley published before this,[5] I emphasized the broad coverage of industry and the role of proto-industrial development in the years long before 1780. But the focus of Crafts's analysis in his book and in later articles was to centre on the slow rate of productivity growth during the Industrial Revolution, especially during the period between 1780 and 1820. The brunt of the explanation for disappointing results as indicated in the newly estimated growth rates was borne not by a large agricultural sector, but by a large and sluggish industrial sector.

Britain was a much more industrial nation in the eighteenth century than once thought, but in Crafts's view much of this industry was traditional and overmanned. T. S. Ashton's spectacular 'wave of gadgets' was confined to a few small industries, notably cotton and iron which failed to overcome the deadweight of the older industries until after the 1830s. Crafts's new output and growth estimates were presented in the framework of macroeconomic analysis formerly followed by economic historians, but they turned its previous conclusions on their head. For his new estimates found no radical discontinuity in national income, industrial output, capital formation, gross domestic product per head and productivity.

Following soon on Crafts's new gradualism came Wrigley's continuity thesis.[6] Based on an ecological insight into the predominance of organic over inorganic resources in industry, it argued for limits to growth before the mid-nineteenth century. Resource factors were reinforced by a distribution of the labour force towards rural and traditional industrial occupations. 'Slow growth' and 'continuity' have thus become positions imposed on the period. These positions on the economy have fitted well with revisionist views in political and social history seeking constitutional continuities between *ancien régime* aristocratic oligarchies and 'gentlemanly capitalism'.

The new edition of my book is a challenge to the orthodoxy which now prevails on the dimensions of the eighteenth- and early-nineteenth-century economy. It is also a restatement and reformulation of my position in the first edition that the key to the Industrial Revolution was to be found in the dynamics of technological creativity and the structures of industrial communities. Orthodoxies have their fellow travellers for a time, but ultimately the statistical reworking of the same body of data must end in intellectual rigor mortis. The study of the Industrial Revolution will either be abandoned, or must seek out new frontiers of primary microeconomic research and new frameworks of analysis.

One such new framework must be women's industrial work, and female consumption of manufactured commodities. The hidden bias in all the existing estimates of productivity growth and distribution of the labour force is that they are based on male occupational categories. A male industrial revolution has been presented to us as the general experience. If women's workforce contributions, women's property-holding and capital investment were counted, what difference would this make to accounts of productivity growth? If women's consumer decision-making, and family incomes rather than male wage rates were considered, what difference would this make to currently accepted views of the passive roles of home demand and international trade, and of stable, then steadily rising standards of living? In current accounts of the slow productivity growth of British industry during the eighteenth and early-nineteenth century, traditional, male labour surplus industries take the fore while new manufacturing industries deploying cheap female labour in conjunction with improved forms of economic organization and new machinery are excluded, or their place is understated. Narrative accounts along with partial quantitative indicators built up from specific regional and industrial studies provide insight into more rapid industrial transformation than ever conceived within the blinkered framework of current national accounting categories.

Another framework is the extent of Britain's difference, from the eighteenth century onwards, from her European and Asian neighbours. Perhaps the major contribution of Crafts's and Wrigley's books is their clarification of the distinctiveness of the British path of economic development. But this has been hidden behind more prominent messages of slow productivity change, limits to growth, organic resource bases and traditional labour forces. Crafts compared the rapid labour force deployment away from agriculture in Britain to the still largely agricultural economies of the rest of Europe. This reduction in the agricultural labour force was combined with organizational and technical change to produce a high productivity agriculture capable of feeding a rapidly growing population. Yet international specialization and comparative advantage went to a new, initially small but rapid growth industry – the cotton manufacture. It was not British industry which set the economy apart from the rest of the continent, but British agriculture plus the cotton manufacture.

Wrigley identified two other distinctive features of the British economy. One was its urban growth along with the extent of its rural manufacturing. Population growth over the course of the eighteenth century emerged from rural industrial expansion and an uninterrupted growth in the urban sector. The towns of Britain, especially those of small and medium size, were growing rapidly at a time when those in much of the rest of Europe were stagnating or declining. In 1800 Britain's urban population was surpassed only by the Netherlands, and the Dutch towns had been declining for a century.[7] Many of Britain's smaller towns were heavily industrial, closely integrated with concurrent proto-industrial development in rural hinterlands. Turnpikes, canals and rivers, and a constant traffic of human activity bound the countryside to the town.

Another distinctive feature was Britain's reliance on coal resources since the later eighteenth century. New potentials for growth set her apart from the stagnation facing the Dutch economy.[8] From this time on, Britain, unlike her neighbours, broke free of the limitations imposed by organic, land-based raw materials. Her industries shifted from woollen textiles, leather and construction to iron and steel goods, pottery, bricks, glass and inorganic chemicals.[9] The expansion of the northeastern coalfield was one of the miracles of the seventeenth century, and Newcastle was proverbial for its wealth and population even at the end of the eighteenth century.[10] By this time the other major coalfields of the Midlands and the North were in rapid development and dictated the location of new industry. Britain consumed more coal per capita than any other European country even in the nineteenth century. In 1850 her consumption of coal per capita exceeded that reached by Germany in 1880, but the main industrial use for this coal was in the iron and the cotton industries.[11]

Coal, towns and labour deployment played their part, to be sure, and set a distinctive path for Britain apparent in all the available macroeconomic indicators. It was not these that set off the discontinuity, however, but a concentrated technological breakthrough combined with a more broadly-based technological innovation across a range of new manufacturing

5

industries. What the Industrial Revolution involved, as Ralph Davis once wrote, was 'a movement on to quite different paths of industrial development from those that were being successfully followed'.[12] But the backdrop to this intensive capital-deepening kind of transformation, was the expansion of manufacturing usually associated with capital-widening. This too was accompanied in many newer industries by the application of the division of labour, as well as new tools and techniques if not mechanization.

The clustering of a key set of inventions was combined with new forms of work organization, centralized factories and workshops as well as decentralized subcontracting, and new labour forces, especially women, children and other uninitiated labour such as pauper apprentices. Framing this clustering was a rich diversity of technological and organizational change in a broad range of industries. As Mokyr has argued, 'per capita consumption and living standards increased little initially, but production technologies changed dramatically in many industries and sectors, preparing the way for sustained Schumpeterian growth in the second half of the nineteenth century'.[13] These fundamental changes in production systems were achieved by major inventors like Samuel Crompton who wrote that he spent 'four-and-a-half years at least wherein every moment of time and power of mind as well as expense which my other employment would permit were devoted to this one end'.[14] They were achieved by minor manufacturers such as James Bisset who could not brook the prospect of life as a journeyman japan painter, spending twelve-hour days painting snuff boxes with roses and anemones. He escaped by inventing a novel kind of painting on glass, called Imperial, and a whole range of other designer goods.[15] They were also achieved by such as Catherine Willcox, Wedgwood's designer and painter,[16] or the anonymous female spinner and engineer who escaped with Hargreaves when his spinning jenny was attacked by a mob.[17] And they were achieved by the groups of women who applied their own divisions of labour and female work patterns in the proliferating workshops and small factories of the new manufacturing industries.

Such technological and organizational change brought major dislocation to many communities. Manufacture was by no means new to the eighteenth century; cottage industries were widespread over the Scottish Highlands, West Wales, the Yorkshire Dales, the Derbyshire and Cornish countrysides, not to mention Ulster, Kilkenny, Mayo and Donegal. These regions experienced a new pastoralization and with it pauperization as a result of the onset of industrialization on an altogether different scale in a few key regions of mainland England and lowland Scotland. This 'euthanasia of cottage industries' may have been a 'great exercise in Schumpeterian creative destruction',[18] but for the families, and above all the women and children who played such a prominent part in these industries, the results were catastrophic, and entailed a long period of resistance to technology in many such communities.

Technological change and the expansion of manufacturing took shape within this diverse climate of enthusiasm and resistance, and were vigorous enough to produce the discontinuity which distinguished Britain from her continental neighbours. As O'Brien has put it, 'the productivity of the British workforce producing manufactures and urban services had to advance . . . rapidly enough to support the terms and levels of trade between industry and agriculture required for sustained structural transformation'.[19] At the back of all this, Britain had advantages over her neighbours. Over the period from the late seventeenth to the early nineteenth century Britain fought a long series of wars outside her shores. The results were a windfall of colonial markets, a huge navy and army which made international and domestic markets safer for British trade, and, even more significantly, the founding of the Bank of England, the creation of the City, and the shipping and insurance services which dominated world markets.

> Britain, by first obtaining a dominating position for herself in world markets, and then by servicing the commercial and industrial needs of other countries during their industrialization processes, built up an almost unassailable comparative advantage in these fields. In this case at least, then, the role of the external world in Britain's industrialization had a consequence of a permanent nature.[20]

Britain's economy was 'distinctive' in the eighteenth and early nineteenth centuries, not because of resource endowments and agricultural output, but, as contemporaries such as Tocqueville saw, because of the extraordinary industry and inventiveness of her manufacturing people. But distinctive does not mean isolated, for around this lay the allure, the adventure, and indeed the conquest of the world economy. Britain was not the first to understand the crucial role of this world economy: 'the splendid high noon of Dutch wealth and power' was achieved in the seventeenth century from this vantage point. The British learned their lessons from the Dutch, but took that major step into the beyond by connecting their dominant trading position to broadly-based expansion of their manufacturing sector along with concentrated growth in their new leading manufactures, cotton and iron.

This book is an industrial history, and it reasserts the primacy of the industrial experience to Britain's Industrial Revolution. That experience was tremendously varied and fraught with the struggles and controversies of both machinery and the intensive exploitation of labour. This is also a book about the process of restructuring and transformation of production, a process which was spread over a longer period and a broader range of manufacture than once thought. It is, nevertheless, a book about transformations and not about the gradualism and continuity of economic indicators. While these indicators have their place, the estimates on which they are based are fragile and incomplete. They are so far all we have in terms of quantitative estimates, but the story which is told on the basis of such estimates alone is not only not enough, it is also at odds with other narratives of the times. David Landes warned thirty years ago against masking the significance of discontinuities by concentrating on the absence of shifts in quantitative indicators: to him these were the historian's 'butterfly under glass or frog in formaldehyde – without the virtue of wholeness to compensate for their lifelessness'.[21] It is time that this warning was renewed.

Finally, this book forms part of a debate on the Industrial Revolution which I hope will continue to invigorate the subject. Crafts has given us new quantitative estimates of economic growth, and new ways of thinking about the sectoral developments of the economy. Wrigley has given us new ways of thinking about the agricultural and resource base of the economy as well as new estimates of the growth and distribution of the labour force. My book is not simply an account of the industrial facts which they have left out; it is an alternative analysis which questions the interpretations and significance placed upon the economic indicators.

These arguments are developed through twelve chapters. Chapters 1, 3, 8 and 9 are mainly theoretical, dealing with debates and issues. Chapter 1 summarizes the now orthodox quantitative treatment of the Industrial Revolution, the problems with this, and the new issues now opening for research. Chapters 3, 8 and 9 discuss a series of debates over industry, including classical writers such as Smith and Marx, as well as recent discussion of proto-industrialization, flexible specialization, the 'bosses' and labour process debates, and economic and social theories of technological and organizational change. The other chapters marshal both argument and evidence to present a different view of the place of manufacture in the British Industrial Revolution. This includes discussion of agriculture and resources as well as trade and consumption. Chapter 2 on Industries provides a broadly based and up-to-date survey of technological, organizational and productivity change in Britain's major industries. Chapters 10 to 12 provide an in-depth discussion of changes in techniques and work, and their social impact in Britain's two major and contrasting industries, textiles and metals.

This book still challenges the attachment of older generations of economic historians to the years after 1780, to the factory and to the cotton industry. But in this new edition it also challenges the current and now orthodox preference for gradual and continuous change over the discontinuity associated with the Industrial Revolution. That discontinuity was less short and sharp than once thought, but it was nevertheless a transformation, and one in which changes in manufacturing played a prominent part. This second edition, like the first, asks that we reconsider the kinds of changes taking place in the earlier eighteenth century and the context in these years for the rise of household and workshop industries. It asks for a closer analysis of the economic dynamic, the techniques and the labour forces of these cottage and workshop industries, and of the factories which grew up in the midst of some but not all of them. It asks finally that we look on the Industrial Revolution as a more complex, many-sided and long-term phenomenon than economic historians have recently assumed.

This book considers a range of debates over and analyses of industrial change. On specific industries, however, it is selective, and deals in depth with only some of the textile industries and some of the metal industries. Since the first edition, I have been able to draw on new research on the woollen industry by Pat Hudson and Adrian Randall, on the silk industry by Judy Lown and on the lace industry by Pamela Sharpe. But a range of other industries, examined from the viewpoint of their labour forces, work and technologies, remains neglected, including the whole range of food processing, papermaking, glass and pottery, shoemaking, and colonial finishing trades. As a general survey, this second edition, like the first, still raises more questions than it answers. I hope, however, that these will still provide the incentive for new research and new interpretations of the Industrial Revolution.

Part I

MANUFACTURE AND THE ECONOMY

1

CURRENT PERSPECTIVES AND NEW DEPARTURES

The Industrial Revolution has long been a terrain of debate and controversy among economic and social historians. Debates over how much change, how fast, and what impact this had on communities and peoples have been part of the process of making the concept itself. These debates, among what have become rather specialist historians, have in turn affected our wider historical sense of identity. The Industrial Revolution has been conceived of as a period of transition, however long the period and varied its characteristics. It is a part of the 'life story' of the nation, conceived generally as its formative childhood and adolescence. The Industrial Revolution has been the starting point of accounts of political and social change and of the making of the modern economy. The developmental indicators and their trends, centred on the growth of national output, capital formation, demographic growth, and changes in economic and industrial structures, are known just as surely as are the weights, heights, motor skills, speech and understanding of the developing child.

Recently these indicators have been called to account. Quantitative economic historians have re-estimated their trends, and have found the gap between the performance of the expected and the real adolescence of the British economy to be too great to claim a transition even over the long period from the early eighteenth to the mid-nineteenth century. 'Continuity' has replaced 'revolution', bringing a loss of confidence in the stages of the life story. From the Right, Norman Stone dismissed the 'industrial revolution' as the conceptual relic of a few outdated early twentieth-century economists.[1] From the Left, Gareth Stedman Jones described the 'changing face of nineteenth-century Britain' as the discovery of a continuity between eighteenth- and nineteenth-century class formations.[2]

QUANTITATIVE ESTIMATES: A NEW ORTHODOXY

Let us turn now to those analyses which have formed the foundation of our new times of historical doubt. During the 1980s a number of quantitative economic historians applied more sophisticated statistical techniques and incorporated research over the previous two decades to modify the quantitative indicators of output growth, wages and occupational structure. The national accounts and industrial and agricultural output estimates of Deane and Cole had, since the 1960s, provided the basic framework for patterns of economic growth over the course of the eighteenth and nineteenth centuries. Now these estimates were displaced and with them the historical turning points which had framed all previous historiography. Deane and Cole's estimates had confirmed the received picture passed on by T. S. Ashton that 'after 1782 almost every statistical series of production shows a sharp upward turn'.[3] Deane and Cole found industry and commerce growing at 0.49 per cent for 1760–80, but 3.43 per cent for 1780–1801.[4]

The displacement of both estimates and turning points was summarized by N. F. R. Crafts. Gathering together and commenting on earlier work by C. K. Harley, P. H. Lindert and J. G. Williamson, Crafts produced new composite output series for the economic sectors, agriculture, industry and commerce, and government and services. He also produced estimates of the growth of national product and of total factor productivity growth. These estimates are summarized in Tables 1.1, 1.2 and 1.3.

Table 1.1 Output growth, 1700–1831 (% per year)

	New estimates			Old estimates		
	GDP	Industry	Agri-culture	GDP	Industry	Agri-culture
1700–60	0.7	0.7	0.6	0.7	1.0	0.2
1760–80	0.6	1.3	0.1	0.6	0.5	0.5
1780–1801	1.4	2.0	0.8	2.1	3.4	0.6
1801–31	1.9	2.8	1.2	3.1	4.4	1.6

Source: Crafts, 'The Eighteenth Century', table 3.

New estimates based on Crafts and Harley, 'Output Growth', and Crafts, *British Economic Growth*. Old estimates based on Deane and Cole, *British Economic Growth*.

Table 1.2 Estimates of total factor productivity growth (% per year)

Estimates	1760–1801	1801–1831
$\Delta Y/Y$	1.0	1.9
$\Delta K/K$	1.0	1.7
$\Delta L/L$	0.8	1.4
TFP	0.1	0.35

Source: Crafts and Harley, 'Output Growth', table 5.

Table 1.3 Revisions to estimates of industrial output growth
(% per year)

	Original	Revised
a) Crafts		
1760–1780	1.51	1.29
1780–1800	2.11	1.96
1801–1831	3.00	2.78
b) Harley		
1770–1815	1.60	1.50
1815–1841	3.10	3.00

Source: Crafts and Harley, 'Output Growth', table 2.
Original estimates from Crafts, *British Economic Growth*, table 2.6;
Harley, 'British Industrialisation', table 5. New estimates based on
data from Feinstein, 'National Statistics', table X.

New estimates provided evidence for several challenging conclusions on the patterns and structures of British industrialization. First, rates of growth of national ouput, total factor productivity, and industrial output were slow before 1830, and did not demonstrate that sharp upturn previously claimed by historians. The economy did not reach 3 per cent per year growth in real output before 1830. Real income growth was much lower than previously thought, leaving less scope for consumption to rise and less acceleration in productivity growth. Changes in investment proportions were also very gradual over the period, leaving total factor productivity growth at only 0.2 per cent per annum 1700–60, rising to only 0.35 per cent per annum in 1801–31. What increase in growth there was in the later eighteenth century was accounted for by faster growth of inputs rather than extra productivity growth. This demonstrated, contrary to all previous accounts, little effect of technical progress on productivity until well into the nineteenth century.

These new estimates discounted radical economic change, but they did not discount change altogether. For though growth in output and productivity were gradual they did sustain a much-increased population, and a population much more urbanized and more industrialized than either previously or in any other contemporary economy. It was in supporting a substantial proportion of this population *off* the land that Britain measured its achievement in comparison with other European countries.

Crafts, indeed, has described Britain as an 'idiosyncratic industrializer'.[5] Her idiosyncracy is defined by an early start on the road to industrialization, high productivity growth in agriculture which released labour to industry, but comparative advantage in exportable manufactures, especially cotton textiles. This was also a comparative advantage in goods made with relatively more unskilled labour than skilled, and it was this combined with a relatively large industrial sector and a smaller agricultural sector which set the route to later patterns of slow growth.[6]

It was thus the early productivity growth of and 'release of labour' from agriculture which, paradoxically, dictated the speed of subsequent economic growth. The problem of development faced by the British economy in the eighteenth century was not a large subsistence agricultural sector. On the contrary agricultural productivity increased steadily over the century. Crafts estimated that agricultural growth was in fact higher before 1760 than after. The first result of this was a new capacity to sustain higher populations than previously. Rates of population growth rose from −0.3 per cent in 1661 to 0.9 per cent in 1776 and up to 1.5 per cent per year in 1816.[7] Customary restraints on marriage and fertility helped to create conditions for higher income levels by the eighteenth century, and ensuing population growth did not result in the 'Malthusian Trap', that is the reversal of initial gains in living standards. High populations were sustained by agricultural growth initially, and later by more general economic growth, without a large decline in living standards and a reversion to slower population growth.

Not only did agricultural output grow, but so did agricultural productivity based on labour-shedding innovation and investment. In order to feed a higher population and to industrialize, that is to feed those living in towns and engaged in non-agricultural activities, it is necessary to find ways of generating rising output per agricultural worker to allow a 'release of labour' to other sectors. Crafts pointed out that this requirement was met by British agriculture in the first half of the eighteenth century. Productivity growth in agriculture was faster than in any other sector of the British economy, and labour productivity in the sector was the highest in Europe. Not only this, but Britain reduced the share of its male labour force in agriculture, releasing this in the main to industry, and it urbanized, doing both at much greater speed than its European neighbours.

There is so far nothing fundamentally new in this presentation of the British pattern of development, apart from the earlier dating of the rise in agricultural productivity. What Crafts did point out, however, was the coincidence of high rates of agricultural growth along with 'release of labour', yet comparatively low rates of increase of industrial output. This led him to investigate the distribution of the labour force and productivity growth in the manufacturing and commercial sector.

It was clear from the new social tables devised by Lindert and Williamson that Britain in the late seventeenth and early eighteenth centuries had much higher percentages of its population in commerce and industry than previously thought, but the characteristics of employment of this population were only made clear by data from the 1831 census summarized by Wrigley. This revealed that much higher percentages of this industrial and commercial labour force were to be found in retail trade and handicraft than in manufacturing for distant markets. Crafts's breakdown of industrial output also

Table 1.4 Patterns of employment, income, expenditure and residence (%)

	1700	1760	1800	1840
Male employment in agriculture	61.2	52.8	40.8	28.6
Male employment in industry	18.5	23.8	29.5	47.3
Income from agriculture	37.4	37.5	36.1	24.9
Income from industry	20.0	20.0	19.8	31.5
Consumption/income	92.8	73.6	76.3	80.1
Investment/income	4.0	6.8	8.5	10.8
Exports/income	8.4	14.6	15.7	14.3
Urban population	17.0	21.0	33.9	48.3

Source: Crafts, 'The Eighteenth Century', table 1.

showed a large divergence in both the growth of real output across individual industries, and in the percentages of value added contributed by these industries. Industrial output until the nineteenth century was, on Crafts's estimates, dominated by industries which showed little consistent dynamic performance. In his words,

> much of British 'industry' in the first half of the nineteenth century was traditional and small-scale, and catered to local domestic markets. This sector, responsible for perhaps 60 per cent of industrial employment, experienced low levels of labour productivity and slow productivity growth – it is possible that there was virtually no advance during 1780–1860.[8]

Some of those industries which initially contributed relatively small proportions of value added were also the glamorous innovative industries which captured contemporary imaginations – cotton and iron. The remarkable growth in real output of the cotton industry, in particular, from 4.59 per cent per year in 1760–70 to 12.76 per cent per year in 1780–90 should be combined with its contribution to industrial output of only 2.6 per cent per annum in 1770, rising to 17 per cent in 1801 and 22.4 per cent in 1831. Cotton's performance was remarkable, but it was not sufficient to overcome the deadweight of most other British industry, traditionally organized and serving only home markets. It was primarily to this traditional industry that most of the labour 'released' by an innovative agricultural sector migrated, and Britain became 'overcommitted' to these labour-intensive manufacturing activities.[9]

Britain's rapid productivity growth in those manufactures which were

17

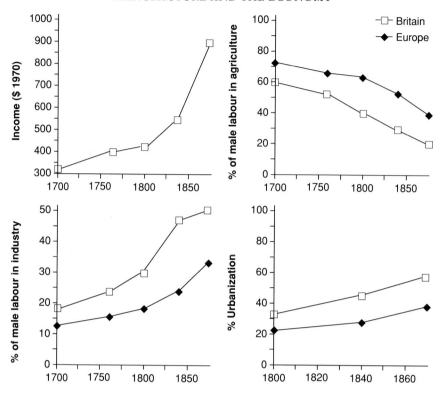

Figure 1.1 Britain's development transition in European perspective

Source: Crafts, 'British Industrialisation', table 2.

traded internationally did give her a large comparative advantage in those activities, and she scooped international markets in cotton. And indeed this was a major achievement, for throughout the nineteenth century cotton textiles constituted the largest part of world trade. This achievement, narrowly based on one industry, accounted for Britain's international position throughout the nineteenth century. As Crafts has pointed out, by the mid-nineteenth century Britain was exporting 60 per cent of its cotton output, in comparison with France's 10 per cent. Cottons accounted for half of British exports during the twenty-five years before then, and Britain controlled 82 per cent of the world market for cotton cloth even as late as the 1880s. Overall, Britain's exports were virtually all manufactured commodities (90 per cent), and she exported a comparatively high proportion of her total industrial output (25 per cent compared to France's 10 per cent).

Yet the end result of this spectacular achievement from what was initially such a new and minor industry in Britain was ultimately disappointing. The British story was one of the 'pain of structural change, but without the reward of rapid income growth'. The success of cotton masked the backwardness of other sectors, and this unique model of success was built on short-term strategies of providing 'low-wage factory fodder' rather than high technology industries and a skilled workforce.[10]

The association of high growth rates in agriculture, urbanization and the deployment of labour to a low productivity industrial sector has provided the basis for a much more far-reaching version of the 'continuity' thesis of the Industrial Revolution. This is E. A. Wrigley's depiction of the period until the mid-nineteenth century as one dominated by 'organic' sources of raw materials and 'natural' technologies. It was an economy of definitely limited growth prospects, confirming the Malthusian and Ricardian barriers of population growth and resource scarcity. Nature, not technology, dominated the economy of the so-called Industrial Revolution. Williamson had pointed out that Crafts's estimates confirmed the classical economists' pessimism that between 1761 and 1831 the difference between the rate of growth of capital and that of output was trivial and failed to offset the impact of increasing land scarcity. Wrigley reinterpreted the analysis of Adam Smith and Thomas Robert Malthus to underwrite the new estimates. He argued that the classical economists were right to argue as they did – 'their reluctance to envisage the possibility of large gains in individual productivity finds support in . . . Crafts's estimates'. Their systems were dominated by 'negative feedback loops' – most of the economic changes taking place until the 1830s and 1840s were thus best understood within the framework they posed of constraints of land or resource scarcity and population growth. The break beyond these barriers only came with the deployment of inanimate sources of energy and inorganic sources of raw materials.

> The natural technology of the day, though demonstrably capable of substantial development, especially under the spur of increased specialisation of function, was not compatible with the substantial and progressive increase in real incomes which constitutes and defines an Industrial Revolution . . . the raw materials which formed the input into the production processes were almost all organic in nature, and thus restricted in quantity by the productivity of the soil.[11]

Power sources and raw materials, based as they were in natural substances, under this regime, were subject like agriculture to declining marginal returns to land.

Wrigley placed eighteenth- and early nineteenth-century England in an advanced stage of the organic economy. His advanced organic economy had moved beyond the balance between energy gained and energy expended, and contained some anticipations of the future. But it was still strictly limited by fixed supplies of resources. Improvements in the efficiency of producing food and raw materials might release substantial amounts of the workforce from these activities, but all still depended on the flow of these resources whose size was ultimately limited. There was so far no access to capital stocks of energy which could sharply increase the quantity of energy per head.[12]

It was the use of coal which moved Britain into the advanced organic phase. For this reduced its dependence on organic raw materials. Coal output rose in Britain by 1700 to between 2.5 and 3 million tons, five times the output of the whole of the rest of the world.[13] This coal produced heat for domestic uses, replaced wood in processing manufactured commodities, and led to a change in building materials from wood to bricks. 'The transition to a partial dependence upon inorganic *stocks* of energy rather than upon organic energy *flows* played an important role in allowing the English economy to expand without debilitating pressure on the land in the early modern period.'[14]

The strictly limited possibilities to be expected from advanced organic growth were also revealed in the structure of the labour force. The growth of labour productivity in agriculture was, as we have seen, paramount over that of other sectors in the eighteenth century, and it was indeed the largest employer of the adult male labour force. But the proportions employed in agriculture were falling rapidly, as was the weight of the sector in the economy as a whole. Productivity increase overall thus depended not just on agriculture, but increasingly on other economic sectors. Most industrial employment was not, however, centred on high-productivity industries, that is, those deriving the greatest gains from coal-using resources and inanimate technologies. It was found in the retail trades and handicraft industry.

In spite of comparatively high urban populations, most of the labour force was working in occupations supplying goods for local markets. Those working in factories or proto-industrial workshops made up only 10 per cent of the adult male labour force. The bulk of industrial working men, by contrast, were employed in industries whose work practices were traditional, and whose opportunities of making gains from specialization were limited by the small size of their markets. These were reinforced by rapidly growing numbers in personal service, urban labouring, and clerical jobs whose productivity was probably static.[15] As late as 1831–41, at least two-thirds of the total increase in adult male non-agricultural employment were in occupations such as building labourers, butchers, alehouse keepers, shoe-makers, tailors, blacksmiths and bakers.[16]

Britain became significantly more industrial over the course of the eighteenth century, but much of this industry was rural and traditional handicraft manufacture. The release of labour from agriculture supported this industrial expansion, and allowed a significant increase in population without pauperization. The population history of England, as revised by Wrigley and Schofield, however, reveals that, despite considerable growth in numbers and the disappearance of major crises of mortality, there was no significant discontinuity in demographic *behaviour* in England from the sixteenth to the nineteenth centuries. The population regime was driven by marriage, and this changed as a lagged response to changes in the standard of living.[17]

The redeployment of labour from agriculture to industry was confirmed in a steady decline over two hundred years in the number of marriages in parishes under the influence of seasonal agricultural variations, and the steady increase in marriages in those not subject to such seasonality.[18] The picture again was of steady continuous industrial growth, rather than any discontinuity. It was achieved primarily through redeployment of labour away from agriculture, a process which had reached its limits by the nineteenth century. The consequent pressures on manufacturing profitability were only then solved with labour-saving technological change and a new resource base.

Industrialization in Britain, as conveyed in the historical orthodoxy which now prevails, was, rather than a series of distinct stages, a peculiarly 'fractured' process.[19] In Crafts's view, productivity growth in industry was skewed in the direction of one or two industries, and 'not only was the triumph of ingenuity slow to come to fruition but it does not seem appropriate to regard innovativeness as pervasive'.[20] For Wrigley, the eighteenth-century economy, in spite of considerable inventiveness, much of which was directed to greater specialization and division of labour, remained dependent upon organic resources and human and animal sources of energy. The Industrial Revolution occupied a transition time between the organic and the mineral-based economy determined by the random resort from this time to the use of coal-based energy.

The traditional stages of models of industrialization were broken by these new models of 'change' but 'continuity', yet the new models were but stage theories in another form. For the developmental indicators were still known, *post hoc*. Measures of economic and productivity growth, and analyses of social and economic structures were still considered in the light of other more recent industrial transitions.

QUESTIONS

The steadiness, 'continuity', and distinctly 'unrevolutionary' character of Britain's industrialization are now a very acceptable story, for it fits with all kinds of other historical orthodoxies. It fits well with the anti-Whig school of constitutional and social history which prefers a history of stable but civilized change. What was once the English Revolution has been transformed into an accidental event with few long-term consequences. Thus the *ancien régime* of the confessional state, based on deference, religion and a cohesive society, survived the eighteenth and early nineteenth centuries substantially unchanged. Social historians too have turned to addressing the continuity between eighteenth- and nineteenth-century social protest and radicalism. Chartism was no longer the herald of the class struggle. It was rather a chronological extension of radical democratic movements from the eighteenth century, concerned not with class but with political representation. Old analyses of the sources of social conflict in economic hardship prevail once again over histories of alternative radical social and economic critiques. What emerged from this 'continuous' history was a British economy and society never fully committed to industrial growth. The landed aristocracy, metropolitan finance and 'gentlemanly capitalists' prevailed over an anti-competitive and paternal economy at the end of the nineteenth century in a manner not so very different from that of the seventeenth century.

The universalistic characteristics of economic, social and political life in the eighteenth and early nineteenth centuries had once been centred on revolutionary or at least modernizing tendencies. Now these were discarded in favour first of the complexities and particularities of these features, then in favour of the overwhelming hold of traditional social structures and an expanding but largely unreformed industrial sector.

It is time now to return to the place of the complexities and particularities of British industrialization. The novelty they introduced has, under the terms of the recent orthodoxy, been hidden by statistical aggregation. The nature of such aggregation is to smooth discontinuities, to mask the selective unbalanced growth of the economy. Changes in one or a few branches might take a considerable time to spread to the rest of the economy, or to have an important effect on the whole economy. The process of 'construction' was also in some senses one of 'destruction' – a better term might be 'restructuring'. Aggregate indicators only demonstrated the compensating effects of gains and losses of such changes, but were unable to reveal the process of change itself. Individual industries might, on aggregative output data, appear to have undergone no change over a period, but might in that same period have undergone dramatic changes in their labour forces, technologies and location. This was clearly the case for the silk, copper and woollen industries during the eighteenth century, and will be demonstrated in Chapter 2. The national accounts framework which now dominates the new orthodoxy of the Industrial Revolution gives only one side of the story, that provided by performance according to predetermined indicators. Those indicators, like child development trends, highlight the norm not the individual – they smooth disparities into continuities. Indeed, shifts in the aggregate measures of productivity growth are less likely to show up as significant during periods of rapid and fundamental economic transition than in periods of slower and more piecemeal adjustment. The story of these changes, their transitions in work and life styles, the specific effect on communities and individuals of their gains and losses, will be lost to us if we look only to the indicators of economic performance. Many of these will reveal significant increases in growth rates only some decades after the changes underlying these have occurred.

Once we believed that the child was precursor to the man, childhood a preparation for adulthood. But the impact of psychoanalysis has been to seek a return to the lost childhood, to seek an understanding of it and to reconstitute a 'life story' so as to arrive at a self-knowledge. In this psychoanalytic age it seems right to question the models, development paradigms, and growth norms by which we have so far judged the economic performance of nations and communities. It is time to question the norms, for what are these but constructs, fantasies, narratives of our own times? And it is time to return to the period of the Industrial Revolution as to a recovery of the child lost.

First we must turn to judgements on rates and discontinuities of growth. Even with the revised estimates, it is apparent that between 1831 and 1861 national income was growing four and a half times, and per capita income six and a half times, faster than rates estimated for the first six decades of the eighteenth century. The economic lead Britain had achieved by the time of the Great Exhibition could not have been accomplished in the mere twenty years beforehand. A discontinuity did occur, and the productivity of the British industrial and commercial workforce had to rise fast enough to pay for food and resources for itself and its rapidly rising numbers of dependants. That productivity growth required, in turn, technological and organizational change in industry. Rates of increase in output and productivity levels have been judged in recent accounts against those of recent industrializers, not against rates prevailing earlier or among other contemporary neighbours. Part of the reason for this is the lack of reliable estimates, so comparison is made where and when the data do exist. But such judgement must also answer the question 'how big is big?' Initially low rates of increase are less important than the fact of a new trend of continuing and accelerating growth.[21]

Industrial transformation was vital to the Industrial Revolution, and it is this that the orthodoxy finds lacking. The work of Crafts, Wrigley and others can be combined with research on proto-industrialization to show industrial expansion extending back to the sixteenth century. This industrial expansion before and during the early years of the eighteenth century raises the base from which we measure growth in the later years of the century. Growth rates do then appear to be lower than those calculated by earlier historians. The implication of this, however, should not be to downplay growth rates in the period between 1780 and 1830 with hindsight from those of later in the nineteenth century, but to re-examine industrial growth in the eighteenth century from the backdrop of the early modern economy.

The national accounting framework deployed by Crafts and the occupational distributions relied on by Wrigley use the new social and occupational tables of Lindert and Williamson.[22] These tables give a higher

23

profile to the industrial sector than did the earlier estimates of King, Massie and Colquhoun, and they fit well with work on the importance of proto-industrialization. But these tables are prone to error margins as high as 60 per cent, and estimates for shoemakers, carpenters and others are 'little more than guesses'. These occupational data, as well as those of the 1831 census, are based entirely on information for adult males. As will be clear from later parts of this book, women and children were a vital and growing pillar of the manufacturing workforce. There is no accounting for dual occupations or by-employments which were widespread at the time; indeed there was a common overlap between agrarian and industrial occupations. We cannot be as confident as the orthodoxy suggests of the occupations and social structure of early industrial Britain.

Nor can we be so confident of findings of the poor performance of the industrial sector. Estimates of sectoral outputs and inputs rely on multipliers from a handful of examples and a sample of industries. Industries left out of the picture because of lack of consistent long-run data include food processing, metal wares, distilling, furniture, shipbuilding, chemicals, engineering, pottery, glass and clothing. Subsectors of included industries are presumed to grow at the same rate as a single 'representative indicator'. Furthermore, the weights used to construct the overall index cover industries and activities which include not more than 57 per cent of total industrial output.[23]

National income accounting, by itself, is not adequate to the task of presenting national economic activity. Major problems of underestimation arise for activities embedded in unquantifiable and unrecorded non-market relationships.[24] In periods of fundamental economic change, the proportion of total industrial and commercial activity showing up in the estimates is likely to change radically over time. Furthermore, entry thresholds in most industries, and especially new industries, were low. And industrial expansion often took place first and foremost among a myriad of small firms which also left few records. Innovation in product and techniques was often most rapid in the pygmies rather than the giants of an industry. For a number of industries, there is a strong case for arguing that there was a period during the eighteenth and early nineteenth centuries when more market power was held by smaller and medium-scale firms than before or after. On current indices their contribution is missed.

Assessing the performance of industry during the eighteenth and early nineteenth centuries runs into the unresolved problem of 'misplaced aggregation'. The growth paths of individual industries deviate widely from the average path for industry as a whole. Cotton was notable, iron somewhat less so. The contributions made by improvements in productivity to the promotion of long-term growth varied from industry to industry, and did not necessarily show up in rates of growth of output for each industry. The building industry is a good example, an industry which increased its contribution to industrial production from 11 per cent in 1770 to 25 per cent in

1841, but is presumed to have done so at constant or rising costs per unit of output.[25]

Slow industrial growth in the British economy of the time is explained in the current orthodoxy by the inordinate weight within the industrial sector of industries which underwent little technological change, combined with the concentration of labour in these same industries which in the main supplied local markets. Quantitative historians made an analytical division between 'modern' industries, that is the new proto-industrial and factory industries dealing in tradable commodities, and 'traditional', that is, locally based, handicraft industries. This division of the economy into traditional and modern sectors was based on economic theories of trade and development popular in the 1950s and 1960s. This new historical version distorts the characteristics of manufacturing in the eighteenth century, and hides major sources of productivity gain in manufacture. Rigid associations of productivity gain and technical progress with concepts of large-scale production, factories, powered machinery and capital-deepening pervade the new orthodoxy on the Industrial Revolution. In practice it was and is very difficult to make clear-cut divisions between the traditional and the modern, the tradable and the non-tradable, as there were rarely separate organizational forms, technologies, locations or even firms to be ascribed to either. Eighteenth- and nineteenth-century cotton manufacturers typically combined steam-powered spinning in centralized factories with large-scale employment of domestic hand-loom weavers using traditional techniques. The small metalworking shops of Birmingham, Sheffield and Lancashire fall into the Crafts and Wrigley classifications of traditional, handicraft employments, although they typically developed their high technology in the luxury goods trade of the home market and also broke into and extended foreign markets. Artisans in the sector frequently combined occupations or changed these over their life cycle in such a way that they too could be classified in both the traditional and the modern sector. Firms primarily concerned with metalworking, a 'traditional' sector, also diversified into metal-processing ventures, the 'modern' sector, as a way of generating steady supplies of raw material. The traditional and the modern industrial activities were often inseparable and mutually reinforcing.

Neither was technological and organizational change the sole preserve of the 'modern' sector. A study of individual industries in the next chapter will show the extent of technical and organizational change within the 'handicraft' occupations. The division and specialization of labour were an altogether more complex affair than the basic sectoral divisions of the economy. Wrigley found most industrial labour in occupations which he identifies as 'traditional' – the food and drink trades, shoemaking, tailoring, blacksmithing and trades for luxury consumption. But early industrial capital formation and enterprise typically combined activity in the food and drink or agricultural processing trades with more obviously industrial activities. Innkeepers and victuallers were common mortgagees and joint owners of metalworking enterprises. Peter Stubs, the Lancashire tool maker, became T. S. Ashton's pre-eminent industrialist. Yet he appeared in 1788 as a tenant of the White Bear Inn in Warrington. Here he combined the activity of innkeeper, maltster, and brewer with that of filemaker, using the carbon in the barrel dregs left from his brewing activities to strengthen his files.[26] There are many examples of this kind of overlap between services, agriculture and industry. Entrepreneurs and artisans diversified their portfolios and their activities to reduce the risks attendant on trade and harvest fluctuations, and also stood to gain from the external economies created by overlaps such as those found by Peter Stubs.

An account of the industrial sector must rely on far more than estimates of national industrial output, or even an aggregation of estimates of production and productivity change industry by industry. Statistical results themselves are not sufficient for such an assessment, unless supported from an external context of broader historical evidence. The well-documented studies of particular industries, regions and manufactures suggest more rapid rates of growth and greater productivity change than conveyed in the series devised by the orthodoxy. Growth rates of individual sectors, on their own, do not tell us about the processes underlying growth. Such processes involved industrial restructuring, including technological change, organizational or locational change and market readjustment. It is in understanding these processes, and not just in setting out new revisions of trend rates of output growth, that we find the key to the Industrial Revolution. It was in ways of working, of doing and making things that lives were changed.

It is thus that technology must remain crucial to the story of the Industrial Revolution. The new orthodoxy uses as a proxy measure for technological change total factor productivity growth. It measures this as a residual after accounting for inputs of labour and capital, and finds it wanting. On this basis, technology has been edged out of the story. But as we shall see in the following chapter, the processes and impact of technological change are very difficult to measure. This does not, however, provide grounds for discounting a wrenching and compelling force for change.

David Landes once wrote of the great achievements of the factory system and large-scale power technologies with the one caveat: 'The labouring poor, especially those by-passed or squeezed by machine industry, said little but were undoubtedly of another mind.'[27] He has since come to reconsider this presentation to powerful effect.

> What needs stressing . . . is the force with which technological change impinged on the livelihood of workers and often translated into protest, much of it violent. Changes may have been making their way in some regions more than others, in some industrial branches more than others, and slower than some enthusiastic scholars may have thought.

But don't tell that to the people affected: the pauper apprentices taken from their parents and assigned to labour in mills, the women who were sent to work in the factories where their husbands or fathers would not go, the displaced craftsmen, the residents of once-green valleys now renamed the Black Country, the Irish immigrants who did the dirty work; or for that matter to the winners of the new, industrializing world: the managers, merchants, and shopkeepers, the new-skilled and the 'labour aristocracy', the multiplying professionals in growing towns and cities.[28]

NEW DEPARTURES

Challenges to the current historical orthodoxy of slow continuous growth during the Industrial Revolution have arisen recently on several fronts. These focus on the regional dimension of economic change, on technology and work organization, on the labour force, particularly its gender distribution, and on trade and consumption. Research in these areas has challenged both the continuity thesis of the Industrial Revolution and assessments of the industrial sector. These topics will be dealt with in depth in later chapters of the book; recent findings and their implications for current orthodoxies will be summarized here.

Regions

Pat Hudson has pointed out the extent to which aggregate analysis conceals significant spatial differences in development, averaging out the effects of the dynamism of some regions with the stagnation or decline of others. The uneven and unbalanced nature of industrial growth was above all a discontinuous transformation of different parts of the country.[29] There were obviously always regional differences in growth rates and industrial change across the country, and these remain to this day. Studies of local industries or other such case studies cannot however substitute for the attempt to place industrialization in a national and an international framework.

Nevertheless, there was an important 'regionalization' to the Industrial Revolution which is bypassed by aggregate data. This 'regionalization' furthermore became a part of the discontinuity and the transformation of the Industrial Revolution. A unique form of regional specialization took place between the eighteenth and the first half of the nineteenth century. Before the eighteenth century, pre-industrial regions were relatively cut off from one another, their communications networks oriented to the metropolis or international ports. From the mid-eighteenth century these were displaced by internally integrated regions concentrating on an interrelated set of industries. Cotton textile production, once distributed albeit in a small way across the country, became the industry of South Lancashire and southern

Scotland. Yorkshire took over the woollen and worsted industry, increasing its share of national woollen output from 20 to 60 per cent during the century. The metal and hardware trades found their home in the Midlands, South Yorkshire, South Lancashire and the Glasgow region. The coalfields might dictate industrial locations, perhaps only in the first instance. But this was enough to create the base of business enterprise, capital and labour forces reinforced by new regional externalities.[30] Sometimes the fact of the location itself, the novelty of enterprise, and the mix of activities were a strong enough brew.[31]

The new canal networks reinforced these internally unified, but separate, regions. They were succeeded by railways which structured freight rates to favour short-haul traffic, and with this regional economic activities.[32] Regional factor markets, with wage differentials and specific credit institutions prevailed.[33]

Regionalization during the eighteenth and early nineteenth centuries did not mean industrial production for local needs or home markets. For it was international trade which provided the incentive for the specialization of both proto-industrial expansion and concentrated industry. London, however, was not the centre of this spatial dynamic. The new export trades were conducted, not through London as in the seventeenth and early eighteenth centuries, but direct from the ports of the new industrial regions. First Newcastle and Bristol, then Liverpool, Glasgow and Hull became the hubs of new resources, industrial products and world trade.

Hudson has elsewhere described this regional dynamic for each of the specific areas of England, and I will not repeat this here.[34] The regional framework must always be present in any underlying analysis of industrial change and restructuring. It is dealt with in later chapters of this book as integral to industries, industrial decline and industrial organization.

Technology

It is technology above any other feature which is associated in the popular imagination with the Industrial Revolution. Contemporaries defined the transformation of their times in terms of a 'revolution in machinery'.[35] Writers on the Industrial Revolution from Toynbee to Landes placed changes in technology at the heart of their story. Ashton encapsulated the Industrial Revolution in a 'wave of gadgets'.

But the new orthodoxy discounts all this. Crafts concluded that for most of industry 'not only was the triumph of ingenuity slow to come to fruition but it does not seem appropriate to regard innovativeness as pervasive'.[36] Wrigley saw strict limitations in the gains to be made from the 'natural technology of the day'.[37] Crafts does concede that technological change did finally provoke a switch in the direction of economic growth, but the inventions in cotton textiles were 'random exogenous shocks'.[38]

Technological change and its effects are notoriously difficult to measure. The concept of total factor productivity growth, often used as a proxy for technological change, leaves much to be desired in the very nature of its restrictive assumptions. It is a measure which takes no account of innovation in the nature of outputs or of changes in the quality of inputs, including labour, materials and intermediate goods. It is a measure which fails to account for product innovation and qualitative improvements in the means of production. National income accounting unduly restricts the concept of technological change. Our knowledge of the timing and impact of innovation must depend on a broader background of research on science, economic organization, market developments, new products and processes, skills and workpractices.[39]

Not only is the definition and measurement of technological change upheld in current perspectives deeply suspect, but so too are failures to account for the 'discontinuity' of a clustering of key innovations. Mokyr has divided the innovations of the Industrial Revolution into 'macro' and 'micro' inventions, pointing out that the 'clustering' of inventions between 1765 and 1800 was unprecedented. A small number of macroinventions or major breakthroughs raised rates of return on improvements, and led to a whole series of microinventions and 'learning by doing'.[40] These inventions in textile machinery, power, and metal processing occurred together, creating a 'critical mass'. Their success, and the many microinventions, those improvements and adaptations that came to account for most productivity gains, depended not on chance, but on Britain's large skilled labour force. Its base of skills, not just in local crafts and luxury trades, but in adaptive mechanical techniques in metalworking, precision instrument making, and chemical processes, created the means by which the Industrial Revolution became 'not the age of cotton, or iron, or of steam; it was the age of improvement'.[41]

The glamour sectors were not the monopolists of innovation. Indeed early textile innovations – carding and scribbling machinery, the Dutch loom, the knitting frame, the flying shuttle and the jenny, silk-throwing machinery and finishing techniques in bleaching and calico printing – were all developed within rural manufacture and artisan industry, and few were initially developed for the high-profile cotton industry. The metalworking trades were proverbial for skill-intensive hand processes and hand tools. The stamp, press, drawbench and lathe were developed to innumerable specifications and uses, and new malleable alloys, gilting processes, plating and japanning were at least as important. Other industries experienced some form of transformation in materials or division of labour, if not in the artefacts of technological change. There are no productivity estimates for the range of hand tools and early machine tools in the metal industries, but their significance to overall productivity growth is a recurrent theme of economic history.[42]

Other forms of innovation also affected 'traditional' industry and handi-craft production. The wool textile sector moved to new products – for example, from heavy serges to mixed stuffs – to reduce finishing times. New industrial uses for coal affected brewing, brickmaking, malting, sugar and soap-boiling as well as metallurgy and metalworking. Changes in materials had similar effects on saltmaking, hatmaking and luxury metalwares. Innovations in putting-out systems, wholesaling, retailing, credit and debt, and artisan co-operation were devised as ways of retaining the essentials of older structures in the face of new more competitive environments. Customary practices and ways of working were not static, but these too evolved to match the needs of more market-orientated production.[43]

Innovation was 'discontinuous' and clustered, but it was also embedded in a context of adaptive technical skill and rippled outwards to widespread 'improvement'. This innovation was also in the things that mattered. As Landes argues,

> the British innovations had wider economic consequences because the demand for these products was potentially larger and supply more elastic (compare cotton and silk for supply and cheapness); and be-cause they had wider ramifications within the larger economy (thus multiple uses of iron and the general applicability of advances in power technology). They were the stuff of an industrial revolution.[44]

Labour forces

The one distinctive feature of the eighteenth and early nineteenth centuries pinpointed by Crafts and Wrigley is one of structural change – the shift of economic activity and labour forces away from agriculture to industries and services. Current estimates of the distribution of the labour force between agriculture and other employments have been based on Wrigley's calculation of the numbers which the expanding agricultural sector could support off the land. Census data on adult male labour for 1831 showed that only 10 per cent of this workforce were employed in industries serving distant markets. Lindert's estimates for industrial occupations in the eighteenth century relied on adult male burial records.

Yet it was not the men who mattered in many of the new industries. The labour force was not homogeneous, and the classic period of the Industrial Revolution was marked by the unprecedented incorporation of female and child labour into manufacturing industries. It is hard to quantify the amount of female and child labour, as such labour was usually excluded from official statistics until the mid-nineteenth century. But equally, male labour inputs have been assumed from occupational categories, notwithstanding high levels of unemployment and underemployment in many male occupations.

There are many good reasons why women mattered to manufacturing to a greater degree than they had done in the past, and indeed were to do so later in the nineteenth century. Female labour supply was high at the time, encouraged by population growth, the age structure of the population, feminine-skewed sex ratios and agricultural innovation which shed higher proportions of female than male labour. British industry used this labour force as a cheap and flexible input, and one which was furthermore experimented on with new work disciplines, new forms of work organization and new technologies.

The fact that only 10 per cent of adult male labour was to be found in the modernized progressive sectors, as Wrigley points out, does not tell us a great deal. For the preferred labour force for precisely these sectors was overwhelmingly young and female. Access to cheap supplies of labour, especially that of women and children, was integral to the spread of manufacture from the early modern period. But this labour was also endowed with special attributes of flexibility, dexterity and discipline which made it particularly suited to eighteenth-century technologies and work organization. Estimates for labour inputs and distribution of labour need to be disaggregated into gender and age differences, skill and labour intensity. There was a special place for women's and children's labour in the early industrial period which has only recently found a parallel in the decentralized production processes in manufacturing in Third World and advanced industrial countries.[45]

Trade and consumption

Current perspectives on the Industrial Revolution focus almost exclusively on supply-side considerations. Foreign trade once ranked as of 'central importance' in the expansion of the economy,[46] or as the 'spark' which set the Industrial Revolution on its upward path.[47] But it has since been dethroned. Quantitative historians have argued that foreign trade was not essential to Britain's economic growth, and could indeed have been replaced by domestic demand or supply. Exports, furthermore, did not initiate growth, for the terms of trade were falling during key periods of expansion.[48] It has been argued that demand was not an independent variable in the process of economic growth, because it must itself arise from increasing incomes or from a reallocation of incomes.[49]

These general points have been elaborated for Britain's Industrial Revolution. It has been argued that export growth was internally generated – exports were driven by needs for imports, in turn giving trading partners purchasing power to buy British goods. Furthermore, the role played by external factors depended on appropriate economic responses in the internal economy.[50] Crafts's reassessment of Britain's economic growth during the period did not change the estimates of exports provided by Davis and Deane and Cole. But it removed international trade from the front line of analysis

31

9246

for the sources of the Industrial Revolution. Crafts restated the basic pattern of British trade during the period as the export of manufactured goods in exchange for food and raw materials. He found changes in these broad categories over the whole period of the mid-eighteenth to the mid-nineteenth century, however, to be relatively minor: 'the industrial revolution saw the consolidation of existing tendencies'.[51]

The result of these analyses was, for a time, to turn research away from international trade and other aspects of demand. But new research on the framework of international trade, on the rise of consumer demand, and on the impact of mercantile trade on sources of capital formation and institutions of credit and commerce is now reversing this trend. O'Brien has pointed out the role of British naval policy and military expenditure in making the international and domestic market safe for British trade. This also allowed British industry and commerce to capture the lion's share of international markets in manufactures and services.[52] The trade generated with Britain's American colonies was unmatched by European rivals,[53] and it was in commodities in which techniques of mass-production were most easily developed. The demonstration effect of internationally-traded commodities also rebounded on the home market; more household production was replaced by commercially produced goods.[54] This was a long-term process, not confined to the classic years of the Industrial Revolution, but nevertheless the extension of access to a range of cosmopolitan commodities also expanded the markets which in turn generated greater specialization and improvements in production processes.

Recent research has in these ways sought a reintegration of international trade and home markets. New analysis relies on a broader view of the gains from trade than that identified in contributions to gross national product (GNP). As O'Brien has summed it up: 'Attempts to apply counterfactual logic and the Ricardian theory of comparative advantage to denigrate the role of foreign trade in the first Industrial Revolution are no longer convincing.' The significance of trade was not 'as expendable as cliometricians suggest'.[55]

Research on international trade may yet hold the key to much more. Whatever their views on reducing the relative importance accorded to trade, the quantitative historians did not accumulate new data on exports and imports. They used data compiled by Davis, Schumpeter and Deane and Cole in the 1960s. The accumulation of more data on textile prices and the quantities and values of colonial wares might change much more than our assessment of the role of international trade. For on these prices depend estimates of the value of output of individual industries, especially the textile industries. Higher growth rates in these industries would imply higher growth rates in the economy overall.[56] New quantitative data, combined with qualitative research, could point yet again to 'a major discontinuity'. No longer can we be so sure, as Crafts has argued, that 'the dimensions of economic change in Britain during the Industrial Revolution are now reliably measured'.[57]

Doubts on the now orthodox interpretation of the Industrial Revolution have generated a whole series of new departures in research areas. These areas and their findings will be explored throughout this book. What we must first turn to is an account of industrial growth over the eighteenth and early nineteenth centuries. For it is industry which must bear the brunt of debate over continuity and discontinuity, traditionalism and technological change.

2

INDUSTRIES

British industry during the eighteenth and early nineteenth centuries is now believed to have undergone much more limited change than was once thought both by previous historians and by contemporaries. Eighteenth-century political economists thought they were living through times of great progress, with a great expansion of industry and widespread technological change. Defoe's *Tour through the Whole Island of Great Britain* in 1720 declared:

> New discoveries in metals, mines and minerals, new undertakings in trade, engines, manufactures in a nation pushing and improving as we are; these things open new things every day, and make England especially shew a new and differing face in many places, on every occasion of surveying it.[1]

His words were echoed by economic writers throughout the century, who also urged yet more mechanization, or, like Anderson in the 1760s, were inspired to catalogue new industries and inventions.[2]

Yet today historians can identify dramatic increases in output in only a few very small industries, while most industry simply expanded on the basis of older methods along with population growth. An index of industrial production was drawn up by Hoffmann in the 1950s. This index formed the basis for views held on rapid acceleration of industrial growth by Deane and Cole, Hobsbawm, Landes and other historians. But Harley, then Crafts, changed the weighting of Hoffmann's series. Hoffmann used data available for only 56 per cent of the industrial sector, and his index thus gave virtually double weighting to two atypically fast-growing industries – cotton and iron. Harley and Crafts adjusted this index, giving lower weights to these leading industries, but without the addition of any further industries. The result was a much smoother trend rate of growth.[3]

NATIONAL STATISTICS

The overall picture showed that industry grew rather slowly over the period, with the result that the growth of real Gross Domestic Product (GDP) was much less impressive than was once thought. The economy did not even reach 3 per cent per year growth in real output until after 1830. And the growth of industrial output did not show that rapid spurt forward once thought.

Table 2.1 Estimates of industrial output growth (% per year)

Dates	Original	Revised
1760–1780	1.51	1.29
1780–1800	2.11	1.96
1801–1831	3.00	2.78

Source: Crafts and Harley, 'Output Growth', table 2(a).

Estimates of industrial output have been aggregated from estimates of output growth and value added for a selected number of industries. These estimates indicate that industrial growth in the first half of the eighteenth century was fairly equally spread across the main traditional sectors, that is the textile industries, building and the leather industries. Together these accounted for two-thirds of industrial output. The divergence in industrial performance starts from the 1760s, when cotton starts its rapid growth, and iron too starts to move sharply upwards. But the new progress of these industries has to be placed in the perspective of their size, as indicated in their contribution to value added. Together they contributed less than 10 per cent of output in 1770, despite growth rates then of 6.20 per cent and 4.47 per cent per year respectively.

The differences between the trend growth paths of most industries and those of the few industries which did experience rapid growth in output have been illustrated in two trend paths: the first includes all the industries in the Crafts sample; the second excludes cotton, iron, steel and coal (see Figure 2.1).

It is on the basis of such output data and estimates on the industrial distribution of the labour force that Crafts summed up the peculiar nature of British industrial growth. Much of British 'industry' was 'traditional and small-scale, and catered to local domestic markets'. This sector employed 60 per cent of the industrial workforce, had low levels of labour productivity and slow productivity growth – 'it is possible that there was virtually no advance during 1780–1860'. By contrast, productivity growth in exportable manufactures, that is cotton and iron, was rapid.[4]

It seems appropriate now to assess estimates of output growth in Britain's industries, and the conclusions drawn from these estimates on the extent of or lack of change in production processes. The first problem with these estimates is that they are based on a sample of industries; many manufactures are not included because of lack of data. These include food processing, pottery, glass, lead, engineering and metal manufactures, distilling, brass, chemicals, furniture, clothing and luxury manufactures. Estimates of output for industries which are included in the index are subject to wide margins of error. Customs and excise figures used as evidence for several industries are not corrected for the effects of smuggling, evasion and corruption of officials.[5] It has been argued that the total effect of these problems on the index of industrial output was likely to have been small, but no evidence is provided for the size of their effects on individual industries.[6] Estimates for some industries, such as coal, diverge substantially from those provided in recent industry studies. Crafts's estimate for coal in the first half of the eighteenth century is only half that given by Flinn, and 14 to 24 per cent less than that given by Flinn for the period 1750–1815.[7] A greater problem arises from estimates for whole industries based on data from case studies of individual firms. Those firms which left records were often the larger not the representative firms. Large-scale firms in the seventeenth century were more likely to leave records than were small firms in the nineteenth century. Hence we know so much about Ambrose Crowley and his giant seventeenth-century ironworks, and so little about the typical early nineteenth-century Birmingham manufacturer. Indeed, for a number of industries, there is a strong case for arguing that there was a period during the eighteenth and early nineteenth centuries when more market power was held by small and medium-scale firms than before or after. If indices of industrial growth are based only on output figures left by a few large-scale firms, the contributions of these representative firms are missed.

The large proportion of British industry which has been placed in the 'traditional' category is also an 'unknown territory'. We do know that some at least of this industry experienced technological and organizational change, yet the effect of such changes did not appear in estimates of final output. One reason for this is that some industries experienced 'learning by doing' improvements rather than great breakthroughs. Another is that their type of change was not associated with 'artefacts' such as new machines or new factory buildings. Examples are artisan metal trades which developed new skill-intensive hand processes, hand tools, and new malleable alloys; wool textile manufacturers who moved over to new products requiring shorter finishing times and new marketing initiatives; and builders who introduced 'general contracting' and housing estates to replace the old master builder.

There are further good reasons why industries which underwent periods of fundamental transformation in their technologies, organization and markets seemed not to show the results of these in higher output results for some years to come. The economy-wide effect of any single innovation or even set of innovations might be very small, or might take a long time to make its impact. This was the point of David Ricardo's famous chapter 'On Machinery'. In the short run, innovation might only increase unemployment and put downward pressure on wages.[8]

The growth rates of any single industry, furthermore, do not tell us about

Table 2.2 Growth of real output in industrial sectors

	Cotton	Wool	Linen	Silk	Building	Iron	Copper	Beer	Leather	Soap	Candles	Coal	Paper
1700–60	1.37	0.97	1.25	0.67	0.74	0.60	2.62	0.21	0.25	0.28	0.49	0.64	1.51
1760–70	4.59	1.30	2.68	3.40	0.34	1.65	5.61	−0.10	−0.10	0.62	0.71	2.19	2.09
1770–80	6.20		3.42	−0.03	4.24	4.47	2.40	1.10	0.82	1.32	1.15	2.48	0.00
1780–90	12.76	0.54	−0.34	1.13	3.22	3.79	4.14	0.82	0.95	1.34	0.43	2.36	5.62
1790–1801	6.73		0.00	−0.67	2.01	6.48	−0.85	1.54	0.63	2.19	2.19	3.21	1.02
1801–11	4.49	1.64	1.07	1.65	2.05	7.45	−0.88	0.79	2.13	2.63	1.34	2.53	3.34
1811–21	5.59		3.40	6.04	3.61	−0.28	3.22	−0.47	−0.94	2.42	1.80	2.76	1.73
1821–31	6.82	2.03	3.03	6.08	3.14	6.47	3.43	0.66	1.15	2.41	2.27	3.68	2.21

Source: Crafts, *British Economic Growth*, table 2.4

Table 2.3 Value added in British industry (£m, current)

	1770	%	1801	%	1831	%
Cotton	0.6	(2.6)	9.2	(17.0)	25.3	(22.4)
Wool	7.0	(30.6)	10.1	(18.7)	15.9	(14.1)
Linen	1.9	(8.3)	2.6	(4.8)	5.0	(4.4)
Silk	1.0	(4.4)	2.0	(3.7)	5.8	(5.1)
Building	2.4	(10.5)	9.3	(17.2)	26.5	(23.5)
Iron	1.5	(6.6)	4.0	(7.4)	7.6	(6.7)
Copper	0.2	(0.9)	0.9	(1.7)	0.8	(0.7)
Beer	1.3	(5.7)	2.5	(4.6)	5.2	(4.6)
Leather	5.1	(22.3)	8.4	(15.5)	9.8	(8.7)
Soap	0.3	(1.3)	0.8	(1.5)	1.2	(1.1)
Candles	0.5	(2.2)	1.0	(1.8)	1.2	(1.1)
Coal	0.9	(4.4)	2.7	(5.0)	7.9	(7.0)
Paper	0.1	(0.4)	0.6	(1.1)	0.8	(0.7)
	22.8		54.1		113.0	

Source: Crafts, *British Economic Growth*, table 2.3.

the processes underlying growth. Some of these processes involved industrial restructuring. This might include technological change, organizational or locational change, and market readjustment. But the downside of this process would also be branches of the industry eliminated, markets abandoned, redundant workers made unemployed, and obsolete machinery scrapped. In the short term there are costs to all of this. We might look, for example, to processes of change in the silk, copper and brass industries during the later eighteenth and early nineteenth centuries, years covering the American War of Independence and the Napoleonic Wars. Throwing mills were introduced in the silk industry, a substantial portion of the industry was moved out of London, and the source of raw silk was moved from the Mediterranean to the Far East.[9] There were, to be sure, negative growth rates in the industry in the 1790s, but this was also the time when these key changes were occurring. And by 1811–21 and 1821–31, rates of growth of output were comparable to those of the cotton industry. The copper industry experienced rapid growth in output until the 1790s, but faced organizational change then, after an attack by copper consumers and miners on the smelting cartels. Output faltered over this period, but by 1811–21 growth of real output in the industry was back to over 3 per cent per year.[10]

Growth trends in an industry which might appear stable or even falling are no indication in themselves of a simple continuation with traditional methods. Those periods when individual industries experienced their greatest innovation did not necessarily coincide with periods of highest rates of growth of output.

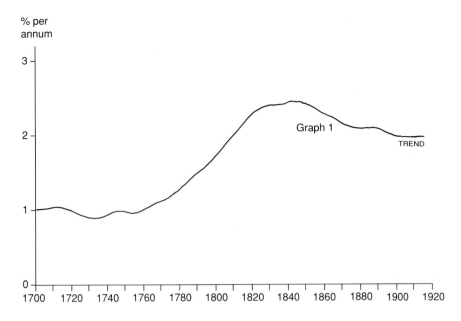

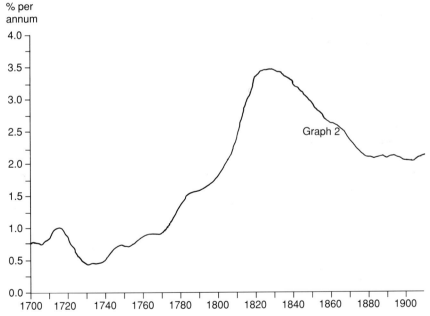

Figure 2.1 Trend growth of industry

Source: Crafts, Leybourne and Mills, 'Britain', pp. 132 and 140.

Note: Graph 1 represents the trend growth of Crafts's industry sample excluding cotton, iron, steel and coal, and Graph 2 the trend growth of Crafts's complete industry sample.

With these overall indications of the progress of British industry, and questions we can raise about just how much these indicators tell us, we will now turn to look at the patterns of growth in various industrial groups.

THE TEXTILE INDUSTRIES

The textile group of industries contained Crafts's 'glamour industry', cotton, and three 'traditional industries', wool and worsted, linen and silk. We can compare their relative positions within British industry, and their performance in output.

A comparison of these industries shows that the 'traditional' woollen industry still dominated the whole industrial sector at the beginning of the nineteenth century, and was still more important in terms of value added than the cotton industry until the 1820s. The traditional textile industries did show substantial increases in their growth rates over the period 1700 to 1830, not steadily and sometimes not rapidly. But whatever they did accomplish was clearly overshadowed by cotton's amazing growth. Landes contrasted the two periods of the cotton industry's expansion by pointing out that in 1760 Britain imported only 2.5 million pounds of raw cotton to feed an industry dispersed through the countryside, but in 1787 she consumed up to 22 million pounds. The industry was second only to wool in numbers employed and value of production, and most of the fibre was being cleaned, carded and spun on machines. For this was the period of the great textile innovations – Kay's flying shuttle, Hargreaves's jenny, Arkwright's water frame and Crompton's mule, to be followed at the end of the century by the power loom and the dressing frame.[11]

The cotton industry's spectacular growth was made from a small base. The orthodoxy stresses its minimal contribution to value added in the last third of the eighteenth century. The advantages of the 'small industry' were obvious: rapid organizational and technological change in the early stages brought few costs in terms of obsolescent capital and redundant labour within the industry itself; these costs were borne by the other textile industries. Behind the rapid increases in output lay mechanization and the factory system, but the form which these took and the lengths to which they went were not quite what they have been made out to be. In 1780 Britain had no more than 15 or 20 cotton mills, and seven years later there were 145 Arkwright-type mills. Before the end of the eighteenth century there were 900 cotton-spinning factories. These ranged, however, from 300 Arkwright-type factories – purpose-built buildings of several stories employing over fifty workers – through 600 'factories' using jennies and mules, some of which were little more than sheds or workshops employing around a dozen workers.[12] The industry's capital in the late 1780s was still predominantly spread over hand or domestic processes, especially weaving.

The place given to cotton in general industrial growth must depend upon

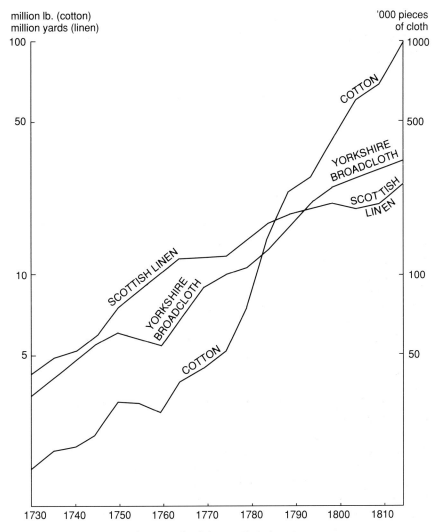

Figure 2.2 The growth of the textile industries, 1730–1815

Source: Pawson, *The Early Industrial Revolution*, p. 103.

the sectoral weights given to the sector. These weights have been the subject of much debate, but thus far most of this has centred around the choice of price indices, and the techniques for applying these.[13] But cotton's position could equally well be affected by the quality of the yarn whose prices are included in the series. If it is possible to show higher price reductions over the later eighteenth century in low count yarns, the growth of the industry appears correspondingly higher.[14] It is, furthermore, almost certainly the case that estimates for cloth output included only unfinished cloth. The finishing processes, bleaching, dyeing and printing added greatly to the value of the industry; indeed Chapman has calculated that their inclusion would be likely to double the gross value of output in the industry in 1797. The result would be a value added of £17 million, and a contribution to national income of 7 per cent.[15]

On current estimates, the woollen industry appears to be a good candidate for theories of steady continuous growth, for output grew by only 150 per cent over the whole of the eighteenth century. But behind these overall trends of change lay remarkable change in the geographical location of the industry, and much higher rates of increase in output for the Yorkshire branch of the industry, as illustrated in Figure 2.2 (see page 41). In the early eighteenth century the geography of the industry was much as it had been in the Middle Ages, that is to say, concentrated in East Anglia, the West Country and Yorkshire. The rapid growth of a worsted industry and of a dynamic woollen branch in Yorkshire from the end of the seventeenth century was reflected in the eighteenth-century growth of Leeds, Bradford, Huddersfield, Wakefield and Halifax. Yorkshire's share of national production grew from 20 per cent to 60 per cent. The intensive growth and concentration of the industry in this one region meant not gradual change in the industry but a regional revolution in organization and products.[16] The new importance of the West Riding of Yorkshire was complemented by the decline over the century of the industry in Suffolk, Essex and the West Country, and by the early nineteenth century in Northamptonshire and other parts of the Midlands and the South.[17] The major gains of the industry in one region smoothed out the losses in the rest of the country.

Behind the growth of output from Yorkshire lay the appearance of new factories along with changes in technology. Some of these factories were substantial in the worsted sector, but the woollen industry boasted a whole range of small mills for spinning with jennies or small mules, and for fulling, carding and scribbling. They had a central source of power, usually a waterwheel. The growth in the numbers of these mills was rapid in the later eighteenth century, then steadied off.

Changes in technology were also clear in the distribution of labour costs across the processes of the industry. Where, earlier in the eighteenth century, hand spinning absorbed most of the labour, there was a sharp reversal in the positions of spinning and weaving at the end of the century. Spinning was being mechanized, and hand weaving now absorbed the highest labour costs.

By the mid 1830s Yorkshire had 600 mills; there were only 242 in 1800.[18] Horsepower and numbers employed made these small affairs by today's standards, or even by comparison with a state-of-the-art cotton mill at the time. But nevertheless these were mills, using power and new machinery and making a different product from other parts of the country, and all of these produced a distinctive growth and regional concentration of the industry.

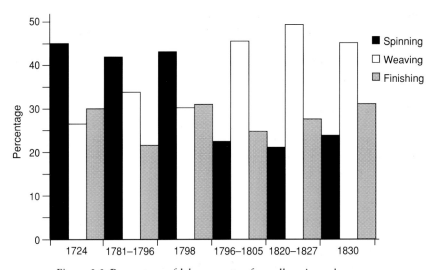

Figure 2.3 Percentage of labour costs of woollens in each process

Source: Berg, 'Factories, Workshops', and Hudson, *Genesis of Industrial Capital*, p. 150.

The silk industry bore the handicap of an expensive luxury commodity facing fierce foreign competition. Yet it was a technological leader from the first quarter of the eighteenth century in the use of water-driven machinery and the factory system. These changes were reflected in rates of increase in output by the 1770s of 3.4 per cent per year, a faster advance over previous growth rates than shown by any other textile industry, including cotton. But silk then entered its years of restructuring in the face of shifting world input and product markets. The effort only bore fruit after the end of the Napoleonic Wars, with growth rates rising to the levels held by cotton in the second two decades of the nineteenth century.[19] By this stage, however, cotton was the dominant textile industry; silk started small and stayed that way.

In aggregative accounts of industrial growth the linen industry does not even rate a nod, but this is another instance of the blinkered lenses of the national accounts shutting out a sight of regional and provincial economies. In England linen had long been a widespread local industry producing for domestic consumption; in the course of the eighteenth century it became much more market-orientated. Output doubled in the second quarter of the eighteenth century, and did so again in the third quarter. But it was Scotland that made the industry its own. The Act of Union of 1707 gave the Scots access to English and especially colonial markets; linen was a key export under the old colonial system. The industry quickly became concentrated in parts of five counties: Forfarshire, Lowland Perthshire, Fife, Lanarkshire and Renfrewshire.[20] And the value of linen produced in this one part of

Britain rose from £103,000 in 1728 to £1,116,000 in 1799; the English performance pales into insignificance beside provincial ratings like this.[21] In Scotland at least it was not enough to pin an Industrial Revolution to the cotton industry; linen was part of the story too.

MINING AND METALS

The fuel which was the key to the British path of technical transformation was coal. It is coal which forms the centre-point for Wrigley's great transformation to a 'mineral based energy economy'. Increases in its use during the eighteenth century had led to a departure of the 'advanced organic economy' away from its 'pure' form.[22] Holland had peat, and for a time exploited its cheap fuel supplies with great success to develop the great manufactures of the Dutch golden age: brewing, distilling, salt refining, bleaching, dyeing and printing textiles, brick- and tile-making and shipbuilding.[23] But the golden age was short-lived, and Dutch industry was soon facing rising marginal costs and competition with British industry.

This pivotal industry rates, however, with Crafts's traditional sector, that producing 'non-tradables'. But coal is in some dispute. Crafts himself, in later work, groups it with cotton, iron and steel as an export staple to be extracted from the general picture of the trend growth of industrial production.[24] Mokyr put all factories, transport, mining, quarrying, metallurgy, paper and potteries in the 'modern' sector.[25] And current estimates of growth in output range widely with Crafts's estimates falling well short, especially in the first half of the century, of those provided by Flinn.

Even these estimates move in doubtful territory. No national coal statistics were collected until 1854; estimates made on the period before are concocted from a number of series, random figures and estimates of varying degrees of reliability, and are no more than a guide. What they do indicate is a tenfold growth in British coal production between 1700 and 1830. Growth accelerated steadily up to 1815, with some periods of sudden spurts. Per capita consumption nearly doubled by the mid-eighteenth century, and tripled by 1800.[26]

Behind these national aggregates lie regional disparities much as we find in the textile industry. During the eighteenth century the North-East held sway; almost half of British coal was produced there early in the century. But by 1830, though still the largest producer, its share of total output had fallen to one quarter.[27] The pits on Tyneside were state-of-the-art: large in scale with an average workforce of 300 compared to 80 for the whole industry, and technological leaders with highly rated workforce and management skills.[28] But coal was needed by the iron industry, and later in the eighteenth century other regions – South Wales, Staffordshire and Yorkshire – as well as Scotland and the West Midlands took off.

Table 2.4 Estimated output of coal, 1700–1830, by mining regions ('000s of tons)

Mining region	1700	1750	1775	1800	1815	1830
Scotland	450	715	1,000	2,000	2,500	3,000
Cumberland	25	350	450	500	520	560
Lancashire	80	350	900	1,400	2,800	4,000
North Wales	25	80	110	150	350	600
South Wales	80	140	650	1,700	2,750	4,400
South-West	150	180	250	445	610	800
East Midlands	75	140	250	750	1,400	1,700
West Midlands	510	820	1,400	2,550	3,990	5,600
Yorkshire	300	500	850	1,100	1,950	2,800
North-East	1,290	1,955	2,990	4,450	5,395	6,915
Total (tons)	2,985	5,230	8,850	15,045	22,265	30,375
(tonnes)	3,033	5,314	8,992	15,286	22,621	30,861
Annual compounded rate of growth (%)		1.13	2.13	2.15	2.65	2.09

Source: Flinn, 'History of the British Coal Industry', p. 26.

It is a classic one-liner that the coal industry's achievement was based not on mechanization, but on greater inputs of capital and labour. The one input which made mineral-based powered technologies possible was dug from the ground by a hugely expanding army of miners working with muscle, pick and shovel. But the coal which made the steam power possible was also extracted from deeper pits with the aid of such power. The first uses to which the steam engines were put were the draining of deeper seams, then the winding of coal.

The rapid expansion of coal production was bound up with break-throughs in the iron industry and with steam power, both of these accomplished within the first two decades of the eighteenth century. Iron's progress is the other great success story conceded in current assessments of the Industrial Revolution. For iron, as in other metal smelting and refining, the major technical changes of the period were those that saved on raw material costs, not on labour. Darby first smelted iron using coal converted into coke as a substitute for charcoal in 1709. But it took until the last third of the eighteenth century before production methods across the industry seriously changed. Rates of growth of output jumped to 4.47 per cent per year in the 1770s, to 6.48 per cent in the 1790s, and up to 7.45 per cent in the first decade of the nineteenth century, after which the industry encountered a crisis of overproduction.[29] 1775 was the beginning of a new era when the wider application of steam power made for a stronger blast and raised the efficiency of smelting by coke.

Restructuring brought geographical concentration in South Wales, which produced 40 per cent of total output, the Midlands, and later in Scotland.[30]

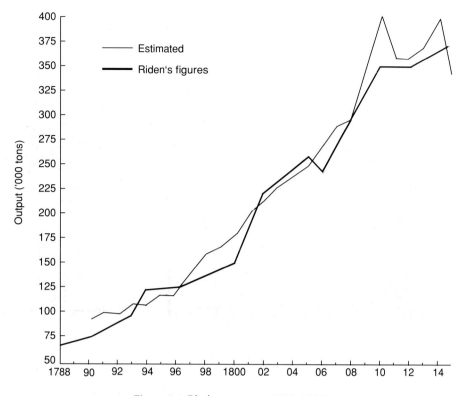

Figure 2.4 Pig iron output, 1788–1815

Source: Davis and Pollard, 'The Iron Industry', p. 83.

And capacity grew. Average output per blast furnace grew from 300 tons in 1720 to 1,500 in 1805 and 2,600 in 1826.[31]

Iron's progress must be held in some perspective. Cotton may have been a small industry in 1770, and iron was certainly two and a half times its size in terms of proportions contributed to value added. By 1801 iron was contributing only a slightly higher proportion of value added than it had in 1770, and by 1831 had reverted to its former position, while cotton had upset all the old distributions. The iron industry's growth in value added between 1770 and 1831 was less than that of coal.[32]

The diffusion of coke smelting put pressure on the old refining techniques. Puddling and rolling replaced them and made it possible to substitute for the expensive imported bar iron, traditionally used in metalworking, the new home-produced pig iron. In the early eighteenth century Britain produced 20,000 to 25,000 tons of pig iron per year; most of this went on to be refined as bar iron, converting to 15,000 to 18,000 tons a year. But this was nowhere near meeting the needs of Britain's metalworking industries. It

46

Plate 1 Painting of Thorncliffe ironworks, near Sheffield, 1811 (Chapeltown and High Green Archive)

provided no more than a half, possibly only one third, of the total consumption of bar iron; the rest was imported mainly from Sweden.[33] Even in the early nineteenth century the Sheffield cutlery and steel industries relied on imports of high-grade iron.

Other non-ferrous industries experienced expansion, but some hiccups as well. Exports of these metals more than quadrupled over the century.[34] Cornish tin production rose from 1,323 tons in 1695–1704 to 2,658 in 1750–9, and further to 3,245 tons in 1790–9. Cornish copper ore production rose from 6,600 tons in 1725–34 to 46,700 tons in 1790–9. On Crafts's estimates copper was a high-growth industry until the 1790s; its growth rate of 5.61 per cent per year for 1760–70 was higher than that of any of the other industries he surveys. But there was a sharp setback in the 1790s with negative growth rates from then until the second decade of the nineteenth century. What happened during these years was a reorganization of the industry including an attack on the copper cartels. Production probably faltered, but statistical returns at the time certainly did so, and it is difficult to discover at just what rate output was rising.[35] Whatever the extent of the setback, there were few long-term repercussions, for output was back to increases of well over 3 per cent after the first decade of the nineteenth century.

It was not just the production of basic metals which made great advances, but that of all sorts of metal goods. Their progress is not measured by the growth of the iron or copper industries alone, for as we have seen Britain imported high proportions of its needs for bar iron throughout the eighteenth century. Their raw materials were, furthermore, a range of metal alloys whose invention in the eighteenth century generated further extensive product innovation in final outputs. Well before the Industrial Revolution, the West Midlands, South Yorkshire and North-East Durham were well-established centres of the metal trades. In 1677 Andrew Yarranton described how the iron manufactures of Stourbridge, Dudley, Wolverhampton, Sedgley, Walsall and Birmingham were diffused all over England. The Crowley Ironworks in North-East Durham was established in 1682 in Sunderland, moving in 1690 close to Newcastle. And Defoe wrote in 1724 of 'the continued smoke of the forges' at Sheffield which were 'always at work, making all sorts of cutleryware'.[36]

There are no consistent indices of output for metalwares, and Crafts gives output figures only for pig iron over the whole period, and for copper ore only until 1771. Some indication of the growth of metalwares can be derived from data on exports. Wool dominated the export trade at the beginning of the eighteenth century, but this domination was gradually broken down throughout the rest of the century by the expansion of other industries. Britain's exports became much more diversified, and by the 1770s wool made up only about one half of exports. Textiles' position was brought to the fore again with the rise of cotton exports towards the end of the century. But in the meantime the largest group of exports outside textiles was comprised of metals and metalwares. Initially these exports were comprised of handicraft metalwares, hardware and guns. But new iron processing, copper smelting and tin processing techniques expanded the refined metals exported, and formed the basis for new manufactures in heavy iron wares, brassware and tinplate.

Elizabeth Schumpeter estimated that exports of wrought iron rose from 21,693 cwt in 1700 to 464,931 cwt in 1800. Exports of iron nails rose from 10,839 cwt in 1700 to 37,162 cwt in 1800. Exports of wrought copper rose from 1,636 cwt in 1700 to 96,199 cwt in 1800. Exports of wrought brass also rose to a similar extent over the century, but increased by nearly three times between 1775 and 1800.[37] Joshua Gee, a political economist, had noticed in the 1720s the technical advances and growth of the copper and brass industries, and he connected these to the growth of the new hardware, steel and toy trades of Birmingham.[38] Much of the output of the metalwares industry was also used for home consumption. This relied in turn on substantial imports – two-thirds of its needs, of high-grade bar iron. Imports of bar iron in tons rose from 16,949 in 1700 to 38,155 in 1800; in value terms they rose from £169,024 to £472,732.[39]

The expansion of home and overseas markets in metalwares created the stimulus for technological change – stamps, moulds, processes for boring and rolling metals – and extensive division of labour. Most of this expansion was, however, based on domestic industry and workshops, not on the factory system.

Iron's uses for girders, iron sheets, plates, pipes, railings, buildings and bridges generated a whole series of improvements after puddling in the 1790s. Bigger and better-designed furnaces and larger-scale integrated plants helped to provide the output for domination in world markets and for new construction and engineering materials at home.

Table 2.5 provides some disaggregation of the metals industry, if only for the early nineteenth century. But even this can mask the degree of change. The category for 'hardware and cutlery' must have changed its composition

Table 2.5 Exports of refined metals and metalwares, 1814–16 and 1844–6 (£'000)

	1814–16	1844–6
Finished goods:		
Hardware and cutlery	1612	2181
Hand guns and swords	123	268
Gold and silver plate	112	131
Brass, copper and tin wares	248	148
Iron nails	118	140
Watches and clocks	55	78
Instruments	103	101
Machinery: steam engines	–	319
other	28	614
Total finished goods	*2399*	*3980*
Semi-finished and constructional goods:		
Iron bolts, rods, castings	236	571
Iron rails, etc.	–	n.a.
Other iron wares	548	834
Copper sheet and nails	328	775
Tinplate	232	580
Total semi-finished goods etc.	*1344*	*2760*
Refined metals:		
Iron	205	1842
Steel	32	266
Lead	306	268
Copper	55	759
Other metals	147	96
Total refined metals	*745*	*3231*
Total	*4488*	*9971*

Source: Davis, *The Industrial Revolution*, table 15.

and quality many times over the eighteenth and early nineteenth centuries. But the whole of this varied production is lumped in a single category in official statistics and given a fixed valuation per hundredweight.[40]

The new proliferation of metalworking was founded for the most part not on machines, but on labour and skill. The puddling and rolling of iron were based on the skills and the sweat and muscle of newly specialized workers – the furnaceman and the puddler. The emergence of this freshly skilled workforce arose in turn out of a long tradition of artisan skills in mineral fuel technology. Metalworking covered not only the hardware and cutlery trades, but machine- and toolmaking. Processes here were improved by new handtools for turning, cutting, piercing and stamping metal goods. Improvements in water power and the introduction of an effective rotative, then rotary, steam engine, while they did not immediately affect most of these small-scale trades, did demand new millwrighting and engineering skills, and especially skills in the precision metalworking of large objects in iron such as cylinders, crankshafts and piping. A new range of engineering tools for boring, planing, turning and cutting accompanied these skills.

We have no means of estimating quantities of new tools and machinery produced. From 1780 until 1825 the export of machinery (though not of steam engines) was prohibited, and after that such exports were only permitted under special licence until 1843. In spite of these prohibitions, much machinery was smuggled abroad. Most of the machinery used at home was made at this stage in machine shops attached to factories or works, or in shops producing a range of engineering and general hardware goods. Even in the last half of the nineteenth century, output estimates are available for only one or two leading machine tool firms.[41] The only major centres of engineering technology by the early nineteenth century were Boulton and Watt's Soho Works, Maudslay's London Workshop and the Woolwich Arsenal.

What has been estimated is steam engine production. A vigorous academic industry in steam engine counting for the eighteenth century has produced the estimates shown in Table 2.6.

OTHER INDUSTRIES

Current orthodoxy tells us that rapid transformation was confined to cotton and iron. The rest of industry, if it did not sleep, simply kept pace with population growth. But what was the rest of industry? When Hoffmann first estimated output for the industrial sector, he could find data for only 56 per cent of industry, and this was used to represent the whole. After deducting for cotton and iron, Crafts is left with 43.2 per cent of the industrial sector containing 'observable' industries.[42] We have dealt already with wool, linen, silk, coal and copper. Of the industries that are left, only building and leather are given any notice, and this for their high relative weight in value

Table 2.6 Steam power in British industry, 1800

Industry	Numbers	Percentage
Mines and quarries	1,064	48.6
Metal manufacture and		
mechanical engineering	1,263	12.0
Textiles	469	21.4
Food, drink, tobacco	112	5.1
Total manufacturing	906	41.4

Source: Von Tunzelmann, 'Coal and Steam Power', table 8.1, p. 78.

Note: The column 'numbers' refers to the number of enterprises which use steam power, and the column 'percentage' describes their share in the individual branch of enterprises.

added combined with the traditionalism of their processes. Beer, soap, candles and paper are 'observed', but passed over as insignificant. Other industries – shipbuilding, chemicals, distilling and food processing, glass-making and potteries, hatmaking and clothing – were 'unobserved', and therefore ignored.

Let us look first at building and leather. The value added by building rose both absolutely and proportionately over the whole period; building's share of total value added in industry was 17 per cent in 1801, and 23 per cent in 1831. And this was supposedly achieved with no change in methods of production. This stagnation is certainly overstated if civil engineering is included. Mechanical methods of preparing clay and making bricks were gradually introduced over the nineteenth century. Key inventions, especially the wire-cut brick, were made in the 1830s, but did not come into effective use until the latter half of the century. There were already more than 230 patents connected with brickmaking by 1856, but diffusion was slow.[43] In spite of this, results were clear-cut: at the beginning of the nineteenth century brickmaking was local, unmechanized and small-scale; by the century's end, mass-production by machinery predominated.[44] Production units were still small. Clapham worked out that even in 1870 there were about 1,770 works, and an average of 12.7 work-people per works.[45] Apart from brickmaking, a range of technical improvements in woodworking was introduced from the beginning of the nineteenth century.

Overall, expansion in the industry was rapid. Brick production doubled over the period 1815 to 1849, and rose more than in proportion to population.[46] The building industry absorbed high proportions of the male labour force, and responded to building booms in the mid-1820s, the later 1830s and 1847. The result was decennial net increases in housing rising from 216,000 in 1801–11 to 516,000 for 1831–41.[47]

Building and the leather trades are the industries singled out in current

Plate 2 The art of hat-making (Mary Evans Picture Library)

accounts of the Industrial Revolution for their high labour forces deployed to relatively uninspiring effect. They were among those occupational categories where Wrigley thought it unlikely that output per head had been rising more than marginally for generations.[48] If we add up the men aged 20 and over occupied in 1831 as carpenters, masons and bricklayers, these comprised 15 per cent of the adult male labour force. Building was by far the largest male employment after agriculture. But what kind of employment was this? It was seasonal, cyclical, erratic. For much of the time the occupational category was a cover for unemployed men. Numbers in occupational categories, especially in this case and in that of shoemaking too, are no measure of labour input. If processes were slow to change in building, organization led the way to change. The eighteenth century saw the rise of speculative building, general contracting, housing estates and building societies.[49]

The leather industry was another large industry which experienced little technological innovation before the 1830s. In 1770 it contributed the highest proportion of value added in industry after wool, but unlike building its share of industrial production fell steadily thereafter. Between 1770 and 1831 its share of value added fell from 22.3 per cent to 8.7 per cent.[50] Most

Table 2.7 House-building and brick output, 1791–1850

Decades	Output of bricks (in millions)	Houses built (in thousands)	Implied bricks per house (in thousands)
1791–1800	6,400	188	34.1
1801–10	8,250	255	32.4
1811–20	8,630	345	25.0
1821–30	12,310	480	25.6
1831–40	13,370	586	22.8
1841–50	10,560	423	25.0

Source: Feinstein, 'National Statistics, 1760–1920', table 17.5, p. 388.

Note: The value of column four was calculated by dividing the value of column two by the value of column three. Higher levels of brick usage in the fourth column for the first two decades are likely to be accounted for by canal building.

shoemaking was a widely practised local craft. Entry to the trade was relatively easy, so that like building it became a sponge for excess male labour. Mechanization did not come until the 1850s, but the putting-out system emerged from mid-seventeenth-century wholesale manufacture. Wholesale production, first for army orders, then for other markets, moved from London to Northamptonshire and Staffordshire. These trends were intensified into the mid-nineteenth century.[51]

The ambiguous showing of leather and building in the stakes for productivity growth must not, however, be allowed to cast a shadow over the achievements of other industries. Food processing, chemicals, glass and pottery, paper and shipbuilding all experienced major technological or organizational changes in the period. On Crafts's measures, brewing increased its value added by four times between 1770 and 1831; paper rose eight times. The other industries are among the 'unobserved'. We can still, however, ask what happened to them. Dutch and German potters in the seventeenth and early eighteenth centuries produced the first good imitations of Chinese porcelain. The British made a close substitute, using coal fuel and new materials. Wedgwood combined this with the factory system and effective marketing.[52] The British upstaged the French in glassmaking at the end of the eighteenth century with the coal-fired reverberatory furnace.[53] Exports of glass and earthenware rose spectacularly from 785,975 pieces in 1700 to 30,281,388 in 1800.[54] The growth of potash and soda production and salt refining in the chemical industries was outstripped by the invention and production of sulphuric acid and its derivative, chlorine for bleaching, all of these first and foremost Scottish industries. The paper industry was revolutionized at the end of the eighteenth century by machinery for making continuous sheets in place of moulds for separate sheets. The process was perfected and introduced in England, and called the Foudrinier machine. Its impact was to cut production time for a sheet of paper from three weeks to three minutes.[55]

Merchant shipbuilding was a big industry in the ports, and the British picked up the innovative initiative from the Dutch. The shipbuilding skills of the Dutch were noticed at the beginning of the eighteenth century and described by Henry Martyn, who connected the rise of the herring fishery with the invention of interchangeable parts in the building of fishing boats:

> Busses and other things, are works of great variety: to make them, there is as great variety of Artists; no one is charg'd with so much work, as to abate his Skill or Expedition. The model of their Busses is seldom chang'd, so that the Parts of one would serve as well for every Buss; as soon as any such thing can be bespoke in Holland, presently all the parts are laid together, the Buss is raised with mighty expedition.[56]

It was a wood and sail industry, but innovation in designs and production systems was important. In some of these the naval dockyards led the way, incorporating leading engineers and introducing flow-line methods.

Table 2.8 Ships built at the major shipbuilding centres, 1787–99

	Number	*Tonnage*
London	576	129,557
Newcastle	419	92,794
Hull	458	57,746
Sunderland	318	56,420
Whitby	234	54,704
Liverpool	322	48,955

Source: Pawson, *The Early Industrial Revolution*, p. 126.

Then there is food processing, 'unobserved' apart from brewing. In a country still predominantly agricultural this was one of the most prominent of manufacturing activities. The food and drink trades brought agriculture and manufacture together. Multiple occupations and partnerships were common in manufacture at the time, and the most common connection for many manufacturers was one with the food or drink trades. Brewing grew most rapidly with the largest-scale firms. Distilling followed suit.

The eighteenth century was also the heyday of colonial groceries and other raw materials. Processing these created new industries – sugar houses, cocoa and coffee works, tobacco processing. Many of these groceries were processed around the ports – in Bristol, Glasgow and London. Large-scale production and technological innovation in these commodities was already well known in Amsterdam. These industries were famous in their time, and were described as technological leaders whose example also affected other trades. John Cary, the Bristol sugar merchant and political economist, delighted in a catalogue of technological achievements in sugar refining, distilling, tobacco manufacture, woodworking and lead smelting:

> There is a cunning crept into the trades – the clockmaker hath improved his art to such a degree that labour and materials are the least part the buyer pays for. The variety of our woollen manufacture is so pretty . . . artificers, by tools and lathes fitted for different purposes, make such things as would puzzle a stander by to set a price on, according to the worth of men's labour.[57]

The desirability of some of these manufactures and the novelty of their processing methods were not enough to overcome the fact that they were luxury commodities. The value added by these colonial food industries cannot have been much more than 1 per cent of Europe's total industrial output.[58]

Industrial raw materials imported from Asia and the Americas undoubtedly had a larger effect on industrial expansion, but this has not yet been measured. Cochineal, indigo and other dye products contributed to dye works and printing houses. Chapman has estimated that if the value added in these finishing industries, along with bleaching, is added to Crafts's estimates for value added in cotton, then estimates for the sector would nearly double.[59] Furs, especially beaver furs, were processed in a rapidly expanding hatting industry in the London workshop economy. Fish and whale oil and log wood were integrated into other processing industries. The impact of some of these industries may not have been great in terms of value added. But they were part of a system of trade which included other export industries – cotton, iron, shipbuilding – and like these were among the more advanced manufacturing sectors. They were a focus for technological and organizational innovation, and generated external economies in the ports and other regional centres where they concentrated. If the overall size of these industries was small, the demonstration effect was large. And the goods produced generated more desire for commercially produced manufactured commodities, and escalated the advance of industries connected to the world economy.

We have seen that current estimates of productivity growth and growth of output point to rapid change in only a handful of industries. But as this chapter has set out, growth rates for a large range of industries were, for at least part of the period, respectable, and in some cases very substantial. Many industries also underwent a phase of rapid technological or organizational change late in the eighteenth century or early in the nineteenth century. These phases of restructuring did not necessarily produce instant results. Nevertheless, the high industrial growth rates which the orthodox view sets forward for the years after 1830 were the results of changes in technology and organization in the eighteenth and early nineteenth centuries.

3

MODELS OF INDUSTRIAL TRANSITION

There have been many theories of the sources of the Industrial Revolution, but a limited few of these address the economic and social changes within industry. Indeed significant attention has shifted recently far from the entrepreneurs, inventors and workers at the centre of industry towards the long-term processes of demographic change and resource endowments.[1] Debates on randomness and contingency, sectoral shifts and levels of capital investment[2] have pushed industry to the sidelines.

Models of industrial change which look, however, to the social structures of industry, its organization and techniques, were popular in earlier accounts of the Industrial Revolution, and some of these have been rediscovered and developed anew. This chapter will accordingly discuss Adam Smith's theory of the rise of industry, Marx's theory of manufactures and modern industry, and theories of proto-industrialization. All of these theories draw attention to the connections between agrarian change, commercial capitalism and the growth of handicraft production in rural cottages and urban workshops. They find in these connections the roots of subsequent mechanization and factory organization. The chapter will then relate the limitations of these theories to recent ideas on regional transformation and consumer demand.

ADAM SMITH AND NATURAL PROGRESS

For the economic and social historian, Adam Smith's *Wealth of Nations* has always provided the first systematic analysis of the division of labour and increasing returns. Smith provided a much more far-reaching historical model linking industrial, agricultural and urban growth in his lesser-known Book III, 'Of the Different Progress of Opulence in Different Nations'. The connections Smith set out in this model have come once again to the fore in recent historical work on agriculture and urban growth.[3] His analysis of distinctive types of manufacture, and his observations on the organization of industry and mercantile trade, provide major insights into the transitions in eighteenth-century industry.

Smith specifically deployed a development model to understand the economic history of Europe. He called this the 'natural progression' of economic development. The 'natural' in this phrase was not the actual, but an ideal type. The components of the model were agricultural surpluses, markets, and urban manufactures and services. Increasing productivity in agriculture created the base for urban and industrial growth. The 'natural progress' was from agriculture to manufacture and thence to foreign commerce. 'Manufactures for distant sale' might 'grow up of their own accord, by the gradual refinement of those household and coarser manufactures which must at all times be carried on in even the poorest and rudest countries.' Based on domestic raw materials, they generally sprang up in an inland country which produced an agricultural surplus that it, in turn, found difficult to trade, owing to high transport costs. The surplus, however, made basic needs very inexpensive, encouraging the immigration of a larger labour force. These workmen

> work up the materials of manufacture which the land produces . . .
> they give a new value to the surplus part of raw produce . . . and they
> furnish the cultivators with something in exchange for it that is either
> useful or agreeable to them . . . They are thus both encouraged and
> enabled to increase this surplus produce by a further improvement and
> better cultivation of the land; and as the fertility of the land had given
> birth to the manufacture, so the progress of the manufacture re-acts
> upon the land and increases still further its fertility.[4]

This 'natural progress' provided a close interaction between agricultural and industrial growth, and a solid basis for sustained regional development. Smith believed that his model came close to reality in the the histories of some parts of England, and in America. In England, some cities had arisen on the basis of rural industries which complemented regional agricultural surpluses: 'In this manner have grown up naturally, and as it were of their own accord, the manufactures of Leeds, Halifax, Sheffield, Birmingham and Wolverhampton. Such manufactures are the offspring of agriculture.'[5] Of American development, he wrote, 'Compare the slow progress of those European countries of which the wealth depends very much upon their commerce and manufacture, with the rapid advances of our North American colonies, of which the wealth is founded altogether in agriculture.'[6]

Unlike these model cases, however, Smith found the actual course of European development to be the reverse, that is not from agriculture to industry and commerce, but from foreign commerce and industry to agriculture. The 'unnatural' course of European economic development had been based on policies which favoured the development of luxury manufactures using foreign raw materials, manufactures introduced to substitute for former imports. Such industries had usually been the 'scheme and project of a few individuals' and were established in maritime towns or inland cities 'according to their interest, judgment or caprice'.[7] The results were the exploitation of the countryside by the town, turning the terms of trade against agriculture, and an unstable industrial sector. 'Manufactures for which the demand arises altogether from fashion and fancy, are continually changing, and seldom last long enough to be considered as old established manufactures.'[8] Smith believed that the capital created by a merchant 'who was not necessarily the citizen of any particular country' was an unstable possession until part of it was reinvested in the land. An economy with a strong agrarian base was more likely to have a strong and stable political and social structure.

Smith's aversion to merchants and the industries they fostered for international luxury markets was clear in his conclusions on the different routes to urban growth.

> It is thus that through the greater part of Europe the commerce and manufactures of cities, instead of being the effect, have been the cause and occasion of the improvement of cultivation of the country. This order, however, being contrary to the natural course of things, is necessarily both slow and uncertain.[9]

The Smithian model of integrated agricultural and industrial development and complementarity between the town and the country has been recast in recent analyses of regional growth, urbanization and consumption. Industrialization as a regional phenomenon is now a starting point for analysis. The agrarian setting and social institutions in different regions are a determinant of industrial structures and vitality.[10] The success of industrial transition in different regions was dependent on the degree of conglomeration of multiple industrial activities, all interconnected, providing externalities and supporting overheads.[11] While agriculture may have passed at some point from being one of the key activities of a region, the principle of new activities arising on the basis of local surpluses, and in turn newly stimulating the local economy, remains. The regional model is thus fundamentally a Smithian construct.

NEW THEORIES OF REGIONAL AND URBAN GROWTH

Recent accounts of urban growth and manufacture also have a Smithian framework. Smith's model addressed the recent rise of Britain's new industrial towns. Their growth and the broadly-based urban growth in Britain in general over the seventeenth and eighteenth centuries have been compared recently by Wrigley to urban decline in the rest of Europe. The great cities of Europe (described by Smith as 'unnatural' extensions of commerce, monopolistic restriction and mercantile greed), whose growth was founded in the early modern period on long-distance trade, went into decline, falling victim to the new vitality of local rural-based manufacture.[12] Britain's new industrial towns, based on regional growth, home markets and agricultural development, not only survived, but grew rapidly.[13]

The interdependency of agricultural and industrial growth was also to be found in the distribution of income and consumer demand. Hohenberg has analysed rural–urban dynamics in a closed economy model of income distribution. The early modern city played an important part in manufacture. The model related incomes and, with this, demand in urban centres to conditions in the countryside. Agricultural productivity is related to property incomes. Improvements in productivity raise the share of income going to profits, reducing the shares going to wage payments and rents. A rising population would lead ultimately to diminishing returns in agriculture and, with this, higher rents. Diminishing returns in the countryside, reducing productivity and bringing high grain prices and lower discretionary incomes, would rapidly affect rural manufacturers. The rising population which brought higher rents would, in this model, also entail higher urban incomes, since the holders of power and property lived in the towns. Taxes and government revenue would also flow into the towns. Those in the central city might thus for a time retain their prosperity, buoyed up by high rents and property incomes, but demographic crisis would eventually cut rental incomes and break the urban boom.[14] This interdependent cycle would only be broken with rising agricultural surpluses, and such surpluses depended in turn on market incentives.

Market incentives would sustain the urban and industrial economy by providing new consumer demands. Demands for basic consumer goods were necessary to promote urban industry; such demand needed to be generated not only within the towns themselves, but in surrounding rural areas which held the greatest part of the population. Rural areas thus had to become commercialized; market-oriented work and market-oriented household consumption were the vital aspects of rural expansion needed to sustain urban expansion. Changes in rural household behaviour towards greater consumer demand were the key to what Jan de Vries has called the 'industrious revolution'.[15] This will be explored at length in Chapter 6. But the basic connections between town and country, and industry and agriculture in these recent historical models are based in Smithian concepts of market expansion and commercialization: 'as the fertility of the land had given birth to the manufacture, so the progress of the manufacture re-acts upon the land, and increases still further its fertility'.[16]

The Smithian model was based in agricultural and regional growth with international trade emerging out of this base. Where industry was, instead, the child of international trade and mercantile schemes, growth was erratic and the conditions of labour poor. Putting-out systems which were tied to the dynamics of international markets did not necessarily provide any mechanism for transitions in the economic and social organization of industry. From Smith's viewpoint such industries were frequently under-capitalized, deploying underemployed rural labour. They generated extremes of poverty and luxury, not the roots of industrialization. Smith used the linen industry of Scotland as a good example. Most of the labour went into the preparation and spinning of the yarn, and 'our spinners are poor people, women commonly, scattered about in all the different parts of the country, without support or protection'. But the great merchants and master manufacturers wanted to sell the final cloth as expensively, and to buy the yarn as cheaply as possible. 'It is the industry which is carried on for the benefit of the rich and the powerful, that is principally encouraged by our mercantile system. That which is carried on for the benefit of the poor and indigent, is too often either neglected or oppressed.'[17]

Alongside models of the rise and expansion of industry based mainly on Smith, are others more directly concerned with the processes of industrial production. These have taken their inspiration primarily from the Marxian analysis of the transition to industrial capitalism, and the rise of 'manufactures and modern industry'. This analysis has been important in recent years in shaping our ideas and assumptions about the creation of an industrial labour force and about the transition in the organization of industry from craft to factory production. The Marxian analysis is another historical model; its focus is based not in market expansion as with Smithian models, but in transitions in the production process. As a model it highlights key connections and tendencies, and is not intended as historical description.

MARX ON PRIMITIVE ACCUMULATION

The first analysis of industrial expansion before the factory, to which most historians have been tempted to look back, is Marx's model of the phase of manufacture, and, with this, his theory of primitive accumulation. Classical Marxist questions concerning the nature and mechanism of primary accumulation, the role of merchant capital, and the advance of the division of labour informed a widespread debate on the nature of the transition to industrial capitalism. Marx defined primitive accumulation as the necessary prehistorical phase of capitalism. It was the process which initially created the capital–labour relation.

Primitive accumulation was, in the first instance, associated with agrarian change and enclosure movements. The industrial side of the model is, at first, difficult to see. And the agrarian bias of primitive accumulation fitted well with a separate English historical tradition on the decline of the peasantry. Primitive accumulation influenced the tradition of Tawney and the Hammonds, and was also basic to the beliefs of the Oxford founders of economic history – Toynbee and James E. Thorold Rogers, a former Drummond Professor. It is to this historical tradition that we look to find the strongly-held belief that the robbery of his just rights from the labourer took the major form of the robbery of his land. Thorold Rogers, on the basis of his massive and much-praised *History of Agriculture and Prices*, denounced the practices of landlords and the government from the Middle Ages through to recent times.

> We have been able to trace the process by which the condition of English labour had been continuously deteriorated by the acts of government. It was first impoverished by the issue of base money. Next it was robbed of its guild capital by the land thieves of Edward's regency. It was next brought in contact with a new more needy set of employers – the sheepmasters who succeeded the monks . . . the agricultural labourer was then further mulcted by enclosures . . . The poor law professed to find him work, but was so administered that the reduction of his wages to a bare subsistence became an easy process . . . The freedom of the few was bought by the servitude of the many . . . Such was the education of which the English workman received from those evil days . . . He may have no knowledge, or a very vague knowledge, as to the process by which so strange, so woeful an alteration has been made in his condition. But there exists, and always has existed, a tradition, obscure and uncertain, but deeply seated, that there was a time when his lot was happier, his means more ample, his prospects more cheerful than they have been in more modern experience.[18]

This historical tradition, however, neglected the industrial side of the peasantry's decline. And Marx too wrote less, and less systematically, on the association between the spread of domestic industry and primitive accumulation. He did, however, write of primary accumulation as the first stage on the way to industrial concentration. He regarded the private property of the worker in his means of production as the foundation of small-scale industry, and small-scale industry as the necessary condition for the development of social production and the free individuality of the worker himself.

He argued that the destruction of the subsidiary trades of the countryside went hand in hand with the expropriation of a previously self-supporting peasantry. Only through the destruction of rural domestic industry could an adequate home market be provided for the capitalist mode of production. Yet he also pointed out that such domestic crafts did not simply disappear before the emergence of large-scale industry. This 'manufacturing period' did not 'carry out this transformation radically'. It always rested on the 'handicrafts of towns', and the domestic subsidiary industries of rural districts, but it destroyed these in one form and resurrected them again elsewhere. It produced 'a new class of small villagers who cultivate the soil as a subsidiary occupation, but find their chief occupation is industrial labour, the products of which they sell to the manufacturers directly, or through the medium of merchants'.[19]

Primitive accumulation was thus associated with manufacture. Primitive accumulation was meant to accomplish the separation of the labourer from his means of production, but did not necessarily mean removing him from the countryside. For, as Marx argued, the merchant capital which commissioned a number of immediate producers provided the 'soil from which modern capitalism has grown', and here and there it still forms an aspect of what Marx called the 'formal subsumption of labour', that is, where capital took over an available and established labour process. The changes taking place in domestic industry during primary accumulation were a good example.

'MANUFACTURES' AND 'MODERN INDUSTRY'

Elsewhere in *Capital* Marx also set out the definition of a stage in the development of the capitalist labour process which he termed 'manufacture'. Manufacture described a phase of handicraft workshop industry, a phase which preceded that of modern machine production. He was concerned with the organization and technological developments which set 'manufacture' off from previous industrial production. As a new form of organization, 'manufacture' described a workshop of handicraftsmen under capitalist control, carrying out one or a variety of tasks. As a new technology, it introduced the division of labour, though operations done by hand were still dependent on the skill of individuals and retained the character of a handicraft.

It becomes clear that Marx was more concerned to point out the limitations of the system of manufactures than to detail the variety of its manifestations. He noted three basic inadequacies of the system. First, because a hierarchical structure was inserted into the division of labour, the number of unskilled workers could not be infinitely extended. Hierarchy entailed the power and influence of skilled workers, and this prevented the full application of the division of labour.[20] Second, the narrow basis of handicraft itself excluded a really scientific division of the production process into its constituent parts. The division of labour could only go so far, for all parts had to be capable of being done by hand and forming a separate handicraft. The third and greatest problem, however, was the inability of capital to seize control of the whole disposable labour time of manufacturing workers.

> Since handicraft skill is the foundation of manufacture, and since the mechanization of manufacture as a whole possesses no objective framework which would be independent of the workers themselves, capital is constantly compelled to wrestle with the insubordination of the workers.[21]

The best historical example Marx could find to fit the criteria of his model

63

of manufacture was the engineering workshop of the late eighteenth and early nineteenth centuries. In spite of the allusions to rural industry and centralized production, then, Marx's model of 'manufactures' seems to have been a large workshop in the hands of a capitalist and organized on the basis of wage labour. Though Marx clearly intended it to be an abstract model, he included many historical signposts. The image of a handicraft-workshop economy preceding the rise of the factory system has been readily accepted with little enquiry into 'manufactures' as a model rather than as an historical description. But it seemed very aptly to encapsulate the structures of some of the leading workshops and proto-factories of the day. There was the minute division of labour of the pin manufactory described in Diderot's *Encyclopédie*. The pin, the smallest and most common of all manufactured products, demanded perhaps the most operations before entering into commerce. The essay on the pin describes eighteen different stages in the manufacturing process.[22]

There was also the division of handicraft skills in the Birmingham toy trades described in 1766:

> There a button passes through fifty hands, and each hand passes perhaps a thousand in a day – likewise, by this means, the work becomes so simple that five times in six, children of 6 or 8 years old do it as well as men, and earn from 10 pence to 8 shillings a week.[23]

The Boulton and Watt works in 1790 seemed the epitome of the order, regularity, and systematic layout emphasized by Marx.[24] Other manufacturers, such as Robert Peel in his Bury calico printing works in the 1780s, deployed unskilled labour under close discipline and supervision in much the manner described by Marx.[25]

These examples have frequently been accepted as indicative of the character of manufacturing organization in the country as a whole; or other manufacturing systems, such as 'putting-out', have been analysed purely in terms of 'manufactures'. Both systems are regarded as the first stage of that two-step phase by which workers were deprived of their control of product and process. But clearly the processes Marx was concerned to highlight were hierarchy and the division of labour. The manufacturing workshop was an example, an image of this. It was not a descriptive category meant to encompass a stage of capitalist development, for such workshops were of minimal significance beside rural decentralized industry. The break constituted by the minute division of labour in manufactures was followed by a second step, the centralized organization of the factory system. The phase of 'manufactures' was thus an innovation in organization, but one which obviously paled by comparison with the later innovation of the factory system. 'Manufactures' is credited with giving the capitalist, rather than the worker, control of the product, while the factory achieved this control over the production process itself.[26]

Applications and problems

The Marxist view of the system of manufactures is obviously 'retrospective', its vantage point progressive modern industry. The linear framework of the model of manufactures has, however, been incorporated into historians' discussion of industry before the factory system; it has also significantly affected our histories of workers' resistance. For just as the history of production was divided into control over product versus control over process, so eighteenth-century workers' struggles were divided off from those of the nineteenth century. Under manufactures, it has been assumed that each worker or group of workers still controlled, in some degree, the speed, intensity and rhythm of work, while later, under the factory system, machine-based modern industry was more profitable because it succeeded in taking away this control.

The model of manufactures was useful in highlighting the features of some of eighteenth-century industry, but it was a model and as such excluded the complication and variety of production processes. It was also a linear model, looking forward and back and not to either side, thus failing to place this manufacture in its own wider historical context. The clearest instance of both these problems is the model's failure to deal adequately with the features of the putting-out system and other related domestic forms of manufacture. This neglect did not, however, prevent economists and historians from applying Marx's model. Maurice Dobb, in particular, presented a clear and provocative account of the domestic system.

> The domestic industry of this period, however, was in a crucial respect different from the gild handicraft from which it had descended: in the majority of cases it had become subordinated to the control of capital, and the producing craftsman had lost most of his economic independence of earlier times . . . The craftsman's status was already beginning to approximate to that of a simple wage-earner; and in this respect the system was much closer to 'manufacture' than to the older urban handicrafts . . . The subordination of production to capital, and the appearance of this class relationship between capitalist and the producer is, therefore, to be regarded as the crucial watershed between the old mode of production and the new, even if the technical changes that we associate with the industrial revolution were needed both to complete the transition and to afford scope for the full maturing of the capitalist mode of production.[27]

The model of manufactures does, however, have much more to offer in recent research on the transition from artisan to factory production. Research addressed to different types of factory production has set out a new model of the 'small scale or unmechanised factory'. This model, deployed by Goldin and Sokoloff to analyse the early phases of American industrialization, is used to analyse the sources of productivity growth in a range of industries outside of textiles – clock- and gunmaking, hat- and shoemaking, umbrella and hardware manufacture. These new-style factories were to be distinguished from artisan workshops by size (6–15 employees), division of hand-performed tasks, use of simple tools, supervision and a more disciplined work regime. These latter features were reflected in the significantly higher proportion of female and child labour.[28]

This Sokoloff model of sources of productivity gain in organizational change, bringing hierarchy, division of labour and greater intensity, is a modern-day version of Marx's insights on the phase of manufacture. Other alternative models such as this and 'flexible specialization' will be explored at greater length in Chapter 9.

PROTO-INDUSTRIALIZATION

Where Marx himself did not dwell on the domestic system as the key manifestation of early modern manufacture, a recent historical school has identified rural putting-out systems with a distinct historical phase which preceded and paved the way for industrialization proper. The point of this model was to direct historians to the regional and rural economy, not simply agriculture, and to the country cottage rather than the urban workshop, for the crucial transitional phase of economic development, a phase now popularly known as 'proto-industrialization'.

Economic historians have long recognized the existence and importance of the great increase in commercial manufacturing production in the countryside between the seventeenth and nineteenth centuries. This rural industry, practised in conjunction with agriculture, has now, however, been elevated into the matrix of early modern economic and social change which paved the way for the factory system and wage labour: in short, industrialization at a later date. Developments from the seventeenth to the nineteenth century are encapsulated in the following key changes. The world market for mass-produced goods grew at such a pace from the later sixteenth century that traditional urban manufacturers could not efficiently respond, hampered as they were by guild restrictions and high labour costs. Complementary agricultural development entailed increasing regional differentiation between arable and pastoral regions. A regional symbiosis based on comparative advantage ensued. An underemployed peasantry in pastoral regions became the basis for an expandable and self-exploiting industrial labour force, and the industry it took up improved the seasonal employment of labour. The possibilities of alternative industrial employment released the traditional limits placed on population growth by the size of landholdings. Rural workers, living as they did in a world of traditional peasant culture and values, took less than the customary urban wage for their industrial work and laboured more intensively in the face of falling wages. In theory they had access to agricultural work which allowed them to produce part of their own subsistence. Their dispersal across the countryside furthermore made it difficult for them to organize so as to prevent price reductions by merchants. Access to this cheaper labour force therefore gave merchants a differential profit, one which was above the usual urban rates. This differential profit in turn provided a major source for capital accumulation. Proto-industry is credited not just with the sources of labour and capital, but in addition with the entrepreneurship and the technical and organizational changes that led to the first major increases in productivity before the factory.[29]

It is important to note that the emphasis given in this theory to cottage manufacture and putting-out systems is nothing new. Its proponents acknowledge their debt to later nineteenth-century German authorities such as Sombart, Troeltsch and Schmoller, and to the classic English economic histories by Unwin, Wadsworth and Mann, and Court. And recent English economic historians of the seventeenth and eighteenth centuries had already drawn attention to the demographic, agrarian and social organizational implications of the spread of rural industry.[30] But unlike this work, proto-industrialization implied systematic theory and predictive hypotheses.

If we wish to spell out more fully the definition of proto-industrialization, we can look to the criteria drawn up by Franklin Mendels who coined the term itself:

1 the unit of reference is the region;
2 rural industry in the region involved peasant participation in handicraft production for the market. Thus industry was seasonal and provided an income supplement, though it could ultimately be a full-time family occupation;
3 the market for proto-industrial goods was international, not local;
4 proto-industrial manufacture developed in symbiosis with commercial agriculture;
5 towns in the region provided a locus for marketing, finishing and mercantile activity.

This definition of proto-industrialization went with a series of hypotheses.

1 The higher incomes derived from handicraft production led to population growth, breaking the balance between labour supply and local subsistence; that is, handicraft generated the labour supply of the Industrial Revolution.
2 Population growth and proto-industrialization soon generated diminishing returns, prompting changes in organization as well as new techniques which saved labour. In other words, proto-industrialization created pressures leading to the factory system and to new technology.
3 The profits from proto-industry accumulated in the hands of merchants,

commercial farmers and landlords; that is, proto-industry led to the accumulation of capital.

4 Proto-industry required and generated specialist knowledge of manufacturing organization and commerce; that is, proto-industry provided a training ground for and a new supply of entrepreneurs.

5 Proto-industrialization and regional agricultural specialization go hand in hand; that is, proto-industrialization leads to agricultural surpluses and reduces the price of food.

Proto-industrialization is thus credited with creating the key changes in the use of land, labour, capital and entrepreneurship which made the Industrial Revolution possible.[31]

The most widely-explored aspect of Mendels's original theory has been the demographic. Incentives to the emergence of domestic industry, it is argued, were strengthened by population pressure and magnified by the existence of partible inheritance. Simultaneously, income-earning activities such as handicraft production outside agriculture released the traditional social controls on marriage – inheritance and patriarchal control. Mendels argued on the basis of evidence from Flanders that earlier marriage and rapid rates of population increase were associated with areas of proto-industry. But the demographic evidence, despite the energy devoted to collecting it over the past decade, has not given us the clue to causation. Did the characteristics of proto-industry generate a growth in population, or was higher population the factor which attracted rural industry to an area?[32] Not only were the connections of the model tenuous, but the results of its application to explain the economic history of various regions have proved enormously variable. Mendels called his proto-industry the first phase of the industrialization process. Yet, in fact, for every area that made a successful transition to the factory system – Lancashire, Yorkshire, Lille, Alsace, the Rhineland, Saxony – there were many more which headed straight for de-industrialization – the West Country, East Anglia, the Cotswolds, rural Warwickshire, Bedfordshire, Ulster, Brittany, Flanders, Silesia, Languedoc, Bavaria and Bohemia.

The discussion of these larger macroeconomic implications of proto-industry has complemented a debate at another level on the microeconomics of the proto-industrial manufacturing unit. The most sophisticated work from this new perspective has questioned the meaning of the division of labour in proto-industry. It has shown that there was little marked division of labour in the proto-industrial household. Several members of one household might carry on the same operation side by side, or alternatively individual processes might be put out to separate households. It was 'not the rule' for a proto-industrial household to be a 'miniature factory'. It was difficult to get a proper ratio of numbers employed in the different operations in the small unit of the proto-industrial household. The most important form of the division of labour was not the technical division of labour analysed by Marx and the nineteenth-century economists, but a division of labour in the society and economy at large, that is, the specialization of regions in the mass-production of a small number of articles.[33]

The sexual division of labour characteristic of such rural industry was also different from that imagined in more traditional literature. The characteristic household structure and production unit were not dominated by a servant class, but by families which had recently turned to early marriage and more children to meet the needs of a new production process reliant on child and female labour. This household production unit reveals not a division of labour but the reverse – a new lack of separation between the work of men and women. As Hans Medick has put it, 'proto-industry brought the man back to the household'.[34]

The main reason for the success of this system of capitalist production, it is argued, was the built-in tendency to workers' self-exploitation. Even where guild artisans might mass-produce a commodity, they could not compete with rural labourers who had to be content with lower wages, both because they lacked corporate protection and because they had access to cheaper food. The higher profitability of rural industry did not necessarily imply higher productivity; if anything, productivity probably stagnated in the countryside until the connection between proto-industry and agriculture was weakened.

Proto-industrialization is used by historians as a phase or stage of development in much the same way as is 'manufactures'. Like 'manufactures', it, too, was said to 'contain the seeds of its own destruction'. For the same limitations of the high marginal costs of geographical dispersion and lack of regulation over work rhythms and quality pushed the putting-out system either into full factory production or into de-industrialization. Recent research has, however, diverged from Mendels's former unilinear framework. Historians have enquired into the reasons for the different outcomes of proto-industrialization. And they have tried to explain these by differences among regions in their internal economic, political and institutional environments, as well as in patterns of world trade. Although it is now accepted that the experience of proto-industrialization varied from region to region, the explanations given for this are based on two conflicting theories: one a theory of comparative advantage; the other a theory of noneconomic motivation.

Mendels and Jones explained the different regional specializations of Europe in terms of comparative advantage. According to Jones, comparative advantage accounted for the emergence of the North and Midland areas of England as the major manufacturing counties in the eighteenth century, while the southern regions de-industrialized and turned to the higher returns to be gained in agriculture. Areas of light and heavy soils adapted differently to the new crops and rotations of the Industrial Revolution, revealing a higher comparative advantage in agriculture in the light-soil regions of the South.[35] Similar regional differentiation is said to have taken place on the Continent. But this mode of reasoning is really very unsatisfactory. Regional specialization and centres of proto-industry are explained by results – areas became proto-industrial because they did – and because they were good at what they did.

To this theory of comparative advantage is joined a simultaneous belief in the role of nonmarket behaviour or pre-industrial values. The emergence, success and ultimately the limitations of proto-industry are all explained by these values. And historians also appeal to these to explain away the continued existence of dispersed manufacture after the factory system. Proto-industry sometimes led into de-industrialization, it is argued, because of the subsistence orientation of workers.[36] And economic historians have long explained away that age-old *bête noire* of the success story of the Industrial Revolution – the handloom weaver and sweated industry – by appeals to the values of handicraft workers or family production units. The values of the family economy are thus left to account for a great deal, but we know little of what these values were. Yet it is precisely these nonmarket values, those unanalysed areas of custom and culture, which determined the way in which individuals, families and communities reacted to new economic settings and constraints. This is not to say that they dwelt in a nonmonetary world or 'moral economy' which simply clashed with the market values of commerce and industry when these came to the countryside, but rather that they participated in this market with a different code of rationality, consuming at times when 'economic man' saved, playing at times when 'economic man' worked. A recognition and analysis of this plebeian culture are vital to the understanding of the dynamic of this period of 'manufactures' or 'proto-industry'.[37]

MANUFACTURE AND PROTO-INDUSTRY: APPLICATIONS?

If we now look in more depth at the problems raised by the way in which the model of proto-industrialization has been used, we find them mirroring those of the model of manufactures. Both models assume the factory to be the ultimate method of organizing labour, and modern power-based machinery to be the best-practice technology. The arrival of both made the Industrial Revolution, and they apparently eclipsed all other forms of technology and organization. But what do we know of these other technologies and manufacturing structures? Eighteenth-century manufacture was practised in all manner of different settings; it was organized along many different lines, each of which was 'rational' or legitimate in its own environment. Putting-out systems coexisted with artisan and co-operative forms of production, and all of these systems frequently interacted with some type of manufacture or proto-factory. This was often the case within any one region. There was, for example, the Kentish Weald in the sixteenth and seventeenth centuries. It had a rural textile industry organized on a putting-out system which employed peasant labour, but it also had an important iron industry organized in centralized units around water-powered blast furnaces.

Even within one industry, these diverse forms of organization prevailed at the different stages of production. In eighteenth-century West Yorkshire, small artisan clothiers built and used their own co-operative mills for some of their preparatory processes. In eighteenth-century Lancashire, the Peels centralized their calico printing and spinning establishments, but ran extensive putting-out networks among weavers. In eighteenth-century Birmingham, small artisans in the hardware trades gathered together to build a centralized processing unit which supplied their brass and copper, and they 'put out' the production of parts and pieces in much the same way as did the lockmakers of the West Midlands and the nineteenth-century watchmakers of Coventry. How, then, did these many systems of manufacture succeed for so long in organizing work?

For an answer to this we might turn first to the economics of work organization. For it is here that we find some systematic attempt to compare the efficiencies and advantages of the different types of work organization at any one time. Williamson, who compared several different modes of organizing a batch industry such as pinmaking, assessed each mode in terms of its efficiency and its socioeconomic implications. Putting-out systems were compared to co-operative forms, and both in turn to capitalist subcontracting and factory hierarchies. On such assessments the factory system still appeared 'superior' in terms of efficiency to the putting-out system, and the putting-out system was better in turn than artisan ownership. The putting-out system had key disadvantages as compared to factories: high inventories, high transportation costs, poor work intensity, embezzlement and poor quality control, and poor adaptation to sudden changes in markets or technique. In turn, the putting-out system has been deemed on such assessments to be preferable to artisan systems, for putting-out allowed the diffusion of knowledge of new materials or mixes of materials, and it ensured better quality control of a standardized output. These advantages compounded cost advantages associated with the exchange of materials and the final product.[38] The economists of work organization, for all their claims to independent judgement of a wide range of forms of work organization, ultimately confirm the old linear framework of artisan stage succeeded by putting-out stage, with both finally eclipsed by the factory.

Marx and the historians of proto-industry adopted the same framework. Marx's analysis of the 'system of manufacture' and his historical view of production in the period just prior to the Industrial Revolution were mainly confined to the large workshop deploying the division of labour; while the proto-industry model has in general been applied only to the rural textile manufacture deploying putting-out systems. The large, hierarchically-organized workshop was seen by Marx to be the most advanced form reached by manufacture before the limitations of the system became obvious. The historians of proto-industry have similarly regarded putting-out in such a light. They have certainly recognized that putting-out was not the only way of organizing industry before the factory. Indeed, they have distinguished between the 'Kauf system' (or artisan production) and the 'Verlag system' (or putting-out), but only to point to putting-out as the superior and dominant mode of organization before the factory system. It is back to Clapham's Industrial Revolution that we must go for any understanding of the polymorphic nature of industrial organization in this period. Clapham pointed out in 1930 that the Britain of a hundred years before had abounded in ancient and transitional types of industrial organization. While putting-out prevailed in much of the Scottish linen industry, in Dundee the spinners dealt directly with the manufacturer. While the woollen industry of the West Country and the worsted industry of West Yorkshire were model examples of putting-out, the woollen industry of the West Riding was the seat of that independent artisan production which received the praise of Defoe, Josiah Tucker and David Hume. And the survival of these small independent clothiers was ensured well into the nineteenth century, when in face of the advantages of machinery and concentration in some processes they formed the co-operative or company units of which Clapham and more recently Pat Hudson have written.[39] When factories were forming in Lancashire, we must also remember what Faucher said of Birmingham in the 1830s:

> The industry of this town, like French agriculture, has got into a state of parcellation. You meet . . . hardly any big establishments: . . . whilst capitals tend to concentrate in Great Britain, they divide more and more in Birmingham.[40]

OTHER ALTERNATIVES

Artisans, co-operatives and centralized manufacture

If we look at two alternatives to the putting-out system – artisan production and centralized manufacture or proto-factories – we find many instances of their widespread use and success. In other European countries and in earlier centuries artisan production had emerged as an alternative to both the medieval guilds and the putting-out systems dominated by merchant capital.[41] In an urban context, artisan structures or small commodity production also developed their own dynamic, sometimes alongside old guild-

72

dominated production or as a form of production appropriate to unincorporated towns and areas.[42]

Artisan-organized production was a dynamic industrial structure of the urban villages, suburbs and unincorporated towns of eighteenth-century Britain, in areas such as Birmingham and the London suburbs. It was a system of production which was not constrained by guild regulations but, nevertheless, it did not operate purely according to the dictates of market forces; rather it was mediated through artisan customs and values. These customs and values, even in a guild-free environment, were expressed through journeymen's associations, as in the *compagnonnages* of eighteenth-century France, or simply through those principles of mutuality and co-operation contained in the 'custom of the trade'.[43]

Yet we know virtually nothing of the place of artisan structures or of co-operative alternatives in industrialization. These have been by and large disregarded by historians, written off as primitive structures of prehistory or as utopian failures. Economists and economic historians have nearly always taken the side of the winners and have written for them. Industry, like labour, needs its sympathetic historian, one who would recognize all those forms of enterprise other than the factory. Integral to many such artisan systems of production were co-operative systems which were sometimes resorted to in order to ensure sources of materials or to complete a necessary stage of production involving centralized or mechanized processes, as we found in the metal and textile industries. A tradition of co-operation was also started in many trades as a temporary expedient for dealing with cyclical fluctuations.

In our attempt to uncover the history of some of the neglected artisanal and co-operative structures, we might take our inspiration not from Marx or the proto-industry model, but from eighteenth-century observers. For as we have seen already, Adam Smith regarded putting-out industries as a major source of labour's exploitation, but artisanship he credited with the most favourable of working conditions. With artisan structures, too, were to be found particular forms of artisan discipline and technology.

Time was a discipline which structured the artisan's life to an enormous extent. He or she worked within the limits of set delivery times of raw materials, availability of assistants who might have a different time economy, set dates for markets and fairs, and the time patterns of other social and income-earning activities. It is also striking that the theory of proto-industrialization has shunned technological change, assuming static technologies before the eighteenth century. But the significance, ubiquity and flexibility of handtools like the stamp, press, drawbench and lathe, cemented artisan industry in Birmingham in the eighteenth and nineteenth centuries. As a witness to the Select Committee on Arts and Manufactures wrote in 1824,

Our Birmingham machines are rarely, if ever mentioned in the scientific works of the day. The Birmingham machine is ephemeral . . . it has its existence only during the fashion of a certain article, and it is contained within the precincts of a single manufactory of a town.[44]

And the inventions, improvements and adaptations made by these small artisans were often kept secret, incorporated in the special skill which guaranteed their craft superiority.

The organizational and technological achievements of these artisan systems may be compared to the assessments of recent quantitative history. This history, as discussed in Chapters 1 and 2, finds most industry during the eighteenth century dogged by slow productivity growth. This is explained by traditional small-scale organization and slow mechanization, in contrast to cotton's factory system and mechanized powered technologies. But innovation in industries organized on a small-scale basis was, as demonstrated, widespread. And the potential in such small-scale industries for dynamic expansion forms the basis for an alternative model of industrial transition.

Flexible specialization

'Flexible specialization' is the term devised for a recent model of craft production and industrial development. In this model craft production was not a prehistory to, but an alternative to mass-production and the factory system. Artisan production was not necessarily equated to low-productivity traditional activities; craft economies could equally be the basis for a highly innovative small-scale capitalism. Small producers offered economic advantages of creativity, nimbleness and easy entry; they could develop 'flexible technologies', easily changed across products and activities, as well as skill-intensive processes and a range of product choices for localized and regional tastes.[45] This model brought regional conglomeration, technological initiative and market diversity together as the framework for dynamic craft economies. It offered an alternative kind of industrial transition, but as a model it had many weaknesses. A full discussion of these problems belongs to later sections of the book.

Apart from these artisan and co-operative manufacturing systems, which flourished alongside putting-out, there were those forms of industrial production which were centralized from the outset, as in mining and metal processing, and in the proto-factories which existed in the silk industry, in calico printing, in pinmaking, and in some of the factory colonies of the West Country woollen industry.[46] The calico-printing proto-factories have been described as the 'missing link' between the proto-industrial and modern industrial system in the textile industries. Such works were organized along the lines of Marx's workshop-manufactures, based on elementary

74

labour-intensive techniques, the disciplining of the labour force, and the maximization of skills deriving from the division of handicraft labour.[47] The structures and dynamics of these forms have been revived recently in the Goldin-Sokoloff 'small-scale factory'.

Although textiles formed the largest industry in the period before the factory, this does not mean that other industries organized around some central plant – as in mining, smelting, forging, brewing or distilling works – should be excluded from consideration as proto-industrialization. Many such activities entailed some change for better or worse in the local economy. The existence of centralized plant and processes did not prevent a seasonal or even family division of labour between industry and agriculture in much the same manner as in the textile putting-out industries. The same thing occurred frequently in mining and early iron forges and furnaces. One industry, such as metalworking, contained classic 'proto-factories' such as the Crowley ironworks, and at the same time the extensive division of labour found in a putting-out framework as in Peter Stubs's Warrington filemaking business. There was the Bristol wireworks producing pins in a proto-factory side by side with dispersed and impoverished nailmakers exploited in a highly-developed putting-out system. The textile industry, too, easily assimilated partly-mechanized mills into a countryside dominated by dispersed man- and womanpower.

Diversity and change

This diverse range of manufacturing structures coexisted within and across industries; in addition, these structures were rarely static. Either they adapted to changing market conditions with more or less success in their individual industries and regions, or industries changed their organization not in a linear but more frequently in a cyclical pattern.[48] There was no one pattern and no one criterion for the choice of a type of industrial organization. Profitability and labour costs were important determinants for the development of each structure, but, as we have seen, in a transitional capitalist society they were not the only ones – custom, community and patriarchal discipline played at least as significant a role in artisan, co-operative and proto-factory alternatives to putting-out. This range of industrial structures also implied a range of different types of labour discipline and technological change. Yet we also know little of these.

Not only must we learn more of these alternative manufacturing structures, but we must more clearly assess the accomplishments and difficulties of the putting-out systems so frequently equated with proto-industrialization. Just how adaptable, for one, was the putting-out system to changes in demand?

Fabrics, of whatever fibres, in England or elsewhere, readily became identified in pre-industrial manufacture with particular regions . . . conservatism of method could almost be described as an endemic disease. Although the system knew little fixed capital, it had much human capital, which means minds as well as hands; to re-tool a factory or scrap a plant is often much easier than to bring about a fresh approach in management or to retrain a workforce with inherited ways of doing things.[49]

SOCIAL VALUES

To conclude: the period just before industrialization was characterized by a multiplicity of different organizational structures of manufacture. Historical theories of why these organizational structures arose and how they changed during industrialization reach back to Smith and forward to theories of 'flexible' and network capitalism. The resilience of organizational structures was determined by their own special adaptability to the market, but it was also significantly affected by a range of nonmarket values and institutions. The directions of technological change and the choice of economic structures were, in other words, partly dependent on these social values of domestic workers and artisans. The strength of such values reverberated in the resistance to factories and to mechanization, ultimately determining the location of much factory-based industry. In moving beyond the market we can also start to account for all those nonwaged activities in which a largely underdeveloped workforce engaged in order to make up a daily subsistence. Credit and debt, perks and customary rights, and even embezzlement intersected with the extra-economic relationships of the various forms of community – familial, civic as well as trade-based – which made up the texture of the working man and woman's daily life.

We must seek to delve into those interstices of economic and customary relationship, interstices which have been neglected in economic history. Primitive accumulation and proto-industry have drawn our attention to the problem and to the years of transition before the Industrial Revolution, but the research still remains to be done to give these years an historical existence of their own.

4

AGRICULTURE, RESOURCES, ENVIRONMENT

Adam Smith believed that agriculture was the foundation of economic development. Historians of proto-industrialization have looked to the countryside for the most significant manufacturing development of the eighteenth century. What precisely was the relationship between agriculture and industry over these years, and what made this relationship so special?

AGRICULTURE'S SUBORDINATION

The experience of technical and institutional change in the agricultural sector requires its own separate study, one which this book cannot attempt to offer. What we shall do here is examine the extent of interdependence between the agricultural and industrial sectors. Historians are keen to point out connections between agriculture and industry, but they have generally treated agriculture as the passive partner: the receptacle of raw materials and labour, there to be exploited by the industrial sector.

The timing of the Agricultural and Industrial Revolutions has confused the connection we seek. For most of the great agricultural innovators such as Turnip Townshend, Coke of Norfolk and Robert Bakewell coincided with, rather than preceded, the great industrial inventors – Arkwright, Watt, Darby and others. Agriculture thus took second place, its pace of innovation only complementary to and much slower than industry's. But this subordinate place was created partly out of the now outmoded economic models previously absorbed by economic historians, and partly out of a vulgarized Ricardian perspective which pervaded much nineteenth-century economic debate. The latter conveyed the impression that agriculture was the ultimate limitation on economic growth. It was a view aptly expressed by J. S. Mill:

The improvements which have been introduced into agriculture are so extremely limited, when compared with those of which some branches of manufactures have been found susceptible, and they are, besides, so very slow in making their way against those old habits and prejudices,

77

which are perhaps more deeply rooted among farmers than among any other class of producers, that the progress of population seems in most instances to have kept pace with the improvement of population . . . It has not, hitherto, indeed been at any time the effect of an improvement to drive capital from the land, nor consequently to lower rent.[1]

This kind of anti-agrarian prejudice has produced an enormously mistaken view based on a rather insignificant place for agriculture in British industrialization. Indeed, the early decline of the relative importance of agriculture in the distribution of national income and of the labour force reflected as much an increase in its own productivity as it did the very rapid progress of industry.

Recent research has now established that most of the key technical and organizational changes in agriculture took place in the seventeenth and early eighteenth centuries and not later.[2] Agriculture, in fact, played a dynamic role in the wider economy, for early and inexpensive technical improvements increased labour productivity and made it possible to produce much more food at lower unit costs. New population estimates also demonstrate a sustained rise in population, not just from the middle of the eighteenth century, but from its very beginning. And statistical evidence, which if anything underestimates the improvement, shows that the most substantial increases in output probably took place in the first half of the eighteenth century, not the last half.[3] This chronology of improvement now makes a strong case for the close interdependence of agriculture and manufacturing, with the springs of much manufacturing improvement to be found in the early dynamism of the agricultural sector.

Estimating increases in output and productivity growth in agriculture over the eighteenth and early nineteenth centuries is by no means straightforward. Historians are agreed on the precocious development of Britain's agricultural sector. By 1840 Britain had a very low share, by other European standards, of labour in agriculture; England in 1841 had 27.3 per cent of the adult male labour force in agriculture in comparison with levels of over 50 per cent in the rest of Europe. Output per worker grew, it is estimated, by 60 to 100 per cent between 1600 and 1800, in comparison with a rise of only 20 per cent in France.[4]

Estimates of output have been calculated from the national accounts estimates of value added and from value added estimates adjusted for changes over time in per capita food consumption. Alternatively they have been calculated directly from data accumulated on the output and prices of individual products.[5] These estimates show similar results in output increasing by a factor of between 3.37 and 3.56. But estimates do differ on the timing of these increases. Deane and Cole's series showed little growth in the first half of the eighteenth century, and much more in the latter half. Newer estimates by Crafts and Jackson find most eighteenth-century growth in the

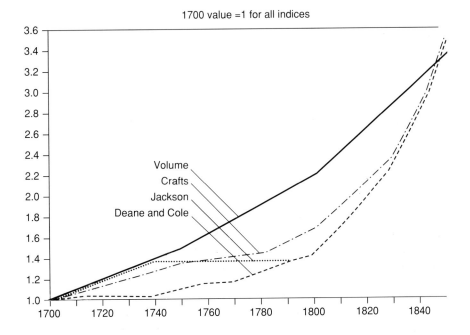

1700 value =1 for all indices

Figure 4.1 Indices of agricultural output

Source: R. C. Allen, 'Agriculture and the Industrial Revolution', Fig. 5.1, p. 101.

first half of the century.[6] And estimates drawing on physical output data show steady growth in output and productivity improvement over time. There is still no agreement on whether output grew or stagnated during the last half of the eighteenth century. The implications of the fate of late eighteenth-century agriculture are, as we shall see, very important for industry.

Estimates of productivity growth also vary according to procedures of estimation. The most recent estimates by R.C. Allen indicate that over the period 1700–1850, land grew by 37 per cent, labour by 16 per cent and capital by 93 per cent. Inputs thus grew by a factor of 1.45, and output, as we have seen, is accepted to have grown by 3.37 to 3.56 times. Total factor productivity then grew by a factor of 2.34 to 2.46 between 1700 and 1850.[7] Total factor productivity growth in agriculture grew at approximately 1 per cent per annum, a rate faster, according to Crafts, than industrial productivity growth for much of the eighteenth century.[8]

Probate inventories indicate a substantial rise in yields per acre, from 10 bushels in medieval times to approximately 27 in 1850. Half the gain in output per worker in the South Midlands between 1600 and 1800 was accounted for by the rising size of farms. Only 12 per cent of farms had more than 100 acres in the early seventeenth century, in contrast to 57 per cent in the early nineteenth century. Economies of scale were clear – labour costs per acre on a 400-acre farm were 40 per cent those of a 25-acre farm.[9]

CONTRIBUTIONS TO INDUSTRY

Agriculture is generally considered to have made four types of contribution to industry. In the first place, it created a food surplus to feed a growing and increasingly urban population. Second, it helped to widen home and foreign markets. Third, it provided a source of capital. And, finally, it helped to condition a labour force and acted as a source and training ground for early management.

Agricultural surpluses

The achievement of feeding Britain's rapidly expanding population for most of the eighteenth century was a great success story of the Industrial Revolution. It is estimated that in the period 1650–1750 London's population rose by 70 per cent, expanding its proportion of national population from 7 to 11 per cent. In order to feed this population as well as that of the rest of the country, and still to export corn, output would have had to rise by at least 13 per cent in the period.[10] The growth in yields was impressive from the seventeenth century, and before the mid-eighteenth century Britain was no longer in danger of mortality crises. Allen has calculated that without agriculture's contributions to rising output during the eighteenth century, positive growth in per capita income would have been reduced to almost nothing.[11] For the first half of the nineteenth century, the rate of growth of GDP would have been reduced by one-fifth.

What was the effect of this growth in food supplies and the high productivity of British agriculture? There is first the question of the timing of increases in agricultural output and productivity. Recent assessments which find greater gains in agriculture in the period before 1750 must be placed in the context of the timing of population growth. While population was rising from the early part of the eighteenth century, its major acceleration was in the second half of the century, just at the time when the growth of agricultural output was slackening. The result was that agricultural output did not keep pace with demand; imports and food prices rose.[12] Allen points out that rising food prices hurt the poor, while they brought rising rents to landowners.

The timing of productivity growth is at issue among historians, but rapid productivity growth is not. Rapid productivity growth in agriculture helped to keep in check imports of food and raw materials; it reduced downward pressure on the terms of trade between manufactured exports and imports.

Table 4.1 Output of principal commodities, 1700–1850

	1700	*1750*	*1800*	*1850*
Part A. Major commodities				
corn (million bushels)	65	88	131	181
meat (million lbs)	370	665	888	1,356
wool (million lbs)	40	60	90	120
cheese (million lbs)	61	84	112	157
Part B. Volume in 1815 prices (millions of £s)				
corn and potatoes	19	25	37	56
animal products	21	34	51	79
Total	40	59	88	135

Source: R. C. Allen, 'Agriculture and the Industrial Revolution', table 5.4, p. 109.

Note: Corn includes wheat, rye, barley, oats, beans and peas, net of seed and oats consumed by livestock. Animal products include meat, wool, dairy products, cheese, hides, and hay sold off the farm.

The sources of this increase in output have been variously explained by the agricultural innovations of the seventeenth and early eighteenth centuries – the irrigation, drainage, multiple crop rotations, and fodder and root crops described by others. To these, along with concomitant changes in agrarian structure – the decline of the peasantry and the rise of large-scale capitalist farming on a landlord–tenant basis – have been ascribed the increases in the agricultural surplus. But the gains from these innovations on their own have been questioned recently; most of the gains in agricultural productivity have been explained not by technology or institutional change, but by the increase in the size of farms which went with these changes.

What effect did greater agricultural surpluses have on manufacturing industry? Their main effect was to release the old pre-industrial clamp of land limits and population pressure. Formerly there was little scope for the development of manufacturing, as diminishing marginal returns on the land placed an ever-recurring barrier on both sustained population expansion and new patterns of demand. Technical progress in agriculture effectively extended the area of agricultural production, allowing real wages to remain the same or even rise in spite of population pressure. Higher real wages might indeed be spent on a greater number and range of consumer goods and not simply spread over more and bigger families. For productivity gains in agriculture enabled a smaller percentage of the labour force to feed the whole, and labour could be released into manufacturing, trade and distribution.

But, in effect, it was not labour which was released, but labour time, for men and women moved only partly out of agriculture and soon found, in a combination of rural manufacturing and extensive cultivation, new economic incentives to increase their numbers. Innovations in agriculture, in addition, ultimately favoured grain-importing areas. For the same volume of manufactured goods, these areas could gain more foodstuffs and, therefore, support a higher population.

There is also the paradox to be explained of both a high growth in productivity in agriculture and rapid industrialization. The high productivity of agriculture did not, after all, lead to Britain becoming the granary of Europe. This paradox was solved by Adam Smith in his 'rich country – poor country' comparison of England and Poland.

> The most opulent nations, indeed generally excel all their neighbours in agriculture as well as in manufactures; but they are commonly more distinguished by their superiority in the latter than in the former . . . In agriculture, the labour of the rich country is not always much more productive than that of the poor; or, at least, it is never so much more productive, as it commonly is in manufactures . . . The 'cornlands' of England . . . are better cultivated than those of France, and the 'cornlands' of France are better cultivated than those of Poland. But though the poor country, notwithstanding the inferiority of its cultivation, can in some measure, rival the rich in the cheapness and goodness of its corn, it can pretend to no such competition in its manufactures.[13]

Ricardo, in his theory of comparative advantage, and more recently Crafts, have reiterated the point. Crafts has argued that while the growth of agricultural productivity over the eighteenth century was higher than that of industrial productivity, *some* British industry was growing at much higher rates than both. Britain's exportable manufactures, especially cotton textiles, experienced such rapid gains in productivity growth that supply prices for cotton yarn and woven goods were 25 per cent lower than those of her nearest rival, France. Britain's greater *relative* efficiency in a small group of manufactured commodities made international specialization in these more profitable, and agricultural goods became importables.[14]

Even when net barter terms of trade turned against Britain, it was still profitable to continue exporting manufactured commodities. Agricultural productivity, as O'Brien has argued, rose rapidly enough to support her manufacturing sector, but 'not fast enough to shift the country's comparative advantage back towards agriculture'.[15] Institutional barriers in the system of landownership along with the Corn Laws, furthermore, made sure that landowners did not exert themselves to maximize returns on their already advanced agricultural sector.

British agriculture had by 1700 already made the remarkable achievement of feeding nearly half the population occupied in non-agricultural pursuits.

But its successes after this in achieving large-scale increases in food output may have been less significant than once believed.

Markets and trade

Apart from releasing the British economy from the locks of a pre-industrial economic cycle, agricultural improvement provided a more precise foundation for industry through its impact on trade and on capital and labour markets. The food surpluses which allowed cities and industries to grow in turn created the mechanisms of trade and specialization which widened home and foreign markets. The precise connections and timing of the relations between agricultural improvement and greater demand for industrial commodities are difficult to specify, for consumption in the eighteenth century is a subject based on hypothesis and impressionistic evidence. Historians debate whether the home market was stagnating or buoyant in the first half of the eighteenth century. They are clear that agricultural prices fell steadily over these years. But whether this was due to a series of good harvests or to agricultural improvement, or simply to limited population pressure, is unclear. The sustained effect of agricultural improvement is now accepted as very significant. But the effect, in turn, of these years of cheap grain on the market for industrial commodities is still a puzzle, for the higher real incomes, which cheap grain implied, could be spent on more and better food, or on manufactured commodities. Recent estimates give more weight to the former than was previously thought. Good harvests, furthermore, affected the distribution as well as the level of incomes, and these could have moved in opposite directions. There seems to be no clear hypothetical relationship between food prices and industrial demand. Data linking food prices and industrial output in the early half of the century do indicate that falling food prices in years of peace were accompanied by rising industrial output, but in the last half of the century rising food prices and industrial output went hand in hand.[16] The effect of agricultural improvement and good harvests on rural incomes, and with this on industrial demand, needs a more critical approach. The data indicate some association, but the effect of a favourable conjuncture of harvests, agricultural change and population growth still seems open to uncertainty.

We can look first to changes in the intersectoral terms of trade between agriculture and industry. Before 1745 industrial and agricultural prices moved together; but between 1745 and 1810, there was a shift in the terms of trade against industry. The result was a rather limited increase in the consumption of manufactured commodities by those in the agricultural sector; this was only one-third during the same period that saw industrial output increased 3.7 times.[17] After 1800 the case was even clearer that the home market for manufactured goods was provided not by agriculture, but by the urban economy and the industrial and service sectors.

The idea of a favourable conjuncture of harvests, agricultural change and population growth is an attractive one, but evidence is gathering against it. The first objection relates to the effect of this conjuncture on the distribution of income as a whole and is one that is fairly easily accommodated. The second questions the real gains of the labouring poor and is much more difficult to answer. First we must look at the differential effect of the harvest on the various landed classes and on the relations between town and country, agriculture and industry. As the great decline of the English peasantry had already happened by the 1730s and the greatest proportion of land was worked by tenant farmers paying money rents, we must also consider the effect of the harvest on these farmers and on their landlords, for their expenditure patterns were very different from those of the rural poor. The immediate impact of the harvest would be faced by tenant farmers who experienced declining terms of trade with industry. If wages were based on subsistence, lower food prices might mean lower labour costs, but not if wages were inflexible, for the result might then have been fewer working hours and therefore lower total income for farmers.[18] There was also an expanding middle-class market which maintained its momentum even against the erosion of the higher food prices which came in the latter half of the eighteenth century.[19] This market and the higher urban-industrial demand for foodstuffs which it simultaneously encouraged also prevented agricultural prices from becoming fatally depressed when higher agricultural productivity did encourage a downward trend of prices.[20]

An equally important connection between agriculture and industry was established through the landlords, for the movement of property income affected urban and rural industry alike. A simple model can go far to explain the impact of the distribution of agricultural income on the growth of manufactures. Cities and their industries might prosper in spite of high food prices and the lower discretionary incomes of the poor, for they were dependent on property incomes which rose with higher rents. But rural crises could also be transmitted eventually to the towns as landlords faced greater difficulty in collecting rents and struggled to maintain property incomes, while the state also faced problems in collecting taxes.

The problems of the countryside would be exacerbated by a constant syphoning-off of the surplus to the benefit of the towns and by unproductive expenditure on various forms of conspicuous consumption. Attempts to maintain property incomes during such reversals would deprive both agriculture and rural industry of capital and incentives. The limitations inherent in these rural–urban connections were broken, however, by the introduction of convertible husbandry. For the new agriculture both created greater food surpluses and called for more investment in enclosure and transportation.[21] The local impact of these improvements was to drive away industry to other areas. Agricultural improvement was also supposed to have raised the demand for wage goods from other areas, because the wage labourer as well as farmers, traders and town-dwellers bought their necessities and decencies instead of making their own.[22]

If we look to the winners among the contenders for England's agricultural surpluses in the eighteenth century, these were neither farmers nor labourers, but landlords. Rising agricultural prices in the second half of the eighteenth century favoured rising rents. But the market potential generated by rental income for the new mass-produced domestic manufactured goods was distinctly limited. Spending went on stately homes, servants and imported handicrafts. The conventional perspective on the relation between agricultural improvement and the expansion of trade has hinged on new rural expenditure patterns arising from that period of good harvests and agricultural improvements in the middle of the eighteenth century, characteristically dubbed 'the golden age of the labourer'. But before accepting this perspective we must know more of the conditions of the rural poor and something of the impact on this community of the composition of the market itself.

By the eighteenth century it was already the case that most rural inhabitants were at least partly dependent on money wages. But new food surpluses did not necessarily bring better conditions or even higher wages, because the results of improvement varied according to the different agrarian economies. As Hoskins has shown for the village of Wigston in Leicestershire, the agricultural improvement of the period went hand in hand with agrarian reform, which brought money but not wealth to the community.

> The domestic economy of the whole village was radically altered. No longer could the peasant derive the necessaries of life from the materials, the soil, and the resources of his own countryside and his own strong arms. The self supporting peasant was transformed into a spender of money, for all the things he needed were now in the shops. Money which in the sixteenth century had played merely a marginal, though a necessary, part, now became the one thing necessary for the maintenance of life. Peasant thrift was replaced by commercial thrift. Every hour of work now had a money-value, unemployment became a disaster, for there was no piece of land the wage earner could turn to. His Elizabethan master had needed money intermittently, but *he* needs it nearly every day, certainly every week of the year.[23]

The greater need for money at the time coincided, Hoskins shows, with rapidly rising poor rates. He states that 'farming had been revolutionised since the early 1600s, but the farmer's household probably enjoyed little more in the way of comforts and amenities in 1820 than their ancestors had in 1620'.[24]

Historical judgement is also confirmed by contemporary observation. Eden in his extensive survey of the poor found that there was, if anything, a close connection between poverty and the market. Northern families preferred their subsistence economies to the shops, for though the clothing they produced was of a higher cost in terms of materials and time than most shop goods, it was also of higher quality. Workers in the Midlands and the South bought most of their clothing from the shopkeeper, and 'in the vicinity of the metropolis, working people seldom buy new clothes: they content themselves with a cast off coat, which may be usually purchased for about 5s. and second hand waistcoats, and breeches'.[25] And while markets did not mean wealth to the rural labourer, neither did they mean any connection between high real wages and local food surpluses. National and international corn markets, intercepted at various levels by myriads of corn middlemen, broke any local connection between the prices of food and the harvest. Not just the price of food, but the wages prevailing in most rural industry, were set by international not local markets.[26] Certainly the home market grew in the eighteenth century, but its expansion was based on changing social relations and not on a national trend of rising living standards.

This pessimistic interpretation of the growth of the market goes against the grain of much economic history of the period. But it tells the story of large regions of the country frequently neglected by economic historians. For Wigston was a Midland village, open-field, highly populated, and with a substantial proportion still holding land in 1750. It was slipping towards pastoral agriculture in the mid-eighteenth century, but until enclosure it contained a higher proportion of peasants than more arable areas of older enclosure and more consolidated landholdings. The latter areas had made their transition to 'agrarian capitalism' in the preceding two centuries.[27]

Just as the experience of the growth of the market was regional, not national, so too was the course of real wages which supposedly contributed to a widening market. The traditional division in the mid-eighteenth century between the earlier period of high real wages and the later period of falling real wages was tempered by the different agrarian and industrial economies between regions. Historians are now careful to point out, in addition, the frequent divergence between real wages and real incomes. Real wages were augmented, they argue, by higher labour inputs, through more intensive labour and more productive contributions from women and children.[28] Even optimistic interpretation of eighteenth-century living standards remains equivocal. Wrigley and Schofield, on the basis of the Cambridge population data, argue that it is probably true that 'the secular tendency in standards of living as reflected in real wages was steadily upwards from the mid-seventeenth to the late eighteenth century, but that thereafter there was a sharp fall for about a generation before a resumption in the upward movement in the early nineteenth century'. The rising trend of real wages may have contributed to increasing nuptiality, but 'there are far too many uncertainties about the measurement of trends in real wages or in family purchasing power more generally to press the analysis very far'.[29]

Capital and labour

Equally tenuous is the conventional idea of agriculture's contribution to capital and labour markets. The narrow debate on the extent to which landlords invested in industry has really ended in stalemate. For while politics and prestige as much as profit influenced their business decisions, who can estimate the indirect effect?[30] Conventional dealings in the land market, in setting up trusts and obtaining mortgages, took on a new dimension in the commercial and industrial entries to the portfolios administered by provincial attorneys.[31] There seems, in addition, to have been no fixed division between agricultural and industrial capital. For many 'industrialists' moved their capital freely between the textile industry and traditional investment in the grocery trades, warehousing, agricultural processing and milling. The eighteenth-century Essex clothier Thomas Griggs alternated between the manufacture of textiles and the retailing of groceries; in addition he invested in real estate, fattened stock for winter markets, and malted barley for retail. Stubs, the Warrington filemaker, also worked the property markets, kept an inn and was a successful brewer.[32] Chapman argues that the records of 1,000 early eighteenth-century textile entrepreneurs from the West Country, East Anglia and the Midlands show a close connection between agricultural and industrial investments. In these areas, unlike the West Riding which was known for its yeoman clothiers, this connection did not represent a direct involvement in both farming and manufacture. There was, rather, a direct connection between investment in textiles and investment in secondary agrarian activity. Many entrepreneurs divided their capital between the textile industry and the more traditional pursuits of malting, brewing or innkeeping in an attempt to limit their commitment to any particular industrial activity. The linkage existing between these agricultural and industrial pursuits formed a basis not just for the movement of capital from the land to manufacture, but also for the reverse movement. For when the older textile centres declined, assets were easily shifted back to agricultural processing, retailing and real estate.[33]

There are many examples of landlords and farmers investing in industry, most often however in rentier-type activities such as the leasing of mineral rights, mines and water power sites. If we look at the case of large landlords, it does seem that on balance more capital flowed towards the land than away from it.

Lower down the social scale the capital-flows from agriculture to industry may have been much greater. Small producers commonly invested in land and housing alongside industrial enterprise. Farms and smallholdings provided security for raising mortgages and assets for future transfer into industrial capital. This was the pattern of close interaction between industrial and property investment in the West Midland and South Yorkshire

Table 4.2 Capital in English and Welsh agriculture, 1700–1850
(£m in 1851–60 prices)

	1700	*1750*	*1800*	*1850*
Landlords				
structures, etc.	112	114	143	232
Tenants				
implements	10	8	10	14
farm horses	20	20	18	22
other livestock	41	53	71	85
Total	183	195	242	353

Source: R. C. Allen, 'Agriculture and the Industrial Revolution', table 5.4, p. 109.

metal trades. Capital from farms and smallholdings also went into the West Riding woollen industry.[34]

Was this capital agricultural or industrial in its origins? This section has argued that there was no clear-cut division between the two sectors. Early industrial capital formation and enterprise frequently combined activities associated with land and agriculture with more obviously industrial activities. Family investment and inheritance strategies among smaller industrialists included extensive land and property-holding along with management of trusts. These were particularly developed for widows, daughters and under-age children.[35] It was the family, not the agrarian basis of British capitalism, which reinforced the agricultural–industrial framework of capital formation.

If the route to industrial capital formation from agricultural improvement was so convoluted, then the agricultural foundation for an industrial labour force was no less complicated. It was once argued that agricultural improvement was labour-using rather than labour-saving, so that most of the industrial labour force must have arisen out of population growth.[36] But historians have returned to the older theories that labour was 'released' by agriculture. Crafts has emphasized the rising productivity of agriculture along with the falling *relative* share of the labour force in the sector.[37] Was this labour 'released' then reabsorbed by the rising industrial sector? The answer now appears to be no, for rural unemployment was an endemic feature of the English countryside from the eighteenth through the first half of the nineteenth century. First, it is not all that clear that local rather than national agricultural improvement and agrarian reform did increase employment. This view rests on a failure to take account of the newly pastoral regions. Furthermore, it concentrates on the labour-intensive nature of the enclosing process itself. This and the wartime movement towards arable production were both relatively short-lived phenomena. The employment levels of areas that converted to pasture plummeted. Wigston's labouring requirement for its 3,000 acres in 1832 was only forty labourers, about one-quarter to a third of the labour needed in the old open fields.[38] But this unemployed labour force did not leave to flood new factories, nor did it, for that matter, become a fully-fledged or even semi-proletariat.

The decline of Wigston's peasantry and its village went hand in hand with an increase in its population, for it became one of the many industrial villages which attracted the dispossessed from all round about to enter the domestic industry of framework knitting. The argument as put by E. L. Jones is that the workforce which engaged in by-employments 'acquired the technical expertise of industry'. Not only this, but it was being separated from the land and indeed from the ownership of all but a few tools and its own labour power. It worked for wages, bought its food and broke out of old customs of marriage and inheritance. It was a labour force which was being conditioned into that 'malleable and trained workforce' so 'central to an industrializing economy'.[39] But how accurate a picture is this of a very distinctive kind of labour force? Just as I have questioned the perspective on rural industry which sees it only as a problem of the transition to industrialization, so I would also argue that the existence of a rural industrial labour force does not provide any evidence of a direct role for agriculture in the formation of an industrial proletariat. The same historians who point to the modern characteristics of this rural industrial labour force also explain away its continued existence in the nineteenth century in face of the factory system by an appeal to its backward social values.[40] Agricultural improvement and agrarian reform did not create a 'semi-proletarianized' workforce on its way to the factory, but a rural domestic industrial workforce with its own internal dynamic. And where this rural industry did not emerge, unemployment was frequently the ultimate result of agricultural improvement. Even in those regions of arable farming, enclosure was frequently labour-saving, especially on larger farms such as the new estates created for tithe compensation.[41]

Extensive evidence for these arguments has been gathered in recent years for the South of England and the South Midlands. In counties across the South and the South-East, improvements in arable cultivation, greater specialization of labour, enclosure and increases in farm sizes led to rural unemployment, and especially female unemployment.[42] In the South Midlands, bigger farms and more arable cultivation reduced the workforce, and again especially the female workforce. And the industry which, according to the models, ought to have soaked up this labour was not nearly widespread enough to compensate for the decline in full-time agricultural jobs.[43] Pauperization rather than proletarianization was the result.

AGRARIAN STRUCTURES AND THE RISE OF INDUSTRY

Much the most significant connections between agriculture and industry were established via changing agrarian institutions and property-holding. Different regional social structures engendered different industrial and technological experiences. Agrarian institutions hold the key to why industries arose in some areas rather than others, why they declined or moved to new frontiers, and why they adopted very different forms of organization. Joan Thirsk maintains that the rise of domestic industry is not to be explained by demography but by the existence of certain types of farming community and social organization.[44] The longer historical perspective shows that industrial by-employments were not particularly new for the seventeenth and eighteenth centuries. In mineral areas, for example, agriculture and industry were ancient by-employments – it is hard to say which started first. The reason for the rise of rural industry was not to be found in entrepreneurship, easy supplies of raw materials or even market demand, but in the economic circumstances of an area's inhabitants. The common factors in these circumstances were: (1) a community of small freeholders or customary tenants with good tenure; (2) pastoral farming, that is, dairying or breeding; (3) no strong framework of co-operative agriculture, but, rather, equal division of landholding.[45] Owners of circulating capital looked for labour in areas of weak manorialization which allowed immigration and the division of property among small cultivators. Areas of new settlement gave some livelihood to squatters, but areas of equal partition had also resulted in farms so small that the peasantry took to industry to supplement their small agricultural incomes. The Kentish Weald, North-West Wiltshire and central Suffolk provided examples of the first, and the Dales of the West Riding examples of the second, where

> They knitted as they walked the village streets, they knitted in the dark because they were too poor to have a light; they knitted for dear life, because life was so cheap.[46]

The simple correspondence between areas of partible inheritance combined with pastoral agriculture and the location of the early domestic industries is, however, complicated by a number of factors. The seasonal interdependence of pastoral agriculture and domestic industry may have been a result rather than a cause of the location of rural industry. For the intensification of interregional economic competition in the seventeenth and eighteenth centuries can explain industrial location at least as well as the seasons can. Any divergence between regions was accentuated by improvements on the supply side of agriculture. Arable regions with surplus crops 'scooped' the urban markets, leaving less favoured regions to turn to livestock and rural industry.[47] But if the precise direction of these agricultural influences is unclear, the differences between the various systems of property-holding and their implications for industry are very complicated indeed. The first problem is that the division between partible inheritance and primogeniture is a very blurred one. In spite of the minimal difference in the end-result of inheritance by one system or the other,[48] it does seem that partible inheritance tended to be confined first to areas of sparse population – to forest areas with the fringe benefits of forage and domestic industry – second, to areas of dense population supported by fishing or small industry, or finally to rich pasture land. In areas like these the survival of the family did not hinge on the distinction between land and goods. But arable areas shared little prospect of an extension of land use, and there primogeniture supplemented by cash legacies tended to dominate society. It was when the shift was made from portions in kind to portions in cash that areas of primogeniture became associated with large farms and large cash portions; areas of partible inheritance went with dual economies, poor farms and small portions.[49] The latter encouraged the expansion of rural industry; for most members of the family, this provided the opportunity for making their small stakes in the land a viable basis for subsistence. In areas of primogeniture, however, younger sons who inherited cash legacies and the skilled crafts of their fathers were freed from the land to go and make their fortunes, and so became quite different recruits for industry.[50] Though one of the common features of many areas of domestic industry was weak manorialization or no strong framework of co-operative agriculture, this is not to say that communal agriculture and industrial by-employments did not coexist. Wigston was a case in point; so too was the woollen area of the West Riding of Yorkshire.

For most cottagers and smallholders, however, the kind of inheritance that was most important was not that of a tenure but that of use rights. David Hey has shown that it was not so much equal partition that was crucial as the existence of common rights, for these offered opportunities for squatters. Settlements near West Bromwich in the seventeenth and early eighteenth centuries consisted of small groups of cottages around the heath, and the population kept cows and sheep and took up industrial employments.[51] Indeed, common rights afforded the opportunity to take up by-employments. E. P. Thompson has described what he calls this 'grid of inheritance':

> The farmer, confronted with a dozen scattered strips in different hands, and with prescribed stints in the commons, did not feel fiercely that he owned the land, that it was *his*. What he inherited was a place within the hierarchy of use rights; the right to tether his horse in the sykes, the right to unloose his stock for grazing, or for the cottager the right to get away with some timber foraging and casual grazing.[52]

The complications of the agrarian environment and the ultimate implications of these for industry make it difficult in the end to chart any simple general rules. There were certainly many proto-industrial communities to be found in environments which did not in any way fit the partible inheritance/ pastoral agriculture model. The rural industries of the South of England – wool in East Anglia, pillow lace and straw plait in Buckinghamshire, Bedfordshire, Hertfordshire and Huntingdonshire, calico printing in Surrey, silk in Essex – were all set in areas of old enclosure and arable agriculture. The open-field arable villages of Leicestershire provided the setting for a knitting industry, and the arable Western Lowlands of Scotland held a substantial rural spinning industry.[53]

Different agricultural and landholding systems might be preconditions for purely agricultural or semi-industrial regions, but research has not yet established just what the connections were. They could as well help to explain the emergence of different types of industry or at least of industrial organization. The West Midlands metal industries of the early eighteenth century were both highly specialized and localized. The scythesmiths were to be found in the southern parts of the region close to the fielden parishes of Worcestershire and Warwickshire. They ran large-scale farms and large workshops containing as many as eight anvils and six bellows. Their trade demanded more skill and capital than the other metal crafts and did not lend itself to putting-out arrangements, so that scythemakers retained all the stages of production in their own hands. Lorimers and saddlers' iron-mongers were concentrated in Walsall where they held small parcels of customary or freehold land in this relatively urban community. The nail-workers had very small holdings and practised their trade as a seasonal occupation alternating with agriculture. Unlike the lorimers, who used their smallholdings to raise mortgages in order to finance their industrial capital, the nailers used their plots to eke out a subsistence which they failed to maintain out of the measly piece rates paid by nail factors and putting-out ironmongers.[54]

Different inheritance systems and the differential decline of manorialism also help to explain the emergence of different industries and different industrial organizations within the West Riding of Yorkshire. The tradi-tional woollen industry found its context in an area of large fertile holdings dominated by traditional manorial controls over land tenure. More copy-hold land was retained, and the commons were not enclosed until the late eighteenth century. This industry was organized on a 'Kauf system' basis; the independent farmer-weaver, not the factory system or the putting-out merchant, remained the pillar of the industry into the nineteenth century. The new worsted industry by contrast emerged in an area of early enclosure, and enfranchisement with partible inheritance, while economic and social divisions between an increasing landless element and a small elite of large-scale merchant capitalists, who operated a putting-out system, paved the way for the factory system.[55]

Commoners

The impact of inheritance systems and patterns of enclosure on industrial initiative was one way of looking at agricultural institutions; another was the impact of such institutions on labour and the poor. New enclosure acts at the end of the eighteenth century were directed toward the enclosure of the commons. Forest, fen, hill and vale villages with common pastures housed many small cottagers. These were independent labourers, the 'last of the English peasantry'. They drew part of their own subsistence from the commons, and provided a part-time labour force for agriculture and for the woollen, linen, and small metal trades. This common-right economy was associated by contemporaries, not with pauperism, as in those areas of large-scale enclosed agriculture, but with independence, thrift and industry. A 'country farmer' wrote that common rights supported not just small farmers, but 'the cottager, the mechanic, and inferior shopkeepers . . . this common-right is an incitement to industry, and also an encouragement to the young men and women to intermarry, and is the means of support-ing their children with credit and comfort, and of course renders them very valuable members of society'.[56] The commons provided some of the conditions during the eighteenth century that gave some labour in the countryside that 'independence' praised by Adam Smith:

> Nothing can be more absurd . . . than to imagine that men in general should work less when they work for themselves, than when they work for other people. A poor independent workman will generally be more industrious than even a journeyman who works by the piece. The one enjoys the whole produce of his industry; the other shares it with his master . . . The superiority of the independent workman over those servants who are hired by the month or by the year, and whose wages and maintenance are the same, whether they do much or do little, is likely to be still greater.[57]

Smith argued, further, that the produce of such independent labour was frequently ignored by the government and by political arithmeticians: it often consisted of goods which were consumed at home by the family or by neighbours and were never retailed through the market.[58]

These institutions of common right, inheritance, manorial systems and poor law arrangements provided the framework for social differentiation, for entrepreneurial initiative and for labour forces with some industrial experience. Research would no doubt reveal more of the complexities of the relations between agrarian institutions of property-holding and industrial organization and technology. The land may hold the key to the distinctive technological and organizational traditions of the different regions of Britain. The different coalmining technologies of Staffordshire and the North-East, the method of wage payments peculiar to Cornish mining areas, the contrast between the industrial organization of Shropshire and neighbouring Staffordshire, and other regional peculiarities noticed by Sidney Pollard, owe much to local traditions, and these traditions in turn find their context in the complicated local variations in the holding and transmission of landed property.[59]

These tantalizing connections between agrarian relations and industry can only be explored region by region. A link between changes in agriculture and the rise of manufacture exists, but we are no longer sure of the effects of agricultural change on the supplies of labour, capital and organization to new and older industries. As with agrarian relations, the strength of the link and its direct and indirect effects vary enormously between regions. This is not to dismiss the agricultural foundation of the age of manufacture, but to point to the complications of this foundation and the many different edifices that might be erected on it.

RESOURCES AND ENVIRONMENT

Resources are rarely seriously considered by historians to rank among the prime determinants of industrialization. Recently a greater sensitivity to environmental and ecological issues has brought about a re-examination of the resource base of industrialization. During the early phases of industrialization, the raw materials of manufacturing were crucial; technology had not yet developed to the point where substitute inputs could easily be developed. Even in our own times the limitations placed on economic growth by non-renewable resources in coal and oil have not been overcome by technological change, for nuclear power has not proved to be the 'free lunch' it was at first believed to be. Thus we have turned once again to consider the connections between the environment and industry. Historians too are reassessing and recasting the place of natural resources in Western industrialization.

Clearly British manufacture was not dependent upon local resources. Fine woollens were spun and woven from wool imported from Spain, France and Italy. Flax for the linen industry was imported from Ireland; silk was imported from the Mediterranean, then the East. Bar iron for the fine metal and cutlery trades was imported from Sweden and Russia; furs for the hatting trades were imported from North America. Above all, cotton was imported from India, then America. Britain's industrial dependence on these resources, however, was a major impetus to the expansion of European trade in the years leading up to the Industrial Revolution. Her acquisition and exploitation of these resources had an irreversible impact on the economies and ecologies of those lands brought into the orbit of British trade and empire. Eric Wolfe has argued, 'European merchants . . . invaded existing networks of exchange and linked one to the other. In the service of "God and profit", they located sources of products desired in Europe and developed coercive systems for their delivery.' One such product was furs; the quest for these 'was to have a profound impact upon the native peoples of North America and their modes of life'.[60]

The local resources that did matter to a much greater extent were mineral fuels. Minerals formed the core of some industrial regions, but were not enough in themselves to explain the emergence or success of industry. An important part of metal manufacturing depended on cheap but bulky energy inputs and raw materials for processing. A ton of refined iron took 10 tons of fuel and a ton of refined copper 20 tons of fuel to process in the eighteenth century.[61] Long distances from coal reserves made mass-production diffi-cult. Equally, an iron industry dependent upon charcoal was dispersed and small-scale, precluding concentration at sites favourable to the market or the labour force.[62] Coal and other mineral reserves were also an incentive to innovation, for their working created challenges just out of reach of existing technologies. Not just industry, but enterprise and innovation were attracted to areas in the vicinity of coal reserves.[63]

Large deposits of coal and low-value minerals could support the growth of heavy industry and rapid urbanization. There was salt, potash and gypsum supporting the chemical industry of Cheshire and North Yorkshire, and the coal and local clay deposits of Staffordshire, together with china clay from Cornwall, gave rise to the potteries.[64]

Trends in the output of coal have already been set out in Chapter 2. Consumption per capita rose from 9 cwt in 1700 to 16 cwt in 1750, and up to over 27 cwt in 1800 and 37 cwt in 1830. This great increase in output over the course of the eighteenth and early nineteenth centuries was achieved within the basic confines of the same coalfields in production in 1700. There was some shift of centres in the North-East, and the opening up of the eastern part of the South Wales coalfield took place in the later half of the eighteenth century. But otherwise, greater output was achieved by more intensive development and deeper mining.[65]

The history of one region of rich coal reserves bears examination. This is the Tyneside industry, otherwise known as the 'black Indies' or 'England's Peru'.[66] The Newcastle coal trade was well known from the sixteenth century, not just for household fuel, but for industry. Nef estimated, and his views have since been rehabilitated, that, by the end of the seventeenth century, approximately one-third of Britain's coal output was used in industrial processes – lime-burning, smithying, metalworking, malting and brewing, salt and soap-boiling, starch- and candlemaking, food processing and sugar-refining, textile finishing, smelting, brick- and tilemaking, glass-making, and in the manufacture of alum, copperas, saltpetre and gun-powder.[67] On Tyneside an early coal-based industrialization provided a mature coal industry which proved crucial to the distinctive path of British industrialization.[68]

By the later seventeenth century the Tyneside region was famous for its

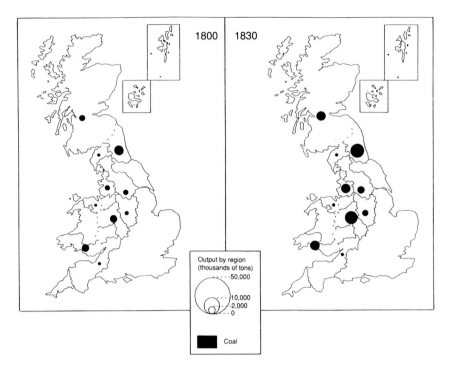

Figure 4.2 Coal output by region, 1800 and 1830

Source: Von Tunzelmann, 'Coal and Steam Power', p. 73.

coal, but also well known for a whole series of industrial undertakings using the coal – salt, glass and lime works, shipbuilding, copper and iron.[69] One of these was the Winlaton ironworks founded in 1691 by Sir Ambrose Crowley; by 1728 the Crowley factory was said to be the largest manufacturing complex of the day with its forges, mills, furnaces, warehouses and workshops.[70]

Wrigley has placed coal at the centre of the meaning of the Industrial Revolution. Its own pre-industrial production technology made available a source of inanimate energy whose impact dwarfed any other alternative.[71] Coal produced a new source of heat, and was used across a range of textile, bleaching and dyeing industries; it produced a source of power effectively harnessed with the advances in steam power. Coal, when the means were found of using it to smelt iron ore, also brought the substitution of mineral for organic raw materials across a range of industries. The results flowing from this key resource were, according to Wrigley, 'opportunities opening up over a vast new terrain'.

In the new regime huge industries could develop for which the productivity of the land was an irrelevance since agricultural products did not
figure amongst their raw materials – metal manufacture, machine tools
and engineering; pottery, bricks, glass and ceramics; heavy and fine
chemicals; shipbuilding; the manufacture of road and rail vehicles;
electrical goods; most durable consumer goods industries.[72]

Wrigley's dating of this transformation is an elastic process stretching
from the sixteenth century to the last half of the nineteenth century.
Tyneside's experience showed the impact which coal could produce in one
region during an otherwise 'pre-industrial' period. British industry on a
broad basis was deeply rooted in coal-using technologies from an early date,
and the skills and processes associated with these eventually built up to a
cumulative wave of technological change.[73] Despite this, coal resources by
themselves were not enough to explain industrial transformation. They had
to be deployed, and workers, craftsmen and entrepreneurs had to invent,
and use, these resources so as to grasp these great new opportunities.
Whatever the time span for the use of coal in industry, the key inventions of
smelting iron with coal, puddling and steam power were achieved in the
short period from 1760 to 1790, if we include the classic inventions of
Darby's smelting with coke, Cort's puddling process, and the Watt steam
engine, or the period from 1709, if we also include earlier and less successful
versions of these.[74] The existence of coal resources, and Britain's long
experience in using them, are not enough to explain this series of events.
Tyneside's early success story built on coal was soon eclipsed by that of
Lancashire and the West Riding, whose emergence as successful industrial
regions was caused by a quite different range of factors.

The extent to which coal provided a release from the limits to growth was,
furthermore, subject to strict constraints, as Ricardo clearly understood.
Mines were not fundamentally different from land in being subject to
diminishing returns. 'The metals, like other things, are obtained by labour.
Nature, indeed, produces them; but it is the labour of man which extracts
them from the bowels of the earth, and prepares them for our service . . .
But there are mines of various qualities, affording very different results, with
equal quantities of labour.'[75] Coal was a non-renewable resource; the extension of its margin was measured in the depth of the pits and the numbers of
miners. Like land, it was subject to diminishing returns. Ricardo, however,
also believed that the pressure of diminishing returns was an incentive to
technological innovation, which in turn could hold back for a time a general
tendency for the rate of profit to fall. Though the cotton industry spread
fastest in areas of cheap coal, the most rapid rate of diffusion of the Watt
steam engine, and subsequently the high-pressure steam engine, was in areas
where coal was more costly.[76] Using coal may have been one technological
breakthrough; saving it proved to be of far greater significance.

5

INDUSTRIAL DECLINE

Industrial transformation in the eighteenth and early nineteenth centuries meant not only the rise of new industries and the reorganization of the old. It also entailed the decline of old industries and erasure of old methods of production. Earlier chapters have pointed out the significance historians attach to the spread of the rural domestic industries in the sixteenth to eighteenth centuries, and the bridge these industries formed between agricultural and industrial development. Now we shall examine some of the failures of this rural manufacture or proto-industrialization. We shall trace the road to decline in some of these industries and production methods over the eighteenth century.

Joan Thirsk has described the growth and wide geographical dispersal of industrial by-employments in the seventeenth century. Most of these industries grew up within a pastoral economy, though some found a more suitable context in the towns. The manufacture of starch, needles, pins, cooking pots, kettles, frying pans, lace, soap, vinegar and stockings, as well as the more conventional iron, glass, brass, lead and coal industries, now employed large numbers of part- and full-time workers. Divisions in the quality of commodities coincided in many cases with divisions between town and country industries. The best knives were made in Sheffield itself; the inferior and cheaper ones in the villages round about. Coarse pottery was made in the country, while delftware and creamware were crafts of the large towns. Woollen and worsted stockings were made in the country; jersey stockings in Norwich and London; and silk stockings only in London.[1]

Some areas of the country were already industrialized regions by the seventeenth century. Most parts of Staffordshire, for example, supported industry of some kind. There were wood turning, carpentry and tanning in the Needlewood Forest, coal in south Staffordshire, as well as iron and metal goods including locks, handles, buttons, saddlery and nails, and coal and iron in Cannock Chase. Kinver Forest in the South-West had scythesmiths and makers of edge tools, and there were glassworkers on the Staffordshire–Worcestershire border at Stourbridge. Burslem in the North-West had a pottery industry, and there was ironstone mining in the North-East.

98

Leatherworking and textile weaving in hemp, flax and wool were scattered throughout the country.[2] In Essex by 1629, 40,000 to 50,000 people were said to be wholly dependent on the manufacture of the New Draperies. These rural workers were 'not able to subsist unless they be continually set on work, and weekly paid'. A trade crisis in 1629 meant the 'instant impoverishment of multitudes of those poor people'.[3]

We know of the emergence of these industries in the sixteenth and seventeenth centuries, and subsequently of the factory-based textile industries and large-scale metal manufactures which formed the basis for industrialization in the late eighteenth and early nineteenth centuries. But we know little of the course of economic change between these two periods nor of what happened to all those industries set up by hopeful projectors before and after the Civil War. Here we shall look at the forgotten side-effects of the greater regional concentration of industry and the development of factory production. Industrial decline is a subject curiously neglected by economic historians who are generally more concerned to point out the triumphs of industrialization and the growth of new regions. They have assumed that most regions of domestic industry went on to join the story of the factory system, and for those that did not do so immediately it was apparent that the effect of economic growth from the late eighteenth century onwards was to generate employment opportunities in hand-domestic as well as mechanized sectors. We are aware of a whole series of traditional domestic industries which were eclipsed in the course of the eighteenth and early nineteenth centuries, but know little of the course of their decline and nothing of the short- if not long-term effect of this de-industrialization. Sidney Pollard has admitted industrial decline as part of a European pattern of ebb and flow between regions,[4] and Eric Richards has postulated an association between the decline of a whole series of traditional domestic industries and a contraction of employment opportunities for women over the course of the nineteenth century. Richards argues that not only did employment for women in agriculture fall in the nineteenth century, but women's hand trades withered away. The new cotton industry did generate jobs for women but these were concentrated in only a few regions, and other new industries created few employment opportunities. 'For women the gradual loss in employment in the traditional lines was probably greater than the creation of new opportunities.'[5]

The greatest decline of these traditional industries probably took place in the years just following the Napoleonic Wars. But a substantial revolution, if not actual decline, is also evident over the course of the eighteenth century. Historians who have acknowledged this decline ascribe it to a number of factors: a regional phenomenon reflecting changes in comparative advantage;[6] the failure of traditional entrepreneurship and labour;[7] or a specific outcome of cyclical downturn in the middle of the century.[8] Be that as it may, the most striking change in the industrial structure of the country between the end of the seventeenth century and the middle of the nineteenth was its geography. The urbanized industrial zone of the seventeenth century extended along a right-angle connecting Bristol, London and Norwich. By the nineteenth century this zone had shifted north and north-west to the coalfields of the West Midlands, the West Riding, Lancashire and South Wales. The old manufacturing centres of southern and eastern England had languished or disappeared.[9]

DISPERSED INDUSTRY AND REGIONAL FACTORS

The decline of these centres and the emergence of new industrial areas can be analysed in terms of regional development. A new type of industrial region emerged in the later eighteenth and early nineteenth century. This differed from earlier and indeed later regions. Earlier proto-industrial and pre-industrial regions existed side by side, relatively cut off from one another, due to poor interregional transport and little economic complementarity. Proto-industrial regions connected much more significantly to the metro-polis, and through this to international markets. Industrial concentrations in these areas were very mixed, comprised of small towns and villages, and often spread over wide areas. They frequently lacked the scale and external economies which came to characterize regions of the Industrial Revolution.[10]

There were also important political factors behind earlier regional struc-tures. Much proto-industrial development found its framework within what was an age of absolutism and mercantilism. Industries were thought to be sources of military and thus of political power. Industrial self-sufficiency in many provinces and towns became a goal of economic policy.[11] Industry was also a means of poor relief and social control. Economic policy in some areas and especially in towns was directed to stabilizing the volume and type of industrial production in order to pre-vent dearth and unemployment.[12] Debates on trade and industrial policy during the eighteenth century focused in much the same way as they do today on the issue of unemployment. Projectors and inventors couched their schemes in terms of how many jobs they would create.[13] John Cary wrote: 'new projections are every day set on foot to render the making of our woollen manufactures easy, which should be rendered cheaper by the contrivance of manufacturers not by the falling price of labour; cheapness creates expense, and expense gives fresh employments, whereby the poor will be still kept at work'.[14] Postlethwayt feared that English industry would be undermined by foreign imports, and thought that the best security was the 'home market' provided by the 'cultivators of the soil', and that 'every machine tending to diminish their employment would really be destructive of the strength of society, of the mass of men and of home consumption'.[15] The result was a state infrastructure of subsidies, monopolies and protective tariffs primarily directed towards reinforcing existing regional leads and lags.[16]

The regions built up under this framework of dispersed industry and state policy went into decline during the course of the eighteenth century, to be replaced by distinctive, much more specialized regions. These new regions were marked by a geographical concentration of whole sectors of production. Regional capital markets and intraregional labour migration, regional ports and mercantile facilities, and provincial capitals with their own political and cultural priorities developed to reinforce the industrial dynamic at the core of South Lancashire, the West Riding, the West and East Midlands, the North-East, South Wales and the South-West of Scotland. These regional economies were also canal economies.

> Dense patches of the [canal] network . . . developed highly integrated economies largely separate from one another . . . the canal-based economies became more specialised, more differentiated from each other and more internally unified.[17]

The result, for a particular stage of economic development, was not isolation but innovation. Britain's pioneering industrialization was grounded, according to Pollard, in a set of regions, each internally integrated in such a way as to foster innovation, and, in Chandler's terminology, to focus the economies of scope as well as of scale.[18]

Before the rise of these new industrial regions, however, a number of early and proto-industrial regions had appeared. With their fate was bound up the livelihoods of large numbers of rural and urban small producers and poor landless labourers. For agricultural advance during the seventeenth and eighteenth centuries, as we have seen, was labour-shedding, especially in areas turning to large-scale arable cultivation.

While peasant society was mean and poor, the coming of some domestic industries could make the difference between destitution and decency for the poor and dispossessed. Defoe in the early eighteenth century reported on the living conditions of some of the leadminers of Bassington Moor in Derbyshire, where he found a woman and her family living in a cave.

> The habitation was poor, 'tis true, but things within did not look so like misery as I expected. Everything was clean and neat, though mean and ordinary. There were shelves with earthenware and some pewter and brass. There was . . . a whole flitch or side of bacon hanging up in the chimney and by it a good piece of another. There was a sow and pigs running about at the door, and a little lean cow feeding upon a green place just before the door . . . a little enclosed piece of ground was growing with good barley.

The woman's husband worked in the leadmines for 5d a day, and when she could she worked ore for 3d a day. Defoe was amazed that 8d a day was enough to maintain a man, his wife and five small children, but declared that they 'seemed to live pleasantly'. The children looked 'plump, ruddy and wholesome and the woman was full, well shaped and clean'. He found nothing there which looked like the 'dirt and nastiness of the miserable cottages of the poor'.[19]

But other contemporaries saw different conditions, for such industry was as uncertain as the volatile trade which encouraged it. An observer in 1677 wrote that

> though it sets the poor on work where it finds them, yet it draws them still more to the place; and their masters allow wages so mean that they are only preserved from starving while they work; when age, sickness and death comes, themselves, their wives or their children are commonly left on the parish.[20]

The variable conditions of these areas of industrial by-employment even in the seventeenth century were dramatically accentuated by the nineteenth. Some areas had declined into terrible poverty. Hoskins found that the peasant society of Wigston Magna, practically all framework knitters by the 1830s, lived in overcrowded streets, only to die at alarming rates of puerperal fever, consumption, and infant mortality. 'Wages were low, housing conditions worse than they had been since the sixteenth century, unemployment had become endemic.' And the trade declined amidst all those depressing institutions of decline – truck payments, debts and proliferating middlemen. By 1845 knitters could rarely earn more than 7s a week, and young people were finally giving up this low-paid trade for a new one, sewing and stitching gloves.[21]

The decline of industries in the South of England took place earlier, but the effect on local communities, at least in the short term, was no less devastating. E. L. Jones has charted the grim litany of regional decline in Berkshire, Dorset, Hampshire, Wiltshire, Norfolk, Suffolk and Essex, areas which dropped an average of eleven places in the county league table of wealth between 1693 and 1843. Ironworking left Kent, the Sussex Weald, then the Forest of Dean in the course of the eighteenth century. The woollen cloth industry disappeared from Kent in the late seventeenth century and was finally eclipsed in the later eighteenth in Surrey, Berkshire and Hampshire. It dwindled in Exeter, and by the early nineteenth century was contracting in Somerset, Wiltshire and Gloucestershire. Neither carpet weaving, cotton spinning, nor stocking knitting sustained a hold in the South. By the nineteenth century, boot- and shoemaking had disappeared from Berkshire, the making of wire buttons from Dorset, and wool and fur hatting from Gloucestershire.[22] Beside these regions, where industry contracted over the eighteenth century, may be placed others which saw new industries and innovations spurt briefly and retreat thereafter. Pollard names ten regions which 'saw significant innovatory change in the period between the 1760s and 1790s'. But of these he found that Cornwall, Shropshire, North Wales and the Derbyshire uplands fell by the wayside after making their vital contributions, and Tyneside and Clydeside had to find a 'second wind to survive as industrial centres'.[23]

REASONS FOR DECLINE

What were the causes of these different regional experiences of expansion and decline? Many historians are quick to point to the inexorable emergence of 'comparative advantage' between industry and agriculture in various regions. Some regions were better suited to take up the new agricultural techniques of the period, while others had distinctive industrial advantages. Regions then specialized accordingly. Sidney Pollard charges a more specific set of factors with the subsequent decline of industrial regions, including exhaustion of minerals, discovery of cheaper alternative supplies, locational shifts elsewhere, new developments in transportation which made the region less favourable than its rivals, or the fetter of small size.[24] The natural resources which had formed a *raison d'être* of an industrial region might be depleted, as happened with copper in the Lake District, iron ore in Shropshire, and lead in Derbyshire. Even if such resources remained, new sources, richer, of better quality, or easier to access, might be discovered, throwing traditional sources of supply into decline. Markets might decline with changing fashions, and the region fail to adapt to new tastes, as was the case with the Norwich worsted manufacture during the eighteenth century. There was also, as Pollard has argued, the reluctance of many erstwhile successful industrial regions to accept change: 'pride, conservatism, self-satisfaction, misplaced hopes, misunderstood market signals' leading to 'loss of market and momentum when change becomes necessary'.[25] We need to consider the course and causes of industrial decline in the case of several regions and industries, looking first at the most celebrated case of decline – that of the traditional cloth industries of East Anglia and the West of England. Some contemporaries attributed the failure of these regions to a lack of basic raw materials, for example coal and water power. Yet, as Jones has shown, the persistence of the blanket manufacture at Witney was specifically attributed in 1809 to cheap local labour offsetting the 'want of vicinity to coal'. The Wiltshire mills had access to Somerset coal, and the competition of agriculture for water power in the South hardly accounts for the extent of market retreat.[26] As we shall see, more weight should be placed on the social and institutional factors, and we need to re-examine the meaning of comparative advantage as an explanation for regional growth and decline.

THE OLD CLOTH REGIONS

The cloth industry of Essex was the first major southern industry to collapse. In the seventeenth and eighteenth centuries it dominated the life of four large towns as well as a further dozen towns and large villages: it contributed something to the income of most Essex families. Defoe had seen

> the villages stand thick, the market towns not only more in number but larger and fuller of inhabitants and, in short, the whole county full of little endships or hamlets and scattered houses, that it looks all like a planted colony, everywhere full of people and the people everywhere full of business.[27]

By 1800 the cloth industry was gone. The two regions had specialized in says and bays, that is, cloth which was half worsted and half fulled. Rural weaving, which had been widespread, was the first to decline, disappearing soon after 1700. At this time the few surviving village firms all ceased, and weaving continued for a time in the towns. Spinning, however, was widespread through the countryside, and in the 1740s it was thought that the majority of women were employed in it. In addition to wool, fustians and cottons were manufactured across North-West Essex into Suffolk. These new textiles had caused smallholders to settle in the area, growing woad for dyeing, and this survived until mechanization in the North at the end of the century. The cloth trade, however, collapsed even before mechanization posed any threat.

The first casualties were the small centres where most of the clothiers were master weavers with a small capital. The major centre was Halstead, where long-established family businesses also maintained extensive interests in farming, malting and milling, following the classic pattern of pre-industrial capital formation. Most of the men were weavers and the women spinners. But apprenticeship suddenly declined after 1780, population fell soon after, and by 1791 it was reported that the industry was in a declining state: there were only four clothiers left, and by 1800 even these were gone. Other Essex cloth towns declined even earlier. The centuries-old cloth trade of Coggeshall, buttressed by very substantial business, was in decay by 1720. In 1733 it was petitioning Parliament for help; in 1740 there was a major poor law crisis; a short recovery was followed by collapse again in the 1760s. The early 1790s saw the last workers' procession and the dissolution of the Cloth Workers' Company. Even Colchester, known for its high standards and pre-eminent craftsmen, failed to escape the general malaise. A decline from 1700, punctuated by occasional booms following on the end of wars, escalated after the 1760s to a state of bankruptcy.[28]

The booms were memorable. Defoe remembered that

> after the late plague in France and the Peace in Spain the Run for goods was so great in England and the Price of everything rose so high that

the poor women in Essex could earn one shilling to one shilling and sixpence per diem by spinning . . . the poor farmers could get no dairy maids . . . they all run away to Bocking, Sudbury, to Braintree and to other manufacturing towns in Essex and Suffolk. The very Plowman did the same.

But this prosperity was not long-lasting, for 'As soon as the demand slack'd from abroad all these loose people were turn'd off, the spinsters went to begging, the weavers rose in rebellion.'[29]

Norfolk's industry was in trouble from the first decade of the eighteenth century, thanks to the transfer of the stocking manufacture. There was a petition to Parliament in 1709 on the decline of trade, followed by riots against printed calico ten years later. Norfolk staggered under the blow of competition first from East India goods, then from Yorkshire worsteds, and finally from cotton. Prosperity returned in the 1750s and 1760s followed by decline again in 1765. Trade picked up in the 1770s, but was low again in the 1780s.[30] Stumbling between periods of stagnation and activity, the worsted industry did continue to grow until the 1770s, and, though it saw the occasional light of prosperity until the 1820s, it was by then well on the wane behind the rising star of the West Riding.[31] By 1820 *Rees's Cyclopedia* could report that the manufacture of worsteds had transferred to Yorkshire and that the manufacture of camlets, calimancoes and bombazines had disappeared from Norwich.[32]

The cloth industry of the West Country held out until the early nineteenth century, but it was subject to fluctuating fortunes for most of the eighteenth. While output of broadcloth in Yorkshire doubled between 1727 and 1765, that of the West Country did not grow at all – it stagnated right up until 1770. The little improvement which followed was eclipsed by a severe depression in Gloucestershire in 1783–4, and the last five years of the decade in no way overcame this. A growth in demand in the early 1790s, however, encouraged manufacturers and workers to acquiesce in the use of spinning machinery. The industry grew in Wiltshire and Somerset, making great advances in Frome. But by 1800 there was more unemployment in Wiltshire and Somerset. An air of confidence appeared once more in Gloucestershire in the early 1820s. But except in Trowbridge the small clothier was replaced by the large factory, though domestic handloom weaving continued in the West. The crisis of 1826 was the real dividing line, and while the industry picked up again in the early 1830s, it had actually shifted in location from the Upper Stroudwater Valley and the region below the Cotswolds to concentrate around Stroud and the Nailsworth Valley. But the West did not take up steam power; by the 1830s it had lost almost all its manufacture of cheaper cloth, and like Essex and Norfolk was experiencing population decline.[33] The pattern and timing of decline in Essex, Norfolk and the West Country were also those of Suffolk, Coventry, Worcester, Dorset and Exeter. The serge industry of Exeter, which claimed an export trade of £500,000 in 1700, had ceased to be of any importance to the city by 1800.[34]

COMPARATIVE ADVANTAGE

The explanations given for the decline of these old cloth regions are as varied as those for the rise of the industrial North. They range from geography to institutions, including the characteristics of management and labour. Though Clapham dismissed the significance of water power and coal as factors behind the shift of the industry to the North, a new form of natural determination has arisen based on the theory of comparative advantage. It is E. L. Jones's view that regions progressively discovered their comparative advantage in either agriculture or industry and increasingly concentrated resources in the one or the other. The kinds of agricultural innovation which occurred in the seventeenth and eighteenth centuries favoured the light land soils of the South, where agriculture became the more profitable activity. In the North and the Midlands, on the other hand, domestic industries gathered in areas suited only to pastoral husbandry, and these industrial occupations became relatively more profitable even before other advantages of coal and water power came into play in the later period of mechanization.

> The North and some Midland districts became more industrial precisely because the readier uptake of the 'new' crops on the light land in the south had made them relatively poorer agriculturally. North and south thus evolved as complementary markets which it became worth linking by better communications.[35]

The decline of the Essex cloth industry was a pre-eminent example of this. Though the decline of the industry was blamed directly on its product specialization, there had to be some reason why clothiers did not introduce new product lines. Specialization in bays and says with limited markets in Spain, Portugal and Latin America made the link with Lisbon crucial, and the series of eighteenth-century wars was disastrous for trade. But in Essex the traditional dual occupations of farming and textiles formed the basis for some clothiers to strengthen their ties with farming, especially after 1700 when both the profitability and the social standing of agriculture improved.[36] It had also long been customary for West Country clothiers to buy estates and become gentlemen clothiers. But it was in addition evident that the spread of investment across industrial- and agrarian-related pursuits was part and parcel of the pre-industrial pattern of capital formation.[37] That resources were shifted over to agriculture and away from industry was nothing new. What was new was the extent and the timing of this shift of resources. Jones points out that in Gloucestershire this transfer of capital into land was said to have caused the failure of clothiers whose assets were no longer liquid enough to tide them over trade depressions. But more important was a prolonged and unfortunately-timed withdrawal from industry into agriculture which seemed to coincide with the recognition that local industrial investment was no longer rewarding. This argument seems to fit the experiences of Essex, Berkshire and Norfolk, which were in decline even before the threat of mechanization. Subsequently this was reinforced by the dictates of sources of power.

> On the clays and lowland heaths of the south and east, with little or no alternative to 'mother and daughter power', no escape from the spinning wheel or hand loom, cottage industry contracted in the face of competition from machines . . . Handicraft workers cut their prices to the bone in order to match machine production . . . the operators of water driven textile mills cut their prices when in turn they were also faced with competition from steam. Coal beat them. Without it areas with waterpower alone followed handicraft districts into industrial oblivion.[38]

Comparative advantage in agriculture cannot, however, provide a sufficient explanation for industrial decline in the old clothing districts. For it explains much of what occurred by the end result, failing to provide enough in the way of independent factors contributing to industrial decline. Reasons behind the original aptitude of regions for the one pursuit or the other are not explored. It is also clear that, although the cloth industry in the southern regions did not entirely de-industrialize, it shifted resources into more profitable agricultural pursuits. It is clear that the capital and labour of the failing cloth industry also provided a congenial environment to attract a whole series of smaller domestic industries in silk, lace and strawplait manufacture, glovemaking and shirt-buttonmaking, until these industries too faced the threat of the machine.

INSTITUTIONAL FACTORS

If comparative advantage in agriculture is not reason itself for the shift away from the southern cloth manufacture, what other explanations are there? There were several notable institutional rigidities. The first was restrictions on capital and entrepreneurship. Monopoly restriction on markets and credit was exercised by a small group of London merchants called the Blackwell Hall factors. By manipulating credit the factors apparently split the clothiers into a small wealthy group and a large group of men with inadequate credit. High and inflexible wage rates in the South have also been blamed for industrial decline. It is often argued that in the late seventeenth century the many competing occupations in Kent and the high price of food in the Home Counties so forced up wages that Kentish clothiers could no longer compete with lower-wage areas. But in the remainder of the southern cloth industry wages were by the second half of the eighteenth century lower than in the North. The final rigidity was the polarity of master and man in the South compared to the socially more uniform small weaver communities of the North. This produced more forceful workers' resistance to mechanization in the South.[39]

The limitations of entrepreneurship do seem to have played a contributory, if not decisive, part in the route to decline. It was said of the West Country that it was founded on a monopoly erected and supported by great capitals and this led to conservatism. Most have accepted Josiah Tucker's well-known comparison of Yorkshire and the West Country. In Yorkshire

> Their journeymen . . . if they have any, being so little removed from the Degree and Condition of their masters, and likely to set up for themselves by the Industry and Frugality of a few years . . . thus it is, that the working people are generally Moral, Sober, and Industrious; that the goods are well made, and exceedingly cheap.

In the West Country

> The Motives to Industry, Frugality and Sobriety are all subverted to this one consideration viz. that they shall always be chained to the same Oar (the Clothier), and never be but Journeymen . . . Is it little wonder that the trade in Yorkshire should flourish, or the trade in Somersetshire, Wiltshire, and Gloucestershire be found declining every Day?[40]

More recently several historians have made a similar observation on the deficiencies of entrepreneurship: 'All through the eighteenth century the Company [of Weavers, Fullers and Shearmen] was inbreeding, with the same families and their ideas preserved like heirlooms.'[41] Although, as Julia Mann points out, clothiers, small as well as large, abounded in the West Country in the eighteenth century, the conditions for the survival of the small man became more difficult over the period as divisions between 'respectable' and 'inferior' clothiers sharpened. Mann, however, blames the clothiers for being too easy-going, 'faithful for too long' to the older types of cloth.[42] Yet another failure lay in marketing; this explains the continued specialization in the same product lines and the same markets. For all the West Country cloth exports went through Blackwell Hall. There were no public cloth halls in the West Country or Norwich where clothiers could exhibit and sell their wares.

> Export outlets in the West Country were entirely, if somewhat indirectly through the Blackwell Hall factors, controlled by merchants in London . . . They were not experts in handling cloth. The merchants in Leeds and Wakefield were a different species. Cloth was their life, their sole interest . . . The difference between the ways in which the West Riding trade was handled by the active merchants of Leeds,

Wakefield (and eventually Halifax) and the exports of every other production area from Norwich down, which were all monopolized by non-specialist London traders often working within the restrictions of the trading companies themselves, accounts in good measure for Yorkshire's growing supremacy in the eighteenth century.[43]

The social divisions which inhibited enterprise also provoked extensive workers' antagonism to technical and organizational change. Though decline in the South had set in before the time of water- and steam-powered factories, this is not to deny the role of earlier technical innovation. The examples of resistance to machinery are legion throughout the eighteenth century. In Essex class conflict was often acute. Weavers in the towns shared identical working conditions and were well placed to combine. The weavers' revolt of 1715 extinguished any idea of a factory system. There was a big strike in 1757 when Colchester employers demanded the return of thrums (the ends left on the loom after weaving). Weavers in Barking fought against the wool mill (for cleaning and loosening wool) in 1759. There was also some resistance to the flying shuttle, though it was introduced from the 1750s. Spinning remained backward, and there were no jennies until 1794. But cheap domestic spinning labour seemed a viable alternative, and it just did not seem profitable to invest in machinery at a time of imminent industrial collapse.[44]

In the West Country, weavers faced an almost continuous decline in wage rates, at least until the middle of the eighteenth century. Spinners' earnings were more volatile, but, when they fell, a widely-dispersed body of female spinners had no organization to marshal resistance. The wretched state of these spinners and other clothworkers in Gloucestershire was more often expressed in embezzlement and shoddy work. By the 1780s the clothiers of Minchinhampton sent all their wool to be spun outside the area, for 'Our poor spoil their yarn by dirtiness, bad spinning, dumping and frequently putting several workers' yarn together and many other frauds.'[45]

Spinning occupied women over a wide area in what were otherwise purely agricultural districts. Though there were spinning jennies and carding engines in Yorkshire from the 1770s, few were introduced into the West Country until the 1790s. A jenny set up in Shepton Mallet in 1776 was destroyed by a mob. Elsewhere until the 1790s it was only on the fringe of the industrial area that machinery was set up. The fierce resistance to the jenny at Keynsham among colliers and their wives, dependent upon the supplementary income from spinning, may have eroded the industry there, for, whatever the reasons, the industry left the area soon after.[46]

Within the West Country, Wiltshire and Somerset continued to be much more hostile to machinery than Gloucestershire. A mob destroyed an advanced scribbling machine in Bradford-on-Avon in 1791. Workpeople rioted against the flying shuttle in Trowbridge in 1785–7 and 1810–13, postponing its introduction there and in West Wiltshire until the end of the Napoleonic Wars. Weavers were still rioting against the flying shuttle in Frome in 1822. Resistance to finishing machinery was even more celebrated, in Yorkshire fuelling the classic Luddite attacks, and just as strongly resisted in Wiltshire and Somerset. Unlike the clothworkers of Gloucestershire who had long ago adopted the gig mill, those of Wiltshire and Somerset believed the machine would be the first step to the introduction of the shearing frame, and it remained rare in these counties until the end of the wars.[47]

The greater resistance to the jenny in the South and the East can be accounted for by the much greater importance of hand spinning to the subsistence of poor women and rural families generally. There were fewer poor women dependent on spinning alone in the North, and anyway those previously employed in the wool trade could get employment well into the nineteenth century in spinning worsted, for which the jenny was little used. In the South and the East, it was not just machinery but the decline of the worsted trade itself which removed the mainstay for thousands of women and children in the villages of Norfolk and Suffolk. The concentration of industry did bring more employment and higher wages for women in the districts where mechanization was introduced, but it spelt doom to thousands of women in scattered outlying parishes.[48]

NEW RURAL INDUSTRIES

But where the cloth industry declined in the South of England, other smaller domestic industries grew up, some of them continuing into the later nineteenth century. Comparative advantage in agriculture did not prevent the emergence of new industries there when the old cloth centres declined. However, it would be a big mistake to regard these industries as a replacement for the old cloth industries. In the first place, they were smaller and poorer than their great predecessors. And, in addition, they were sometimes not real replacements at all. In Northamptonshire, for example, shoes apparently replaced worsted, but in fact they were made in different areas and employed different sections of the country population.[49]

The decline of several Essex towns was stayed by the silk manufacture and by the substitution of bunting for the more expensive worsted previously made. This coarse cheap fabric continued to employ women in and around Sudbury until the 1870s.[50] The ancient bone and pillow lace industry in the early eighteenth century was the staple of women and children in Bedfordshire, Buckinghamshire, Northamptonshire, Devon, Dorset, Somerset, Wiltshire, Hampshire, Derbyshire and Yorkshire. By the end of the eighteenth century the industry had concentrated in the first three of these counties, and by 1780 was employing 140,000 there and over the borders of Huntingdon, Hertfordshire and Oxford. The finest and most expensive lace was made in the West Country – Honiton in Devon and

Blandford in Dorset. The trade, however, gradually declined with competition from foreign lace and in some cases from machinery. In Honiton in 1820 only 300 lacemakers remained out of the 21,000 formerly employed.[51] The domestic lace industry appeared to go into a general decline from 1815 to the 1830s, under those dual threats. While the Nottingham industry had been steadily improving, the pillow lace industry had been 'constantly deteriorating and excluded by the price'. The demand for cheaper products favoured the Nottingham machine-made lace industry. The threat from the handworkers of France was countered by the machine. 'By the 1830s, the industry had disappeared from a number of places and almost everywhere prices and wages had fallen, and employment had become very intermittent.'[52] But a new wave of demand for lace of all kinds, including in particular handmade lace, appeared in the 1840s, and the industry gained a new lease of life. Prices and employment reached a high point. After this the industry lasted until 1880.

In addition to lace there was straw plaiting which spread quickly in the borders of Buckinghamshire, Hertfordshire and Bedfordshire. It was also introduced into North Essex in the late eighteenth century, and in 1840 was still keeping women, children and old men busy in the Halstead, Braintree and Barking districts. Straw plaiting had started in the late eighteenth century and spread rapidly just at the time when the decline in wool spinning had left many women unemployed. There were good wages until the end of the Napoleonic Wars. The introduction of hats from Italy was a temporary setback, and the industry recovered for a time by importing Italian straw. Wages, however, fell to 5s–7s a week and stayed there until the industry finally died in 1870.[53]

The appearance of lace and strawplaiting in southern arable farming regions may have been connected to contemporary agricultural change. As Keith Snell and Robert Allen have argued recently, the kind of agricultural changes which took place in the South and the East probably reduced the potential for the participation of women in the agricultural labour force.[54] This was not nearly so marked in western pastoral regions, for such regions did make available some comparatively well-paid agricultural and alternative female employment. Because farming activities were reduced for women in the South and the East, a labour force was left to take up lacemaking and straw plaiting. It could just as well be argued, however, that the attractiveness of these industries after the mid-eighteenth century might itself have contributed to the sexual division of labour in agriculture.[55]

There was a rapid increase in glovemaking from the end of the eighteenth century, and this industry found its urban headquarters in Woodstock, Yeovil and Worcester, with outworking villages in Oxfordshire, Somerset and Worcestershire. Worcester and its outlying villages claimed 30,000 workers in the 1820s, Somerset had 20,000, Hereford 3,000. But there was a great decline after Huskisson's withdrawal of the import restrictions on

French gloves.[56] By 1832 output at Worcester was one-third of what it had been in 1825.[57]

Dorset had further cottage industries in string, pack thread, netting, cordage, and ropes with sailcloth and sacking. It was well known, too, for its wire shirt-button industry which in 1793 employed 4,000 in the town and neighbourhood of Shaftesbury. But this industry too bowed out in the 1830s, to competition from horn and pearl buttons.[58]

The decline of the older domestic manufactures in the South of England was thus much more complicated than is generally allowed for. The decline of the older woollen manufacture was of course dominant. Wool, which was Britain's chief home as well as export industry, provided 70 per cent of domestic exports in 1700 and 50 per cent in 1770. The enormous effect of its transfer from the South to Yorkshire, which produced 20 per cent of output in 1700 and 60 per cent in 1800,[59] outweighs all other trends. But still the South did not entirely turn to agriculture – new cottage industries developed on the burial mounds of the old. The reasons for the decline of the old cloth centres cannot lie entirely in a comparative advantage for agriculture in the South, because the appearance of these new industries, limited though they were in extent and long-term success, contradicts that case. The argument of comparative advantage is, in addition, an anachronistic one, because investment decisions were based on a long tradition of mixed portfolios and responses to the trade cycle. Bankruptcy, not comparative advantage, determined the allocation of resources between the industrial and agricultural sectors.[60]

OTHER REGIONS

Other regions of Britain played an important part in the early phase of industrialization, but failed to sustain their leadership. Cornwall was one such area. Early and rapid growth was based on the tin and copper industries. Because coal was expensive, the area was the first to use the Watt engine, and tin and copper mining and smelting became the basis for one of the most advanced engineering centres of the world. But in the middle of the nineteenth century mining suddenly declined and the region was rapidly transformed into a holiday resort. Shropshire was another such early developer. A technological leader in ironmaking and -using, it fostered brickworks, potteries, glass and chemical works, armament works and engineering plants. But the region went into decline; the absolute growth of iron output from Shropshire peaked in 1869, but the county's share of national production fell from 27 per cent in 1796 to 10 per cent in 1830.[61] The problem here does not appear to have been depletion of mineral resources, but instead failure to use them effectively. Local iron-using industries were not built up, and a decline in the relative wages of iron-workers soon resulted in the emigration of skilled men. Even South

Staffordshire and the Black Country failed to stay the course. Rich in coal, iron and water power as well as generations of skilled metalworkers, the area developed some of the earliest canal networks and glass, engineering and armament works. There was substantial expansion in heavy industry in 1810–30 but the area rapidly declined after 1860. The place of North Wales was also ambiguous. With supplies of coal, slate, iron, lead, copper and water power it created ironworks, copper-smelting plants, engineering works, brick- and limeworks. It built up cotton mills, and woollen-, linen- and ropemaking industries. Yet even before the depletion of its coal, copper had given out in the 1820s, and cotton spinning declined by the 1830s. It too became a recreation area. Derbyshire was rich in lead ore and water power. It had a long tradition of domestic textile work with leading textile innovations including those of Arkwright, Lombe, Paul, Hargreaves, Cartwright and Strutt. Its attraction to early cotton entrepreneurs was based on its low wages and absence of any history of machine-breaking, as well as its proximity to the framework-knitting centres which created cotton twist. But the cotton industry only lasted fifteen years in the area before shifting to Lancashire.[62] During this time the centuries-old leadmining industry also suffered a demise. The industry's peak output was in the mid-eighteenth century, but technical changes at the end of the century both displaced the smaller investor and increased productivity. Trouble was obvious in the first years of the nineteenth century when the exhaustion of ore shoots, deeper working and drainage problems led to a reduction in mining output. The industry was in severe decline by the 1830s.[63]

The decline of the Weald was a classic case of a 'failed transition' from proto-industry to industrialization. The Weald was, at the beginning of the seventeenth century, a leading industrial centre, known internationally for its iron, cloth, glass and timber products. The region's famous iron industry was in decline long before the rise of coke-smelted iron; the cloth industry had disappeared even further back. The reasons for this decline did not lie in depleted natural resources, nor in comparative advantage in agriculture. Loose land controls had brought immigration, population pressure and poverty. Entrepreneurship and technical expertise were not based in the region, but came from outside mercantile groups and groups of migrant foreign craftsmen mainly from France and the Low Countries. There was little overlap in capital and technology between the different industries, and no external economies. As each individual industry declined, mercantile metropolitan capital switched not into the region's agriculture or even any other activity, but into foreign investment and government stocks.[64]

Abortive development also featured in Ireland, where the cotton industry had made a brief start in the areas around Belfast, Dublin and Cork. Cork was already in decline in the first decade of the nineteenth century as large general manufacturers collapsed following the decline in the Atlantic trade in provisions. An industry which employed about 80,000 in 1810 succumbed by the 1820s to international commercial crises and stagnation in the home market. The crisis of 1825–6 caused the greatest run of failures in the history of the industry, and, around Bandon, where coarse cords were manufactured, a slump in the mid-1820s followed by the advent of the power loom had a devastating effect. Bandon decayed, its inhabitants choosing emigration. Other areas responded to the challenge of improvements in flax spinning, and many Belfast cotton spinners opted out of cotton and transferred operations to the linen manufacture.[65]

None of these regions succeeded in accumulating the 'critical mass' of industrial activity, or in taking part in the 'economics of conglomeration'. They did not develop the sequence of industries which came to characterize the manufacturing regions of the Industrial Revolution. Glasgow and the Clyde valley followed the sequence of linen and tobacco to coal, to cotton, and iron, and on to engineering, steel and shipbuilding. The North-East started with coal and salt, glass and chemicals, then iron, followed by steel, shipbuilding and engineering. Lancashire had wool and linen, then cotton, coal, chemicals, metals, iron and engineering.[66]

CYCLICAL FACTORS

The fortunes of those regions which dropped out of the industrial vanguard in the course of the eighteenth and early nineteenth centuries were partly set by cyclical swings over the period. Industries highly dependent on export markets suffered deeply from the setbacks of the numerous eighteenth-century wars. Deane and Cole saw a definite discontinuity in economic growth in the second quarter of the century. They found a turning point in the rate of growth in total output and incomes as well as in the growth rates of particular industries in the 1740s. The downturn in economic growth was closely connected with the depression in agriculture in the 1730s and 1740s. This view and the estimates it is based on are now subject to substantial criticism.[67] The impact of war over the period was, however, probably felt in the index of industrial production, for most eighteenth-century wars had a particularly adverse effect on the home market.[68] Taking the available estimates of output along with contemporary observation, there still seems some evidence for an industrial setback in the years before mid-century.

Complaints of depression in the woollen industry in the 1730s were complemented by an obvious need for export subsidies in the linen manufacture. Innovations in cotton technology – the flying shuttle and roller spinning stood out – took until the 1760s either to spread significantly in the one case or to be perfected in the other. The hosiery industry expanded rapidly in the later seventeenth century and first quarter of the eighteenth, then slackened. Imports of raw silk increased slowly until 1740 then fell to levels lower than at the beginning of the eighteenth century and revived only in the 1750s. The hosiery industry in Nottingham and Leicester fell into widespread poverty in the 1740s and 1750s. Military expenditure during the War of the Austrian Succession boosted the output of Birmingham only slowly. The pottery industry, after undergoing a great transformation in 1690–1720, was in crisis in the late 1750s, and only revived in the third quarter of the eighteenth century. The output of the paper industry, after rising fourfold between 1710 and 1720, stagnated until 1735–45. Domestic consumption of copper and brass fell between 1725 and 1745, exports were booming but prices low. Tin had become almost unsaleable by the late 1740s. The throughput of the English iron industry stood at 26,000 tons in 1625–35 but at only 20,000–25,000 tons in the 1720s. In Phyllis Deane's words, 'The evidence suggests that the English iron industry in the first half of the eighteenth century was scattered, migratory, intermittent in operation and probably declining.'[69]

Whether there was a general mid-century cyclical industrial *malaise*, or whether this was recession and crisis in only a selected group of industries particularly affected by war, the result was regional industrial decline in the old industrial South. This may have been enough to set the seal of de-industrialization on some of those areas of former proto-industrial splendour. But it only brought to a head the many underlying institutional problems of the older industrial regions. Long periods of stagnation and at best uncertainty made the prospect of new frontiers all the more appealing. For the largely rural industrial workforce the effects of industrial decline in a region and mechanization in at least some of the major industries brought labour redundancy on a huge scale. The West of England cloth industry was such a case; mechanization and decline went hand in hand, with the worst consequences of labour redundancy felt by women spinners located not only in the woollen centres, but spread over a broad swathe of the agricultural landscape.[70]

6

TRADE, CONSUMPTION AND MANUFACTURING

Major sources of markets for the manufacturing sector were trade on the one hand and home demand on the other. The patterns of English trade over the sixteenth to the eighteenth centuries have been described many times before. These need to be put together with patterns of European trade at the time, and both related to the fortunes of the manufacturing sector.

FOREIGN MARKETS

Home demand always provided by far the most significant part of the market for the new manufactures. For the period 1700–10 to 1780–90 the home market absorbed 92 to 95 per cent of total output; foreign demand was responsible for only 5 to 9 per cent of the increase in England's total product. But the role of foreign demand grew sharply thereafter, so that between the 1780s and the 1860s it absorbed 30 per cent of UK additional output; in the period 1783–1803 the incremental ratio of exports to national product was as high as 40 per cent. From the end of the American War of Independence to the first years of the nineteenth century exports were a powerful engine of growth.[1] This is not to say, however, that external demand provided an exogenous cause of the Industrial Revolution. The main growth of Britain's industrial exports from 1790 to 1870 was under-pinned by falling relative costs and prices. But the rapid expansion in trade earlier in the eighteenth century was more closely tied to the entry of the re-export trade in exotic commodities and the rise in population in England's 'free trade zone' of England, Wales, Scotland, Ireland and the colonies in North America and the West Indies.[2]

Hobsbawm once termed foreign trade the 'spark' which lit the Industrial Revolution. Much research has accumulated to disprove this proposition. Yet there is a sense in which he was correct. For many of the parameters which set the terms for the rise of new European industries in the early industrial period were to be found in international trade. The new dimension in trade was a greatly expanded trade with Asia, Africa and the Americas from the seventeenth century. An Asian and American version of a com-

116

modities trade based on luxury goods developed to underpin a whole new system of international trade.

In the years of commercial expansion from 1769 to 1800 population rose rapidly in Europe. The fastest growing populations were those of Scandinavia, England, Belgium and Portugal. France's population rose at a rate of 0.23 per cent per annum, with the highest rates of growth in the South and the East. Italy's population grew fastest in the South, increasing 80 per cent from 1700 to 1800, 50 per cent in the North and 20 per cent in the central region. Spain's population rose 44 per cent overall, while Catalonia's tripled and Valencia's doubled. This population was also more urbanized by later in the century; 7.6 per cent of Europe's population lived in cities over 10,000 in 1600; 10 per cent in 1800.[3] These rising European populations, increasingly concentrated in towns and cities, contributed to rising demand for manufactured commodities. These commodities were produced, from the seventeenth century onwards, not within the framework of the local economy but within the world market.

European trade with Asia, Africa and the Americas grew rapidly from the seventeenth century. The flow of bullion and the silver trade integrated Asia and Europe. Asian goods – spices, coffee, tea, indigo, silk and cotton textiles – flowed West, interacting with the flow of new colonial products from the Americas. Export surpluses in Asia, the Baltic and the Levant were met by inter-European trade. French and Dutch export surpluses with Spain facilitated bullion supplies to maintain the Asian trade. Only the Americas constituted an important early industrial export market. The African market took only firearms and linen; the Asian virtually nothing. But colonial staples from the Americas and Asia stimulated profitable processing and finishing industries: sugar refining, tobacco processing and calico printing, the fundamental industries underpinning the re-export trade.[4]

It was the re-export trade, the Atlantic economy and the expansion of manufactured exports which set the framework for the markets behind the Industrial Revolution, and this chapter will therefore concentrate on this aspect of foreign trade.

Jacob Price has reduced the overall framework of the growth of Britain's foreign trade to three related phenomena:

1 growing demand in Britain for exotic products and for European industrial raw materials;
2 increasing demand in Northern and Western Europe for British re-exports of exotic commodities;
3 rising demand by the American colonies for British manufactures and re-exports.[5]

All of these parts were interdependent. Domestic industries needed imported raw materials. These were paid for by re-exports of exotic commodities from the American colonies and Asia. Slaves were bought in Africa

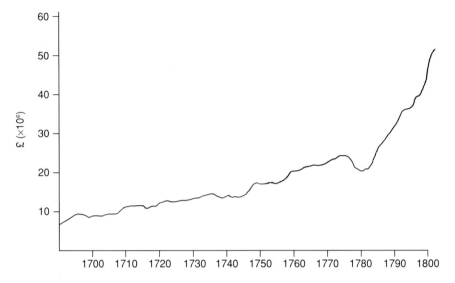

Figure 6.1 English foreign trade in the eighteenth century (net imports plus domestic exports; official values)

Source: Engerman, 'Mercantilism and Overseas Trade', figure 1.

Note: The statistics are for England, 1697–1774, and for Great Britain, 1772–1800.

with Birmingham ware and Mediterranean and Asian commodities. Linen was exported to America from Bohemia, Westphalia, Ulster and Fife. All of this was co-ordinated by merchants in the long-distance trade in London, Bristol, Liverpool and Glasgow.

This 'Atlantic economy' relied for its labour force on slavery: 1.3 million slaves entered the Americas in the seventeenth century; 5.8 million in the eighteenth. 'Almost the whole of the increment to non-bullion trade between Western Europe and the New World from 1600 to 1800 depended directly and indirectly on the exchange of tropical foodstuffs, tobacco and industrial raw materials, cultivated basically with slave labour and exchanged for manufactured goods and commercial services produced by Europeans.'[6]

Britain's external trade grew from 10 per cent of GNP in the mid-eighteenth century to 18 per cent by 1800; most exports were manufactured goods. The share of exports in industrial output grew from one-quarter at the start of the eighteenth century to over one-third at its end. Imports were increasingly made up not of manufactures, but of non-essential foodstuffs such as sugar and tea. Estimates of the volume of trade for England alone show that 46 per cent of English imports by the mid-eighteenth century were made up of imports from Asia and America. Re-exports came to approximately one-half of domestically-produced exports at some points in the century.

Table 6.1 Exports and industrial output

Year	Gross industrial output (in current prices) (£ million)	Exports (£ million)	Ratio of exports to gross industrial output (%)	Increase in exports as a proportion of increase in gross industrial output (%)
1700	15.6	3.8	24.4	56.3
1760	23.6	8.3	35.2	2.5
1780	39.9	8.7	21.8	46.2
1801	82.5	28.4	34.4	

Source: Engerman, 'Mercantilism and Overseas Trade', table 2.

The crucial part played by the re-export trade, and its subsequent impact on the expansion of trade with the Americas, was reflected in the rapid changes in the geographical distribution of trade. At the beginning of the eighteenth century four-fifths of British exports found an outlet in Europe; by the end only 30 per cent. Exports to Southern Europe grew by only 50 per cent; those to Northern Europe fell as these areas became protectionist. But meanwhile the share of British exports going to the Americas rose from 10 per cent to 60 per cent. The re-export trade played a crucial part in creating the later markets in the Americas for domestically-produced European goods. Most of the growth in British exports from the end of the eighteenth century was in exports of domestically-produced commodities, especially for those that could be mass-produced for colonies with European settlers.

Exports to North America were now predominantly printed textiles, blankets, nails, ropes, buckets, handtools, copper and wrought-iron products, linens and sails, earthenware, buttons, buckles and fancy cloth. This broad base of the British export trade developed through the eighteenth century. After the 1780s and until the early nineteenth century British foreign trade increased dramatically, but now this was a trade based narrowly on cotton textiles.

These broad outlines of the structure and directions of British trade in the eighteenth century can now be investigated more closely. We look first at English exports, then at the impact of mercantilist policies, and subsequently at the role of the re-export trade.

ENGLISH EXPORTS

English trade in the first instance was dominated by commerce rather than by industry. Between 1660 and 1701 the re-export trade grew from negligible proportions to one-third of total exports. It was this trade that provided the basis for the wealth of the merchant classes. The eighteenth

Table 6.2 The composition of manufactured exports

	1700 %	1750 %	1800* %
Woollens	85.0	61.9	22.1
Linens	–	3.3	2.9
Silks	2.2	2.5	2.0
Cottons, etc.	0.6	1.3	35.4
Metals	3.2	9.2	15.2
Rest	9.0	21.7	22.5

Source: Engerman, 'Mercantilism and Overseas Trade', table 4.

* Based on average of 1794–6 and 1804–6. If the 1800 data from Mitchell and Deane, *Abstract of British Historical Statistics*, were used, cotton's share would have been only 24.1 per cent.

century opened with a period of growth followed in 1722–4 by a slump after the South Sea Bubble, and another depression in the early 1750s. There was another major commercial crisis between 1772 and 1774, but there were good years on either side.[7]

Woollens and worsteds accounted for most of English exports in the eighteenth century, but their role and growth by this time were already diminishing relative to other commodities. Up to the 1760s exports of woollens and worsteds grew at 0.9 per cent per year as against 1.6 per cent for total English exports. There was a more rapid rise in exports of linens, cottons, metals, metal manufactures and coal. The share of woollens in total exports fell from 70 per cent in 1700–9 to 44 per cent in 1760–9. There was a widening in the base of the British export trade from the seventeenth century; exports of pig iron doubled between 1760 and 1788 and increased fourfold between 1788 and 1806.[8] All the main British industries in fact contributed to the increasing ratio of exports to national income up to the 1780s. This broadly-based export trade was overtaken from the 1780s until the end of the Napoleonic Wars by a dramatically increasing foreign trade sector, but one based narrowly on cotton textiles. For most of the early nineteenth century, trade returned to its broad base, and the incremental ratio of exports to output fell as the home market absorbed much of the additional production.[9]

Most of England's woollen exports (92 per cent) in the first half of the eighteenth century went to the rest of Europe. Even so, there was during this period a decline in these exports to several European countries, which was offset for a time by a rapid increase in exports to Spain and Portugal. The trend to industrial self-sufficiency in many European countries was paralleled in Britain. The Scottish and Irish linen industries were developed, and by the 1770s supplied most of the requirements of England and the colonies. The result for Germany and Holland was a 50 per cent reduction in their linen markets in Britain. Over the eighteenth century, England's trade with Europe became more concerned with the import of industrial raw materials, especially from the Baltic and the Mediterranean. The dynamic element in the export trade passed to exports to the colonies. There was a rapid rise in the West African demand for English exports in the 1740s, and a new shift in exports to Asia with military establishments in Bengal and Madras. Further export markets were developed in Ireland, and while privileged markets in the American colonies were disjointed with the War of Independence, exports resumed rapidly thereafter.

Table 6.3 Destination of English exports

Year	Europe %	Americas %	Rest of world %
1700	85.3	10.3	4.4
1750	77.0	15.6	7.4
1770	49.2	37.3	13.5
1797–8	30.1	57.4	12.5

Source: Engerman, 'Mercantilism and Overseas Trade', table 6.

Table 6.4 Source of English imports

Year	Europe %	Americas %	Rest of world %
1700	66.3	19.9	14.7
1750	55.3	30.1	14.7
1770	45.1	36.4	18.5
1797–8	42.4	32.1	25.5

Source: Engerman, 'Mercantilism and Overseas Trade', table 7.

From the end of the eighteenth century, the transformation of the English cotton and metal industries was recasting the trade connections and industrial specialisms of Europe. In Pollard's view, industrialization now took on a European framework, and complex regional interrelationships of trade and specialization were developed. British yarn fed German looms; British iron German metal goods. Lancashire and Yorkshire concentrated on coarse-quality manufactured goods, the French on high-quality fabrics; the British on pig iron, the French and Germans on finished metal goods.[10]

The changing base of British trade during the eighteenth century from a broad to a narrow range of manufactured commodities has been associated with characteristics of industrialization. Earlier historians, especially Ralph Davis, associated the industrial expansion of the mid-eighteenth century with the export trade but emphasized the modest impact of this: traditional industries expanded but did not industrialize. The much more narrowly focused trade of the later eighteenth century was based on rapid technical change in a new industry with new markets. The stimulus for this new industrial expansion and rapid spurt in trade was not previous commercial expansion but supply-side factors, notably technical change. As Davis put it, 'The Industrial Revolution in fact involved a movement on to quite different paths of industrial development from those that were being successfully followed.'[11]

Cotton goods exports rose to nearly half of all British exports during the first half of the nineteenth century; the whole textile sector accounted for 79 per cent of all manufactured exports in the mid-1830s. From the 1830s, however, other industries took a growing part. The place of the metals industries shows a particularly interesting development from their position in the eighteenth century. The share of all metals industries in manufactured exports grew from 12 per cent in 1814–16 to 27 per cent in 1854–6. But these were different kinds of metal goods from those which had played an important part in mid-eighteenth-century trade. From the finished metal goods and consumer products of the eighteenth century the composition of metals exports had shifted to refined metals, semi-finished goods, machinery and engineering products. Davis wrote that the diversification of the export trade, interrupted at the end of the eighteenth century, was resumed again 'on the basis of the rolling mill, the steam hammer and the locomotive engine'.[12]

Conventional wisdom in the past decade has attempted to downgrade the role of foreign trade in the Industrial Revolution. Davis saw it as less significant during the later eighteenth century than before or after. Crafts and Mokyr found a declining ratio of exports to national product and to industrial output over the years between 1780 and 1840.[13] Crafts argued further that increases in exports during the eighteenth century were the result of gains from specialization in international trade rather than a net addition to aggregate demand. 'In general, it would seem that growth was determined by the supply-side factors over the long run.'[14] The expansion of trade in the period, however, was limited by the backwardness of the rest of the world – the productivity gains of Britain's leading industries were not matched in the countries from which she was importing.[15]

Estimates of the macroeconomic significance of foreign trade of course depends on estimates of output and income, which are themselves open to debate. Recent research arguing for faster growth rates in the cotton industry, and with this faster growth rates overall throughout the period 1770–1831, also implies greater significance of foreign and colonial trade in quantitative terms in the late eighteenth century.[16]

The significance of foreign trade, however, extends beyond these macro-economic estimates. For the level of Britain's exports of manufactured goods, both as a proportion of total exports and as a proportion of industrial output, was unprecedented in Europe. Exports grew in surges, and they were highly concentrated in textiles, iron and metalwares. Key industrial regions were closely interconnected with the erratic movements of international markets and European and colonial wars.[17]

MERCANTILIST POLICIES

The rapid rise of the re-export trades and of European trade with the Americas and the East Indies took place within a framework of a mercantilist economic policy and a military policy directed to naval power abroad.

The age of exploration was followed by mercantilist visions of national power and profit in the wider world economy. Political power within Europe was sought through protectionist trade policies and the acquisition of colonies and gold bullion. These policies were to enhance domestic production, especially of manufactured goods, to gain control of international shipping and to acquire more bullion. Gold reserves would provide an indication of positive trade balances, and colonies would provide economic benefits to the metropolis. Both were achieved at the cost of extensive military expenditure to open and defend trade routes and to defend parts of individual European empires.[18]

The effect of these perspectives in the seventeenth and early eighteenth centuries was to generate the rise of the great Dutch entrepôt. Any understanding of the domination of British trade during the eighteenth century must depend upon a prior knowledge of Dutch trade. The Dutch came to dominate in the shipping, warehousing and re-exporting of bulk commodities, but simultaneously dominated the rich trades. They used their position in the Asian and American luxury trades to transform their European domination of the shipping of Baltic grain, timber and shipping stores. The Dutch now turned to dominate trade in colonial raw materials and semi-processed manufactures. Their position as re-export centre for these goods in the seventeenth century led to their development of manufacturing and processing industries in these as well as the rich trades. But in the eighteenth century mercantilist trade policies in other European countries became protectionist industrial policies, and Dutch markets for these rich trades were cut off throughout Europe as other European countries established their own entrepôt industries.

Certainly a rival like Britain posed this threat, and could furthermore combine it with her own naval and shipping prominence. Commercial power was further enhanced for the British by the Navigation Acts from 1660 designed to ensure transportation of colonial goods in British ships, and, even better, to have certain colonial goods, such as tobacco, sent to Britain before being re-exported elsewhere. The whole system of trade protection was also a system for raising government revenue. Tariffs on foreign-produced commodities provided the means to pay for the military arm of national power. The British Navy and its enormous build-up during the period were integral to the rise of British trade hegemony. The Navy captured and maintained a fortified network of bases in the Mediterranean and along the perimeters of the Atlantic, Pacific and Indian Oceans in order to protect British ships and cargoes. Naval convoys defeated long-running piracy supported by the French and at times by the Spanish, Dutch and Americans against British trade. The Navy went on to keep open trade with Europe even during the Napoleonic blockade. Merchants and industrialists throughout the century lobbied for the use of force and diplomacy to open and to maintain markets. Over the whole period between 1688 and 1815, there was a huge growth in British commitment to international commerce, and along with this a great vulnerability to hostile forces outside the kingdom. Taxpayers endorsed policies to defend British interests in the Atlantic, Mediterranean and Indian Oceans.[19]

The backdrop to this policy was a century of war. Between 1688 and 1802 Britain declared war against foreign powers eight times, and mobilized its army and navy for half the years of that century. Her great enemies were France and Spain, countries which maintained great land armies. Her way of dealing with this was through a series of alliances with Dutch, Austrian, Russian and Prussian governments and the use of their troops as well as foreign mercenaries. But the bulk of government military spending went into the navy, and throughout these many campaigns the British remained in command of the North Sea and the English Channel, and made great gains on foreign trade routes. This was the 'British way of warfare' which brought great territorial and commercial opportunities overseas at the cost of taxes, but not of wartime destruction. Meanwhile other European countries bore the brunt of successively ruined capital stocks, agriculture and infrastructure as armies marched back and forth across Europe.[20]

Throughout Britain's eighteenth-century wars with France and up until the end of the Napoleonic Wars there was little contemplation of free trade policies. Britain's international and domestic markets had been assured by British military policy. It was with the backing of the British Navy and Army that British industries and commerce captured 'inordinate' shares of world markets in the new commodities and services.[21]

The military policies which brought British domination of the re-export and colonial trades also brought these trades into prominence as the basis for new manufacturing industries, as new consumer industries and as a focus for government intervention and taxation policy.

THE RE-EXPORT AND ENTREPÔT TRADES

It was perhaps paradoxical that the very commodities which formed the basis for the great expansion of overseas trade in the eighteenth century were also those which were most heavily taxed and most interfered with by governments. The tax revenue which sustained naval and military power was raised through indirect taxation on those food and manufactured commodities which most appealed to bourgeois tastes and consumption. Taxes fell most heavily on beer, spirits, tobacco, sugar, other tropical groceries, salt, soap, starch and candles. Many of these entrepôt trades were subject to strict government regulations which varied across European countries, and inspired state-backed initiatives in export processing plants and import substitution. The demonstration effect of these imports on European taste and demand encouraged import substitution industries across Europe. It was in this sense that, as Jan de Vries has put it, 'the European economy . . . gained more from its non-western imports than from the colonial export markets it acquired'.

The colonial staples from the Americas and Asia stimulated profitable processing and finishing industries in many European cities – sugar refining, tobacco processing and calico printing were the fundamental industries underpinning the re-export trade. Other industries such as the china and porcelain trades were direct import substitutions for the Asian trade. In Britain the trade in imported chinaware was established from the 1690s – dealers or 'chinamen' bought goods from the East India Company sales in London. But from the late 1740s English porcelain factories were set up, in London first, and then in Staffordshire, with distribution networks centred in London.[22] The new china trade, then the porcelain works and potteries, were an integral part of the rise of the colonial tea, coffee and cacao trades. The trade in the colonial staples and the processing industries feeding on them were great stimuli to urban growth throughout the seventeenth and eighteenth centuries. Marseilles, Bordeaux, Nantes, Barcelona, Amsterdam, Glasgow, Bristol and Liverpool benefited from the trade and manufacture in these colonial commodities.

The Dutch led the way from the seventeenth century in developing industries based on colonial wares. They specialized in finishing processes in commodities stockpiled for world trade. The Dutch developed dyeing, bleaching and printing expertise in the calicoes, dyestuffs and chemicals they traded. The sugar refineries and tobacco-processing plants were the leading centralized manufactures of their time. Indeed Holland was an exhibition centre for textile machinery, copper stills, presses, saws, shipbuilding innovations and scientific and consumer novelties.[23] The Dutch sugar industry rose to new heights in the first half of the eighteenth century. Between 1700 and 1748 the number of refineries in Amsterdam rose from twenty to ninety-five. Behind this expansion lay the Dutch attempt to conquer the Portuguese sugar empire in Brazil – a response to the rise of the English sugar-producing colonies in the West Indies. Sugar was a highly competitive industry; business ingenuity was at the forefront of success in markets dominated by a long-term fall in prices.[24]

The Dutch success in exploiting the commodities trade for her own industrial development was also being followed in Britain. Britain was the channel through which the largest part of tobacco imports from America passed into Northern Europe. Bristol and Glasgow not only dominated the trade; they processed the product before re-exporting the bulk of it to their European neighbours and colonial dependents. The tobacco lords in Glasgow in the eighteenth century dominated entire industries in the West and Central regions of Scotland. The Clyde ports developed as centres for their investment not just in tobacco processing but in sugar refining, the rope and sailcloth industries, the glass, linen and bleaching industries, and the mining and metallurgy industries.[25]

Perhaps in no export finishing and processing trade were the connections between taxes, government intervention and industrial development so closely interlocked as in the calico printing trades. The introduction of oriental printed silks and subsequently Indian printed cottons into European markets in the later seventeenth century was one of the most remarkable examples of innovation in pre-industrial long-distance trade. Printed textiles extended the new European artistic taste for the 'oriental' which coincided with the consumption of exotic spices, coffee and tea from the Orient. Indian producers were able to meet the increase in European demand using traditional techniques and to challenge European markets in silk and linen. The result was a rapid restriction of the trade throughout several European countries and the transfer of finishing processes from the East Indies to European centres.

From the 1660s Asian textiles penetrated European, African and American markets at a rapid rate, and European countries soon started to regulate or to ban these imports. European governments also used infant industry trade strategies to encourage the growth of these textile industries at home. English trade policies allowed Asian textiles to enter the home market, and fostered protection of home dyeing and printing processes. Then in 1721 further legislation banned Asian finished and unfinished textiles from the home market. The result was that British textile manufacturers moved into the production of mixed fibres and cloth, then into cotton. 'Cotton represents the prime example of a major European industry adopted, nurtured and brought to successful maturity in the context of oceanic trade.'[26]

In Britain the state imposed a series of discriminatory taxes and bans on printed calicoes from the beginning of the eighteenth century. But the printing was still carried out on linens and fustians, and the bans did not affect the export from Britain of printed calicoes. In France the import, production and use of printed calicoes were banned in 1686, but the ban was not successfully enforced. The Spanish banned the import of printed calicoes from 1720, but not their domestic production. There were no restrictions on the trade in Holland, nor in a series of German and Swiss towns. Printing works proliferated in Amsterdam, Bremen, Frankfurt, Hamburg, Neuchatel, Lausanne, Geneva and Basel. Swiss entrepreneurs later moved into Italy to start cotton works to feed the trade. The popularity of the textiles overcame all attempts by governments to prevent competition with domestic traditional textile industries. The different responses of the state in different countries resulted instead in varying degrees of success in import substitution.[27] Calico printing works flourished in a framework of high degrees of protection – in the case of Britain this was also protection in domestic markets, at least from unprinted calicoes. The result here was not just import substitution of finishing processes, but of the linen and cotton industries as well.

These printing works were set up rapidly, they were concentrated manufactures employing several hundred workers in any single works, and they were urban manufactures. Government protection in this case, unlike that in so many attempts at import substitution, brought advantages giving these large-scale manufacturers a lead in accumulating profit and acquiring a commanding position in the industry. This allowed them to dominate expansion into the cotton manufacture, and to diffuse centralized production processes into that industry. In Britain, Robert Peel took calico printing from London to Lancashire and forged its vertical integration with a domestic cotton industry.

Cotton became the first fully mechanized factory industry. Quantitative economic historians have emphasized its small place in accounts of national output. But its demonstration effect was large, and even more significant was its place in the Atlantic economy and long-distance oceanic trade. British trade and military policy had ensured the largest share of gains ensuing from trans-Atlantic and Asian trade during the eighteenth century, and this helps to explain the dominance of the British cotton industry over world markets during the nineteenth century.[28]

The entrepôt trades, demand and the Industrial Revolution

Trade in colonial commodities had become an important part of North European economic activity by the mid-eighteenth century, and it was beginning to leave an impression not only on habits of consumption but also on habits of investment and spending.[29] The fortunes and crises of European regions became closely entwined with events thousands of miles away. Areas such as Yorkshire and the West Midlands produced in part for overseas markets and depended on imported resources – 'the political sensibilities of the colonists had a direct effect on the fortunes of the weaving and spinning communities scattered over the Yorkshire hills'.

Trade also affected non-industrial sectors, notably financial and commercial services, and domestic infrastructure in transport, docks and waterworks. Jacob Price identified the broader impact of the dynamic commerce of the eighteenth century in this commercial framework and social overhead capital which was a great utility to the entire economy in the ensuing era of industrialization and subsequent export growth. Most important to this social overhead capital were the commercial and financial institutions: banks, clearing-houses, insurance companies, Lloyd's exchange, the stock exchange, and commercial practices and law, as well as commercial education.[30] Trade furthermore generated enormous mercantile expansion, and the progression of mercantile activity into finance and specialist trading enterprise. This activity branched out against the background, first of the Atlantic economy, then of the Empire.[31]

The creation of the demand and increased consumption which fuelled the rise of the colonial and re-export trades in the first place is still to be explained. Recent reassments of economic growth in Britain by Crafts and others have attributed most of the growth to changes in agricultural productivity, changes which reached their most significant levels in the seventeenth and eighteenth centuries. Yet other research has shown that agriculture's contribution towards widening the domestic market for industrial expansion was slight. Farmers, labourers and even landlords provided poor prospects for industrial markets. O'Brien argued that only 6 per cent of the increment to expenditure on manufactures between 1700 and 1800 was due to higher wages paid to workers released through increases in agricultural productivity. In addition, there was only a small shift in the terms of trade between agriculture and industry in the long period of stable prices between 1650 and 1750. This may have raised expenditures on industrial goods between 3 and 8 per cent. Though most of the increase in agricultural output during the eighteenth century was sold on the home market, increases in agricultural productivity cannot be credited with the main source for increases in domestic purchasing power.[32] There is little evidence of rising real incomes of the mass of the population until the early nineteenth century, and even less of participation in revolutionary fashion-orientated consumption. Upper-class families valued traditional commodities for dynastic reasons.[33] Tradesmen and professional families, however, took quickly to the new commodities, initially in London and Edinburgh, but soon throughout the country, especially in urban areas. Bourgeois consumption and urban growth in Europe and the New World provided most of the market for the new luxuries and their import substitutes in the seventeenth and eighteenth centuries. On the one hand the trade in colonial staples was a great stimulus to urban growth in Europe – Marseilles, Bordeaux, Nantes, Glasgow, Bristol and Liverpool were but some of the beneficiaries. Yet this was also a time of urban stagnation in Europe – large cities and traditional urban centres fell into decline, mainly in Spain and Italy, and to a lesser extent in Belgium and Germany.[34] It was not these centres, however, which provided the springs of urban consumption and export-orientated industrial production, but smaller towns and newer commercial centres which provided for a resurgence in urban growth in Europe from the mid-eighteenth century. In England this urban expansion took place without a pause right through the early modern to the industrial period.[35]

These towns and cities expanded on the trade from the colonies, but they also provided the commercial framework and the mercantile connections which organized foreign trade, the entrepôt industries and, subsequently, regional industrial development. The markets for the new industrial commodities were provided in the first instance from bourgeois consumption and the demands of the non-agricultural sector, and in the second instance by exports. These two sides of the demand for manufactured commodities were closely interdependent. Bourgeois consumption expanded the way it did because of the incentives and demonstration effect offered by international trade. It is, therefore, important to go on to examine the middle-class market, fashion and urban demand.

CONSUMPTION AND FASHION

Changing tastes among the eighteenth-century middle classes were fostered by international trade. Jones has argued that there was a new passion for oriental designs brought by maritime expansion, and that the French in particular dominated European culture and dictated fashion. Both of these influences were reinforced by urbanization and the growth of London. The new fashions for calico-printed fabrics and chinoiserie were particularly important in creating demand in the cotton industry and in the small metal trades; new calico printing techniques and the invention of japanning were direct results. The markets for such goods expanded rapidly, fostered by prosperity among the middle class and the class of small tradesmen. The development of retailing through shops and commercial travellers promoted a national market for these goods.

At one level, demand for the new manufactured commodities of the eighteenth century was determined by fashion. There were social hierarchies of fashion. Manufacturers took advantage of existing demand to release the potentialities of latent demand. Boulton and Watt, for example, sought out wealthy customers – the 'legislators of taste'. Then Boulton made goods accessible in price and place of sale to a mass market. 'It would not be worth my while to make for three countries only; but I find it well worth my while to make for all the world.'[36]

Boulton made commemorative issues of goods for royal birthdays, and sent new patterns to members of the aristocracy. He then produced a similar commodity in a variety of materials accessible to all levels of society. The classic example was the shoe buckle. The 'gradations of society' were codified in a whole 'protocol of shoe buckles made in every size and every material from diamonds to paste, from gold to pinchbeck'.

The variety of the great will ever be affecting new modes, in order to increase that notice to which it thinks itself exclusively entitled. The lower ranks will imitate them as soon as they have discovered the innovation.[37]

The theory of emulation can only explain a portion of eighteenth-century consumption patterns. Equally important was the place of consumer expenditure in cementing social connections and family relationships. Aristocratic consumption frequently had dynastic motivations, while that of the gentry and middle classes conveyed protocol and a sense of belonging as well as the stability of family connections.[38] Furthermore, studies of fashion and consumerism in the eighteenth century have been confined for the most part to the gentry and the wealthier tradesmen. The consumption of the bulk of the middle ranks and of wage earners is not included. We have to turn to recent studies of probate inventories to discover more about the consumption habits of a broader spectrum of the population. This research indicates an overall increase in the ownership of all household goods during the first part of the eighteenth century. Kitchen and chinaware, clocks, pictures, mirrors and curtains became more common everywhere. Patterns of consumption of household goods do not, however, coincide directly with other economic indicators. During the period 1715–25, for example, imports of tea and coffee rose rapidly, but imports of china, pottery, printed goods, paper and beer remained steady. Changes in national income, and even in wage trends, were not automatically reflected in the frequencies of ownership of household goods.[39]

Probate inventories for the period do not indicate any great increase in mean wealth in consumer durables, but households did turn to the purchase of more innovative and impermanent objects instead of older, traditional wares.[40] Regional contrasts indicate that the North-East was much more deeply affected in its household possessions by its trade with London than were Liverpool and Glasgow by foreign commerce.[41] By the end of the eighteenth century, however, Glasgow, at least, presented a combination of new manufacturing wealth with fashionable consumerism. Displays of conspicuous consumption by manufacturers demonstrated their credit-worthiness and social distinction.[42]

Flexible markets and mass-production

To what extent did the expansion of consumption in this broad middle-class and middling group in Britain and the American colonies form the basis for mass-production methods? The place of fashion and the impact on tastes of the new colonial wares lead us to doubt the simple-minded search for mass markets. Research on flexible specialization emphasizes different national and regional markets. This has looked to the heritage of craft industry, and

Table 6.5 Ownership of goods, 1675–1725

| Social status | Number of inventories | Mean value | | Clocks %* | Pictures %* | Looking glasses %* | China and hot drink utensils %* | Knives, forks %* |
		Total inventory £	Household goods £					
Gentry	122	320	55	51	33	62	13	11
High trades and professions	152	193	97	34	35	62	18	7
Intermediate trades	344	157	32	25	29	56	19	11
Low trades	435	92	19	18	15	37	7	3
Widows and spinsters	217	82	18	13	12	36	6	4

Source: Weatherill, Consumer Behaviour, table 8.1, p. 168.

* % of inventories.

has related its history to flexible markets. It asserts the existence of a choice of technologies, related in turn to product choices. It thus calls for new attention to consumption and design.[43]

It is argued, for instance, that regional differences in tastes and markets in early modern France in the eighteenth and nineteenth centuries accommodated an expansion of the market for manufactured goods without homogenizing it. The demand for manufactured goods arose from regionally-based groups of nobles and commoners, and tastes and markets differed from region to region. Guild standards of quality continued to maintain a hold, and the country was specializing from the eighteenth century in the production of a wide range of high-quality goods. Even in the nineteenth century, the railways did not lead to the creation of mass markets but were used to make the flexible production capacities of the districts more accessible to the whole country.

In Britain, by contrast, mass urban markets for cheap consumer goods emerged early. This was fuelled by a high rate of urbanization and population increase. Colonial markets demanded a limited range of similar goods. A significant amount of diversity still prevailed, however, throughout the United Kingdom; provincial tastes differed and an abundance of skilled labour underpinned a long tradition of artisan production.

Flexible production techniques held sway through a large part of the nineteenth century in the production of silk textiles in Lyon, printed cottons in Alsace, ribbons, hardware, special steels and luxury engineering in St Etienne, hardware in Birmingham, and cutlery and edge tools in Sheffield and Solingen. In these regions, manufacturing units were mainly small, that is with less than fifty workers, their workforce was skilled, their machinery multi-purpose, and their products varied. Even larger firms were more like a collection of artisanal workshops under one roof than the organizational innovation represented by the factory system.

The big contrast was with the United States, where the imposition of standardized tastes entailed mass-production techniques. There, labour was in short supply and a tradition of guild organization and standards was missing. Employers had the motive to invent labour-saving machinery and customers were ready to buy standardized goods. This difference in consumption patterns allowed for the rapid development of mass-mechanized and large-scale production.[44]

This recognition of national and regional differences in tastes and their implications for production methods is illuminating, but misses the point about manufactured consumer goods in the eighteenth century, both in Britain and in colonial America. Few of these goods were completely standardized, nor were they 'mass-produced'. Most were made in small and medium-scale workshops, factories, and domestic units organized on a putting-out basis. Wide product ranges and customizing for particular markets were common.[45] Goods expressed individuality and luxury through visual diversity. This visual diversity was achieved through colour, ornamentation and lighter products – lightweight cottons instead of heavy worsteds, printed calicoes instead of fancy weaves, mahogany rather than oak furnishings, japanned ware and ormolu rather than inlaid ornaments, brass and plated ware rather than silver and pewter. These goods were produced in an enormous range of variety and design using techniques of specialization, division of labour and even mechanization.

Britain's industrial towns indeed moved very quickly from the production of basic commodities to an immensely varied output to supply its colonial and home markets. The fustians of Lancashire and Yorkshire were replaced by a whole range of fine cottons and lightweight high-quality woollens and worsted. Birmingham and Sheffield were even more notable. Their cheap hardwares, guns, swords, knives and nails had provided one of the early props of the Atlantic trade. But subsequently their 'toys', tableware, cutlery, silver and silver-plated ware provided the household decencies and semi-luxuries of the expanding middle classes of industrializing Britain and her settler colonies. The manufactures of these towns, especially Birmingham, were at the leading edge. Birmingham was also the inventor of new commodities, apparently import substitutes, but, much more significantly, applications of orientalism brought into Europe by the Dutch and British East India Companies, and recreations of designs based in classical antiquity.

COLONIAL WARES AND WOMEN'S DESIRES

Colonial wares played a special part in generating tastes for lightweight, colourful and ornamental commodities. For these colonial wares were 'exotic'. The fascination of consumers for goods which expressed the 'exotic' was part of a broader cultural fascination with the 'oriental' during the eighteenth century.[46] The age of exploration was succeeded by long-distance trade and colonies – the novelty of other worlds was comprehended for many Europeans as a novelty of material possessions. Exotic commodities in food, dress and furnishings expressed their cosmopolitan culture. European fashion in the eighteenth century was dominated by the 'oriental' – 'chinoiserie' in textile design, japanned and caned furniture and china were popular even among small tradesmen. Classical designs – popularized by William Hamilton – among travellers to the south of Italy in the eighteenth century were followed by the Wedgwood and Boulton adaptations such as Portland ware. This ethnicization of taste was also reflected in the perception of the New World through the consumption, even down to relatively low income levels, of sugar and tobacco products, and among higher classes in the trade in fur hats. The transformation of taste and design was the move from exotic imports to import substitutes and subsequently to new industries providing consumer decencies. In the commodities themselves, and in

133

their decoration and design, the New World was brought into the old, and ancient oriental cultures grasped in modern western terminology.

The early association of such consumer goods with the exotic, luxury, sexuality and imports was one way in which women became part of the story of eighteenth-century consumption. An alternative image was the domestic woman. The origins of the ideal of 'domesticity' lay in the commercial expansion of the sixteenth and seventeenth centuries. The domestic industries of Joan Thirsk's consumer culture of the same period were based on the role of the wife as decision-maker in consumption. Linked with this view is recent research on probate inventories and diaries which has emphasized the domesticity and family basis of women's consumption.[47]

This domestic view of consumption, however, can be seen as an aspect of a more broadly-based gendered view of trade. The domestic material culture may have been perceived as feminine, but commerce equally was associated with feminine behavioural traits. Most of the commodities upon which the era of commercial expansion was based were those associated with domestic possessions: lightweight clothing and furnishing fabrics, mahogany for furniture, colonial groceries, dyes, china; and such items, in turn, encouraged European manufacture of ornamental and lightweight metalwares for use in the home, and the development of new products in clothing and pottery.

The desire for consumer goods soon reached down from middling groups who could afford the foreign imports and import substitutes based on them to the lower classes. The ability to acquire such goods, however, depended in the first instance on higher wages and incomes, and in the second on a change in behaviour away from non-market to market production. A shift in household activity towards activities generating money income and away from those of home production and leisure was necessary to provide the means to fulfil desires for commodities. This shift in household behaviour was primarily a shift in the use of women's time from labour in the home for domestic consumption to labour in the marketplace for wages in order to buy different consumer goods – printed calicoes instead of home-spun linens. The trend was first noticed in clothes, and fabrics. Benjamin Franklin sent a package of English cloths to his wife in 1758, desribing them as: '156 yards of cotton, printed curiously from copper plates, a new invention, to make bed and window curtains. Also 7 yards of printed cottons blue ground, to make you a gown.'[48]

One English pamphleteer wrote, 'As ill weeds grow apace, so these manufactured goods from India met with such a kind reception that *from the greatest gallants to the meanest Cook Maids*, nothing was thought so fit to adorn their persons as the Fabrick from India.'[49] Young spinners were condemned by moralists for spending the money they earned in domestic manufacture in 'buying fine clothes and other gawdy gew gaws'.

The desire, and behind this the incentive to shift household activity, had to be there in the first place. It was this shift in household behaviour, constituting what Jan de Vries has recently called an 'industrious revolution', which was necessary to the Industrial Revolution. The shift from relative self-sufficiency to market-oriented production by most household members would involve a reduction of domestically-produced goods, many of which were formerly produced by the women of the household. Thus the wife or other female members of the household took a greater part in decision-making over commercially-produced consumer goods. 'The household strategies that fostered the industrious revolution placed the wife in a strategic position, located, as it were, at the intersection of the household's three functions: reproduction, production, and consumption.'[50]

The incentive and the desire were to a great extent based on women's decisions within the home. Their work for wages in the new rural and later factory industries created the products; it also created the market for these goods. The goods, in turn, had to be desirable – the goods that women wanted – clothing fabrics, china eating utensils, light furnishings and new domestic drinks and foods. They reflected fashion and, beyond this, the romance and the desire of the exotic. An 'industrious revolution' in household behaviour and consumption among the working and middling groups of craftsmen, tradesmen, manufacturers, officials and professionals was fired by the desires provoked by trade, colonial enterprise and urban growth. These desires were felt and transmitted probably more significantly by women than by men. We must seek for the origins of the Industrial Revolution not just in women's labour, but in women's wants and desires.

7

WOMEN, CHILDREN AND WORK

The transformation of agriculture and industry during the eighteenth century was reflected in the changing characteristics of the labour force. Recent economic historians have drawn attention to rapid productivity growth in agriculture which entailed structural shifts of labour away from agriculture to other sectors of the economy. These sectors were not, they have pointed out, the new high-productivity factory industries, but slow-growing traditional industries. Such findings, however, have all been based on evidence for the adult male labour force. The impact of women's labour and wages, and the role of children's labour, have not been considered in the construction of indices of economic change, because long runs of quantitative data on occupations, labour-force participation and wages are not generally available. Women and children were rarely recorded in the eighteenth century in official statistics, legal records or wage books in terms other than widow or spinster. This is not, however, grounds for excluding descriptive and analytical consideration of their impact on current understandings of this classical phase of industrialization.

It is now apparent that the eighteenth-century economy was much more industrial than was once thought. Higher proportions of the population were occupied in industrial urban and rural crafts and in proto-industrial manufacture than Gregory King and Joseph Massie estimated at the time. New estimates of England's social structure show that even before the beginning of the eighteenth century most families were occupied not in subsistence agriculture, but in market- based work. Families occupied in industry, building and commerce comprised 27.7 per cent of the population in 1688, but 36.8 per cent in 1759.[1]

Industrial employment was higher than supposed in our older accounts of the eighteenth century. It was also substantially higher than the levels found in other European countries in the early nineteenth century – 18.5 per cent of the male labour force was occupied in British industry in 1700 compared to Europe's 12.6 per cent; 29.5 per cent in 1800 compared to Europe's 18.6 per cent.

Changes in employment in manufacturing will be my main concern in this chapter. It should be remembered, however, that agriculture and services still occupied the greatest part of the population. Furthermore, more women, in absolute numbers, were occupied in agriculture and domestic service in the eighteenth and early nineteenth centuries than in any other income-earning activity. Lindert and Williamson found 24.6 per cent of families occupied in agriculture in 1759 and 14.6 per cent in 1801–3. Unspecified labourers provided another 15 per cent at both these times. Patrick Colquhoun estimated there were 910,000 domestic servants in England and Wales in 1806; 800,000 of these were female.[2] But trends of female employment in these two sectors diverged in the nineteenth century.

Agricultural innovation included a transition to more arable cultivation and to larger farms; these innovations shed labour, but they shed much higher proportions of female labour than male. Numbers working in agriculture fell between 1700 and 1800, then rose again until 1851. The total then, however, was still less than it had been in 1700. But family labour, including that of children and youths as well as women, fell away. The share of adult males in the workforce rose from 39 per cent in 1700 to 54 per cent in 1850, but by 1851 at least one-third of these were only casually employed during the peak seasons. Robert Allen puts the change thus:

> In 1700, the agricultural workforce had been built around family labour supplemented by young adults in their late teens and early twenties hired on annual contracts as servants. These categories were still present in 1851, but the workforce had become much older, more male, and more erratically employed.[3]

Women's traditional labour in the harvest and in dairying was curtailed over the course of the century. Male labour became concentrated at harvest time, and women's employment was confined to periods of low labour costs and low demand for labour during the year in activities such as weeding, stone gathering, hoeing and spreading manure. More arable cultivation and bigger farms, as a result both of enclosure and of the amalgamation of farms, meant proportionately fewer women employed in dairying.[4]

Women's employment in domestic service, on the other hand, increased over the eighteenth century; there is a consensus that the occupation became feminized over the period, and there are indications of a rising number of middle-class consumers from the end of the eighteenth century, with their expenditure increasingly related to the domestic sphere. By 1851 servants accounted for 10 per cent of the labour force, with women outnumbering men by nine to one.[5] But here too estimates are subject to large errors; those who gathered data in some eighteenth-century surveys and even in the 1851 census failed to separate out personal service from work in husbandry and even on occasion from retailing and household manufacture. There may, therefore, have been smaller proportions of the population occupied in personal domestic service in both centuries than we now think.[6]

It is the increasing proportions of the labour force in manufacturing which have attracted the attention of most economic historians. In the view of recent historians, manufacturing and commerce became overendowed with labour relative to capital, and many industries were technologically stagnant. The evidence for this view lies largely in the characteristics of the distribution of the adult male labour force; relatively little of this was found in progressive manufacturing industries serving distant markets.

If we move beyond the adult male labour force to consider the place of women's and children's labour, what difference will this make to our picture of the manufacturing sector? Women's labour-force participation has so far been cut off from the whole discussion of productivity change, shifts of labour and incomes between sectors and output growth. Male occupational structures, on the other hand, have formed the basic building blocks of all these macroeconomic estimates. Recently development economists have recognized major ramifications on development strategies of failures to take into account gender divisions within the workforce and the household.[7] An historical blindness to gender divisions has also been responsible for significant miscalculations on issues such as agricultural improvement and enclosure, and the standard of living.[8]

WOMEN AND MACROECONOMIC INDICATORS

Failure to take account of gender divisions may also have affected macroeconomic indicators of the Industrial Revolution. If it was the case that higher proportions of women than men were occupied in the newer progressive manufacturing sectors, then the distribution of the labour force between different industries would be changed, and with this productivity estimates based on these. We can, indeed, ask to what extent our views of the low productivity of British industry in the crucial years of the Industrial Revolution have been distorted because we have been looking at the industrial distribution of the wrong workforce. It was the female not the male workforce which counted in the new high-productivity industries. Women's labour was, on the other hand, also heavily concentrated in traditional labour-intensive activities. As the relative significance of traditional and dynamic industries changed, so too did distributions within the female workforce.

The relative place of the textile industries needs to be set in the context of wider industrial output. The textile industries as a whole contributed 45.9 per cent of value added in British industry in 1770 and 46 per cent in 1831. What had changed over the period was the contribution of the individual industries. Cotton's place grew from 2.6 per cent to 22.14 per cent, and wool's declined from 30.6 per cent to 14.1 per cent. But the workforce remained predominantly female throughout the period. In 1770 14 men were needed to make 12 broadcloths, but an additional 17 women and 27 children

Plate 3 Flax spinning in County Down (Mary Evans Picture Library)

were also required.[9] In the Yorkshire worsted manufacture female spinners outnumbered woolcombers and weavers by three to one.

The linen industry contributed more to value added in 1770 than the iron industry, and only approximately 2 per cent less than did iron in 1831. Adam Smith calculated that, in addition to flax growers and dressers, three or four spinners were necessary to keep one weaver in constant employment.[10] In Ireland female linen spinners were more vital than were male weavers to the viability of the linen-manufacturing household for much of the eighteenth century. Linen yarn had a ready sale both within the linen industry itself and as warps in the cotton industry. Households could be formed entirely of women, or it was not uncommon for cottiers 'who have families of industrious females to take larger portions of flax ground'. Weavers, on the other hand, either had to have female spinners in their households or they had to buy their yarn on the market. And 'as the extension of the industry led to geographical specialization, the trend of spinning households entering into a direct cash nexus independent of a familial relationship with male weavers, became more important'.[11]

Silk contributed 4.4 per cent of value added in 1770, the same proportion as coal; by 1831 the position of coal was more important at 7 per cent, but equally silk's contribution had grown to 5.1 per cent. This too was a women's industry. In 1765, the proportion of women and children to men in the London trade was fourteen to one; and there were 4,000 in the Spitalfields trade.[12] In addition to this, the industry was scattered by the late eighteenth century over twenty counties and fifty towns, with one mill in Stockport employing 2,000. Women were employed in both the throwing and the weaving sections of the industry, including large numbers of colliers' wives in the suburbs of Coventry.

These were women's industries, and even in the face of the technological innovation and factory organization that raised some of them by the early nineteenth century into 'dynamic' industrial sectors, they remained women's industries. For many 'dynamic' sectors, it was the distribution of the female labour force, not the male, which counted. We have seen how women suffered disproportionately to men in the decline of the old cloth regions of the South of England. Yet women also gained disproportionately in some new but dynamic sectors of industry – especially cotton. Often these were women in different parts of the country and in different age groups.

The cotton industry, the key 'dynamic' sector credited with much of the productivity increase of the industrial sector, employed higher proportions of women and children than of men in factories in both the eighteenth and the early nineteenth centuries. The few large-scale cotton mills of the eighteenth century employed roughly equal proportions of men and women, and of adults and children. The cotton factory labour force of 1818 showed that women accounted for a little over half of the workforce, and children accounted for a substantial proportion. In Scotland, these pro-portions were even more marked. Women and girls made up 61 per cent of the workforce in Scottish cotton mills; outside Glasgow, the women were even more prominent, for they were also employed in spinning throstles and short mules.[13]

Other textile industries employing high proportions of women were lacemaking and stocking knitting. Lacemaking was exclusively a female trade. From the late seventeenth century the industry was important in Devon, when Honiton lace was popular, and employed approximately 4,000 in the Colyton district alone. It occupied 21 per cent of the population of the town of Colyton, making it a major industry.[14] With the rise of the pillow lace industry late in the eighteenth century, the numbers employed were estimated as high as 140,000 for Buckinghamshire, Northamptonshire and Bedfordshire.[15] Handknitting ranked with spinning as the main women's industry in rural areas all over the country, and in Scotland and the dales of the West Riding long after the introduction of framework knitting. Even after the introduction of the frame, used initially by men, women were occupied in seaming, finishing and winding. Increasingly, as apprenticeship regulations were bypassed, women also worked the frames.

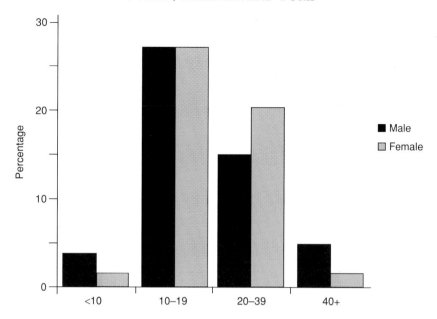

Figure 7.1 Workers in the cotton industry by age and gender, 1819
Source: Berg, 'What Difference did Women's Work Make?', figure 1.

It is apparent that when we write of industry in the eighteenth and early nineteenth centuries, we are including a largely female workforce. Of course there were many other predominantly male industries which also contributed substantial proportions of value added: the leather trades, building and mining. But these are also classic examples of traditional industries which underwent very little innovation over the period. Indeed the building trades and shoemaking were sponges for casual surplus labour.[16] The iron industry is the counter-example, but if we compare its industrial significance to textiles, we find that it contributed much smaller proportions of value added in industry: 7.4 per cent of value added in 1801 in comparison with cotton's 17 per cent. Furthermore, while men worked in iron, other contemporary metal*working* industries which were also undergoing rapid innovation employed a mixed family labour force or high proportions of women and children in home and large-scale workshops. Indeed there was a typical division of labour between women and children making small chains and nails at home while the men worked away in puddling and rolling mills. The Birmingham trades in the eighteenth century encompassed a whole range of new industries deploying new techniques with division of labour: button and bucklemaking, japanning and toymaking. These industries employed a mixed labour force, and systematic data available only from the nineteenth century indicate growing proportions of women and girls.[17]

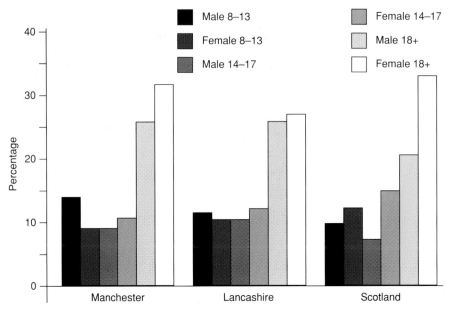

Figure 7.2 Workforce composition according to gender and age in the cotton industry, 1833

Source: Berg, 'What Difference did Women's Work Make?', figure 2.

WHY WERE WOMEN EMPLOYED?

The gender division of the workforce was clearly a major consideration in the demand for labour in manufacturing. Wage rates were one factor; women generally received one-third to one-half of the wage of men. But there is little data on which to construct an index to show any kind of trend. There is, however, enough to indicate the differences between regions. High earnings for women in manufacturing were to be found in areas of the North and Midlands where textiles, metalwares and potteries were expanding rapidly; but also in some southern agricultural areas where lacemaking, strawplaiting and silk spinning were growing quickly. In these areas women's wage rates were at least the equal of those received by local male agricultural labour. Moreover most of these occupations were gender-segregated at least in terms of time and place, so that there was no question of substituting female for male labour as wage differentials changed.

More important in explaining the demand for women's labour than wages was organizational and technological innovation. Women's labour was used in conjunction with these changes to yield substantially higher rates of profit than were possible under earlier manufacturing regimes. Proto-industrialization in some of its forms was associated with extensive division of labour and putting-out or other subcontracting arrangements.

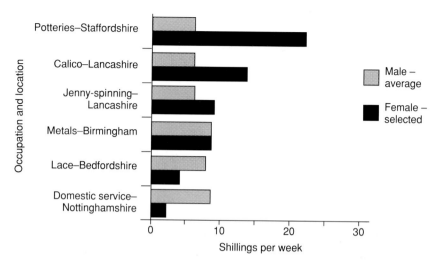

Figure 7.3 Women's wage rates, 1760s (compared to local male wage rates in agriculture)

Source: Berg, 'What Difference did Women's Work Make?', figure 3.

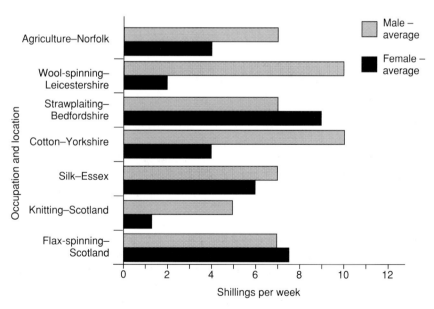

Figure 7.4 Women's wage rates, 1790s (compared to local male wage rates in agriculture)

Source: Berg, 'What Difference did Women's Work Make?', figure 4.

Larger-scale workshops and small factories yielded economies of scale at even such low threshold levels as 6 to 15 employees, due to a division of hand-performed tasks, the use of simple tools, supervision and a more disciplined work regime. Such factories and workshops drew on higher proportions of female and child labour than their predecessors. In industries deploying large-scale production, such as the factory textile industry and papermaking, more capital-intensive processes were associated to some extent with the substitution of women and children for men. But women and children were also assumed to be the key workforce.

FEMALE AND JUVENILE TECHNOLOGIES AND SKILLS

The constraints imposed on the expansion of the textile industries by the supply of spun yarn are the common explanation for the search for spinning machinery and the rise of the first spinning factories. Yet the importance and scarcity of spinning labour implied in these explanations were not reflected in wages: spinning remained an entirely female trade at least until the advent of the larger spinning jennies, and the women who practised it right across the country were invariably among the lowest-paid of workers. Eden found that the earnings of female domestic spinners in Essex, Norfolk, Oxford-shire, Leicestershire and Yorkshire ranged from 3d to 8d a day or from 1s 6d to 3s a week. The women who worked in three Yorkshire cotton mills earned 4s to 5s a week while those employed in the Birmingham toy trades could gain 7s to 10s a week. This range of payment still placed the wages of most women workers well below those of the lowest-paid male labour. Male agricultural labourers earned about 8s a week at the time.[18] The poverty of female woollen spinners was best expressed by Julia Mann who referred to them as 'an unorganized mass of sweated labour'.[19] And Arthur Young attacked the Norwich master manufacturers in 1788 for the wretched state of their spinners:

> The suffering of thousands of wretched individuals, willing to work, but starving from their ill requited labour: of whole families of honest, industrious children offering their little hands to the wheel, and asking bread of the helpless mother, unable through this *well regulated* manufacture to give it them.[20]

And yet such low wages were subject to yet greater reduction. Eden in 1790 found that the war had led to a depression in wages in the Halifax region, and 'many poor women who earned a bare subsistence spinning are now in a very wretched condition'.[21]

The low cost of this women's spinning labour also made it viable to continue using the primitive distaff long after the introduction of spinning wheels and even spinning jennies. This was partly because it was possible for a time to spin much finer yarn on the distaff than on the wheel or jenny, but

Plate 4 Spinning with distaff and spindle (Ann Ronan Picture Library)

the major reason for its survival was that the distaff could tap labour not otherwise in use – that of feeble old women and young children, and the hands of women not otherwise in use when walking, talking, tending animals or watching over children.

At the end of the eighteenth century Eden found the distaff still widely used in Scotland and noted that 'one rarely met with an old woman in the north of Scotland, that is not otherwise employed, but who has got a distaff stuck in her girdle and a spindle at her hand'.[22] Alice Clark cited an eighteenth-century commentator who discussed the choice between the two techniques:

> There are, to speed their labour, who prefer wheels double spol'd, which yield to either hand. A sev'ral line; and many, yet adhere to this ancient distaff, at the bosom fix'd casting the whirling spindle as they walk.[23]

Spinning on the distaff occupied hands otherwise unoccupied, or left the other parts of a woman's body free for yet more work, such as was found by Hugh Miller in the Scottish Highlands even as late as 1823:

Here as in all semi-barbarous countries, is the woman seen to be regarded rather the drudge than the companion to the man. The husband turns up the land and sows it – the wife conveys the manure to it in a creel, tends the corn, reaps it, hoes the potatoes, digs them up, carries the whole home on her back, when bearing the creel she is also engaged with spinning with the distaff.[24]

Hand spinning was assumed to be a female activity. So too was the first mechanized spinning. The early twelve-spindle jenny was a women's technology, or more correctly a girl's. It had a horizontal wheel and a treadle 'which required an awkward posture'.

The awkward posture required to spin on them was discouraging to grown up people, while they saw with a degree of surprise, children from 9 to 12 years of age, manage them with dexterity, which brought plenty into families that were before overburdened with children.[25]

The machine was, however, part of the domestic system and was operated by girls, and, with the adaptation of a vertical wheel, by women. When it came to the Holmfirth district of Yorkshire in 1776 it was 'hailed as a

Plate 5 The flax spinning wheel (Ann Ronan Picture Library)

Plate 6 Spinning jenny (Mary Evans Picture Library)

prodigy'. In the context of fairly competitive yarn prices and little industrial concentration in the early Lancashire cotton industry, the jenny benefited those who owned and operated the machines themselves. It was the cottage producers and those who ran small centralized workshops who reaped the first gains in efficiency from the jenny, and they did so until merchants and factors saw the gains to be had through setting up their own jenny factories.[26] Some women, mainly those in clothworking families, clearly gained from the jenny. It increased their productivity in proportion to the number of spindles, and wages initially increased. As we shall see, however, the jenny came to have a devastating effect on the employment of far more women.

These examples of gender- and age-typing of technologies in spinning were repeated many times over across industries. It seemed that machines and processes were invented with this female and child labour force in mind. Teenage girls were employed to great effect in the new calico-printing processes. Girls, and boys as well, were widely employed with the newer textile technologies in the silk and cotton industries. They were used in the silk throwing mills, where they were taken on from the ages of 6 to 8 'because their fingers are supple and they learn the skills more easily'.[27]

William Hutton remembered being sent to the Derby silk mill when he was too small to reach the machines so that he had to have pattens strapped to his feet.[28] Child and youth labour was widespread in the cotton industry. Samuel Bamford assisted his aunt in the bobbin winding department: his work was 'a piece of bondage, on account of its monotonous confinement'. Ben Brierly remembered the point in his childhood: 'now I must work . . . I was put to the bobbin wheel. How I hated being chained to the stool.'[29] A cotton mill at Emscote was reported to have dismissed girls after their apprenticeship because their fingers were too big to go between the threads.[30]

Patents and contemporary descriptions of new industries frequently pointed out the close connection between a particular innovation and its use of a child or female labour force.[31] Dean Tucker in 1760 described as the key attribute of the division of labour in the Birmingham trades the use of child assistants as an extra appendage of the worker; this use also trained these children to habits of industry.[32] It was widely held at the time that machines for stamping and piercing in the small metal trades extended the range of female employment, especially that of young girls.[33] Girls were specifically requested in advertisements in *Aris's Gazette* for button piercers, annealers, and stove and polishing work in the japanning trades.[34]

Josiah Wedgwood reported to the Children's Employment Commission in 1816 that girls were employed in 'painting on the biscuit mainly, but they also paint upon the glaze and after the second dipping. They work with a camel hair pencil in painting patterns upon the ware, sitting at the table.'[35] The hand-made nail trade relied largely on the labour of women and children. An early nineteenth-century innovation, the 'oliver' or foot-operated spring hammer, allowed a smith to work single-handed, but was responsible for all kinds of deformities in the teenage girls who used it.[36]

These are just some examples of the way in which new technologies and divisions of labour were introduced, then described by contemporaries in terms of the gender and age of the workforce using them. There are two ways of looking at the gender-typing of this technological innovation. The first is that manufacturers and inventors saw the technical and profit-making advantages in using a new workforce which could be integrated with the new techniques, in such a way as to bypass traditional artisan customs and arrangements which would probably have entailed resistance to the technology. They furthermore believed that women and girls had a greater 'natural' aptitude for the manual dexterity and fine motor skills required by the new techniques, and that 'female' ways of working together were more amenable to division of labour than were 'male' work cultures.

The second way of looking at this gendered technology is that inventions and new working methods in manufacture were rather public affairs in the eighteenth century. The advantages of new projects in the seventeenth century, and new manufacturing enterprises in the eighteenth century, were frequently presented to the state or to local communities in terms of their capacities for providing employment.[37] Where the real point of such innovation was to save labour, if it was to be profitable, then it was politically expedient to present technologies in terms of the female and child labour they would employ, rather than the male labour they would save. The efforts of Poor Law authorities to provide manufacturing employment for women and girls, as well as to provide industrial training for young girls in spinning and lace schools, reflected concerns not just over poor rates, but over illegitimacy and in some areas the high proportion of single women among the poor.[38]

Contemporary innovation in processes such as calico printing and spinning was tried out first on a female and child workforce. Processes were broken down into a series of dexterous operations performed particularly well by teenage girls who contributed manual dexterity, learned at home, and high labour intensity. There is increasing evidence of single women and girls working frequently in all-female households or workshops in lacemaking, calico printing, linen spinning and the button manufacture, as well as in more conventional factory arrangements in the cotton manufacture and the potteries. Organizational innovation also tapped married women with children, developing a division of labour based on the adult with child assistants. Women workers in these early factories, workshops and proto-industrial manufactures were employed as they are in the Third World today, not because their wages are lower than those of local male labour, but because whole new methods of production could also be introduced, including management practices, divisions of labour and technologies which bypassed traditional artisan customs and arrangements.

While high proportions of the labour force employed in manufacture were women and child workers, it was also evident that the employment provided by industry was not sufficient. A heritage going back to the sixteenth century of inadequate employment for women and children was only partially made up for by the new manufacturing industries.[39] The demand for labour created by industry was not adequate to the task of soaking up the surplus labour left in the wake of demographic and agricultural change. While factors affecting both labour demand and supply encouraged high rates of female labour-force participation during the Industrial Revolution, the demand created for women's labour was not what models of economic development would predict. To explain this, one area to which we must turn is the effect of technological innovation.

MACHINERY AND WOMEN'S WORK

When the spinning jenny was introduced it met with great resistance in the woollen industry of the South and East because of the greater importance there of hand spinning to poor women. The more limited resistance it met in the North resulted only from the existence there of a more important alternative – the spinning of worsted, for which the jenny was not used.[40] Indeed, in the worsted manufacture the one-thread wheel was common until the end of the century and later.[41] A magistrate in Somerset in 1790 described how he was called in by two manufacturers to protect their property

> from the Depredations of a lawless Banditi of colliers and their wives, for the wives had lost their work to spinning engines . . . they advanced at first with much Insolence, avowing their intention of cutting to pieces the Machine lately introduced in the woollen manufacture; which they suppose, if generally adopted, will lessen the demand for manual labour. The women became clamorous. The men were more open to conviction and after some Expostulation were induced to desist from their purpose and return peaceably home.[42]

The dispute over the introduction of spinning jennies was a long and contentious one. The jenny substantially increased the productivity of women spinners and brought higher wages, though the extent of wage differences was a matter for debate. In the 1760s it was said that hand spinners earned 3d to 5d a day and jenny spinners 1s to 1s 3d. But the opponents of the machine in 1780 estimated the jenny spinners' wage at 8d to 1s a day; while the advocates claimed 2s to 2s 6d for jenny spinners and only 3d to 4d a day for hand spinners. 'For some years a good spinner had been able to get as much or more than a weaver.'[43] Most of the disputes, however, were over the large jenny used in jenny factories rather than at home. Baines wrote of the desperate efforts of workpeople in 1779 to put down the machine. 'The mob scoured the county for several miles around Blackburn, demolishing jennies, carding engines and every machine turned by water or horses, sparing only those with less than 20 spindles.'[44] And Wadsworth and Mann have described part of the country as in a state of 'guerrilla warfare' in the autumn of 1779; the 'spinners' interests were those of every working-class family'.[45] Similar disputes over the taking away of women's labour with the introduction of machinery had arisen even earlier in the silk manufacture. In the 1730s new looms, 'like ribbon looms that could do as much as 8 to 10 hand workers and as cheaply as 6 to 8' were introduced to weave narrow strips of material for buttons. This dispossessed the buttonworking section of the population of their needlework, 'ancient and decrepit men and women, and children'. And in 1737, the women of Macclesfield 'rose in a mob and burnt some looms, and when their leaders were arrested, released them from prison'.[46]

The mechanization that came with industrialization was supposed to have destroyed many of the widespread family-based women's trades. Eric Richards has argued that with industrialization the gradual loss of employment in traditional lines probably exceeded the emergence of new opportunities. The introduction of new technology further increased unemployment for women.[47] And Clapham argued much earlier that spinning machinery, knitting and lockworking implements had left women's hands idle and family earnings curtailed all over the countryside in an age of hunger and high prices.[48] Jones has also pointed out that mechanization drove many of the handicraft districts into industrial oblivion, cutting deeply into the base of 'mother and daughter power' of the South and East.[49]

There was a major decline in cottage industries after 1815. 'The decline of female spinning in particular, probably most marked after 1800 . . . may have aggravated female unemployment and depressed familial income.'[50] But that decline was not final, for to argue thus is to mistake the process of capitalist expansion. The decline of some cottage manufactures could open the way for other, more degraded, employment, and not just domestic service. Technological change and factory production formed but one part of the route to industrialization. The search for ways of using more but cheaper labour more intensively was equally a way of increasing profits and expanding capital. In Hobsbawm's words, 'The obvious way of industrial expansion in the eighteenth century was not to construct factories, but to extend the so-called domestic system.'[51]

Women and labour-intensive technologies

Landes referred to the equal significance of 'capital widening' and 'capital deepening',[52] and Sidney Pollard called the labour-using proclivity of capitalist expansion 'the inner colonization of labour'.[53] In fact, cheap women's labour, driven in the process of mechanization to even lower wage levels, was not simply left unemployed. Women became a source of new cheaper labour in the late eighteenth and early nineteenth centuries for new rural industries in lace, strawplait manufacture, glovemaking and shirt-buttonmaking, and for the new urban sweated trades which arose and flourished from the 1830s onwards.[54] This cheap women's labour was a lucrative source of profit not to be bypassed by manufacturers ready to launch new labour-intensive industries. Women's cheap labour in combination with hand or intermediate techniques long continued to be chosen as an alternative to mechanization. And though mechanization might threaten such labour, new use was usually found for it. When machine spinning came to the linen industry, women's labour was transferred to a lighter and simpler weaving industry. When new techniques were invented which still required some skilled labour, alternative labour-intensive techniques were used or even invented to tap a large cheap female labour force.

The adaptive use of the employment structure to overcome problems of skill or technique was a way of avoiding the necessity of introducing whole new technologies. Perhaps the best example of this development of older as well as new technologies geared to particular labour forces is provided by calico printing. This was an industry which developed labour-intensive

technologies along with an advanced division of labour in order to tap a
female labour force. Fears of competition from inexpensive and labour-
intensive oriental printed fabrics stimulated four technical innovations. The
first was 'picotage' or the patterning of printing blocks with pins or studs
tapped into the blocks. This was delicate work, for one large block contained
63,000 pins, but it was a job done by women who earned 12s to 14s a week
after their apprenticeship. Another labour-intensive process introduced at
the time was pencilling or the handpainting of patterns directly on to the
cloth. This was performed by women who worked in long terraces of
cottage-like workshops under the superintendence of 'mistresses':

> in the shop each woman had her piece suspended before her with a
> supply of hair pencils of different degrees of fineness according to the
> size of the object . . . to be touched, and containing colour . . .
> according to the pattern required . . . a good workwoman might earn
> £2.00 a week, though it was likely most earned a lot less.[55]

The style of patterns changed little from year to year. This laborious work
was done by women, and so was regarded as an unskilled process which
bypassed the employment of the highly-paid craftsmen who engraved and
used wooden printing blocks and, after 1760, copper plates. Copper-plate
printing, introduced in 1760, followed by roller printing in 1785, constituted
the real technical improvements of the industry, but they required the use of

Plate 7 Calico printing – 'pencilling' and block printing (*Supplement to The New
and Universal Dictionary of Arts and Sciences*, 1754)

Plate 8 Block printing (Image Select)

highly-organized and highly-paid 'gentleman journeymen'. Manufacturers such as Peel bypassed these and instead organized 'proto-factories' using elementary labour-intensive techniques and extensive division of labour, along with special training and disciplining of workers. The scarcity, together with the very high status, of skilled calico printers was the main stimulus behind the attempts by entrepreneurs to look for alternative methods of production on which they could employ low-paid women and girls.

Another important new industry which tapped the labour of women and children in declining woollen regions was the silk manufacture. Before and after mechanization silk throwing was carried out by the cheapest labour available – that of women and children. The introduction of silk-throwing machinery simply reproduced the hand procedures on a larger scale. Large supplies of female and juvenile labour were still used to tie threads and assist with winding. Where there were large supplies of such labour, manually-operated winding and throwing mills continued to be used long after water- and steam-powered silk mills had appeared. This was particularly true in East Anglia, and the mills which subsequently grew up in the area remained disproportionately dependent on the labour of young girls, and paid dispro-portionately low wages.[56]

Sexual divisions within technologies

A sexual division of labour between trades and within branches of trades, in fact, complemented a specific sexual division of labour within work processes and technologies. To some extent women were simply confined to the use of more labour-intensive and less efficient techniques where skilled workers were able to restrict entry. Although women were traditionally the spinners, they were only allowed to continue their work at distaff, wheel and jenny after the introduction of the spinning mule, for mule spinning was successfully appropriated from the outset as the preserve of male workers.

Hand spinning of woollens and worsteds was the major industrial employment of women throughout the eighteenth century. Women also dominated the domestic jenny-spinning stage of the cotton industry, and the female spinners formed the backbone of the linen industry, at least until the widespread introduction of Arkwright frames to produce an adequate cotton and, later, linen warp. The productivity of the female domestic linen spinner was doubled by the introduction of the two-handed spinning wheel in 1770, just as that of the cotton spinner was raised several times by the introduction of the jenny. But many women still continued on the older technologies, for the two-handed spinning wheel was not widely distributed until the end of the eighteenth century.

A skilled activity such as mule spinning was so defined from its earliest days in the domestic system, and was assumed to require the use of male

Plate 9 Cylinder printing (Image Select)

labour. Early requirements like strength, skilled spinning, building maintenance and repair skills, as well as a certain amount of capital, accounted for
the 'maleness' of the occupation. But the early application of water power
in the 1790s, which eliminated the need for special strength, and subsequently the introduction of the self-actor in the 1830s, made no difference
to the sexual division of labour. Women were excluded from a technique
which was defined simultaneously as male and skilled.

Female cotton weavers in the eighteenth century were almost invariably
found outside the urban smallware manufacture which also used the Dutch
loom. They worked at the ordinary handloom in the more loosely-
organized country branches of the check, linen and fustian manufacture.
Dutch looms in fact tended to be grouped in the workshops of a superior
class of master weavers, and workers were regarded as skilled, their seven-
year apprenticeship leading on to entry into the small master class. Some
women did weave on the Dutch loom, but these were almost invariably
widows of former smallware weavers. The most common case is exemplified
by the daughter of a fustian weaver who had three looms. At 20 she married
a weaver of checks and stuffs for women's gowns, and they worked together
on two looms. As the children grew up, more looms were added until they
had five. After her husband's death and until she was 70 she kept three
looms.[57]

Cases like this confirm a gender specification of technological development in the eighteenth century very similar to that found in the agricultural
systems of developing countries today. Esther Boserup found that modern
agricultural methods neglected the female agricultural labour force and
caused men to monopolize the new equipment and methods. Women were
left to perform the manual tasks while men used the efficient equipment. The
result was an increase in male labour productivity while women's stayed
static. 'Such a development has the considerable effect of enhancing the
prestige of men and lowering the status of women.'

> It is the men who do the modern things; men spread the fertilizer in
> the fields, women spread manure. Men ride the bicycles and drive the
> lorries while women carry head loads. Men represent modern farming
> in the village; women the old drudgery.[58]

SKILL DEFINITIONS

But there is also an important sense in which the jobs and techniques to
which women were confined should not just be written off as unskilled: the
special attributes they brought to their work processes certainly generated
increases in productivity, and the very definitions of skilled and unskilled
labour have at their root social and gender distinctions of far greater
significance than any technical attribute. As feminists have pointed out,

women are particularly sought out by employers for their nimble fingers, and their powers of concentration on tedious, laborious processes, as well as for their docility and their cheapness. These nimble fingers by repute derive from a long but totally unacknowledged training in household arts and needlework. It was these attributes that formed the background to the acquisition of the knacks, the deftness and the special application with which women worked. But these 'female characteristics' were never regarded as skilled in their own right.[59] In the eighteenth century women were particularly sought out for work characterized by delicacy and repetition – as block pinners and pencillers in calico printing, for the intricate work of stamping and piercing in the button manufacture, for painting and decorating in the toy trades and the potteries, and for stove and polishing work in the japanning trades. Such skilled women were sought out, but still undervalued. In Wedgwood's London workrooms in the early 1770s a skilled female flower painter earned 3s 6d a day, or two-thirds the top rate for skilled male painters who received 5s 6d a day.[60]

Skill has traditionally been associated with masculine virtues. Male skills created a solidarity which extended beyond the workplace.[61] It was also the case that men defined their work as skilled and that of women as unskilled, mainly for reasons of social status. As Phillips and Taylor have described it, immigrant men in late nineteenth-century America entered the female-dominated clothing trade because they were excluded as immigrants from traditional male trades. Facing such social exclusion, they needed to establish and maintain some social status within their own communities and families. Thus they termed the processes they worked on as skilled: those of their women folk as unskilled. Men's struggles to maintain their skilled priority in the workforce against machinery and against the encroachment of unskilled women were thus an important part of their effort to maintain their social status within the community and within their families. This familial, customary and social division of labour then took priority over and largely determined the technical division of labour.[62] The sexual division of labour, therefore, was part of the social hierarchy established among activities. As Maurice Godelier has put it, in primitive societies hunting 'is often more highly regarded than gathering or agriculture. In societies where men dominate, women's tasks are considered inferior only because they have been consigned to women.' In other words, the division of labour is an effect of the social hierarchy and not its cause.[63]

The new industries of the eighteenth century can be seen either as moulders of a new type of industrial workforce, or as a sponge for a traditionally cheap and even more available source of labour. What were the factors, then, affecting women's and children's workforce participation?

EXPLAINING WOMEN'S WORKFORCE PARTICIPATION

Explanations for the unequal and subordinate participation of women in the workforce both now and in the past have been found in issues such as the family economy or family wage systems, household economics, the reserve army of labour and patriarchy. But none of these have addressed the specific historical conditions for women's entry into industrial work in the eighteenth century. Explanations for the special features of women's participation in industry must first be sought in the basic outlines of labour supply and demand. These were affected in turn by three factors: demographic change, institutional change, notably enclosure and the poor laws, and organizational and technological innovation.

If we look first at labour supply, demographic change produced a whole new framework. Fertility increased by a factor of 2.65 between 1676 and 1831; age and gender balances also changed. Children aged 5 to 14 comprised approximately one-quarter of the total population, compared to only 6 per cent in 1951. The high dependency ratio of this young population was cushioned by children earning their way at an early age. Gender balances were also skewed in favour of feminine sex ratios until late in the eighteenth century. A feminine sex ratio prevailed for much of the seventeenth and eighteenth centuries. Women married late and there were higher numbers of single women and widows in the population than there were to be in the early nineteenth century. The average age at first marriage peaked at 30 in the last half of the seventeenth century and stayed high until the later eighteenth century; celibacy also peaked at approximately one-quarter of cohorts reaching marriageable age in the 1670s and 1680s, and was also high in the last half of the eighteenth century. Higher numbers of women than men in the population and higher proportions of women marrying late or not at all were seeking some means of gaining subsistence in the period. They created a ready pool of cheap labour. They were reinforced by large numbers of widows. Between 1574 and 1821 over a quarter of households were headed by a single person; widows accounted for 12.9 per cent of households.[64] Our standard image of women working within the context of the family economy is a great distortion for the eighteenth century. Substantial numbers of women needed to gain an independent subsistence, but, in many cases, wages were pitifully inadequate or highly precarious.

Where women did work within a family economy, their earnings were also very meagre, especially at times in their life cycle dominated by small children. But even these limited earnings, if pooled within a family economy, could help to put together a subsistence. This was another factor which contributed to new departures in female labour supply. Our evidence for wage trends in the Industrial Revolution has thus far been based only on the experiences of adult males. These trends suggest stable or falling real wages at least until 1820, though there was also considerable regional variation.

Low male wage rates where family incomes were at stake had the effect of encouraging high rates of female labour force participation. Among very poor families, all women and children who could find any work did so; amongst those who were poor, but who could eke out a living, the earnings of the head of the household rather than female market wages provided the major determinant of participation rates.[65] In eighteenth-century Scotland, rates for male agricultural labour varied little from the mid-seventeenth to the mid-nineteenth century, yet there is evidence that conditions for many families improved. It is likely that such improvements came about not through higher wage rates or more employment for males, but through more labour by women and children.[66]

Demography and wages trends generated a new women's labour supply in the eighteenth century; agricultural and institutional change, especially enclosure, added considerably to this. Women's income-earning activities were sharply constrained by the enclosure of the commons in the eighteenth century. Enclosure not only cut out vital sources of subsistence in gleaning, wood gathering and gardening, but drastically cut out possibilities for both squatters and copyholders to pursue all sorts of small trades and domestic industries which on their own provided insufficient or volatile returns, but with common rights could in fact provide a subsistence. Other institutional changes, especially changes in the poor law towards the end of the eighteenth century, increased difficulties in obtaining outdoor relief, housing and a settlement, factors which earlier in the century had eased women's participation in the labour force.[67] These institutional changes as well as agricultural innovation caused the classic 'release of labour' from agriculture required by economists' models for the transition to economic development; the labour released was skewed to female labour. We can thus understand the historical origins for a rising female labour supply in the eighteenth century.

FAMILY, STATUS AND TRAINING

Hans Medick has argued that proto-industrial production entailed a change in the division of labour within the nuclear family. Domestic manufacture placed a premium on early marriage and high fertility, as well as the greatest possible work capacity and technical skill of both marriage partners. He argues that 'women were in the vanguard of peasant household industries' and that with the increasing importance of these industries in providing for the family subsistence the men were drawn in from the fields and back to the household. The positive result was a more flexible allocation of role responsibilities for family members than had been the case in peasant families. The old matrimonial control of the young through the allocation of land was broken down by new employment opportunities as well as by land fragmentation. Youths could therefore marry sooner and start their own households;

indeed, they had a positive incentive to do so because the opportunities for maximizing their income depended on their capacity for work as well as the number of child labourers they would produce. The adult proto-industrial worker was unable to exist on his own; his productive output depended on the co-operation of his entire family.[68]

Medick raised the issue of the impact of women's industrial labour upon their status within the household. We might also ask to what extent the participation of women in the newer high-productivity manufacturing sectors, working not just in domestic industry, but in workshops and early factories, affected their household status.

As we have argued already, there is evidence that women did a wide range of work in pre-industrial agriculture and manufacture, and it is difficult to sustain an argument that the advent of proto-industrial manufacture transformed the household division of labour. Caution must rule our statements about the sexual division of labour, for our evidence is very slender for the eighteenth century as well as for the sixteenth and seventeenth: 'We still know very little about sexual divisions within the households of the majority of the rural population, about the different activities and concerns of women and men, old and young, about how socialization took place.'[69]

Households, above all, were complex and varied; it was frequently the case that the household production unit would require labour in addition to that of the nuclear family unit.[70] Where the age and sex ratio of the family unit did not coincide with that of the production unit, journeymen, apprentices or relations might be taken into the household to back up or extend the productive unit. In the Irish linen industry, the need for female spinners could be met by the 'importation of suitable labour into the household'.[71] Households were also extended in times of falling wages, for the reaction of the domestic producer was to increase output. In the framework-knitting industry, as wages fell there was recourse to co-residence rather than reversion to a higher marriage age. In nineteenth-century Shepshed, many framework-knitting households contained resident kin or were shared between two families.[72]

Female households

Another option, allowing production processes to be divided and to use their own markets (as in the case of spun yarn), was to create separate households of young women or of women and children. The premium on the labour of young women appeared clearly in the Irish linen industry, where such households were common in the North-West of Ireland. It was also clear from the complaints of contemporary moralists and economists. Anderson declaimed against domestic industry because the money paid for the making up of manufactures would flow into the hands of the lowest ranks of the people, 'often into those of women and children; who becoming giddy and vain, usually lay out the greatest part of the money thus gained, in buying fine clothes and other gawdy gewgaws that catch their idle fancy'.[73] The wool spinners of Bradford Manor were similarly condemned by the Court Leet in 1687 for asserting their independence: 'Whereat many young women, healthful and strong, combine and agree to cot and live together without government, and refuse to work in time of harvest and give great occasion for lewdness.'[74]

The lacemakers of Colyton also formed female households. Pamela Sharpe found relatively high proportions of single and older women in the town in the seventeenth and eighteenth centuries. Charity and housing policy made it possible for single women to live alone or with other women. These matrifocal households were often also production units.

Status

If we compare the situation of women in the new manufacturing households to their former position within the peasant family economy, their status *may* have improved, depending on the agricultural and industrial conditions which varied over time and place. But where they remained within the family production unit, their labour was still far cheaper than it would have been, and indeed was, in workshops or early factories. Ivy Pinchbeck in fact blames the domestic system for weakening women's former position. The tradition of low wages established within the family industrial unit contributed to the subsequent low wage levels offered to women who did enter the factory. On the one hand, as the workshop trades faced increasing competition from the sixteenth century onwards, they started to exclude women from apprenticeship. On the other hand, the availability of domestic industry within the family economy meant that girls could be usefully employed at home, and this prevented many of them being put out to apprenticeship.[75]

The tradition of service in another household during adolescence, which was an important aspect of sixteenth- and seventeenth-century English social structure, appears to have declined in the eighteenth. There were some communities where, in the earlier period, service was regarded as a 'bleak alternative' for girls who preferred to stay at home until marriage. Some female servants were 'isolated' and 'powerless' compared to the stronger social position of women able to live in the households of parents and kin.[76] But it is also the case that, though such women may have been able to summon the support of their families as compared to more isolated servants in a community, their social position as workers and individuals must have been very constrained by patriarchal authority at home.[77] Such social tensions operated at the level of the household and of the community, and preferences must have been partly conditioned by wider attitudes to women in the community and in the society at large. Social reasons such as these, combined with the availability of more household employment in cottage manufactures in the eighteenth century, may have contributed to a decline in the practice of sending adolescent girls as well as boys into apprenticeship and service.

There is certainly little evidence thus far that women's industrial work had any effect on the sexual division of labour in the home, nor that women were able to reap the gains by partaking equally with men in high-status consumption. The participation of women in manufacturing could well, however, make a difference to their access to and control over family property. In areas such as Birmingham and Sheffield where newer industries were expanding rapidly, the women of the manufacturing classes claimed equal access to family property and wealth. This female access to property may have differed according to region and industry; it certainly fell away in Birmingham during the nineteenth century.

Training

There was also the important role in organizing and training which women carried out in domestic production. Children were integral to the production processes of a great many pre-industrial and proto-industrial manufactures. They were employed from as young as 6 years of age in the workshop trades and at home. Highly-skilled calico printers using both traditional and more advanced techniques relied on children as assistants, and very young girls were widely employed in the bleaching fields. The traditional drawboy looms always relied on a child assistant.[78] In household manufactures their labour was taken for granted. Before the advent of factory spinning 'child spinners were trained by females'. In cotton and in wool, 'the mother was responsible for all the preparatory processes and the training and setting to work of the children'.[79] Children were taught to carry out the same types of industrial activities as women; they formed an equally important part of the proto-industrial labour force and they were invariably trained by women. Radcliffe, the inventor of the dressing frame, remembered how

> my mother taught me [while too young to weave] to earn my bread by carding and spinning cotton, winding linen or cotton weft for my father and elder brothers at the loom, until I became of sufficient age and strength for my father to put me into a loom.[80]

And it was not only the spinning and preparatory processes which women taught but also the weaving. The Hammonds pointed out that women became weavers in considerable numbers at the end of the eighteenth century. Between 1797 and 1799, when there was a great scarcity of Spanish wool, employment was bad and many men enlisted. Large supplies of wool entered soon afterwards, and women filled the men's places. One employer

161

in Freshford, Somerset, had as many women working for him as men. At Bradford in Wiltshire at least two-fifths of the weavers were women. But little was heard of these women afterwards, and the female weavers left in the woollen industry of the South-West were by 1840 employed only in the lighter branches of the industry at low rates of pay.[81]

Keith Snell has argued that women's apprenticeship was widespread in the southern and eastern counties in the first half of the eighteenth century, but fell away rapidly thereafter. Thirty-four per cent of the apprenticeships he examined were for girls and these were appointed to as many as fifty-one trades, more than in the case of men. Many were apprenticed to the same trades as their fathers, and their premiums were comparable to those of boys. Girls apprenticed by the parish were, furthermore, to be found in the widest range of occupations. But by the nineteenth century the number of female apprentices had fallen, women were apprenticed to less than half the trades that men were, and these were largely restricted to the household and clothing manufactures.[82]

Apprenticeship also took on different meanings for men and women. The skill content and the training component of many of the trades to which women were apprenticed were modest, and, for girls in particular, a training in values and behaviour was as much a part of the purpose of apprenticeship as any industrial training.[83] There were orthodox indenture procedures and apprenticeship patterns in the London silk trade, but these did not lead to the foundation of a guild. Apprenticeship for girls was about maintenance and general training before marriage, while boys underwent systematic industrial training and entered a trade guild.[84]

Women trained and supervised the younger members of the family production unit; they passed on 'skills' to the next generation of the industrial workforce and they cared for their children, all as part of one process. Children were involved in the productive activities that women carried out anyway. Even very young children were taught to wind thread and clean wool. George Jacob Holyoake's mother was a self-employed managing mistress of a horn-button workshop attached to their house, and she simultaneously made time to raise her family.[85] The care of children was thus integrated into women's productive activity. The labour, management and training roles of women within the family production unit were all highly significant, but the value placed on them was generally small. Still, the intensity of their labour was shaped by the need to fill the gap between indigence and subsistence, however wide that gap threatened to become.

The low status and value of this women's work, in spite of its acknowledged necessity and significance to the cash earnings of the household, must be largely explained by these workers' continued social subordination within the family. What appears to have happened is that with the rise of domestic industry women's low-paid cash-earning activities became increasingly associated with household duties. Unlike older peasant and artisan families, where late marriage after a period of service or apprenticeship away from the home prevailed, girls now worked in their parents' home until marriage at an early age. They then set up their own production unit within a new family setting and had more children earlier because of the premium on child labour. Their industrial production therefore became intertwined with household formation and what we now call housework. There was no division between their cash-earning activities and household duties.

The family setting also affected the training of girls. Although in many of the textile industries boys and girls were both brought up to assist in all branches of the trade, girls most often combined household chores with casual industrial employment. It was precisely these household chores, especially needlework, however primitive they might be,[86] which gave women the dexterity and diligence they ultimately brought to the production process. But more significantly, this combination of activities also resulted in a very irregular training for women, and it was in the training process, and the customs and conventions associated with it, that entry to a trade was controlled and skills defined. Boys were initially taught alongside girls to carry out the preparatory processes in the textile industries. But for boys, this was a transitory part of their lives. Samuel Bamford expressed his physical frustration with what he clearly regarded as feminine work:

> It was scarcely to be expected that a tall straight round limbed young ruffian like myself with bare legs and feet, bare neck and a head equally bare, save by a crop of thick coarse hair, should sit day by day twirling a wheel and guiding a thread, his long limbs cramped and doubled under a long wooden stool.[87]

However necessary and significant the labour of women in the domestic industries, the control of these industries went to men, while women were relegated to subordinate positions. It is also likely that this subordination of women in proto-industrial production affected the positions of their sisters in the apprenticed workshop trades.

WOMEN'S COMMUNITY NETWORKS

It is difficult to uncover very much about the role of women in eighteenth-century trade societies. We occasionally uncover some evidence of female membership, but little else. And this evidence tells us nothing of the greater part of women's employment in those trades with no formal organization, or in the rural domestic industries. Traditional assumptions of low levels of worker organization among dispersed rural labourers have been discounted by recent research which has demonstrated the high levels of organization among country workers, not only in industrial disputes, but in food and enclosure riots. Bonds were formed among agricultural, urban industrial and rural industrial workers. Protests against enclosure were frequently led by workers from the towns, or industrial workers squatting on the commons. Opposition to enclosure was strongest where open fields and rural industry coincided, and the decline of food rioting in areas of southern England has been attributed to the decline of the industrial communities themselves.

Women were an important section of these rural communities, and frequently played a leading part in local custom and protest; there is evidence that they led food riots, organized gleaning, mobbed poor-law officials and played an important part in instances of rough music or charivari and seasonal rites. There is little evidence indeed to tell us of their role in the details of organizing production, though sense tells us that, in largely female workforces, networks formed among women must have been vital in the training and recruitment of the labour force. Certainly in woollen and worsted spinning, women acted as intermediaries, 'putting out yarn' to their neighbours. Malcolmson cites some telling examples of the force of such female co-operation.

> In June 1753 at Taunton, Somerset, several hundred women assembled in a body to destroy the weir belonging to several grist mills, and thereby prevent corn from being ground at the mills (the men, it was said, 'stood as spectators, giving the women many Huzza's and commendations for their Dexterity in the Work they were about') . . . On a market day at Exeter in April 1757, some Farmers demanded 11s per Bushel for wheat, and were arguing among themselves to bring it to 15s and then make a stand. However, some of the Townsmen getting wind of this plot sent their Wives in great Numbers to Market, resolving to give no more than 6s per Bushel, and, if they would not sell it at that Price, to take it by Force; and such Wives, as did not stand by this Agreement, were to be well flogg'd by their Comrades. Having thus determined, they marched to the Corn-Market, and harangued the Farmers in such a Manner, that they lowered their Price to 8s 6d. The Bakers came, and would have carried all off at that Price, but the Amazonians swore, that they would carry the first man who attempted it before the Mayor; upon which the Farmers swore they would bring no more to Market; and the sanguine Females threatened the Farmers, that, if they did not, they would come and take it by Force out of their Ricks. The Farmers submitted and sold it for 6s on which the poor Weavers and Woolcombers were content.[88]

E. P. Thompson recently gave extended consideration to the role of women in food riots. He has argued that women's prominence in food riots in manufacturing districts was due to their role in the economy, a role which gave them 'authority and self-confidence'. The women had charge of marketing for provisions, of baking, brewing, and feeding the household. They knew about price and quality, and through their neighbourhood connections they also took the initiative in bonding households together in times of protest.[89]

The significance of women's community networks needs to be assessed in relation to recent work exploring the moral economy in industrial contexts. William Reddy demonstrated the existence of a community of shared values and expectations, beliefs and attitudes among eighteenth- and early nineteenth-century textile workers. He argues that gradually this language of the crowd began to recede. Market language, categories and culture became the public code, limiting industrial action and political behaviour to a narrow range of monetary calculations.[90] Applying this model plus Thompson's concept of the 'moral economy of the poor' to the West Country, Randall has also argued for the common basis of strikes and food riots in a strong community consensus. Trade consciousness is thus synonymous with community consciousness.[91] But the explanatory value of this sharp dichotomy between the area of moral imperatives and the market breaks down in areas undergoing industrial change. The dichotomy raises the thorny question of the definition of community.

There were divisions between artisans with a long and stable stake in the community or in the trade society, and casual outworkers in temporary residence. There were divisions created by the differential impact of international price fluctuations on neighbouring communities producing slightly different products. There were divisions inherent in the division of labour itself, especially the division between men and women workers, and between different groups of women workers. Communities were thus bound up not with mutuality, but with division.

Community and the custom to which it is related was neither egalitarian, nor was it free of relations of power and subordination. Divisions of interest within any one community could be marked, yet the 'interests of the community' could be defined in terms of the group which at that moment wielded some authority.[92] Community was frequently invoked when the livelihoods of skilled and craft workers were at stake; rarely when those of squatters, casual labourers and women were threatened. These people were regarded as mobile, anonymous, 'without community'.

Bonds among women and female networks were closely tuned to the family life cycle. The large, youthful labour force of early industrial England made up predominantly of girls and young women cannot be assumed to have found its sole priorities and connections within the 'family economy' of married women and mothers. The changing historical divisions and networks created among working women with the impact of both the new industrial work opportunities and the industrial decline that characterized the eighteenth century need to be examined before historians can pronounce on women's identity with the values of the community.

Part II

PATHS TO THE INDUSTRIAL REVOLUTION

8

MACHINES AND MANUAL LABOUR

The regional and cyclical patterns of industrial advance and decline in the seventeenth and eighteenth centuries continued into the latter part of the eighteenth and into the nineteenth century. These brought with them new technologies which had far-reaching ramifications for the division of labour, including the sexual division of labour, and for community structures. But towards the end of the eighteenth century a rapid process of technological change in selected key industries cemented a new regional and industrial dominance. The paths taken by this new and unprecedented technological advance were as diverse as their industrial settings. The rapid development of a technology of handtools and small-scale machinery, and the rapid proliferation of new hand techniques and skills, were just as notable as the more commonly recognized 'new technology' of mechanized steam-powered processes. Why these technologies arose as they did in their various industries is a question historians have long sought to answer. But looking at the question as they generally do, from hindsight, they have tended to assume the inevitability of only one path of technological change. The possibility of alternative paths which were, for some reason, blocked off in some industries, but allowed to develop in others, has rarely been explored. The way in which technology was developed within various organizational structures and was devised to fit them – artisan or factory, home or workshop, centralized or decentralized decision-making – is rarely considered, for these structures are usually deemed to have been determined by the technology.

We must therefore examine the types of technological advance which corresponded with specific structures of industrial and work organization; we must show how these structures adapted and developed their own technologies. Posing a wide variety of economic structures, and with them technologies, however, only tells us half the story. We must also enquire into the mutability of these structures themselves in response to the concomitant development of labour's skills and forms of organization, and into the familial, cultural and customary constraints on the workplace. These factors have never been considered together: no wonder, for it would be a mammoth task. But because they have only been considered separately we have no real understanding of the relationship between the economic and social history of work and the process of technological change. We shall, therefore, attempt to examine some aspects of this relationship by looking at the parallel but diverse development of two of the Industrial Revolution's most important industries – textiles, and the metal industries.

In the first instance we shall look at present historical analyses of technological diffusion. We will survey the conventional economic theories of technological change and consider the alternative Marxist analysis of the labour process. The substantial contribution of these theories to our understanding of the 'why' of technological change still, however, invites many questions. This chapter will raise those unanswered questions of how the social and economic organization of industry – its industrial structure, the gender, skills and customs of its workforce, and wider social institutions – affected conditions of work and technological change.

Technology lies at the centre of the Industrial Revolution, yet we still have little analytical understanding of the 'how, why and wherefore' of invention and diffusion. For technology is the economist's and the historian's 'black box'. It was fundamental to most other aspects of industrialization, but the contents of that 'black box' are difficult to unravel, and their structure is difficult to perceive. Traditional approaches and some more recent ones accepted the 'black box'; that is, they wrote of technology as an autonomous force. One such account, and an exemplary one, is David Landes's *The Unbound Prometheus*.

Landes provides a lucid and systematic account of the autonomous development of technology in the Industrial Revolution. His is a compelling picture of innovations proceeding forward, within and outside various sectors, in a logical challenge-and-response sequence dictated by the pressures and constraints of the 'interrelatedness' of techniques. He sums up the Industrial Revolution under three technological principles:

1 the substitution of machines – rapid, regular, precise and tireless – for human skill and effort;
2 the substitution of inanimate for animate sources of power – especially ways of converting heat into work;
3 the use of new and more abundant raw materials, and the substitution of mineral for vegetable or animal substances.

He shows how closely each set of technical changes was interrelated with the others. The breakthrough in textile machinery put pressures on raw materials, power sources and the engineering sector, leading in turn to a changeover from a wood to a coal fuel economy, to the introduction of steam as an immensely superior source of power and boundless source of energy, and to advances in engineering which brought standardization, uniformity and precision into machine-making.

While possessing the power of simplification, this perspective also reinforced the old technological determinism of most accounts of the Industrial Revolution. It was a determinism which was also peculiarly parochial in its account of the industrialization process. While presenting a survey of technological development in Europe, it followed the route of the most 'progressive' industries without enquiring into the reasons for the patterns of technological change across Europe's regions. While setting out the remarkable and seemingly unproblematic stages of mechanization in Britain, Landes does not ask why this mechanization took place so much more slowly in Britain than in the United States. In demonstrating the 'backwardness' and eventual upsurge of French industry, he does not ask why the new types of power and coal-using techniques so characteristic of the new British technology were so difficult to adapt to French production processes. Finally, he never asks what impact the new technologies had on skills, employment and labour conditions.[1]

The question of Britain's slow development was extensively debated among economic historians who challenged the view that technological development was autonomous. They looked instead to the economic reasons for why innovation took place in some countries, but not in others. The major economic factors behind the different technologies to be found across countries were the supplies of capital and labour. Economic historians now speak of the capital or labour 'intensity' of various techniques to describe a technology's relative use of the one or the other factor of production. And they argue that different relative endowments of, or costs of, each factor of production between countries or regions either stimulated or retarded innovation. This more relativistic approach to the 'why' of technological change also meant more relativistic consideration of the 'effects' of the new techniques, because the new tools, machinery and processes frequently failed for some time to raise total productivity significantly. This, in itself, was a legitimate reason for slow innovation.

In turning to such debate, economic historians have made much more explicit use of economic theory. But the old economic history contributed much to the economic theory of technical change. The traditional explanations have been simplified, modified and recreated into new theories of technical change. No longer trusting to the old traditions, however, economic historians now turn to economic theory to give 'scientific' credibility to arguments which are not significantly different from the old. But if the economic theory of technical change has not offered a great deal that is new in explanations, it has separated out and clearly specified some of them. Economic historians now draw a distinction between those factors affecting the invention of techniques from those affecting diffusion or innovation. They concede that the springs of invention lie beyond the limits of economic theory, but believe diffusion to lie firmly within its grasp. Diffusion, in turn, is separated off from the impact of technical change. The effects of new technology are conceived to be microeconomic, that is, to affect costs, prices, labour and total productivity in the single firm or industry; or they are conceived to be macroeconomic, to affect growth, economic structure and employment. The jargon of the economist has entered the language of the history of technology such that the diffusion of any technology is categorized into 'inducement mechanisms', 'induced bias', 'learning by doing', 'embodied' and 'intra-sectoral' innovation, and its impact is summed up in terms of the 'residual' input to economic growth.[2] There may be some use to such exercises, but much more interesting, it seems to me, were the areas where history and theory interacted. One such case was the debate on the 'capital or labour intensity' of new technologies.

HABAKKUK AND FACTOR-SAVING THEORIES

H. J. Habakkuk's classic formulation of the problem asked why the British economy appeared to be so prodigal in its use of labour, in contrast to the more mechanized state of the American economy.[3] The 'labour intensity' of British industry had long before been observed by Marx: 'Nowhere do we find a more shameful squandering of human labour power for the most despicable purposes than in England, the land of machinery.'[4]

Habakkuk, however, analysed the speed and character of technical change in both countries in terms of differences not in the supply of labour but in the supply of land. The types of technologies developed in America economized, he argued, on labour because the American industrial wage had to equal average earnings in agriculture. The supply of labour was furthermore 'inelastic', that is, relatively unresponsive to small changes in the wage rate. Geography created great inflexibility in the labour market. In the words of one of Habakkuk's main critics, the essence of Habakkuk's thesis was this: 'If one country has a higher ratio of land to labour than another, all other things being equal, then this country will use more or perhaps better machinery for each worker in manufacturing than the other country.'[5] In Britain, with its small endowments of land, there was a large underemployed agricultural labour force with nowhere else to seek a better living except in industry. The general thickening of population in the countryside therefore made some areas suitable repositories for labour-intensive domestic industries.

Habakkuk did not confine his explanation of technological change to relative endowments of land and labour. For, as he recognized, all techniques depended on the use of some labour. Though some technologies required less labour overall, they may have needed more highly-skilled labour. Habakkuk argued that the more capital-intensive techniques in America did indeed make use of more highly-skilled labour, but this type of labour was also relatively cheaper in America than it was in Britain.[6] Habakkuk's argument made for a powerful model of the economic reasons behind the peculiar national characteristics of technological development, and of the reasons for the faster or slower rates of diffusion of particular techniques.

There was much, of course, which the model left out. First, Habakkuk gave little weight to the impact of natural resource endowments apart from land, such as the effect of the opening up of the Ruhr on German industrialization. Second, when he wrote of the cost of labour he referred only to wage rates, failing to account for the costs of education and of the longer hours and faster pace of work. Third, mechanization might just as well take place because of cheap supplies of labour. For example, the introduction of the sewing machine coincided with the arrival in Massachusetts of cheap Irish labour, and it was this cheap labour that made a factory-dominated clothing industry possible.[7] The point might also be made that the adoption of any capital-intensive technique at one stage might just as well generate the introduction of labour-intensive processes at earlier or later stages of the production process. Some new capital-intensive techniques created demands for craft or domestic work where these had not existed before. And the close connections between the various stages of production meant that attempts to save labour or skilled labour at one stage through mechanization might involve the use of more labour or skills at earlier stages. The choice between techniques according to relative costs of factors of production was furthermore constrained by the structure of the market; for different techniques, particularly in the early phases of industrialization, often made for different qualities of product, higher or lower counts of yarn, coarse or fine cloth, more or less resilient crucibles, more standardized or highly differentiated commodities.[8]

Points like these only made special empirical qualifications to the hypothesis. Some neoclassical economists objected to the whole theory, for it did not fit the idea that innovation was determined by the relative prices of capital and labour. Habakkuk instead explained new technology by a complicated connection between the abundance of land, the high price of labour and the low cost of capital.[9]

The thesis was important to economists for the new departure it made from the neoclassical theory of technical change.[10] For it challenged the view that new techniques appeared in a continuous stream, and that they were the result only of entrepreneurs' attempts to reduce their labour costs. Habakkuk had seen the flaw in this view, and had argued quite correctly that the entrepreneur was more interested in reducing total costs than simply labour costs.[11]

The critique of theories of technical change focused on labour saving has been extended recently by a study of the motivations of patent seekers. Of the 42 per cent of patents which specified a motivation, only 3.7 per cent aimed to save labour.[12] Where inventors and entrepreneurs did wish to save labour, it was usually particular types of labour, especially highly-skilled adult male; or to reduce the bargaining power of unions, and the opportunities for embezzlement of raw materials.[13] Textile machinery in Lancashire was biased against the use of adult male labour; these workers retreated into handloom weaving where wages and incomes declined dramatically. Wages in factories did not fall, except through substitution of female labour, but machinery was speeded up.[14]

The saving of time was a much more significant factor. It can be treated apart from general capital-saving innovation, for it often saved on both capital and labour. It was also true that motives for saving time often differed from those of saving capital. Concentrating production in factories was meant to save time previously spent in roundabout methods of production in the domestic system, but it increased the use of fixed capital. During most of the eighteenth century working capital was much larger than fixed capital, so that saving on work in progress achieved great reductions in total production costs. Innovations in bleaching reduced to a matter of days what had once taken weeks and months. Cort's puddling and rolling processes raised the speed of throughput twenty-five times.[15] Time saving was also achieved through the greater intensity and speed of labour. Innovation was associated with raising the speed of power looms, stretching and speeding up self-acting mules and introducing high-pressure steam engines.[16]

While the theoretical questions raised by Habakkuk's thesis spawned a whole academic industry, the impact of this work was also to generate a series of case studies by American economic historians on the cost structures of various technologies with different rates of diffusion in Britain and America. The most challenging and best-known of these studies[17] did not tell us anything about the origins of British technical change, for all were centred on the latter half of the nineteenth century, but the explanations they offered certainly could provide a basis for rethinking our traditional ideas about the origins of British technology. The purpose of these studies was to provide a critique of standard views on the theme of entrepreneurial failure in the late Victorian economy. Their perspective created a new and wider economic context to explain the so-called retardation of British technology at the end of the nineteenth century. G. N. von Tunzelmann's study of steam power and G. K. Hyde's study of the iron industry offered now classic critical accounts of the speed of Britain's technological takeoff.[18]

Factors which explain the slow diffusion of technology in the later nineteenth century can also help to explain earlier paths of technical change. We can, for example, compare cost and productivity schedules between old and new technologies, and so try to identify the threshold point where it was profitable to introduce new techniques. Such thresholds might be very high, for the costs of change were not only new machines but also new forms of work organization which went with the machines. The spinning mule, for example, drew on a different labour force than did the water frame or the jenny. The water frame, on the other hand, was introduced in large centralized 'factories', unlike the smaller workshops of the early jennies and mules.

Later, powered weaving machinery entailed weaving sheds and other machinery such as dressing frames to prepare the yarn. These costs had to be added to the basic costs of the new machinery. A much later, but well-documented, example is that of agricultural machinery. The introduction of new harvest tools such as the scythe instead of the sickle, and ultimately the reaping machine, required a complete reorganization of the harvest.[19]

New techniques in many industries, furthermore, for some time required different types of raw material and generated different qualities of output. The jenny produced a fine weft, but no warp; the water frame produced a good warp, but inferior weft. The yarn which went to the power loom had to be 'dressed' first. Iron foundries used cheaper materials than the old wood-burning forges; but they produced pig iron which then had to be refined. If different techniques meant some, even slight, differences in output, market structures were to a large extent responsible for the use of newer, older or even compromise 'intermediate' technologies. Different counts of yarn, different qualities of cloth, standardized or quality design, all depended on different technologies.[20]

Social institutions are just as important to the reasons for different but coexisting technologies as are the usual economic factors. But they are frequently difficult to specify. In nineteenth-century Britain, entrenched historical institutions of property-holding and enclosure, along with the layout of the fields, for a long time inhibited the use of reaping machinery. Different institutions of property-holding between regions in the eighteenth century almost certainly affected industrial organization and growth; such institutions probably affected a region's reception to new technology as well.[21]

Apart from sociolegal institutions, there were also the institutions of employer–worker relations. Technologies which were associated with highly-skilled male labour were also frequently constrained by strong trade unions or informal work groups. Employers in several cases sought to escape such constraints by using other techniques which drew on un-organized or unskilled female labour. Calico-printing technologies in the eighteenth century were developed against this backdrop, as were the cloth-finishing techniques in the woollen and knitting industries which fired the Luddite episodes in the early nineteenth century. Later in that century, ring spinning was introduced in America instead of mule spinning for precisely these reasons.[22] Employers in textiles and engineering in this country clearly thought they could dispose of skilled labour by introducing a self-acting mule and semi-automatic machine tools.

RESOURCE SAVING

Habakkuk's work and the many case studies of American technology which it inspired challenged old assumptions about the clear-cut differences between old and new techniques. The latest machinery was not always manifestly superior to the old tools, for the reductions in costs or increases in output to be had were frequently disappointing, or at least ambiguous. Real choices, in addition, had to be made over industrial organization, the division of labour and labour relations, and sociolegal institutions. British historians have not, on the whole, taken up the challenge to analyse these economic, social and institutional determinants of technical change. Two recent studies of the iron industry and steam power specify the strictly economic reasons for these innovations. Both argue, on the basis of a systematic analysis of quantitative data, that the cost of raw materials, in both cases that of coal, was the key consideration prompting innovation. Hyde argued that a sharp increase in the costs of charcoal smelting after the mid-eighteenth century coincided with a drop in the costs of coked pig iron. Very high profits went to those who decided on coke smelting, and in the 1760s average revenue exceeded average costs by £2 per ton. However, the speed of innovation was not just related to cost differentials, but also to prices, for the most rapid diffusion took place in the period of economic expansion between 1775 and 1815. Cost reductions and increases in demand both seemed exhausted after the Napoleonic Wars, though prices were still maintained by the expansion of foreign markets and the slow entry of new producers.[23] Von Tunzelmann's similar study of the diffusion of the Watt steam engine presents the first detailed and systematic comparison of the fixed and variable costs of water power, the atmospheric and the Watt steam engines. He pointed to the long resilience of water power into the mid-nineteenth century, for wheels were cheap, lasted a long time, and called on little labour and no coal. The major costs were water rights and the high cost of installing the wheels. The so-called steam revolution of the 1840s and 1850s was accompanied by only a limited decline in the use of water power – a decline of 9 per cent in the British textile industry, and 14 per cent in Britain as a whole. There was not only a complicated choice to be made between steam and water power, but among different steam engines themselves. In spite of the historical fanfare over Watt's engine, the old atmospheric engine held its own. The speed of diffusion of the Watt engine over the atmospheric was determined not by technical superiority but by the higher fixed costs of the Watt engine, by the length of time the patent had left to run, and by the level of coal prices in the region. Most of the heavily industrialized areas of Britain were regions of cheap coal, and so for some time at least there was little real need to introduce the newest steam technology.[24]

The transition in the resource base of industry away from animals, water and wood to coal, iron and steam power has been seen as the key factor behind rising productivity in British industry in the nineteenth century. This is the transition termed by Wrigley as one from the advanced organic to the mineral-based fuel economy. What is the relationship between this resource base and technological innovation? Clearly the existence of coal was not enough to explain Britain's transition to higher-productivity industry. The coal had been there for centuries, and, as Mokyr has pointed out, the causality ran the other way. Coal consumption rose because technical innovation made it possible to use it more effectively.[25] Furthermore, by the later eighteenth and nineteenth centuries, the object of innovation was not to use coal, but to economize on it. An obvious start was the search for better fuel economy of the steam engine, hence the incentive for developing the Watt, high-pressure and compound steam engines. Similarly, improvements in smelting, especially after the introduction of Neilson's hot blast in 1828, saved on coal.[26]

Resource endowments and scarcities do not, in themselves, offer an explanation of technological change. Mokyr has put the question, is it the scarcity of substitutes or the abundance of complements that drives technological change? Natural resources were no more than a 'focusing device' directing inventive activity into one direction rather than another: 'it worked like a steering mechanism; yet it is the engine, not the steering wheel, that makes a car run'.[27]

Such critical study of two of the most celebrated technologies which are virtually identified with the first Industrial Revolution conveys some of the economic complexities which underlay the process of technological transformation. It conveys a picture of a transformation which was gradual or cyclical, and not instantaneous or revolutionary. But the brunt of the argument still remains within the rather narrow framework of cost-accounting and price responses. Though a great deal can be gleaned about the path of innovation by use of an argument of basic economic rationality, this is an approach which assumes perfect knowledge on the part of its historical actors, and furthermore assumes perfect transferability of labour, capital and other inputs. Labour and capital are treated as abstract entities, and no mention is made of the manufacturing organization or of local customary and historical traditions which could either ensure or long delay an innovation's successful introduction.

EVOLUTIONARY THEORIES

Economists have recently been attracted to the use of evolutionary biological theory for explanations of technological innovation and the behaviour of firms. Darwinian selection mechanisms and adaptive routines have been placed above factor cost-saving and profitability. Economists have looked at businesses as organizations carrying out the 'search' and 'selection' processes to be found in evolutionary biology and genetics. Economic agents are assumed to behave according to routine rules – these rules evolve through a 'search' process similar to mutation in biological evolutionary theory.[28] Capitalist innovation, it is argued, takes place in a context encouraging a variety of approaches, with selection decided by the rules.[29]

The genetic characteristics of industrial organizations are similar to the technological 'paradigms' of firms. Technology and organizational structures, according to this theory, develop along certain trajectories. The past history of an industry affects the parameters of these trajectories, and the breakthrough into altogether new paradigms. There is an extent to which 'how to do things' and 'how to improve them' are embodied in 'organizational or technological routines' which through repetition and incremental improvement make some firms good at exploring certain technical, market or managerial opportunities. There are organizational indivisibilities attached to these routines.[30] The paradigm thesis applied to technology argues that opportunities are paradigm-bound, and there is a gradual exhaustion of technological opportunities along particular trajectories. New paradigms emerge bringing new opportunities for product development, and productivity increases.[31]

The paradigm approach defines industrial performance and structures as endogenous to the process of innovation, imitation and competition. Technological and behavioural variety among firms is both the outcome and a driving force of technological and organizational change. Inter-firm differences in learning result from their own histories, internal organization and institutional context. But these differences in turn become the driving force of change, creating competitive incentives or threats to innovate.[32]

Mokyr has offered the most extended historical application of evolutionary theories. He deploys these theories, not to find further support for gradual incremental economic change, but to distinguish the effects of 'macro and micro inventions'. Macro inventions were large and sudden changes in technology which operated like random exogenous shocks to the system. They were followed by micro inventions, the improvement and development or 'learning by doing' innovation. A small number of macro inventions had enormous repercussions, and they were furthermore clustered in a small number of years.[33]

> The *annus mirabilis* as Cardwell (1972) has called it, 1769, observed the patenting of two of the central inventions of the Industrial Revolution, the separate condenser and the water frame. But in 1783, 1784, 1787, 1793 and 1800 the experience of 1769 was repeated: each of those years experienced more than one major breakthrough.[34]

It was, however, in micro inventions that Britain was said to have a comparative advantage, that is in small improvements and adaptations. The necessary condition for such improvements was a large skilled labour force.

INSTITUTIONAL FACTORS

Quantities of capital and labour are only one side of the coin. There is also the quality of capital and labour; there is the institutional or customary context in which these 'factors of production' grew. Nathan Rosenberg, for one, pointed out the existence of different national technologies.[35] The character of a nation's technology could have important effects on its future capacity for invention and innovation. There were historical reasons, he thought, why nations with a more capital-intensive technology grew faster. Many of the human skills important to economic growth were acquired in the production and employment of a capital-intensive technology. The development of capital-intensive techniques became associated in time with a strategic inventive role for the sector producing capital goods. The development of such a sector which improved the efficiency of producing capital goods would, in time, become a source of capital-saving over the economy as a whole. A special sector producing capital goods was able to develop a base of technical skills and knowledge; it became the institutional means of transferring techniques to other sectors, and of developing new ones. Furthermore, a relatively small number of broadly similar production processes might be developed and spread over a large number of industries. The skills acquired in the production of capital goods and intermediate products could be used throughout the economy.[36]

A special industry and the institutions associated with producing capital goods were important, but even more significant in the early years of the Industrial Revolution were the skills and the labour which made these capital goods. Skills in processing and working metals, and skills in engineering, enabled a new technology to be introduced effectively and to work. Techniques which relied on coal fuels, like iron puddling and new ways of making glass, as well as those which used steam power, were dependent for their introduction, success and repair on new and adaptable skills as well as an old-fashioned practical 'knack' and know-how.[37]

Where other European countries such as France and Italy had large numbers of skilled craftsmen in the luxury trades, Britain's skilled craftsmen specialized in mechanical expertise – clockmakers, shipwrights and makers of navigational and scientific instruments. Further mechanical skills were developed in mining, calico printing, wool finishing and other related industries. Mokyr, like Rosenberg before him, argues that Britain's technical advantage probably lay in these mechanical skills.[38] These skills were developed, and improvements and adaptations followed in the process of 'learning by doing' in the capital goods industries and 'learning by using' in the consumer industries.[39]

'Learning by doing' was the acquisition of knowledge in capital goods industries arising out of the experience of practical production. 'Learning by using' arose from experience in use, allowing both redesigning of equipment

179

and operation of equipment over longer lifetimes. These skills were increasingly fostered in the capital goods sectors through the emergence of prominent entrepreneurs such as Maudslay, Boulton and Watt, Fairbairn and Nasmyth whose apprenticeship schemes became nurseries of creative and adaptive tradesmen.

PRODUCT INNOVATION

An important aspect of technological change rarely singled out by economic historians is product innovation. This type of innovation is generally passed over because it is difficult to separate it out from other types of innovation, and to reduce it to an easily quantified measure of change. As Von Tunzelmann has argued, 'such product innovations could be major like the adoption of cotton, or minor such as fine or fancier kinds of cloth'. Whole new industries in the eighteenth century were the invention of new products, for example the Birmingham 'toy' trades. Just as many patents during the eighteenth century claimed to improve quality as to save capital.[40] Product innovation interacted with process innovation – mule spinning spun yarns of a much higher quality than was possible by hand methods; power-loom weaving developed in coarse and plain fabrics. Some product innovation required supporting changes in machinery; and product innovations at one stage would be process innovations at another, for example new types of steam engine.[41]

Product innovation was also an aspect of the institutional characteristics of technological change. The national characteristics of technology were reflected in types of international specialization. The French specialization in high-quality skill-intensive goods for luxury markets can be compared with the British specialization in medium-quality products for middle-class consumption. But in contrast to America, the British were slow to develop mass markets in key products, and so to take up the American systems of 'interchangeable parts' in its capital goods sector. Mechanization was fastest at the lowest end of the market, for low-quality yarns and coarse cloth, for standard guns and clocks.[42]

RESISTANCE TO NEW TECHNOLOGY

Technological change did not bring a 'free lunch' to everyone. Yet few economists have seriously considered resistance to new technology as anything more than 'rigidity' in the economic system, an 'irritating minor impediment to the inevitable'.[43] In the 1960s David Landes could qualify his vision of the momentum and achievements of technological progress with one reference to those bypassed or squeezed by machine industry. More recently he has considered their plight.

What needs stressing . . . is the force with which technological change impinged on the livelihood of workers and often translated into protest, much of it violent . . . The machine breakers did not need to wait seventy-five years for the new technology to work through its potential to know they were hurting. Their personal experience was for them a good proxy measure of revolution; and for us, with our mighty number play and 20/20 hindsight, it is a fair reminder that there is more to life, work, and death than macro-statistics can tell.[44]

The issue of the reception of new technology has been treated by Mokyr as a problem of 'technological inertia'. It is treated in terms of the actions of interest groups and in terms of value systems. Resistance to technology is given a part role in the decline of British industrial leadership after 1850. Labour resistance and anti-technology ideology took precedence over state incentives to and protection of technological creativity.[45] This approach, while recognizing the existence of technological resistance, still avoids the social and class connections which might go some way to explaining such resistance. Labour was not universally opposed to changing production processes, nor were entrepreneurs all enthusiastic improvers. Regional social structures in the clothing districts of the West of England entailed resistance to new methods by both workforce and clothiers, while the West Midlands was known for the inventiveness of its workforce. A flexible workshop culture in Birmingham and its hinterland formed the basis for a progressive technological stance; in the West Country the textile community became entrenched in its own traditions, vigorously defending its customs and community from any change.[46] A significant part of resistance can also be explained by the division of labour and gender. The response of highly-skilled male workers with traditional craft skills was different from that of skilled workers with mechanical and engineering skills, and different again from that of a newly- emergent factory labour force. A high pro-portion of anti-machinery feeling in the eighteenth century, furthermore, was generated by the taking away of women's labour.

Resistance to technology was an aspect of the very structure of industrial-ization; in the industrial sector, above all, this was marked by unevenness and division. Divisions in experience and reception at the regional and local level were not just about factors of environment and local economy – they were also about the social and economic structure of industry in different places and, equally significantly, about the differences in community struc-tures and traditions. The divisions in the labour force were those between artisans and the rest of the industrial labour force: the growing significance of outwork and its casual labour force and the important place within this 'unregulated' workforce of women's and children's labour. These divisions were not eradicated, but reinforced as the process of technological change became part of the cumulative decline into de-industrialization or alternatively into the 'benign' spiral of growth.[47]

The development of technology is not a self-fulfilling prophecy. At many points there are choices to be made, and these choices have been influenced by market structure, differences in final products and resource costs. Such choices were, however, constrained by institutions and customs which favoured certain kinds of innovation and skill. Economists and historians have, however, reached an impasse with this discussion. Highly abstract but very narrow economic analysis imposed a new economic determinism to replace the old technological determinism. Rosenberg and other economic historians recognized that social institutions were important, but they still kept to a narrow terrain. Only recently has debate moved to the whole sphere of industrial structure and workplace relations. The development of technology was shaped by these factors, as much as it was by conventional economic factors. But economic theory did not give historians the framework they needed in order to include these other more elusive and social factors. And they turned, instead, to Marx.

THE LABOUR PROCESS

Instead of asking what narrow economic costs influenced the diffusion of new technology, a new generation of radicals demanded a total rethinking of technology in relation to manufacturing organization and to the character of work itself. While economists' awareness of the role of raw material costs, labour and capital costs, and demand factors challenged the old technological determinism, it blinkered consideration of the historical contexts of technical change in the pressures and constraints of the wider economy and society. Economists ignored the actual process of technical change within the workplace.

The new challenge was, therefore, to specify the connections between technical change and parallel changes in workshop and factory organization, to relate these to hierarchical organizations in production, and to analyse the impact of a skilled or unskilled workforce. The real questions at issue behind technical change and workplace organization concerned those who claimed the gains of change, and who controlled the pace and direction of work. Where economists regarded technology as an artefact, that is, a newer or older machine, radicals saw it as a process – a combination of tools, machinery, skills, work practices and organization through which production took place.

Two classic texts inspired a whole new enquiry into the source and effects of technical change – Stephen Marglin's 'What Do Bosses Do? The Origins and Functions of Hierarchy in Capitalist Production', and Harry Braverman's *Labor and Monopoly Capital*. The first challenged conventional ideas on the origins of the division of labour and the factory system, arguing that both were introduced not for reasons of efficiency, but because they offered the capitalist the means for greater control of his workforce and an opportunity to claim a higher proportion of the surplus. Contrary to the accepted view that the rise of the factory was caused by the introduction of power-driven machinery, Marglin dismissed the so-called 'technological superiority' of the factory and with this its technological origins. Factories existed well before powered machinery, and what was really at stake in the Industrial Revolution was not efficiency, but social power, hierarchy and the discipline of labour. Marglin also pointed out, and has recently emphasized, the way the factory itself became an impetus to technological innovation. For capitalists sought out and developed techniques which were compatible with large-scale factory organization. The water frame was an example. Originally designed as a small machine turned by hand and capable of being used in the home, it was patented by Arkwright and only thenceforth built as a large-scale piece of machinery driven by water or steam power. Marglin thus argued that, even though the factory did not actually determine prevailing forms of work organization, capitalist control and machines were nevertheless most highly developed in the factory form of organization. It was this high degree of capitalist control in the factory which in turn constrained the development of technology.[48]

Harry Braverman's *Labor and Monopoly Capital* also formulated connections between changes in technology and work organization, but he looked at phases of mechanization as an aspect of the history of the rise of scientific management. Taking Paul Baran's thesis of the rise of monopoly capital, he described the growth of the modern corporation in terms of the rise of automation. His book went back to the Industrial Revolution to seek the origins of scientific management and Fordism, in order ultimately to comment on the implications of a new computer revolution.

Both these texts were published at a time when advanced computing technology and a new microelectronic revolution of the 1970s and 1980s were first becoming apparent. The implications for employment, job structures and manufacturing organizations were predicted to be unprecedented. It was this economic and social context of our own industrial age, as much as the new perspectives of Marglin and Braverman, that challenged radicals to take account in their political analysis of the enormous changes taking place at the basic level of the workplace. Marxist historians thus turned their attention to the 'labour process'. What, then, is the Marxist theory of the 'labour process' which underlay the radical analysis of technological change?

Marx defined the labour process as the basic relation between man and nature which exists in all modes of production. The labour process has three constituents: the work or labour itself, the subject of labour or nature's materials which are worked up into raw materials, and the instruments of labour which mediate between labour and the subject of labour. In the capitalist mode of production, the elements of the labour process are combined to produce surplus value as well as use values, so that the value of the commodities produced in the labour process is greater than its constituent elements. The basic dynamic of capitalism is founded on the drive to increase this surplus value. Marx divided the ways of increasing surplus value into two categories. The first was those ways of increasing what he called absolute surplus value. This was the formal subordination of labour power, that is, labour was coerced into producing more with the same techniques. Longer hours and expansion of production increased absolute surplus value; so too did the greater speed and intensity of labour. The second was ways of increasing relative surplus value. This was the real subordination of labour power, and was carried out through gains in productivity, the introduction of machinery, and the conscious application of science and technology.

Marx connected these ways of increasing surplus value to historical phases in the development of capitalism. These were: first, co-operation, where a number of labourers working together produced more than when each worked separately; second, manufacture, distinguished by increases in productivity through division of labour; and finally, modern industry, defined by the introduction of machinery to replace labour power and to raise the productivity of the workers who remained. Manufacture described the process through which the division of labour splits up productive activity into component parts, separating workers into skilled and unskilled, thereby creating a hierarchy of labour powers. But in manufacture workers still had some degree of control over the content, speed, intensity and rhythm of their work. In modern industry the capitalist took this control. For with the use of machinery work activities could be homogenized, and workers deskilled. Workers became mere appendages of the machine, and capital could appropriate to itself all the functions of specification, organization and control. The historical phases of capitalist production also coincided with the use of different means of increasing surplus value. Co-operation and manufacture were dominated by means for raising absolute surplus value, and these were ultimately limited by the length of the working day. The possibilities for raising relative surplus value which were most obvious in modern machine industry were, however, limitless, for they proceeded through increases in productivity.[49]

This Marxist framework was an important alternative to conventional economic theory, and it inspired a rethinking of technological change among radicals and historians. Most of the first applications of Marx's theory of the labour process, and, with this, responses to and criticisms of the work of Marglin and Braverman, were focused on American examples of technical change and workers' struggles.[50] But a number of recent studies of later nineteenth-century changes in technology and work organization have applied the idea of the labour process, or have made central to their analysis the struggle between workers and employers over the exercise of control at the workplace.

Marx's discussion of the labour process opened a new historical and social dimension in the study of technological change, but the 'labour process' contained many problems of theory and historical validity. Many Marxist historians, whatever may have been the intentions of Marx himself, gave overriding significance to the effects of machinery, or, in Marxist terms, to the 'forces of production'. First, the accepted division between absolute and relative surplus value hinged almost entirely on the introduction of machinery. But Marx's own discussion of the labour process stresses the equally important place of the 'intensification of labour', that is, harder and faster work.[51]

With this in mind, we may cast the empirical validity of 'modern industry' in a new light. What was striking in nineteenth-century Britain was not the power of the machine in displacing labour, but the dependence of most work processes on more and more labour. Even after the Industrial Revolution, the labour process remained 'dependent on the strength, skill, quickness and sureness of touch of the individual worker, rather than on the simultaneous and repetitive operations of the machine'. And where machinery was introduced it 'created a whole new world of labour-intensive jobs'.[52] The reasons for this were not, however, just the conventional economic factors of labour supply, profitability and cost of production, market uncertainties and preferences, technical difficulties and the availability of some intermediate technology. They were also the successful use of the 'intensification of labour' to raise surplus value, and the workplace and wider political disputes over machinery, the length of the working day, and the division and speed of labour.

These disputes produced some remarkable detours and bypasses in the routes of technological change. Wide political struggles in the first half of the nineteenth century to reduce the length of the working day culminated in the factory legislation of 1847 which cut the hours of work in factories from anything up to sixteen hours down to ten. This sharp inroad on conventional means of raising absolute surplus value resulted, however, in the first rapid innovation of the high-pressure steam engine. If the workday was to be cut, manufacturers responded in droves by seeking the means of increasing both the intensity and the productivity of the working hours which remained. Study of the numbers of new and adapted engines introduced, the greater speed of machinery, and the increase in the number of accidents through boiler explosions has established this new burst of innovation.[53] Was its timing, soon after the ten-hours legislation, just coincidence?

Such workplace and political struggle could mean incentives to the development of new and other technologies, as it did in this phase of the steam revolution.[54] But, equally, it could limit the implementation of changes in the structure of the labour force, or the organization of the workplace, which new technologies might allow. The self-acting mule was one such technology. Employers in the 1820s and 1830s actively sought this invention to rid themselves of troublesome skilled mule spinners. Andrew Ure virtually regarded the self-actor as the salvation of capitalism, and Marx several decades later accepted that the self-actor had robbed a particularly militant group of workers of jobs and skills. But, in fact, the self-acting mule did not displace the skilled mule spinner, for existing workplace organization embodied in the minder-piecer system remained and successfully blocked a redivision of labour which might have allowed capitalists to use workers with lower subsistence wages. Yet simultaneously employers found other means of increasing their surplus value through the practice of 'time cribbing', that is, out-of-hours cleaning and oiling of the machinery. Further technical improvements in the self-actor allowed it to be built longer and run faster, and many firms practised 'stretch out' and 'speed up'.[55]

Workplace organization and strategic struggles by workers to deal with the threats to jobs and skills brought by mechanization mattered in many industries. Skilled workers succeeded in maintaining control in the printing industry, in spite of new technology; but they failed to do so in engineering.[56] These are only several examples, among many, of the very different outcomes of workers' struggles.

MARXIST DILEMMAS

Marxists using the labour-process analysis have, however, been overly impressed with the machine, failing to understand the place of the speed and division of labour. In some industries, it was the latter which created the crucial changes that revolutionized an industry. The building industry is a good example. Historians always write about the traditionalism of the building trades, for little new machinery was introduced in the last century. But the key to changes in the production process was not machinery, but the rise of general contracting from the 1830s, that is to say, a transition in the organization of work.[57] Marxists have also accorded far greater power and success to machinery than workplace struggles actually allowed. The old linear framework of technological determinism challenged by economists has not, in effect, been entirely expunged by the Marxists. For though they argue that technological change is the outcome of struggles between workers and capitalists, their search for examples of deskilling, divisions of labour and mechanization in any historical period is inspired by questions and interpretations of production and work suitable only to modern Western capitalist economies. They further seek to situate their individual studies in terms of key turning points that marked out the transition to manufacture or modern industry as the case may be. The result has been a failure to grasp the diversity of the experience of industrialization. There were many alternatives to mechanization in improved hand technology, the use of cheap labour-saving materials, and the division of labour and the simplification of individual tasks, which were developed in their own right. The factory, furthermore, was but one form of work organization among several, including the putting-out system, small workshops and artisan production.[58] But what matters, surely, is not the fact of the coexistence of hand and machine techniques, and centralized and decentralized processes, but the range between these polarities and the different uses and therefore meanings of each. Our task is to look at their relations to each other and the kinds of social and economic pressures which stimulated the cyclical phases of development and the regional concentrations of these many diverse forms of technology and work organization. We must seek to find a nonlinear perspective, one which shows not just the relations between technology and work organization, but also the range of capitalist forms of development. The existence of hand technologies and artisan work organization also reveals the existence of alternative forms which could be exploited just as effectively as the factory and the machine to raise capitalist profit and control. The extent to which this was achieved, however, was a question of struggle within each technology and form of work organization between employers and workers' organizations, customs and institutions.

Another problem of the labour-process perspective is its narrow focus on the workplace and production process. The impact of culture, community and family in the workplace itself is ignored. This is a peculiarly 'male' perspective, and it is not surprising that virtually all of our historical studies of labour processes are focused on a male labour force and male attitudes to work. Although recently social historians have stressed the role of the world outside of work in shaping the structure and attitudes of the so-called labour aristocracy,[59] their example has not been followed in studies of work and technical change. Most of these studies have focused on male industries or only the male workers in those industries – iron and steel, printing and engineering, mule spinning and building. For such industries exemplified the struggles of the skilled craftworker against the inroads of machinery or deskilling. Most have failed to realize that in many industries the term 'deskilling' meant the introduction of women workers. The attributes of the skilled craftworker were still acquired through apprenticeship, 'independence (high enough wages to support himself without recourse to charity or poor law), mobility, mutuality, collectivity and the unspoken but assumed virtue of masculinity'.[60] These ideals were all well and good, but from the viewpoint of only one part of the workforce. What did these ideals look like from the perspective of the ethnic minorities, the women, the unskilled poor who were excluded from the jobs, the public houses and the social institutions inhabited by the skilled man?[61] Analyses based on the division of labour must take account, not only of changes in men's jobs, but of implications for the structure of family employment and, in most of the textile and metalworking industries, of divisions between men's and women's work.

187

This account of the histories and theories of technical change highlights the recent questioning of the neutrality and the 'inevitability' of technological change. Technology, the classical example of a 'black box', is now being opened and its contents scrutinized by economist and social historian alike. But the bearing on technology and work organization of a wider framework of social institutions and customs, the different meanings and values attached to work and production in different historical settings, have as yet received but little attention.

9

THE RISE OF
THE FACTORY SYSTEM

Explanations of technological change provide one route to understanding industrial growth and structure during the eighteenth and early nineteenth centuries. But equally important was organizational change. For manufacturing, the obvious and paramount organizational change was the rise of the factory system. Yet equally important to explaining the rise of the factory system is discovering the range of alternative ways of organizing the production process, and the ways in which these adapted and developed.

Theories of why the factory system arose now take into account the broader organizational framework of manufacture. Debate has focused not just on the factory, but on what styles of work organization and hierarchy prevailed in firms – workshop production, putting-out arrangements or factories. The rise of the factory system has entailed debate over class and organizational efficiency, and over alternative arrangements in 'small-scale factories', and 'flexible specialization'. We will turn first to the factory. Before proceeding further, however, we must settle some definitions.

DEFINITIONS

While the rise of the factory system remains a vital pillar of our ideal of an industrial revolution, there is still no agreement about what a 'factory' was. 'Factories' were seen in the eighteenth century as textile mills which centralized previously dispersed production processes. These mills might include a power source connected to machinery, but not necessarily. Recently historians have adopted a technological or alternatively an institutional perspective. Andrew Ure's extreme version of the technological definition in 1835 was the physical concentration of plant around a centralized power source. In his day this excluded all large-scale activities other than textile mills. At the other extreme were definitions, such as Stephen Marglin's, which identified centralized and hierarchical management rather than a centralized technology.[1] From this perspective the things that mattered were the subjection of the workforce to factory discipline, the 'deskilling' of this workforce and its alienation from production and process. The rationale for the first factories was thus not centralized power or mechanization, but the discipline and division of labour. Pollard argued a middle way: that in some industries technological factors predominated, in others organizational ones. Heaton, long before, pointed out that the factory system pre-dated the use of powered machinery, but it was nevertheless the machinery which gave the factory the edge as a form of industrial organization.

> the modern factory system . . . embodies the use of capital, the congregation of workpeople, the division of labour and the exercise of supervision . . . the major part of the economic advantage of the factory springs from the use of machinery capable of performing work quickly, and the use of power which can make the machinery go at high speed. Until these elements of speed became possible, the factory system did not possess any very great advantage over cottage industry.[2]

The capitalist factory united for a time ownership and managerial control. Under the putting-out system the merchant controlled finance and marketing, and individual small producers the manufacturing process; under the factory system, the manufacturer controlled both.[3] The dispute over the origins of factory production centres on the extent to which technological factors can be disentangled from organizational ones.

The 'factory system' was also a term which frequently hid more than it revealed. For the size and structures of factories varied enormously. There were nothing but contrasts between the small factories set up in hamlets such as that at Cheadle Hulme in 1777 which contained two carding engines and six jennies, and Dale and Owen's New Lanark spinning mill which in 1816 employed 1,600–1,700 workers. While at the end of the eighteenth century there were 900 cotton-spinning factories, 300 of these were Arkwright-type mills employing over fifty workers, and 600 were very small mills using jennies and mules.[4] By 1821, Manchester, the centre for the factory cotton industry, contained only eleven spinning mills of eight storeys and over; most of the spinning mills in the town were between four and seven storeys.[5] These problems of definition reappear in the debate on the technological and organizational origins of the factory system.

ORIGINS OF CAPITALIST HIERARCHY

Historians and economists have long sought the reasons for, and effects of, the transition to the factory system as the predominant form of manufacturing organization. Historians have also challenged its ubiquity in the nineteenth century, and recently economists have questioned its superiority in terms of economic efficiency over other forms of organizing industry. They have asked what technical and organizational advantages factories offered over artisan and workshop systems which allowed them to cut costs and to increase both efficiency and profitability.

Debate on the question has led economists to distinguish between the technical and organizational attributes of the factory, and to separate issues of increasing efficiency from those of raising profitability. Stephen Marglin has argued that economic historians have traditionally ascribed the rise of the factory to advances in technology, failing to distinguish issues of mechanization from those of organization. They have thus been unable to account for the effects of different ways of organizing labour and supervision. The gains from and reasons for the success of the factory system were, according to Marglin, due not to large-scale machinery, but to better control by capitalists of their production processes.[6] At the heart of this explanation was the drive by capitalists for power over the organization of labour and production.

> The agglomeration of workers into factories was a natural outgrowth of the putting-out system (a result if you will, of its internal contradictions) whose success had little or nothing to do with the technological superiority of large scale machinery. The key to the success of the factory, as well as its inspiration, was the substitution of capitalists' for workers' control of the production process; discipline and supervision could and did reduce costs without being technologically superior.[7]

Other approaches gave the factory system more credit for reducing the costs of transacting, costs which arose from opportunistic behaviour by individuals and groups within a firm and such behaviour between firms. Williamson argued that the hierarchically-organized factory was better at quality control, reduced inventories, saved transport and allocated work more efficiently.[8]

These attributes of class and organizational efficiency have not convinced some economic historians. Landes, for example, upholds his belief that large-scale technological change really was the impetus: 'the factory was not just a big workshop – it used power driven machines', and what made the factory successful was the machines.[9] Technology, not simply control over labour, was the driving force: 'what made the factory successful in Britain was not the wish, but the muscle: the machines and the engines. We do not have factories until these were available, because nothing less would have overcome the cost advantages of dispersed manufacture.'[10] In Landes's view, factories in combination with powered machinery were irresistible. He claims that there was virtually no resistance to the early textile innovations, since their superiority was obvious: 'by the 1760s fears over technological unemployment were irrelevant . . . they were not raised against Richard Arkwright, inventor of the water frame . . . the water frame was powered from the start and used in factories.'[11]

Contemporary evidence, however, suggests that the reception of the

191

factory system was much more of a class issue than Landes suggests. There were major riots in 1779 directed against Arkwright's 'patent machines' and larger jennies; the mob attacked ten factories, the largest of which was Birkacre, a mill in which Arkwright was one of the partners. This mill was effectively destroyed, and Arkwright in turn was so alarmed that he put his mill at Cromford into a state of siege. A letter written from Cromford described the preparations:

> In your last letter you expressed some Fear of the Mob coming to Destroy the Works of Cromford, but they are well prepared to receive them should they come there. All the Gentlemen in this Neighbourhood being determined to support Mr. Arkwright, in the defence of his Works, which have been of such Utility to this Country, Fifteen hundred Stand of small Arms are already collected from Derby and the Neighbouring Towns, and a great Battery of Cannon raised of 9 and 12 Pounders, with great plenty of Powder and Grape Shot, besides which, upwards of 500 Spears are fixed in Poles of between 2 and 3 Yards long. The Spears and Battery are always to be kept in Repair for the Defence of the Works and Protection of the Village, and 5 or 6000 Men, Miners etc. can at any Time be assembled in less than an Hour, by Signals agreed upon, who are determined to defend to the very Extremity, the Works, by which many Hundreds of their Wives and Children get a decent and comfortable Livelihood.[12]

Mokyr cites further evidence of the widespread resistance to factories and machine technology. The Lancashire riots of 1779 were suppressed by the army, and the Preston justices of the peace declared: 'The sole cause of great riots was the new machines employed in cotton manufacture; the country notwithstanding has greatly benefited by their erection.' Later, during the Luddite events in 1811–13, the government deployed 12,000 men against rioters, 'a force greater in size than Wellington's original peninsular army in 1808'.[13] Despite such evidence, however, Mokyr, like Landes, finds the resistance to factory technology to be futile and misguided.[14] The question which remained, however, was who was to gain? Manufacturers, as Marglin argued, gained greater control of the production process and higher profits; workers, craftsmen and small producers in some industries, in the short term at least, lost jobs and a degree of autonomy.

The factory system quickly came to be associated not only with mechanized powered production, but with large-scale concentrated manufacture. What were the arguments in favour of large-scale production? Were there alternatives in the form of smaller units and decentralized processes?

SCALE AND INDUSTRIAL ORGANIZATION

Manufacturing organization has been analysed in the main in terms of scale of production. And there have been strong arguments in favour of the view that bigger was better. Larger scale has been associated with greater efficiency, lower relative costs, and greater ability to develop and use new technology. Larger-scale firms were associated with the emergence of hierarchical forms of organization, greater division of labour, and a divide between supervisory workers and unskilled workers.[15] Larger-scale firms were also more amenable to the diffusion of mechanized and powered technologies.[16] In Landes's view, the factories and the machines went hand in hand. There was a factory bias to technological change because (1) that was where the money was; (2) the saving in labour costs was higher because factory wages were higher; (3) the accumulation of small improvements was a function of the volume of investment – the new plant meant new and better equipment; (4) the factory environment was a more favourable environment for the perception of improvements: 'the logic of technology was moving towards even wider mechanisation, toward doing more and faster, thereby enhancing the advantage of mass production and the factory system'.[17] Large factories, furthermore, could deliver lower-priced commodities, and in a mass market with high elasticities of demand, price differences mattered. The great technical innovation, the machine, had an internal logic pushing it in the direction of uniformity and standardization.[18] Thus large-scale production entailing the machine and the factory appeared historically inevitable. Scale economies attributable to the indivisibilities associated with using certain types of machinery were greater than those due from the division of hand-performed tasks.[19]

Then there are all the economies of large-scale production set out by Alfred Marshall: economy of skill, economy of machinery, and economy of materials. The large factory can reap economies of highly-organized buying and selling. It can afford not only highly-specialized machinery, but highly-specialized skill. It can reap economies of entrepreneurship, confining to the entrepreneur the analysis and planning of production. In Marshall's view, the small manufacturer 'must spend much of his time on that which is below him; for if he is to succeed at all, his mind must be in some respects of a high quality, and must have a good deal of originating and organizing force; and yet he must do much routine work'.[20]

These explanations tying the organizational innovation of the factory system to technological innovation have culminated in what has been called the Chandler thesis of the drive to large-scale organization, 'the logic of managerial enterprise'.

FLEXIBLE SPECIALIZATION

It has thus been the prevailing convention, at least since the nineteenth century, to put much of the progress of manufacture down to the economies of large-scale production. Recent work has, however, challenged this.[21] Sabel, Piore and Zeitlin have claimed the existence of a path of industrialization alternative to that of mass-production and the factory system. This path, they argue, was based on craft economies, but not on the low-productivity traditional activities of the village shoemaker and blacksmith. Rather, artisan production was the basis of a highly innovative small-scale capitalism which formed a path termed 'flexible specialization'. Marglin argued that the main advantage of the factory system was a regime ensuring a higher intensity of labour. Piore and Sabel pointed out the indivisibilities, inflexibilities and rigidities entailed in the bureaucratic structures of large-scale production. Small-scale production offered economic advantages of creativity, nimbleness and easy entry.[22] Small-scale firms could develop 'flexible technologies', skill-intensive processes, and interchangeability, providing a range of product choices for localized and regional tastes.[23] Furthermore, in Marshall's view, the lack of a fundamental divide between idea and execution had great advantages: 'The master's eye is everywhere; there is no shirking by his foremen or workmen, no divided responsibility, no sending half-understood messages backwards and forwards from one department to another.'[24] And the small-scale manufacturer could take advantage of external economies, especially in the form of trade knowledge, and in regional concentrations of skills, 'so great are the advantages which people following the same skilled trade get from near neighbourhood to one another. The mysteries of the trade become no mysteries; but are as it were in the air, and children learn many of them unconsciously.'[25]

Economists have recently recognized the advantages of flexibility in the current trends to 'quasi-disintegration.' Recent technological innovation in production processes allowed by developments in microelectronics as well as market uncertainties have increased the importance of flexibility. The Japanese model of 'network capitalism' has demonstrated the positive interdependence of large-scale units and smaller producers, and of alternatives to models based on mass-production: batch production, just-in-time systems and flexible specialization have integrated small-scale production and large-scale inventions. These have a past in the histories of their specific industries.[26]

Definitions and mythology

The whole debate over scale of production – the different advantages of internal versus external economies, standardized versus specialized markets, capital-intensive powered technologies versus skill-intensive, specialized machines – depends upon largely unconscious assumptions about the nature of artisan production versus the factory system. The questions we need to ask are 'what is an artisan?' and 'what is a factory?' Do we owe more of our answer to historical myth than to empirical investigation?

The history of artisans is simultaneously a history of images of small workshops, pre-industrial customs and popular culture. This history carries with it a mythology conveyed in the political and legal documents left by the small producers themselves, and taken up by historians. The mythology constructs binary oppositions between the characteristics of pre-industrial and industrial society, associating artisanship with the archaic, and large-scale factory production with modern industry.[27]

Alongside this runs another mythology on the role of the small producer in industrialization. Large manufacturers in the eighteenth and nineteenth centuries constantly retold myths of humble beginnings. Matthew Boulton, who had inherited a large-scale business from his father, and had married a woman with a dowry of £28,000, told a Select Committee in 1799: 'all the manufacturers I have ever known began the world with very little capitals'. Samuel Timmins, who had also inherited a large-scale business from his father, wrote the classic survey of the Birmingham trades in 1866 to document the case for economic liberalism in the conviction that the factory was an organic development from small beginnings in the workman's cottage.[28]

A mythology of artisan roots thus played a part in the perceptions of small producers whatever their conditions, and in the ethos of large manufacturers. Historians have recently pointed out the vast differences in the types of artisanal enterprise. In some urban trades in eighteenth-century France, for instance, a number of artisans produced for final consumers; but, in the majority of cases, they produced for other intermediaries. Most trades made short runs of different articles sold to order within a range of prices. They depended on constantly changing outlets in dispersed and fickle markets, and an irregular supply of labour employed on piece rates for each job lot.[29]

The historical divide once made by historians between the non-mechanical craft worker and the skilled worker within the factory gates is a misleading one. For the craft worker might work within the framework of small-scale production, and yet experience not harmony, cohesiveness and consensus, but the class conflict of a cut-throat competitive economic environment. In other cases, independent artisan producers moved by choice into the factory, where by subcontracting they could maintain the viability of their small enterprises.[30]

ORGANIZATION AND TECHNOLOGY

Recent research on the enormous diversity of manufacturing organization even within a single industry – with putting-out, workshops and sweating existing alongside and complementary with a diverse factory sector – has muddied the waters of a once clear stream of unilinear development in the rise of the factory system. But myth and history still play their part in the analysis of the capacities of large-scale and small-scale production for introducing technological innovation and increasing efficiency. Crafts and Wrigley have argued that much manufacture in the eighteenth century experienced little technological innovation, and the highest proportions of adult male labour were to be found in these traditional low-productivity industries. Both identify technological innovation with large-scale and factory industry using steam or water power and powered machinery.[31] Sabel and Zeitlin, on the other hand, find technological dynamism in the craft economies, where dispersed labour-using small firms prevailed, and multipurpose machinery was deployed. The artisan firm developed its own highly productive technology – the jacquard loom, the differential gear which allowed rapid change in yarns and weaves, and the techniques of the Birmingham trades – stamps, presses, electroplating and die-sinking which could be adapted to the use of small steam engines, and later to small electric motors. These were the historical antecedents of current developments in microelectronics.[32] Wherein then lies the fount of technological innovation – the factory or the artisan workshop?

In Landes's view, the new machines and the factories that housed them were irresistible – 'the carding machine, water frame and mule were so efficient compared to hand labour'.[33] But on the other hand, the success of the factory was due to the machines and the engines. 'We do not have the factories until these were available, because nothing less would have overcome the cost advantages of dispersed manufacture.'[34] Cheaper production was provided by large-scale producers for the mass market, deploying a tireless, repetitive technology – the machine – which pushed further in the direction of uniformity and standardization.[35] But the modern mechanized technologies of the large-scale factory also hinged on a close dependency on 'traditional' artisan producers. Cotton manufacturers typically combined steam-powered spinning in factories with extensive employment of dispersed domestic handloom weavers long after the availability of powered technology. This spread risks and deployed a cheap labour supply of women and children. The metalworking trades of Birmingham and Sheffield had both large and small firms primarily concerned with metalworking diversifying into large-scale metal-processing ventures as a way of generating steady raw material supplies. They also combined occupations or changed these over their life cycle in a manner which brought the individual manufacturer either simultaneously or in succession into 'large-scale mechanized production' and small-scale 'traditional' activities.

In a parallel vein, the non-factory, supposedly stagnant small-scale sector frequently pioneered extensive and radical technical and organizational change. The classic textile innovations were all developed initially within rural dispersed manufacture. The artisan metal trades, as we have seen, developed skill-intensive hand processes, handtools and new malleable alloys. The wool textile sector moved to new products which reduced finishing times and revolutionized marketing. New forms of putting-out, wholesaling, retailing, credit and debt, and 'artisan co-operation' were devised as ways of retaining the essentials of older structures in the face of a new, more competitive and innovative environment. Customary practices, organizational forms, and 'traditional' technologies were themselves transformed partly in order to combat the spectre of large-scale factory production, and to find other ways of responding to the needs of more dynamic and market-oriented production. Research on proto-industrialization has identified the significance of innovation in organization in the form of elaborate putting-out networks, subcontracting and artisanal co-operative and share ventures, as well as in marketing techniques, credit arrangements and product innovation. It has also emphasized the diversity of such innovation centred on the small-scale unit of production, and the differences in the success rates of such innovation between industry and region.[36]

Organization and labour

The key advantage which manufacturers found in the factory system was the control it allowed over the labour force.

> In his own cottage the worker had control over raw materials and set the pace of his work. His control over raw materials led to endless squabbles over product quality as well as over embezzlement and fraud . . . No wonder that capitalists sought ways of limiting workers' control: organizational forms in which the boss, not the worker, fixed the hours and intensity of work; and where the worker would labour under the eye of a boss so that the fringe benefits (the worker's view of fraud and embezzlement) that accrued from control of raw materials would be harder to come by. The end result of this search was the factory.[37]

Yet it was not just one or the other form of organization which dictated the degree of control over labour. It was also the institutional setting of manufacture, notably the law. Masters had unequal advantage over labour before the law, due to the existence of master-and-servant legislation, which made workmen and women liable to imprisonment for breach of contract of service. This legislation went back to the Statute of Labourers of 1349, and its worst injustices were not removed from the Statute Book until the Master and Servant Act of 1867.[38] The legislation notably became the weapon of smaller employers and explains the widespread practice of long contracts and bonds of service.

Factories may have provided one way of controlling labour, but small producers and manufacturers using putting-out systems exerted control through the law and through extensive credit and debt bondage.[39] Organizational innovation to increase efficiency, profitability or control over labour was thus available to manufacturers in many different forms.

The close interdependencies between small-scale and large-scale producers, and the capacities within both organizational forms for innovation, undermine assumptions of a sharp divide between the factory system and artisan or domestic industry. It is first important to define just what a small- or large-scale producer was, and what the key size differentials within the factory sector were. It is then important to assess the extent to which a type of factory production emerged in the eighteenth century which was small or medium-sized in scale, and which deployed a distinctive division of labour and technologies.

SMALL-SCALE AND LARGE-SCALE FACTORIES

Discussion of the scale of factory enterprise in the Industrial Revolution has, until recently, been confined to differences in the levels and structure of capital formation. Historians have been ready to point out the 'relative' nature of large-scale factory production in the early nineteenth-century cotton industry. Even as late as the 1840s there was still a substantial core of small producers in Manchester; the average primary process firm in Manchester in 1841 employed 260 hands, and a quarter of all firms employed fewer than 100. Before the 1830s new technology was equally accessible to small producers as well as large: small firms took advantage of small steam engines, spinning mules, power looms, water power and traditional building methods.[40] As Gatrell has argued, 'some giants were as labour intensive as some pygmies, and some pygmies were as power intensive as some giants'.[41] The capital requirements of even these small-scale factories, however, lay beyond the reach of traditional mechanisms of upward mobility. These small cotton mills were definitely factories, and not a gradation of the artisan workshop. Further, it was the medium range between small (employing fewer than 150), and large (employing more than 500) which really mattered in the early nineteenth century (see Figure 9.1).

We have seen that in the case of the mid-nineteenth-century cotton industry, there were small factories, employing fewer than 150, large employing over 500, with most actually falling between the two. The definition of small or large changed across industries. The average size for mills varied across the major textile industries: in the early 1830s linen mills employed an average of 93.3, silk 125.3, cotton 175.5 and wool only 44.6.[42] If we go back to the eighteenth century, the variations in size start from a much lower threshold. In 1719 London had 123 calico printers, but of these only three had a large labour force, and large here meant 205, 121 and 49 employees respectively.[43] In 1780 Britain had no more than 15 or 20 cotton mills, but seven years later there were 145 Arkwright-type thousand-spindle

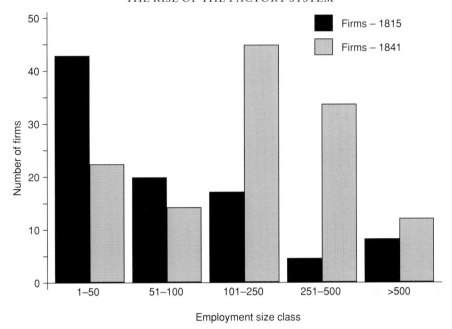

Figure 9.1 Employment size classes in the cotton industry (Manchester, 1815 and 1841)

Source: Lloyd-Jones and Le Roux, 'The Size of Firms in the Cotton Industry', p. 75.

mills. Before the end of the eighteenth century less than a third of cotton spinning factories employed more than 50 workers.[44]

The woollen and worsted industries showed these kinds of contrasts in the nineteenth century. In the 1780s the West Riding had 221 scribbling, carding and slubbing mills in the woollen industry, while in 1800 there were still only 22 worsted mills. By 1835 there were 1,333 woollen and worsted mills, but these averaged a use of 16 horse power. Ninety-one per cent of woollen mills in 1851 employed fewer than 50 workers; 52 per cent of these employed fewer than 10. Sixty-three per cent of worsted mills employed fewer than 50; 23 per cent employed between 50 and 200 workers. 'Small-scale' and 'large-scale' thus carried completely different meanings across a closely related industry in one region.[45]

If we turn from the textile factory sector to other centralized industries, we see that the contrasts over 'small- scale' and 'large-scale' were just as great. In coalmining, 'large' in the pits of Tyne and Wear in 1710 meant 260–325 miners; in 1830 the average workforce there was 300. But for the country as a whole the average coalmine employed no more than 80 pit and surface workers.[46] Similarly, the iron industry contained a small number of celebrated huge firms – the Carron Works with 2,000 workers in 1814;

199

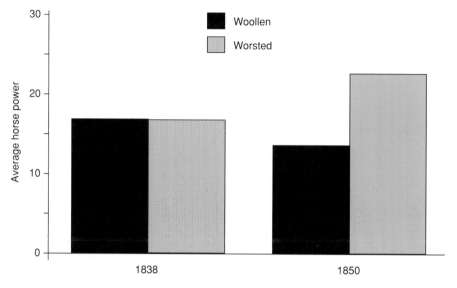

Figure 9.2 Size of woollen and worsted mills (1838 and 1850, in Yorkshire)
Source: Hudson, *Genesis of Industrial Captial*, p. 40.

Samuel Walker and William Yates with 700 workers at one site in 1820; Dowlais in 1842 with 18 blast furnaces, dozens of puddling furnaces and 6,000 employees. But in 1814 the average Scottish foundry employed 20.[47]

Other centralized industries contained a clear divide between a 'large-scale' and a 'small-scale' sector. Brewing is the classic example. Until the 1790s total production was roughly divided between the large common brewers and the small brewing victuallers. By the 1820s, the common brewers were producing approximately 70 per cent of output, while the brewing victuallers produced 30 per cent, but this was still a substantial proportion for the small-scale sector after over a century of competition with the large-scale sector.[48]

For the textile mills and centralized industries, it is clear that the giants were few, and that most production was carried out in 'small'- or 'moderately'-sized units, whose meaning in terms of numbers employed, buildings and horse power differed greatly across industries. Is this a contrast between a small progressive factory sector which took advantage of the economies of large-scale production, and a large traditional sector of small-scale producers? Or is it a contrast between organizational types of factory or centralized production associated with different product types, divisions of labour and technology? We have seen that the new cotton technologies were available at relatively low thresholds – small firms took

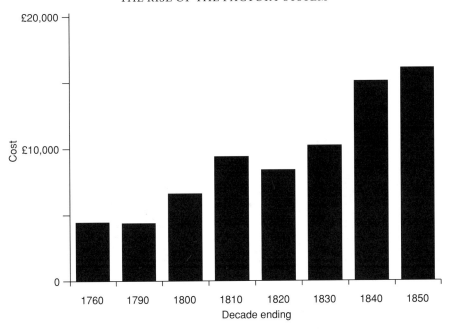

Figure 9.3 Scale of production in the iron industry (initial investment in blast furnaces)

Source: Davis and Pollard, 'The Iron Industry', p. 98.

advantage of small steam engines, and installed small numbers of spinning mules and power looms; they used traditional building methods and existing water-power resources. Is there a case to be made for a special dynamic within the small- and medium-scale sectors of these industries? One way forward is to treat small- and medium-sized factories as a distinctive form of organization. This has been pursued for the manufacturing sector of the American North-East in the early nineteenth century.

American small-scale factories

Historians have only recently begun to examine the distinctive character-istics of the small- and medium-scale factory. A series of essays by Sokoloff, and Goldin and Sokoloff, has examined the characteristics of manufacturing in the North-East of the US in the early nineteenth century. These writers have identified a distinctive set of 'small-scale factories', and have set out the structures of capital in these firms, the age and gender characteristics of their labour forces, their technologies and their organizational innovations. Sokoloff distinguishes the artisanal shop from large-scale textile factories based on the use of sophisticated machinery, and both in turn from what he calls the non-mechanized factory. He argues that the rapid expansion of the

201

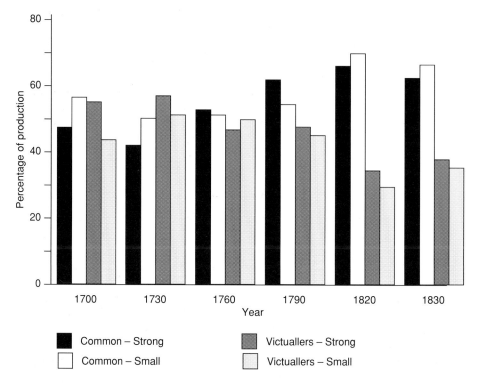

Figure 9.4 Size of firms in brewing (annual production of common brewers and brewing victuallers 1700–1830)

Source: Mathias, *The Brewing Industry in England*, pp. 542–3.

Note: Common brewers were large-scale wholesale producers selling to national markets. Brewing victuallers were small-scale licensed producers selling in local and regional markets. 'Strong' and 'small' refer to different types of beer produced.

manufacturing sector in the North-East was accompanied by a movement toward larger-scale production in a range of industries extending far beyond textiles to include clocks, guns, hats, shoes and umbrellas. Manufacture in these industries became increasingly organized into these non-mechanized factories, and these in turn had an efficiency advantage over traditional artisanal workshops. These non-mechanized factories had scale economies up to a specific threshold size – such economies were virtually exhausted by establishments in the range of 6–15 employees. These economies derived from a division of hand-performed tasks within a firm, the use of simple tools, supervision and a more disciplined work regime. This factory drew on a much higher proportion of female and child labour than its predecessor,[49] and the use of this workforce is explained by the substitution of an unskilled for an expensive skilled male labour force.[50]

These factories were also the focus for a high degree of inventive activity; the expansion of the market with the development of inland waterways, domestic competition and a pre-industrial population with a working knowledge of current technology and the facility to learn from advances in Britain stimulated invention.[51]

To what extent do we find this model of the small-scale factory in eighteenth-century Britain? Are the characteristics of its organization, labour force and inventive activity similar, or does the British case show up other characteristics which might in turn help to offer different explanations of the growth of manufacturing in the American North-East?

Small factories and a workshop economy in Britain

Evidence for the place of such 'small-scale factories', their internal structures and efficiency gains, is less systematic in Britain. Nevertheless, there is certainly a case to be made for an important place for this organizational form in British industry at a parallel stage of development, that is in the later eighteenth century and up to the end of the Napoleonic Wars. Market expansion, regional growth on the basis of the canal economies, and a new departure in the use of child and female labour in textiles, potteries and the metal manufactures were parallel developments. The gains of these small-scale units could also be combined with a significant degree of mechanization, notably the use of water and steam power. The extent of mechanization in these units has been under-recorded because their small size precluded them from coverage under the Factory Acts.[52]

An example of one such small factory can be taken from the calico-printing industry in 1790. Thomas Cooper assessed the needs of such a works as 'a house on the spot, a bleach green with plenty of running water, a printing shop (5 yards wide for a row of tables, nine yards for a double row), a stove in the printing room, a stove room to dry the printed calicoes, a warehouse, counting house, and drug room'. Such an establishment including buildings, raw materials, tools and equipment was valued at approximately £900.[53]

The new consumer industries of eighteenth-century, Birmingham produced all sorts of novelties such as buttons, buckles and jewellery. Such novelties were called 'toys' in the eighteenth century, and the factories producing them, then called 'manufactories', did not rely on centralized power sources. The town was famous for the invention and production of the Watt steam engine, but its own industries drew on very little of this power. These industries did, however, deploy to a remarkable degree the division of labour, specialization, and use of child and female labour which produced productivity gains in America's small factories. Dean Tucker wrote in 1759:

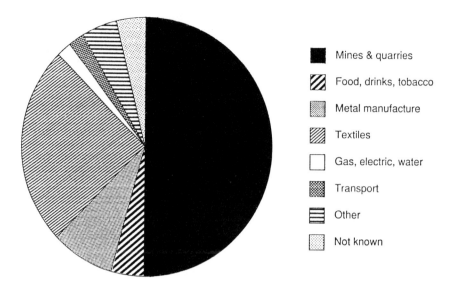

Figure 9.5 Steam power in British industry, 1800 (percentages)
Source: Von Tunzelmann, 'Coal and Steam Power', p. 78.

the labour . . . is very properly proportioned . . . so that no time shall be wasted in passing the goods to be manufactured from Hand to Hand, and that no unnecessary Strength should be employed. For an instance of both Kinds, take one among a Thousand at *Birmingham*, viz. When a Man stamps on a metal Button by means of an Engine, a Child stands by him to place the Button in readiness to receive the Stamp, and to remove it when received, and then to place another. By these Means the Operator can stamp at least double the Number, which he could otherwise have done, had he been obliged to have stopped each Time to have shifted the Buttons: . . . this single Circumstance saved alone 80 or even 100 per cent at the same Time that it trains up Children to an Habit of Industry, almost as soon as they can speak.[54]

The impact of division of labour and specialization took organizational change beyond the factory system. We also see in Britain at the same time the emergence of new departures in the workshop economy, departures deploying an extensive division of labour and multi-plant production processes. Larger manufacturers from Birmingham pointed out that their 'employees' did not necessarily work under one roof, and that, furthermore, some on their premises were contract workers supplying their own tools and only paying rent for their place at the bench. Works arrangements in the copper and gun trades show up a combination of separate but geographically-concentrated workshops.

These were classic instances of what we might term a 'workshop economy', built on specialization and the division of labour, on dispersed units concentrated in specific locations, and on close networking among these units. Alfred Marshall drew on such examples for his concept of the 'industrial district' in his *Industry and Trade* in 1919.[55] He argued that 'industrial districts' such as those found in Birmingham generated external economies of knowledge and skills. Philip Sargant Florence also produced another concept of 'industrial swarming' in the 1950s. Concentrations of skilled labour and of whole complexes of different but related and interdependent industries in specific districts created external economies sufficient to substitute for the internal economies of large-scale production. The result was plant disintegration, but local integration.[56]

Craft, workshop and small-scale economies – end results

Workshop economies, small-scale factories and the craft economies of flexible specialization all held an important place beside the emergent factory system during the eighteenth century. But by the second third of the nineteenth century, the dominant place occupied by smaller- and medium-scale producers was giving way to large-scale concentrated production. This did not, however, imply the disappearance of the small producer. There were still many small industrialists in workshops and domestic production units during the latter half of the nineteenth century. But now, there was a yawning gap between the small producer and the factory.

The artisan clothiers of the Yorkshire woollen industry were successful for a long time – that is, until the last quarter of the nineteenth century – but they were eventually broken by changes in the market and competitive pressures in the industry. They were also undermined by the centralization of finance and the disappearance of community and artisan values, which had previously fostered the self-exploitation of family labour.[57] The Birmingham trades were increasingly subordinated to large capital-intensive firms, at least from the first half of the nineteenth century; the main directions of the trades were mapped out by coalitions and associations of large-scale manufacturers. These big bosses were just as good, if not better, at using and developing the techniques of flexible specialization. From the 1820s on, there was a rise in the size of establishments, the introduction of machinery and falling apprenticeship and wages. It was in this period that the balance of power shifted away from the skilled artisan to the larger-scale unit.[58]

Sheffield's highly-skilled independent artisans developed into the 'little mesters' who proliferated and multiplied, not in times of prosperity but in times of commercial stagnation and distress; their lives were almost totally dictated by a local group of merchant capitalists. They were part of the 'old Sheffield' with its networks of craftsmen in the cutlery and petty trades, and they stood in stark contrast to an urban bourgeoisie linked in with the new heavy steel industry.[59]

Easy entry into several manufacturing industries was still possible for the small producer during the nineteenth century, but now 'easy in' was just as likely to be 'easy out'. Landes summed it up:

> The economic advantages . . . of flexible specialisation are . . . creativity, nimbleness, easy entry. As a result, there will always be small firms, not only for what they offer the buying public, but for the services they can render big business . . . On the other hand, these small firms have serious weaknesses. They lack the credit and resources of big units . . . they are often obliged to operate on the margin . . . which reminds us that small enterprise has its dark side as well as its bright: self-exploitation, inferior working conditions, personal dependency.[60]

At the end of the day, small bosses are still bosses. Pollard has added the further point that the small-scale firm takes the strain of fluctuations; it does not supplant the large efficient plant, but supplements it. The luxury end of the market remains dominated by small producers, but this exists only 'because of the social wealth created by the conveyor belt'.

> Small-scale, perhaps rural industry may seem more attractive to the nostalgic historian, but it cannot begin to match the productivity of mass scale in key sectors: textiles, iron- and steel-making, coal mining, railway transport, shipbuilding, shipping, gas works and electric power stations.[61]

THE LOGIC OF MANAGERIAL ENTERPRISE

The factory system emerged in the eighteenth century within the framework of a dynamic small-producer capitalism. It took until the early nineteenth century in one industry, cotton textiles, for it to become the dominant form of organization. In many other industries the rise of the factory system was a long drawn-out affair taking until the mid- to late nineteenth century. Much research on the size of the firm and profitability follows the tradition of the 'Chandler thesis' of the drive to large-scale organization, or what Chandler calls 'the logic of managerial enterprise'. Large-scale along with high-volume production, the so-called 'American system of manufactures', was combined with carefully-defined managerial hierarchies. The results were economies of scale, but also of scope in keeping to core production technologies; both led to process and product innovation. The advantages went to those who made the first-mover investments to create a managerial enterprise. They gained competitive advantage even across nations, and took the laurels of the second industrial revolution.[62]

Do the lessons of the 'logic of managerial enterprise' also apply to the first industrial revolution? The Chandler thesis of the drive of competitive pressures to large-scale production lies behind many of the associations made between the growth of productivity and the increasing capacity of mines, blast furnaces, mules and looms. But scale and scope also apply to the structures of enterprises.

The modern trend to large-scale organization on the lines indentified by Chandler includes vertical and horizontal integration: economies of scale followed by economies of scope. Yet the British cotton industry remained vertically disintegrated throughout the nineteenth and into the twentieth century. The spinning and weaving sections of the industry remained separate, and marketing was controlled by separate groups of merchants. The historical route to 'scale and scope' in fact had many branches, and the 'Chandler thesis' can provide no exclusive model of the development of eighteenth- and nineteenth-century industry.

Factories arose during the eighteenth century and developed within a plurality of organizational forms suitable to region, market and the economic cycle. The diffusion of the factory system was sometimes long-drawn-out, especially where alternative forms were themselves innovative and highly developed, and where there were not large economies of scale. The transition to the factory system proceeded at a much faster pace where it was combined with rapid power-using technological innovation.

10

THE TEXTILE INDUSTRIES: ORGANIZING WORK

The experience of growth, decline and transformation of the eighteenth-century textile industries frequently passes for the whole story of Britain's economic revolution. Of course, this means a very one-sided, and indeed blinkered, view of economic fortunes and prospects in the period. But we cannot deny the significance of textiles to the British industrial experience. Behind their significance, too, lay a richly textured saga of growth and decline, small-scale industry and large-, home and factory, manual labour and machinery. For the textile industries include far more than the cotton manufacture: there was the experience of work in wool and worsted, linen, silk and framework knitting. How were these other branches of the textile industry organized in the eighteenth century? What were their tools and techniques, and what happened to them? We shall here compare the progress and decline of several branches of the textile industry in the eighteenth century – not just the success stories, but the failures and those which 'also ran'.

Though most historians have been mesmerized by the remarkable growth of the cotton industry at the end of the eighteenth century, what is striking to the historian who takes a longer and broader view over the century is the substantial and impressive growth of all the major textile industries – wool and worsted, stocking knitting, silk and linen as well as cotton, and with the rise of cotton the rapid complementary spurt of calico printing. We have already compared output and productivity across the main textile industries; now we shall look at the origins and forms of development of the various forms of work organization.

What is clear at the outset is the great variety of pre-industrial and proto-industrial structures. The story of textiles, the epitome of the whole story from proto-industry to Industrial Revolution, is frequently carica-tured as a series of transitions from the artisan to the putting-out system, and thence to the factory. But in fact, features of all these types of work organization and various permutations of them existed from the very be-ginning of the eighteenth century within and between the various textile industries. Proto-industry did not, in effect, take on any single type of organization; nor for that matter did it entail any special type of technology.

INDUSTRIAL ORIGINS

Wool and worsted

Before cotton we generally think of wool. What were the main centres of this traditional industry in the eighteenth century? For most of the time, the woollen and worsted industries were spread widely over the country, but they were also specialized by region. Defoe in 1726 found broad cloth and druggets in Wiltshire, Gloucestershire and Worcestershire, serges in Devon and Somerset, narrow cloth in Yorkshire and Staffordshire, kerseys, half thicks, plains and coarser things in Lancashire and Westmorland, shalloons in Northampton, Berkshire, Oxfordshire, Southampton and York, worsteds in Norfolk, lindsey woolseys at Kidderminster, flannels in Salisbury and Wales, and tammeys in Coventry.[1] By 1770, the wool-manufacturing centres stretched from Exeter through Witney and Leicester, out to Newtown, up through Bradford and Kendal and from Galashiels to Aberdeen.[2] In 1792 the inhabitants of most areas of the North and Scotland were occupied in some part of the wool or worsted industries, and there were more so employed in Leicestershire, Oxfordshire, Derbyshire, Norwich and many areas of the West Country.[3] By the last third of the century the real centres of the woollen and worsted industry had concentrated in East Anglia, the West Country, the East Midlands, Yorkshire, Lancashire, the North Pennines and the Scottish borders, but Yorkshire's predominance was already noticeable. Between 1741 and 1772 the input of raw material into the industry had increased by 14 per cent per decade, and by 1770 the output of the industry was valued at £8–10 million. Yorkshire then accounted for one-third of this value and for one-half of the value of all textile exports. In effect the main expansion of the whole industry in the last third of the century was accounted for by the rise of Yorkshire and Lancashire, and it was from the 1770s that the great divide between the West Country and Yorkshire opened up. Between 1770 and 1800 the proportion of wool textile exports going to America rose from 25 per cent to 40 per cent, and virtually all of this increase was supplied by Yorkshire.[4]

Yorkshire's rising supremacy was based partly on wool and partly on the newer worsted manufacture. The manufacture of worsteds had spread first in the sixteenth century with the introduction of the New Draperies in Norfolk, and spread further in the seventeenth and eighteenth centuries with the manufacture of bays, serges and shalloons. It spread rapidly in the West Riding in the eighteenth century; Halifax was the key centre until succeeded by Bradford during the Industrial Revolution.[5]

Yorkshire's rise meant Norfolk's demise, but this prospect was by no means apparent for much of the eighteenth century. Certainly Norfolk's worsteds were of a high quality, but fashions eventually changed against the heavily glazed materials in favour of finer merino fabrics with silk decorations.[6] And by 1770 Yorkshire was producing worsteds to a value equal to Norwich's.[7] Norfolk's original success was, however, based on its successful competition with the West Country woollen industry, for it produced goods at a total cost of some 8 to 10 per cent less than the West Country's, and its weavers' wages in 1760 were 40 per cent lower. Its woollen and worsted industries were expanding rapidly in the first half of the eighteenth century, and at its height Norwich commanded 12,000 looms and 72,000 weavers working to the order of thirty large cloth dyers. The industry grew until the 1770s, after which it went through periods of strength and activity until its collapse in the early nineteenth century.[8]

Colchester, Suffolk, Coventry, Worcester, Dorset and Exeter had likewise all been flourishing centres of the cloth industry in 1700, but by 1800 all were far in decline. The course of decline in Essex was fairly typical. The cloth industry there in 1700 dominated four large towns and a dozen small towns and villages. It contributed to the employment of the majority of Essex families, for most women in the towns and the countryside were spinners. But after 1700 rural weavers were going into rapid decline, and the smaller centres became the first casualties. Local capital was gradually shifted away from textiles and into farming.[9]

The well-established pre-industrial cloth industry of the West Country remained buoyant throughout most of the eighteenth century, but by its end the trade was split. In the area around Stroud in Gloucestershire there was very small expansion, while in Trowbridge and Bradford-on-Avon on the Somerset–Wiltshire border a transfer of production into cassimeres, a fine twisted cloth, cancelled out the decline in broad cloth.[10] Trowbridge in fact prospered, its population rising by 57 per cent between 1811 and 1821. It was the most prosperous centre of the West Country industry, until it too declined in the later 1820s.[11]

Yorkshire's apparently meteoric rise in the eighteenth century was founded on a long period of apprenticeship reaching back to the fifteenth century. Halifax wares were sold at St Bartholomew's Fair and at the Blackwell Hall market in London. By the seventeenth century Wakefield and Leeds were the great wool and cloth markets of the area. Some part of the woollen manufacture was carried on over the whole of the North, the West and parts of the East Riding, though it was very diffused compared to the Leeds, Halifax and Wakefield regions. The main worsted area stretched from Bradford to fifteen miles west and north-west of Halifax, taking in the upper valleys of the Aire and Calder. Halifax, Keighley, Haworth and Colne were centres, with a considerable worsted manufacture also found in the area of Leeds and Wakefield. The woollen district stretched in a pentagon between Wakefield, Huddersfield, Halifax, Bradford and Leeds, with the great cloth market at Leeds.[12] The industry was largely organized in villages which in the seventeenth and eighteenth centuries had grown at the expense of the towns, and even by 1811 most towns were small and contained only one quarter of the population of the whole West Riding.[13]

Knitting

The woollen and worsted industries were complemented by another wide-spread domestic industry in the seventeenth and eighteenth centuries – the hand- and subsequently machine-knit stocking industry. Joan Thirsk has described the rise of the fashion for silk, wool, worsted and cotton knitted stockings, and the wide geographical dispersal of the handknitting industry by the end of the seventeenth century. Although in many areas knitting complemented the woollen industry, the more significant common factor was a large population of smallholders pursuing pastoral farming.[14] Handknitting in Wensleydale and Swaledale was an extension of the old Westmorland industry, and by the eighteenth century desperation pursued the villagers.[15] In Richmond (Yorkshire) 'every family was employed great and small' in the manufacture of knitted yarn stockings for ordinary people. Doncaster's handknitting industry was famous even in the sixteenth and seventeenth centuries, and it was an industry almost entirely in the hands of women.[16]

Machine-knitting came to the East Midlands in the mid-seventeenth century, where it first diffused as the occupation of yeoman knitters of some substance in the villages of South Nottinghamshire, Derbyshire and Leicestershire. But the industry was rapidly urbanized, particularly after the mass migration of framework knitting from London to the Midlands in the first half of the eighteenth century. There were fewer than twelve frames in Leicester in the 1680s, but by 1700 the town had 600. The village industry also continued to grow – 16 per cent of the inhabitants of Wigston Magna between 1698 and 1701 were knitters, while the proportion of knitters in Shepshed rose from 4 per cent in 1701–9 to 25 per cent in 1719–30.[17]

Silk

Machinery came early to the knitting industry, but the development of technology and organization in the silk industry was even more precocious. After the introduction of Lombe's silk-throwing machinery in 1719, mills sprang up all over the country; by the late eighteenth century the industry was still scattered over twenty counties and fifty towns. The largest eighteenth-century silk mill was in Stockport with six engines and 2,000 workpeople. Together with other smaller mills it supplied the Spitalfield weavers.[18] Tightly capitalist from the outset, silk throwing spawned import-ant weaving and ribbon-weaving sectors in London and Coventry. The

Coventry ribbon-weaving industry, in particular, combined traditional artisan structures with new capitalistic methods. In the eighteenth century, the industry moved into a town with long-established textile traditions in the manufacture first of blue thread, then of woollen and broad cloth. But it also spread in periods of prosperity among the wives of the colliers in villages to the north and north-east of the city, and this was soon an area where 13,000 looms supported 30,000 people.[19]

Linen

The rapid growth and early capitalistic structures in both silk and framework knitting were matched by another but equally impressive combination of growth and family production in the linen industry. The eighteenth century saw a rapid increase in the colonial demand for linen for slaves' clothing, coffee and indigo sacks, and mattress covers, as well as in the domestic demand for the 'decencies' made from linen – tablecloths and napkins, towelling, bedding, furnishings, and clothing, especially shirts.[20] An import rather than an export industry, linen accounted for 15 per cent of total imports in 1700, but only 5 per cent in 1800, and sources of supply shifted from the continent to Ireland, to Scotland and to domestic linen production itself.[21] It was an industry with a long history of small-scale production for localized markets. In one sample taken from probate inventories of the late sixteenth and early seventeenth centuries, 14 per cent of agricultural labourers were engaged part-time in working up flax, and a further 15 per cent in working up hemp. The industry flowered between 1740 and 1790 under trade protection. A good deal of it was still hidden away, incorporated into domestic production for family use:

> Tis true the English manufacturer is not publically known, or at least not so much taken notice of as the Scotch or the Irish, but the reason of this is very plain: in this country most of the linen we make is made by private families for their own use, or made and consumed in our country towns and villages.[22]

The commercial industry also provided for several regional economies. It was the staple industry in parts of Yorkshire and County Durham, in several parts of Lancashire ranging from Lancaster and Preston down to Manchester, and in the non-woollen area of Somerset and Dorset, spreading into Devon and Wiltshire.[23]

The Scottish and Irish linen industries arose as staple industries to supply the substantial English demand after English protection sharply reduced continental imports. In Scotland, the industry was encouraged by the new trade opportunities created by the Act of Union, with help from the Board of Trustees which brought over several cambric weavers from France and a man skilled in all branches of linen from Ireland to travel about and instruct weavers in the trade. A visitor to the Highlands in 1725 wrote that 'Every woman made her web and bleached it herself and the price never rose above 2s a yard, and with this cloth almost everyone was clothed.' The manufacture was well-established in Aberdeen and the countryside by 1745; by 1795, 10,000 women were spinning yarn, and 2,000 women and 600 men were employed in the thread manufacture in Aberdeen. It was a staple industry of Glasgow from 1725, and other major centres were found in Forfar, Fife, Perth and Dundee.[24] Even Edinburgh had a high-quality branch. The Irish industry similarly rose to prominence on the basis of English demand. Between 1740 and 1770 cloth exported rose from 6.6 million yards to 20.6, and yarn exports rose from 18,500 to 33,400 cwt. Seven-eighths of these exports went to Britain. The export market in yarn was further stimulated by the expansion of the English cotton industry, which for the first three-quarters of the eighteenth century depended on linen warp for the manufacture of calicoes.[25]

The linen industry also fostered the growth of the cotton industry. The two industries lived together along with a hybrid, the fustian manufacture, for a long time in Lancashire, and in other areas such as Glasgow the cotton industry drew on the older linen industry's skilled labour force. Duties against foreign linen as well as the early eighteenth-century prohibition of Indian printed calicoes stimulated both British manufactures.

> The cotton industry was enabled to grow dramatically once its in-herent technical potentialities were realized because of its long roots in the linen industry. In Lancashire (as in Lanarkshire) there were established skills to be drawn upon and there was a nationwide commercial superstructure of provincial drapers and London warehouse men.[26]

Cotton

As significant as this complementarity between linen and cotton was the developing connection between calico printing and cotton, for a large part of the origin of great demand for cotton textiles in the eighteenth century can be explained by the enormous popularity of the fashion for printed fabrics which emerged in the later seventeenth century. Calico printing, originally established in Egypt, was soon relocated to the main importing centres for London – Amsterdam and Marseilles. It was carried across Western Europe by the Huguenots and was soon also found throughout Eastern Europe. And the British industry, except for the luxury end of the market, soon migrated from the metropolis to the provinces. Chapman and Chassagne have recently demonstrated the significance of the stimulus provided by this industry. By 1792 nearly a million pieces of white cotton cloth were produced in Britain, of which 60 per cent were sent to the printer's. Calico-printing workshops were effectively 'proto-factories', a 'transitional stage in evolution from dispersed domestic manufacture to the factory system'; and a number of leading calico printers were associated with the introduction of mechanized spinning and weaving.[27]

Although calico printing was prohibited in Britain in 1720, printing on linen or cotton–linen mixture was a popular alternative, and the cotton industry soon grew out of the linen or linen mixtures industry. In mid-eighteenth-century Lancashire, a master 'put out' linen yarn for the warp and cotton weft in cops. The spinning was arranged by the merchant or carried out by the weaver's family, and cotton spinning formed the part-time activity of most women of the labouring classes. In Scotland, the weavers of Paisley and Glasgow, already skilled in the production of fine linens, easily turned their hands to fine cottons, notably the Paisley shawls. In the 1770s several thousand looms in the Glasgow area were producing linens, silks, cambrics and lawns; they changed over by the end of the century to fine cottons.[28] Glasgow concentrated on plain and printed muslins and Paisley on fancy fabrics. In Lancashire spinning spread early in the south around Manchester, while weaving was done on handlooms in the north-east corner of the county.[29] The impact of the production of calicoes and muslins was described in 1785 in MacPherson's *Annals of Commerce*.

> A handsome cotton gown was not attainable by women in humble circumstances, and thence the cottons were mixed with linen yarns to reduce their price. But now cotton yarn is cheaper than linen yarn, and cotton goods are very much used in place of cambrics, lawns and other expensive fabrics of flax; and they have almost totally superseded the silks. Women of all ranks, from the highest to the lowest, are clothed in British manufactures of cotton . . . the ingenuity of the calico printers has kept pace with the ingenuity of the weavers and others concerned in the preceding stages of the manufacture, and produced patterns of printed goods which, for elegance of drawing, far exceed anything that ever was imported; and for durability of colour, for generally they stand the washing as well as to appear fresh and new every time they are washed, and give an air of neatness and cleanliness to the wearer beyond the elegance of silk in the first freshness of its transitory lustre.[30]

By the end of the eighteenth century the geographical distribution of most of the main textile industries had undergone great change. Yorkshire now dominated the woollen and worsted industries, though Norfolk and the West Country remained in a strong yet static position. Knitting was now centred on the East Midlands, particularly Leicestershire and Nottinghamshire after framework knitting had shifted out of London, and the formerly widespread country handknitting industry was now more localized in the North and in Scotland. Silk remained a small luxury industry, though organized then along highly capitalistic lines, and received a new fillip in the eighteenth century with the expansion of weaving in London, and later ribbon weaving in Coventry. Linen and cotton became highly concentrated – the one in Scotland and Ireland, the other in Lancashire and Scotland. All the branches of the textile industry in fact went through significant phases of expansion in the eighteenth century, but the remarkable spurt of the cotton industry was unique and soon cast the respectable performances of its predecessors into shadow.

EARLY WORK ORGANIZATION

The organization of production in the early stages of the different textile industries shaped their subsequent paths into industrialization. Elucidating the variety of industrial structures prompts us to seek out the reasons for difference. Mercantile capital intervened in all these industries, but with very different implications for organization. There was in some industries a straightforward correlation between capitalist control, frequently in the form of concentrated ownership, and putting-out systems. But other industries, while using mercantile networks, were run by independent small clothiers who preserved artisan structures. What contributed to the fragility or resilience of these proto-industrial structures? Why did capitalist control intervene more effectively in some, but not others, of these textile industries? The answers to these questions may lie to some extent in costs of production or market structures. But they are likely to lie at least as much in social structure and institutions.

Wool and worsted

At the beginning of our period, the wool and worsted industries in both the West Country and Yorkshire contained an abundance of small clothiers. Julia Mann has argued that until the last half of the eighteenth century the small clothiers of the West Country were a significant part of the local social structure. There was no rigid dividing line between these and other workers; they went poaching in company with cordwainers, shearmen, bakers and glaziers; shopkeepers often carried on a little clothmaking.[31] Heaton describes the textile class of seventeenth-century Yorkshire as mainly small clothiers making one piece of cloth a week and living hand to mouth. There were also yeomen who combined agriculture and industry, either making or finishing cloth, and then there were the large clothiers whose chief interest was cloth manufacture. They were mainly found in the villages near Leeds, where they also kept gardens, orchards and closes for animals. They kept a full set of clothmaking utensils and employed journeymen, women and apprentices. The larger clothiers often bought pieces from small men and sold these along with the cloth of their own manufacture to merchants from London and Yorkshire. The cloth was then taken once or twice a week to the open markets in Leeds, Halifax or Wakefield, or sent in cargoes to Blackwell Hall or Bartholomew Fair. The small clothier's establishment was largely determined by the size of the labour force needed to make a piece of cloth; in the case of the kersey manufacture it took six people sorting, carding, spinning, weaving and shearing for one week to produce one finished but undyed piece.[32]

During the course of the eighteenth century a division arose in Yorkshire between the woollen and worsted branches. The small independent wool clothiers remained much as they had been in the seventeenth century. The father went to market and bought the wool; the wife and children carded and spun it, and some of the wool was put out to be spun in neighbouring cottages. With the help of his sons, apprentices or journeymen, the clothier then dyed the wool, wove it, took it to the fulling mill, and then to his stall in the market. He produced only one or two pieces a week, and kept between three and fifteen acres of land. Some had a horse or ass to carry their burden to market; others carried the pieces on their head or shoulders. It still only cost between £100 and £150 to start out, and the system of open marketing placed the small producer on equal terms with the large.[33]

But this division between wool and worsted was regional before it was industrial. In the more populous areas of the West Riding, especially in the area near to Halifax which was soon to turn to the worsted manufacture, Defoe found the cloth industry organized in a highly sophisticated combination of domestic and workshop manufacture. He found the country 'one continued village' with hardly a house standing out of speaking distance from another; 'at almost every house there was a tenter and almost on every tenter a piece of cloth, or kersey or shalloon'. For two to three miles in almost every direction 'look which way we would, high to the tops, and low to the bottoms, it was all the same; innumerable houses and tenters, and a white piece upon every tenter'.

> Among the manufacturers' houses are likewise scattered an infinite number of cottages or small dwellings, in which dwell the workmen which are employed, the women and children of whom are always busy carding, spinning etc. . . . this is the reason also why we saw so few people without doors, but if we knocked at the door of any of the master manufacturers, we presently saw a houseful of lusty fellows, some at the dye-fat, some dressing the cloths, some in the loom, some one thing, some another, all hard at work.[34]

The worsted manufacture, based on combed rather than carded long-fibred wool, was organized in Yorkshire on a much more capitalistic basis right from the outset. There the small independent clothier never existed; instead there were merchant-manufacturers who resembled the large West of England clothiers. They bought large quantities of wool at big fairs and put it out over a wide area to be spun and woven. The open marketing at the

Leeds cloth hall with over 1,000 stallholders was in sharp contrast to the concentrated industrial structure indicated by the worsted hall at Bradford with its 250 stallholders. The Yorkshire worsted manufacturers ran extensive putting-out networks, commonly distributing wool within a radius of twenty to thirty miles. Woolpacks were often consigned to shopkeepers or small farmers who received a sum for delivering and receiving wool and spun hanks of yarn. 'The mother or head of the family then plucked the tops into pieces the length of the wool, and gave it to the different branches of the family to spin about nine or ten hanks a day.'[35]

Capitalistic structures were, however, by no means necessary features of the worsted manufacture, for in Norfolk independent craftsmen prevailed. In Norwich the weaver was the pivot of the industrial structure. He bought yarn from independent spinners and wove it by himself or with his journeymen who worked either on commission or on the weaver's premises. The cloth was then put out to independent cloth finishers, and afterwards sold locally to drapers or sent to London. Neither, for that matter, were artisan structures natural to the woollen industry. The West Country by mid-century was the living example to contemporaries of monopoly and capitalist putting-out systems.[36]

The sharp contrast between the artisan and capitalist structures of wool and worsted in Yorkshire, of worsted in Norfolk and Yorkshire, and wool in Yorkshire and the West Country cannot be attributed to natural differences in the industries. Neither do such differences account for the early appearance of mills and factories in the different textile manufactures. Mills existed in both industries from the early eighteenth century. And artisan and capitalist alike both made use of water-powered factories, or at least mills. Such mills were used for specific processes of manufacture and were generally incorporated into existing artisan and putting-out structures. Water-powered fulling mills existed from early times, but these were not regarded as factories.[37]

Do labour costs help to explain the different structures of wool and worsted? This seems unlikely, for labour costs were said to be lower in Norfolk than in the West Country, and they were lower in turn in Yorkshire's worsted manufacture. Putting-out systems prevailed in both the West Country and the West Yorkshire worsted manufacture in spite of different labour costs. Markets, to be sure, favoured the new over the old: first worsteds in Norfolk, then those in Yorkshire; and Yorkshire's wool over the West Country's. Guild, corporate or landed regulations played their part in all three regions, but with different results. Putting-out systems in West Country wool and Yorkshire worsted probably owed much of their origin to concentrated ownership; and the local origins of such concentration go back in turn to a range of structural and circumstantial social factors peculiar to each region.

Framework knitting

Artisan and capitalist organizations grew and developed together in the woollen and worsted industries, though both industries were carried out in different regions, even within Yorkshire itself. In framework knitting capitalist relations were an historical development of the eighteenth century. Framework knitting started out as a skilled occupation practised by yeomen of some substance, similar in character to the peasant metal-workers around Sheffield. Early frames were cheap, and in the villages workshops of four to six frames were often built as annexes to houses, with larger production units in the towns. The frame was still, however, costly compared to the capital stock of a handloom weaver. It ranged in price from £3 10s to £18, though many used secondhand frames. The earlier machines of the seventeenth century had cost a great deal more and taken two men to run. Master knitters operated an apprentice-journeyman system, and their capital outlay compared with that of a cutler in the eighteenth century. The technology was soon simplified, and many were able to build their own frames. Many rural stockingers until the later eighteenth century worked three or four days a week at knitting, and carried on another occupation such as farming. During the first phase of its migration to the Midlands the industry was located in villages of middling wealth and relatively egalitarian social structure. Many villages which took up framework knitting had previous traditions, not so much in handknitting as in woollen or worsted weaving; others were located in the vicinity of a metalworking area, as was Nottingham, where stocking machinery was first developed.[38] Knitting villages soon became subject to the pressures facing many areas of subdivided tenancies where a large class of smallholders was emerging.

In the eighteenth century framework knitting became very closely connected with developments in both the silk manufacture and the cotton industry. For it was the stocking frame which created the possibility of abandoning clumsy woollen hose in favour of lighter and more elegant stockings of silk and cotton. The main centre of the industry, originally in London and controlled by the London Chartered Framework Knitters' Company, quickly spread to the Midlands in the later seventeenth and early eighteenth centuries; by the middle of the eighteenth it was focused on Leicester and Nottingham. The wealth and power of the Midland hosiers expanded rapidly as they responded to the caprice of eighteenth-century changes in fashion, using new materials and creating new meshes and new garments on the frame. The London Company's attempts to maintain apprenticeship regulations in the trade throughout the country were ignored by the Nottingham hosiers. Many of these had not themselves served a legal apprenticeship, and they employed unlawful journeymen and women and children in large numbers.[39] The knitters complained of masters who could 'build fine houses and country villas, keep carriages and equipages, go a hunting etc., while begrudging a trivial rise to their workers'.

Apart from sophisticated putting-out networks, the industry also boasted centralized workshops from early in the eighteenth century. Large workshops employing over forty parish apprentices existed in Nottingham from the early 1720s, and Samuel Fellows, one leading hosier, had built a large 'safe box' factory to manufacture imitation Spanish lace gloves in 1763.

> Thus by the time that Hargreaves and Arkwright went to Nottingham, the concentration of both juvenile and adult labour in factories was a fairly familiar idea. The way was prepared for further development of factory industry.[40]

Concentration also extended to entry into the industry. Working framework knitters rarely found their way into the ranks of the hosiers. These latter formed an elite which moved into the same residential districts as the gentry and took their recruits from among the sons of 'gentlemen, farmers and prosperous tradesmen'.[41]

In framework knitting, as in wool and worsted, neither labour costs nor even capital costs contributed seriously to concentration. But the circumstances of markets, and the high incentive to bypass the old guild controls, did open opportunities for a limited number. Reinforced in turn by regional poverty founded on agrarian change and population growth, the hold of the larger clothiers was soon assured.

Silk

Silk was a luxury industry, but it spawned the country's first factories – highly capitalistic enterprises employing child labour – and one of the country's most highly-skilled and traditionally-organized artisan groups, the Spitalfields weavers. Capitalist and artisan confronted each other across the throwing and weaving branches of the trade. And even artisans eventually divided, separating themselves off from degraded outworkers in a split between metropolis and province, and between town and country.

The throwing mills, which sprang up around the country after Lombe's Derby mill first appeared, employed young girls and children. The yarn produced by these mills, was, however, bought by craft-weavers who worked at home or in small workshops. The industry grew up against the backdrop of a series of acts to prohibit the importation of silk goods. In Spitalfields, London, the industry was organized on an artisan basis. Most of the householders were small master weavers who sold their output to mercers or drapers, who in turn retailed to private customers in City shops. A seven-year apprenticeship prevailed and masters kept two to three journeymen by the year. Spitalfields was known at this early stage for its manufacture of elaborate brocades, damasks, velvets and other rich fabrics.

Most of the other silk-weaving centres which became well known by the end of the eighteenth century grew up in the wake of the Spitalfields Acts of 1773.

Under the provisions of these acts the wages of silk weavers were to be fixed in London by the Lord Mayor, recorder and aldermen, and in Middlesex and Westminster by the magistrates. In 1792 the acts were extended to silk mixtures and in 1811 came to cover women as well as men. The acts were established after a period of falling wages and violence in the trade. Samuel Sholl wrote of the early 1770s:

> But in process of time, as there was no established price for labour in England, there was great oppression, confusion and disorder. Many base and ill designing masters took the advantage, in a dead time of trade, to reduce the price of labour. The oppression became so insupportable that a number of journeymen, at the hazard of their lives, resolved to make examples of some of the most oppressive of the manufacturers by destroying their works in the looms. This they effected, but for want of prudence in their conduct, several fell victim to the cause and lost their lives.[42]

The effect of the acts, however, was to prompt many manufacturers to move their trade to other districts. The silk-button trade moved to Macclesfield, a town whose throwing mills were already supplying the Spitalfields trade. Silk weaving spread to the villages nearest the East End of London in the late eighteenth century, and by the early nineteenth into the villages of Essex. Silk ribbon weaving became important in Coventry from the beginning of the nineteenth century, but was built there on the basis of an older silk manufacture going back to the seventeenth century. As the worsted manufacture moved from Norfolk and Suffolk, and as the conditions of the Manchester cotton weavers deteriorated in the early nineteenth century, silk weaving moved in to take its place.[43]

The structure of the Coventry ribbon-weaving industry was perhaps one of the most interesting developments to emerge from this regional diversification. While stocking knitting started as a skilled yeoman's trade which was soon to face a rapid decline in status, ribbon weaving, which developed later, faced pressures which were quite different in the town and country branches of the industry. The trade was important only from the early nineteenth century and was concentrated in Coventry and a number of outlying villages in a twelve-mile radius, including Nuneaton, Foleshill and Bedworth. A distinction between the towns and the villages quickly arose. The first-hand journeymen in the Hillfields area of Coventry were well off, while the trade in the villages was poor, degraded and carried out largely by colliers' and farmers' wives and children. The villagers had no piecelist and were banned from the use of more efficient looms. Weavers in the city and its suburbs were considered to have 'superior habits and intelligence' to the dispersed and ignorant inhabitants of the rural parishes. These were employed chiefly in the single-handed trade and retained most of 'their original barbarism with an accession of vice'.[44] The strength of the urban weavers was largely established through the concentration of the industry in the hands of a small number of manufacturers, and through the weavers' success in preventing an influx of cheap labour. The industry was dominated by only a dozen families whose control extended from the earliest days of silk production to the late Victorian period.[45] The master manufacturers were able to control the industry at least until 1812 by means of the undertaking system. The manufacturer provided the silk dyed in the hank to the undertaker who provided looms and either did the work with his family or was assisted by apprentice and journey hands. Male and female journey hands were required to serve a five- to seven-year apprenticeship.[46]

Linen and cotton

The linen industry was first and foremost a home occupation, widely practised, even after its commercialization, as a basic part of household duties. Never defined as a skilled occupation, it was largely assumed to be a women's preserve. Much of the domestic English linen manufacture was submerged in private family production and use. In Scotland, too, 'Many of the Scotch ladies are good housewives, and many gentlemen of good estate are not ashamed to wear the clothes of their wives and servants' spinning.'[47]

While putting-out systems went hand in hand with industrial concentration in the other textile branches examined thus far, the cotton manufacture tells a different story. Here, from its earliest days, a putting-out type of organization emerged in a more dispersed industrial structure. Cotton's organization was affected by that of its predecessor, fustian. This was a mixed cotton and linen cloth. It was a minor cloth until the mid-eighteenth century, but the rural workers producing it were more caught up in capitalist relations than either linen workers or many wool producers. By the middle of the eighteenth century there was systematic intervention by middlemen and a developed putting-out system, but large merchants did not control the markets or prices of yarn. Fustian masters appeared in the middle of the century. These gave out raw cotton and linen thread to the workers, then sold the cloth so produced to merchants. It seems probable that this prevalence of the small yeoman capitalist was an important factor in the successful growth of the Lancashire cotton trade. He could obtain credit or mortgage his land and become a putter-out. From here he could rise to become a small-scale employer of weavers and thence to the status of merchant.[48] These fustian masters or factors were generally responsible for a large body of small weavers over a wide geographical area. The system had advantages, for the factors did most of the 'managing' of the industry, leaving merchants to concentrate on selling.[49] In spite of this putting-out structure, however, the organization of the industry was hindered by the large number of middlemen, the seasonal labour in agricultural districts, and the delays caused by the small scale of production.[50]

The rise of some of the really big cotton masters and their innovation of the early factory system were closely bound up with the profits of fashion to be gained in calico printing. When calico printing moved beyond London to Lancashire in the mid-eighteenth century, those who took up the business were drawn from the same stratum of society as the cotton spinners, flax spinners and merchants – 'the chapmen or dealers in linen or cotton cloth known as Blackburn Greys'. It was the middlemen suppliers to the Blackburn merchant houses – the Claytons, Liveseys, Peels, Howarths and others – who started out in workshops which grew rapidly in size and efficiency. Peel had early connections with carding and spinning innovations through one of his spinners, Hargreaves, and pressured him into giving up the secret of his invention. Arkwright too was closely involved with calico printing. The increase in the demand for calico to produce the extremely popular printed cloth must have brought great pressure on the cotton spinners. In fact, as Chapman has shown, Peel devoted years to producing the finest possible fabrics for calico printing. He experimented with carding, roving and spinning machinery, building up his own team of artisans to build the machines. By the 1780s fine spinning was virtually an integral part of calico printing so that most manufacturers were calling themselves 'calico muslin manufacturers' or 'calico printers and muslin manufacturers'. And by the 1790s the spread of calico printing was putting a strain on the output of handloom weavers, so that it now became the general practice for manufacturers 'to establish their weaving . . . in all the little villages about [their works] in some of which they put a manager and take apprentices and also give out work to the inhabitants at their houses'.[51]

The calico-printing workshops, or 'proto-factories', formed a nucleus for a series of other workshops gathering together hand technologies, and the cotton industry developed through a combination of dispersed and concentrated, factory and putting-out, forms of production employing a complementarity of mechanized and hand technologies. When Arkwright's water-frame mills started to appear, there already existed small but much more widespread jenny factories and small carding factories preparing cotton for home spinning.[52] But in spite of factories, a substantial amount of spinning, both of high and low counts, was still carried out at home, or in very small factories. Some of these sold their yarn to the larger spinning factories, bridging any gaps during cyclical, technical or labour disruptions.[53]

Where industrial concentration, not production costs or markets, accounted for the predominance of putting-out networks in Yorkshire worsteds and framework knitting, this was not apparently the case in the early days of the cotton manufacture. Here, the market and pre-existing mercantile networks appear to have played the vital role in introducing a new product. Hence the production of this new material was diffused through the putting-out networks of the commercial linen and calico-printing industries. Capitalistic structures came with the new product; they were not imposed upon it. But the market opportunities created by a new product also entailed more open ownership and easier entry than did the concentrated putting-out systems of older textile sectors. This openness was also clearly related to regional social and institutional structures – the absence of corporate regulation over most of the cotton region, and the opportunities for population increase without the widespread poverty experienced in the East Midlands.

IMPACT OF SOCIAL STRUCTURE

The proto-industrialization of the British textile industries in the eighteenth century was thus no single-minded progression, for the starting points of each industry spanned the whole spectrum of work organization. The classic early pattern, combining small independent artisans with agriculture and textiles, existed in some branches of the woollen industry, notably in Yorkshire, but not so much in the West Country; it existed in handknitting and some early framework knitting, and in linen. Some of the textile industries were, however, much more capitalistic, if not at the start then certainly by the middle of the eighteenth century. Putting-out and central-ized processes prevailed from early on in the Yorkshire worsted manu-facture, in the fustian manufacture, in framework knitting, silk throwing, calico printing and cotton.

Why were these structures so different even before the onset of severe pressures from technical change and capitalist competition at the end of the eighteenth century? The origins of these differences lie in several factors. The market played its part, and so did technology. But most influence was exercised by regional and industrial social structures, social structures which went back to the very character of feudalism and the origins of agrarian capitalism.

In the silk industry and in calico printing, a luxury market and tradi-tional urban artisanal social structures encouraged a paradoxical com-bination of capitalistic organization and guild controls. Silk mills and calico-printing workshops were among the most advanced of early factories. But the strength of guild regulations helped to create metropolitan and provincial town and country divisions in both calico printing and silk weaving; divisions which were reflected in the quality of output and the labour force.

The putting-out system prevailed in the Yorkshire worsted industry, the West Country woollen industry, the Midlands framework-knitting industry, and the early cotton industry. The reason again lay largely in local social structures. This is clearest in the divide between the artisan woollen region and the putting-out worsted regions of Yorkshire.

Overpopulated pastoral regions marked by social division also help to account for the social structure of the framework-knitting industry. By the mid-eighteenth century the cost of frames combined with a relatively poor workforce to make for the easy concentration of frames in the hands of putting-out masters. This capitalist concentration and a large, flexible and weakened labour force created ideal conditions for the proliferation of capitalist structures of work organization. Internal control over the size of their labour forces prevented the growth of such capitalistic structures in industries such as the Yorkshire woollen sector and the Coventry silk-weaving trade. Coventry's weavers were protected by a ring of common land over which all master weavers had a right of pasture. This restricted the growth of the town and reinforced the strength of the urban weavers.[54]

What is remarkable is that textiles, the group of industries always singled out as the leader of the Industrial Revolution, and the prototype of advanced factory organization, should not only have started with multifarious forms of work organization, but should have retained these throughout the period of industrialization. Even by the 1820s only some stages of a few of these textile industries relied on factory organization and mechanized power technologies. The significance of these processes and industries, as in cotton spinning, should not, of course, go unrecognized. But it was still the case that decentralized, workshop, artisan and putting-out systems were successful and profitable, and in addition a substantial degree of technological change was compatible with these structures.

ROAD TO THE FACTORY SYSTEM

The artisan systems, putting-out networks and different types of early factories were all transformed over the course of the late eighteenth and the first years of the nineteenth century. The textile manufactures constituted the industry *par excellence* in that large-scale technical change that we call the Industrial Revolution. But it was competition and capitalist pressures, and not new technology itself, which accounted for the new forms of work organization evolving by the end of the eighteenth century. Some of the older types of work organization did develop into a factory system; others never did. Instead they developed their own valid and competitive forms or went into industrial decline. Technological development, on its own, did not have a great deal to do with the outcome. Many of the new techniques developed in the latter half of the eighteenth century could have been adopted across several systems of work organization. Yet some were adopted in only one of the forms they might have taken. This was the case with the development of the water frame and calico-printing techniques inside a factory system. We will discuss their cases more fully in the next chapter. But equally, the development of new technology in this period did not just mean mechanized, power-using techniques. It also included labour-intensive technologies and improvements in hand technologies which could be used in either domestic or factory production.

The particular technological developments of the various textile manufactures and the problems of their reception and diffusion merit a separate discussion, but here we shall concentrate on the historical development of the industrial structure of the textile industries. What happened to the artisan workshops, the putting-out systems and the cooperative factories by the time that the Industrial Revolution reached its peak?

Wool and worsted

The sharp contrast to be found in the early organizational structures of the Yorkshire woollen and worsted industries was intensified during industrialization. The putting-out system of the worsted industry developed into a factory system divided between large mill owners and poor wage labourers. The artisan system in the woollen industry was retained until the mid-nineteenth century, but adapted to needs for space and power by introducing co-operative mills for the use of all small clothiers who subscribed.

Earlier organization in the woollen and worsted industries in Yorkshire first appeared to be moving in quite different directions than this. By 1800, there were a large number of woollen mills containing fulling, scribbling and carding machinery, as well as a number of hand processes; whereas mills were only slowly developed in the worsted industry, partly because of labour opposition to the factory system, and partly because the industry was located in areas with little water power.[55] There were a number of major woollen clothiers around Leeds in the late eighteenth century who ran large workshops resembling miniature factories – James Walker of Wortley had twenty-one looms, eleven in his own loomshop and the rest in weavers' houses. One L. Atkinson of Huddersfield had seventeen looms in the one room. The reasons given by these particular clothiers for direct supervision were 'to have the work near at hand, to have it under our inspection every day, that we may see it spun to a proper length', and 'principally to prevent embezzlement, but if we meet with men we can depend on for honesty, we prefer having the cloths woven at their own houses'. From the 1790s, however, one hears many complaints from domestic clothiers, particularly in the worsted industry, that merchants were becoming manufacturers and so ruining the small independent men.[56]

The development of the factory system in woollens and worsteds ultimately, however, tended to much greater concentration and larger scale in worsted than in wool. The early mills in the woollen industry were not a challenge to but a part of the traditional artisan structure, and most of these mills as well as a number of later cloth mills were 'occupied and run if not entirely financed by small manufacturers previously involved in proto-industry rather than by wealthy mercantile owners'. Water-powered fulling paved the way for the centralization of other processes: soon the water wheels which turned the fulling stocks were turning new scribbling and carding machinery, and eventually even the water frames for spinning worsted.

Both systems of production – artisan and capitalist – could, therefore, generate centralized production processes, in effect forms of a factory system. But these were factory systems which clearly differed in their social relations of production. It was possible, on the one hand, from within and while preserving the artisan system, to make a gradual transition from cottage and cottage workshop to a factory with all the processes of production under one roof. But it was equally possible, on the other hand, for factories to be founded by wool clothiers with the stated purpose of greater supervision, quality control and prevention of embezzlement. Contemporaries were clearly aware of a big distinction between the two types of establishment. The former was generally referred to merely as a 'mill', that is, a centre where domestic manufacturers could bring their own materials to be taken through the mechanized processes of scribbling, carding, fulling and so forth. The latter was truly a factory – an establishment where a manufacturer employed wage-earning labour and with mechanical power made up his own raw materials into yarn and later into cloth. These differences were also reflected in the workforce. By the 1830s, 75 per cent of factory workers in the woollen manufacture were men with experience in the craft sector. Worsted mills, which had a much higher threshold of capitalization, were generally owned by putting-out merchants. The workforce was predominantly female and juvenile, and there was little upward mobility.[57]

The division within the woollen industry between Yorkshire and the West Country also grew wider during industrialization. Where earlier in the eighteenth century there had been a number of small clothiers in the West Country, these appear to have been forced out during this period. At the end of the century there were a number of attempts to exclude the small men coming in on the basis of factors' credit, and a new and very marked division arose between the 'respectable' and 'inferior' clothiers. By the early nineteenth century the small clothier had disappeared in Wiltshire and Somerset, and was replaced by large factories supplying domestic weavers.

Framework knitting

Whereas the putting-out networks in the Yorkshire worsted industry, and to a lesser extent in the West Country woollen industry, developed into a factory system, and in the West Country ultimately into de-industrialization, in framework knitting they developed into sweated

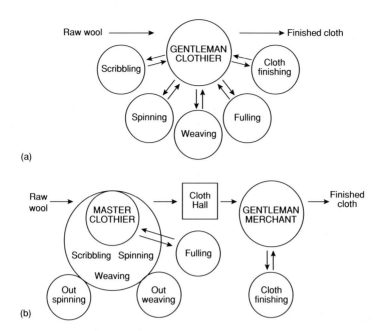

Figure 10.1 Organizational structure of the woollen industry: (a) West of England; (b) West Riding of Yorkshire

Source: A. J. Randall, 'Work, Culture and Resistance to Machinery in the West of England Woollen Industry', in P. Hudson (ed.) *Regions and Industries: A Perspective on the Industrial Revolution in Britain* (Cambridge, 1989), pp. 180–1.

industry. Technological change did to a certain extent increase capital requirements, but most of the increase in capital actually sprang from changing organization in the industry. From the mid-eighteenth century hosiers shifted from small workshops annexed to their homes into greater complexes including a house, workshop, warehouse and rows of brick cottages built for their framework knitters. There was also a new class of bag hosiers renting out frames. One such hosier, Francis Beardsley of Bromscote, died in 1763 possessed of 112 frames in knitters' houses in Nottingham and 25 in villages in the vicinity.[58]

In spite of the earlier existence of open villages and substantial yeoman–artisan connections in South Nottinghamshire, Derbyshire and Leicestershire, framework knitting did not behave like the artisan–agricultural base in the West Riding woollen industry. Instead it declined into a degraded putting-out industry. The structure of the open villages in this area was perhaps not so restrictive as to prevent the influx of population which undermined the artisan. Leicester, for instance, had no belt of common land surrounding it, as had Coventry, to prevent migration from the countryside.

And certainly from the early to mid-eighteenth century, a number of hosiers were employing an unrestricted number of apprentices as well as waged labour. Middlemen appeared in the industry from the mid-eighteenth century, leading to a reduction in knitters' income by 20 per cent, and technical change in the frame again in the mid-eighteenth century resulted in a further reduction in the stockinger's status. By this time the industry was spreading to poorer villages, so that, for instance, in Shepshed it was the poverty of the peasants in the second quarter of the century which formed a precondition for the area's subsequent industrialization.[59]

Silk

Work organization in the silk manufacture was closely tied to conditions in Spitalfields. The decline in the status of the Spitalfields silk weavers by the end of the eighteenth century was hastened in the early nineteenth by the spread of silk weaving about the country in a manner similar to the traditions of silk throwing. Throwsters in Macclesfield now produced for local weavers in the silk-button trade. Those in Leek provided for a family industry carried out in garrets. The industry in Manchester and Essex fed on cheap labour thrown off first by the woollen and worsted industry, and later by cotton handloom weaving. This provincial, as well as foreign, competition had reduced the Spitalfields weavers by the early nineteenth century to sweated labour, and the status of those in Macclesfield and Manchester was soon to take a similar course, after the rapid entry of cheap labour from cotton handloom weaving in the 1820s.[60]

Artisan traditions remained much stronger, however, in the Coventry silk-weaving industry. They were protected by the control exerted over population increase in the city, as well as over entry to the trade. Workers' resistance long prevented the introduction of steam power; no one even attempted to set up a steam factory until 1831, and this was immediately burnt down. Another built in 1837 survived, and after this a number of factories did appear in the city, but the suburb of Hillfields remained an artisan stronghold. The industry, however, became increasingly divided between town and country. Restrictive practices, highly-skilled labour and a high-quality manufacture were the hallmarks of the town, while the villages in a twelve-mile radius around Coventry took the unregulated end of the trade, using largely women workers and less efficient techniques. But even the urban trade fell prey to capitalist pressures in the early nineteenth century. After the Napoleonic Wars a number of small masters appeared employing women and half-pay apprentices. And divisions also appeared among the journeymen. There were the first-hand journeymen who owned their own looms and owned or rented their houses. In 1838, 1,828 of these, 214 of them women, owned 3,967 looms. Then there were the journeymen's journeymen who worked either for first-hand journeymen or in factories. These accounted for 1,225–1,878 men and 347 women, and with their families made up 2,480 workers, of whom 373 worked in factories and the rest for the first-hand journeymen.[61]

The factory system was not the clear-cut outcome of industrialization in any of these textile sectors, except for Yorkshire worsteds. Instead, earlier industrial structures were simply intensified – responding to the pressures for capitalist expansion by accommodating these to artisan institutions, or by giving way to the full exploitation of sweated labour. But factories clearly did appear in the linen and cotton industries. Why did cotton in particular take this new direction, and just what kind of break with the old did it entail?

Linen and cotton

Putting-out systems and artisan production likewise prevailed in the linen industry for most of the eighteenth century, and even after the factory appeared at its end the hand production of linen goods continued to be a staple element of non-commercial or extremely local household production. Putting-out networks and factories came to the linen industry with the commercialization and localization of the industry, but the change was gradual.

The first linen mills were not built in Scotland until the 1780s; they remained insignificant until the first decade of the nineteenth century. Here, as in Ireland, after factory spinning started to displace women's domestic spinning, women were deflected into handweaving, and an oversupply of labour in weaving was already apparent by 1815.[62] Dundee, well known from early in the eighteenth century for coarse linens, was a case in point of one extreme of the variable development of industrial organization in the industry. Until the beginning of the nineteenth century yarn was typically spun by housewives in the countryside who then brought the yarn into Dundee to sell. But manufacturers, finding it difficult to acquire uniform sizes and qualities, started to use agents who purchased directly from householders. A few spinning mills did make their appearance at the beginning of the nineteenth century but they were not significant until the 1820s. By 1822 there were seventeen steam-powered flax mills in Dundee, employing 2,000 people, plus another thirty-two mills in the neighbourhood.[63]

It was in the cotton industry that new organization and industrialization seemed most clearly united. But here too the break with older forms of work organization was not really so marked. As in the other textile manufactures, industrialization brought the intensification of a number of pre-existing forms of work. The domestic system easily accommodated the small mule and jenny factories which first appeared in the 1770s and 1780s. These small factories were set up in hamlets where they formed the nucleus of a village.

An example was the village of Cheadle Hulme whose factory in 1777 contained two carding engines, five spinning jennies and one twisting jenny, though the building was large enough for fifteen jennies, rovers and carders.[64] The jenny mills ranged from the small shop with a hand-carding machine to the water-powered factory containing all preparatory and finishing processes.[65] Spinning mules, at first hand- or horse-powered, were also operated early on in very small factories. Even in 1800 many mule spinners had set up in converted premises, and in a town like Oldham, which later became dominated by very large manufacturers, there were large numbers of small mule-spinning entrepreneurs. These had raised their capital on the strength of connections with the land, with coalmining, or with the domestic textile manufacture.[66]

It was the Arkwright-type mills which marked the really big divide. These were thousand-spindle mills built to use Arkwright's newly-patented water frame. But as will be argued more fully later, this centralization was not caused by the development in technology. It was caused by key business decisions. And these Arkwright mills were still located in the countryside close to sources of water power. They were closely interconnected with the small jenny and mule shops and with domestic weaving run on the putting-out system. Converted premises and mills with many tenancies were in fact the most dominant form taken by the factory system in the cotton industry in the eighteenth century. The first mills in Stockport were silk mills which subsequently declined, to be converted to cotton manufacture. The water power, buildings and child labour were all simply transferred from one textile industry to the other.[67] In addition to conversions there was the widespread practice of renting parts of mills.

Cotton weaving remained a workshop or domestic trade until the power loom started to spread more rapidly after the Napoleonic Wars. But industrialization made important inroads on the workplace of the handloom weaver long before the power loom became a real threat. There was already an important demarcation between the urban and rural branches of the trade. In the towns workshops were substantial, and a journeyman–apprenticeship system prevailed. The Manchester smallware and check weavers were already well organized in trade societies by the 1750s. They were weaver-artisans, self-employed and working by the piece for a choice of masters. The rural fustian weavers, however, were poverty-stricken outworkers.

This rural–urban division in the trade became blurred with the increase of population and influx of immigrants into South Lancashire in the latter part of the eighteenth century. We read a great deal of the declining status of the urban weaver, of his attempts to enforce apprenticeship restrictions and to establish a minimum wage. But we know a great deal less of work relations and the extent of the putting-out system among rural weavers. We do know that the expansion of the cotton industry in the later eighteenth century attracted large numbers of new weavers from amongst small farmers, agricultural labourers and immigrants. 'It was the loom, not the cotton mill, which attracted immigrants in their thousands.'[68]

In the process, rural weavers became increasingly dependent on 'putters-out' who took yarn into the uplands, or upon particular spinning mills, for many early cotton manufacturers claimed to pay hundreds of handloom weavers scattered through the countryside in addition to the employees in their own mills. The dependency and outworker status of these weavers soon also affected the urban weavers. 'The artisan, or journeyman weaver, becomes merged in the generic hand-loom weaver . . . the older artisans . . . were placed on a par with the new immigrants.'[69] Poor outworkers were a cheap and flexible source of labour. Where concern over quality or time-keeping demanded something more, handloom weaving sheds, easily accommodated to existing mill sites, served the purpose.

FACTORIES AND ALTERNATIVES

We have now unravelled some of the threads of development of the diverse structures of the textile industry over the course of the eighteenth and early nineteenth centuries. Let us therefore try to gather together these threads in order to capture the underlying pattern of the web of the eighteenth-century textile industries. The general effect of capitalist competition and technical change at the end of that century seems to have involved an intensification of existing differences in the manufacturing structures of the textile industries, not a trend towards any single structure. Strongly-based artisan systems in the wool and silk industries maintained their structures in the face of capitalist competition well into the industrial period. They did, however, eventually succumb to decline, in some cases taking on all the characteristics of a sweated industry as they fought for survival. In the case of silk weaving, the Spitalfields weavers were sweated workers by the end of the Napoleonic Wars, and the repeal of their apprenticeship laws in the Spitalfields Acts. In the case of the Coventry weavers, the compromise of the cottage factory sustained the artisan until the 1860s when new free-trade developments sacrificed the industry to the flooding of foreign silk imports. Clothiers in the West Riding woollen industry adopted another compromise in the co-operative or 'company mill' which was viable until the 1850s and 1860s, but they too ultimately succumbed under the pressure of falling rates of profit to mass-production in a concentrated factory sector.

Putting-out industries in areas of a strong socioeconomic base and a rising market, or where work processes were more obviously better concentrated, took the road to the factory system. This was the experience of the worsted, linen and cotton industries. Putting-out networks established from early days in areas of population pressure like the East Midlands lent themselves easily, in an industry such as framework knitting, to intensive sweating, as cost-cutting rather than market opportunity determined the constraints on development.

The sweating system and the factory system were the two endpoints which the textile industries reached by the latter half of the nineteenth century. But the forms which industrialization took through the eighteenth and first half of the nineteenth century were based on the different routes of the artisan and putting-out systems, as well as, to a relatively limited extent, of the factory system. The forms of work organization which emerged in the nineteenth century cannot, moreover, realistically be termed endpoints, for the structures of work organization continued to shift as industrialization proceeded. The factory system itself was a term which frequently hid more than it revealed. For the size and structures of textile factories in themselves varied enormously, being also subject to constant pressures for change. For an example of this let us now turn to developments in the size of cotton mills in the late eighteenth and early nineteenth centuries.

The size of cotton mills

The size and structure of mills in the cotton industry raise their own problems for the analysis of work organization. We have seen how artisan and putting-out systems took on many different manifestations and remained as viable industrial structures under certain conditions alongside the development of the factory system. But factories too, even within one textile industry such as cotton, developed in a great multiplicity of forms. Extremely small firms fitted in beside the giants. Some were single-process firms; others combined several processes. Some were multi-storeyed mills with an assembly-line type of organization. Others were a combination of shacks and workshops.

We frequently associate the late-eighteenth-century cotton industry with new machinery and large factory enterprises. In fact, most of these factories were small, and even the great 'cotton lords' spread their resources over several small factories, rather than one large one. Examples of such factories were the well-known, but really rather small establishments of Samuel Oldknow and William Ashworth.[70] Oldknow spent £90 in 1783 renovating a mill in Stockport; in it he kept £57 17s 11d worth of machinery and £261 17s 11d worth of materials, and used this to prepare yarn which he then put out to domestic weavers. From his mill at Anderton, he employed 59 outweavers. By 1786, he was employing 300 weavers with 500 looms from his Stockport mill and 159 weavers at Anderton; in 1804 he had 550 workers at his Mellor mill. Ashworth, at his New Eagley mill, in 1793 employed 50 operatives spinning and carding.[71] Then there were the giants. McConnel and Co. in 1795 had an overall capital of £1,769 13s 1d, and in 1802 employed 312 operatives.[72] In the 1770s and 1780s the Arkwright and Strutt mills were similar to a number of other 'large' establishments in the period.

They were multi-storeyed buildings with 300–500 workers each and valued at £3,000–£5,000. Each mill had its own water wheel, and the group was enlarged by building similar mills close by.[73] Arkwright's first Nottingham mill in 1772 employed 300 and his Cromford mill employed 200.[74] But by 1783 his second Cromford mill employed 800 and his Manchester mill (in 1780) 600.

There survived, however, a number of little workshops with a carding engine, a few spinning jennies, and hand-, horse-, or rudimentary water-power mechanisms. The room-letting or floor-letting system used in Manchester and Stockport was common, and one mill in Stockport had twenty-seven masters employing 250 people in total.[75] These were often small businesses which later grew much bigger. Just as often, however, they were second or third mills owned by risk-spreading and diversifying firms. A firm maintaining several mills of varying scale could experiment with new techniques either in its larger factory or in one or two of its smaller mills. Either way, it would avoid the risk of losing everything. Overall averages confirm this picture. As late as 1835, Ure calculated that the average cotton mill employed 175.5 people. Averages in the larger centres in 1816 were 244 for Glasgow, 184.5 for Carlisle, 418 for Stockport, 211.4 for Mansfield, and 115.5 for Preston. In Manchester forty-three mills employed together 12,940. Of these, seven employed fewer than 100, fourteen employed 100–200, and thirteen 200–400, and only five 400–700.[76]

Concentration of capital

The increase in the size of cotton mills during the first half of the nineteenth century appeared to be a classic case of the capitalist concentration observed and predicted by Marx. Indeed, Engels in 1844 wrote of this ever-increasing concentration of capital in fewer and fewer hands. From the 1830s the small man was being 'squeezed out' as the 'optimum size of firm increased'. But this simplified the picture too much. For in the second quarter of the nineteenth century, capital and credit were available to small as well as to large producers. Even by the 1840s there was still a substantial core of small producers in the industry in Manchester; the average primary-process firm in Manchester in 1841 employed 260 hands, and a quarter of all firms employed fewer than 100.[77]

True, large firms could claim economies of scale, but they were just as vulnerable as the small ones to stoppages, insolvency and recession. Before the 1830s new technology was equally accessible to small producers and large: small firms took advantage of small steam engines, spinning mules, power looms, water power and traditional building methods. The self-acting mule in the 1830s, like the water frame in the 1770s and 1780s, was built to the glory of the cotton lords,[78] but in practice most of the self-actors were built on a relatively small scale and they did not come into their own until the 1860s. At the end of the day, 'some giants were as labour intensive as some pygmies, and some pygmies were as power intensive as some giants'.[79]

Our definitions of size are also relative. For the range between small and large was what really mattered for most firms.

> Firms employing 150 operatives or less, in terms of shares of the total labour force fell from 28.5 per cent in 1815 to only 12.5 per cent in 1841, while firms employing 500 operatives and above saw their share of the total labour force fall from 44.24 per cent in 1815 to 31.68 in 1841. The minimum efficient size is 151 and the optimum unit was a medium sized firm employing between 151 and 500 operatives.

When the prospects and fate of the moderately-sized producers are included, we see that the decline of the small firm was not gradual. It was, perhaps, as rapid as Engels claimed, for if the cotton lords did not take over, moderately-sized but definitely larger firms did. There was a rapid switch in the 1820s between small rented units sharing the same factory premises and larger units which occupied a whole factory.[80]

Conclusions

The coexistence of these many different manufacturing structures across the textile industries and even within the cotton industry itself reveals a great deal about the multiple directions of industrialization. There was obviously no through road to the factory system.

The variety in forms of work organization before the main period of industrialization continued afterwards. The forms taken by these structures may have been influenced by the relationships of power and subordination within and between firms. They certainly also owed much to the social context in which work organization developed. Community solidarity established through forms of landholding, long industrial traditions and customs, and the relative supply and militancy of the local labour force certainly did affect in a multitude of ways the nature of original and later manufacturing structures, as well as the scale of production and the local reception of technical change. It is equally true, however, that markets, monopolistic or competitive pressures, profitability and social status all imposed their own discipline on the subsequent directions taken by manufacturing structures. Artisan, putting-out and factory systems were all shaped during the course of industrialization and all found their own most effective means of responding to the pressure for profits through some combination of increased intensity of work, the division of labour, sweating, mechanization and reorganization. Technologies and the labour forces using them were developed and adapted to these pressures, whether mechanized or not, skilled or unskilled.

11

THE TEXTILE INDUSTRIES: TECHNOLOGIES

The textile industries form a fascinating terrain for the acting out of the human drama of technological change. The technologies fundamental to any production process interacted in a fatal way with the lives of men and women at work, and the community around them. New technologies meant the pinnacles of wealth and success to some; destitution to others. The social divisions they created might appear within one small community, or provoke a great regional split. New technologies were resisted or welcomed; they were stamped with age and gender as were the older methods which had gone before. They created some new jobs, but they also meant unemployment in a whole new way to many others. New methods, new machines did not just mean temporary bad times; they could eradicate a trade and with it the assumption of work for the rest of a person's lifetime. Along with this, the skills which formed a part of any technology were developed, cherished, protected and fought for. With this in view, we turn to the story of technological change in the eighteenth-century textile industries.

Cloth production from time immemorial relied on the two basic crafts of spinning and weaving. Both crafts were practised by enormous numbers of men and women in town and country. Of the weavers we know something. Their craft was recognized, organized into guilds or at the least informal associations, and apprenticeship regulations were enforced. By tradition the weavers were men, with some capital, for their looms were pieces of machinery, but women too practised the craft to a small extent. Of the spinners we know virtually nothing, for these on the whole were women, working full-time or part-time for the market and for family consumption. Their labour was unorganized and unapprenticed; it relied on the dexterity of their hands and a small tool, the distaff or a simple spinning wheel.

Spinning and weaving were both mechanized over the course of the eighteenth and early nineteenth centuries. We hear much of the ingenious machines contrived to carry out these processes, but little of the implications these machines carried for the skills and livelihoods of their working people. Few historians attempt the difficult task of unravelling the precise social, economic or even political implications of a new technique or change in production method. But a description of production processes and their changes in the eighteenth century is vital to our understanding of most social and artisan political movements then and in the early nineteenth century. One historian has argued this for the case of shipbuilding in the eighteenth century:

> The adze, rasp, clave, auger, chisel, hammer, maul, mallet, mooter, saw . . . will suggest a discussion of the degree of specialization, the dangers, the ownership, the employment of these instruments and hence to the social realities of production.[1]

Innovation affected the textile industries long before the eighteenth century. The foot-driven spinning wheel introduced in the sixteenth and seventeenth centuries eventually superseded hand spinning and increased productivity by one-third. The Dutch loom allowed for four times the previous output, while the knitting frame could produce ten times that of the old handknitter. Even the humble flying shuttle doubled productivity. Of course this was small game beside the impressive performance of those spinning frames and mules which by the end of the century had increased productivity by a hundred times.[2]

SPINNING

The most striking series of technical changes across the textile industries in the eighteenth century was centred on spinning in the cotton and then the linen industries. Until this time, women spinners were at a premium, something not, however, reflected in their wages. The three machines which revolutionized the process were Arkwright's water frame, patented in 1769, Hargreaves's jenny, patented in 1770, and subsequently Crompton's mule which came into general use in the 1780s. The invention and early innovation of spinning technology is usually viewed from hindsight as the big break into powered factory production. But if we look historically at these inventions, there was no such break. The chronology of their early development shows us techniques developed out of, and adapted to, basic domestic industry. Although, in some cases, like the jenny, the machine was invented in a factory unit, this was fortuitous, for it was first widely used in domestic and workshop settings. The application of power, associating these machines with factory organization, was another step in the process of diffusion. It was definitely a step distinct from the original invention and use of the machines. Let us now turn anew to the chronology of invention in the textile manufacture, with an eye as much to the continuity as to the novelty of this technical change.

The water frame and jenny complemented each other for some time, for the water frame, though it made possible the use of cotton rather than linen for warp as well as weft, still could not produce a uniformly even yarn. It

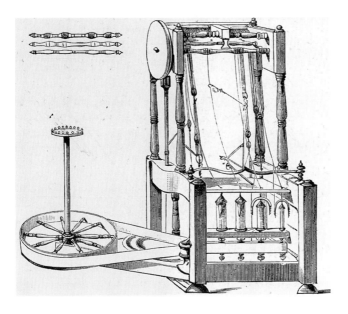

Plate 10 The Arkwright water frame, patented 1769 (Mary Evans Picture Library)

was furthermore, on Arkwright's decision, built on a large scale in water-powered mills. The jenny, however, produced an even yarn, but one too soft to be used for warps, and it was widely worked by hand in the home. The mule, initially also a cottage and hand-powered technology, produced a smooth, strong, fine yarn. All three machines were used until the end of the century, though the jenny was far and away the most important. Colquhoun's estimates of 1789 indicate 310,000 water-frame spindles, 700,000 mule spindles, and 1,400,000 jenny spindles. By 1812, however, the mule had taken over with 4,209,570 spindles as against the 310,516 on water frames and only 158,880 on jennies.[3]

The original Hargreaves jenny was too small to use in woollen spinning, but an improved version spread rapidly in the 1770s. The small jenny factories which spread from cotton into wool had a substantial impact on output, but an ambiguous reception. Where in 1715 seven combers and twenty-five weavers kept 250 worsted spinners employed, hand jennies reduced the weaving–spinning ratio to one weaver to four spinners. In Yorkshire both the jenny and the carding engine were introduced by domestic spinners. The jenny came into general use in Leeds in the 1780s, and by 1793 Benjamin Gott had three or four dozen of these in his large mill at Bean Ing. By this time, however, objections were being raised about the jenny's impact on employment, and in 1806 a group of merchants and master clothiers in Saddleworth met to pass a resolution opposing the factory system in woollen spinning and weaving.[4] In the West Country, until the 1790s, it was only on the fringes of the industry that such machinery was accepted. This was an area which, unlike Yorkshire, was not expanding, and spinning occupied women over a wide agricultural area which offered no alternative employment. The jenny was, on the whole, accepted more easily in the North, and did not pose such a big threat to employment as in the South, for many in the North spun worsted, and the machine was not used for this.[5]

The new spinning technology centred on the jenny was developed within the context of domestic, small workshop and proto-factory production. There was no striking and revolutionary break between mechanized factory technology and cottage manufacture. The jenny could, of course, be worked in the home and was still run by women.[6] It was, however, usually jennies of fewer than twenty spindles which were used at home, and the technique was widely used on this scale. And this was so, in spite of the fact that Hargreaves had actually developed his improved jenny within a factory in Hockley near Nottingham. This factory was owned by Hargreaves's partner, Thomas James, and, though the jenny was cheaper to build and simpler in design than the cottage stocking frame, it was initially kept within a mill which was operated as a 'safe box'. Only trusted workmen were admitted to it, and there were no windows on the bottom floor.

During the 1770s the James–Hargreaves mill was rival to Arkwright's mill. The jennies were also quickly absorbed into the Nottingham hosiers' workshops and warehouses. These hosiers' business premises

> consisted of a few rooms, or perhaps the whole of a substantial house near the centre of Nottingham. The first distinct warehouses were being built by the 'sixties. Apart from accommodation for stock and keeping accounts, the hosiers' premises contained some machinery: several stocking frames to supply urgent or special demands, twisting mills, warping mills and sometimes silk-throwing machines, no doubt based on Lombe's principle. In the country districts, a handful of hosiers also operated fulling mills. It was not difficult to add another room to accommodate a few jennies.[7]

But the jenny which spread around Lancashire at the time and later in the woollen districts was a cottage and small factory technology. Larger jennies were used in the so-called jenny factories. These jennies became linked to machine carding, and it was the small factories containing these machines which spread so rapidly at the time.

Just why the jenny was taken up in the cotton manufacture raises a series of questions about the connections between the organization of the industry and technical change. Stephen Marglin argued that there were no special technical reasons for the factory system; the factory system simply guaranteed to the manufacturer a higher proportion of the surplus and any gains to be had through increased labour productivity. We can take the opposite line, and ask if there was anything inherent in the pre-factory organization of the cotton industry to encourage the introduction of new techniques. The answer to that is yes, but the reasons are not, at first sight, obvious. First, the putting-out system itself did not create any incentives for the introduction of the spinning jenny. For merchants and factors did not control the intensity or efficiency of their labour unless they controlled markets and prices. In the Lancashire cotton industry there was no all-pervasive industrial concentration. Competitive prices were imposed on merchants as well as upon workers; the worker had outlets for his yarn other than any individual factor or merchant. In this setting the merchants had no special price incentive to introduce the spinning jenny, though they did stand to gain from higher and readier supplies of yarn. The ones who stood to gain most were those who owned and ran the spinning jennies themselves. It was the cottage producers and those who ran small centralized workshops who reaped the first gains in efficiency from the jenny, and they did so until the merchants and factors saw the gains to be had through setting up their own larger jenny factories. It was not the putting-out system itself which brought the jenny to the cotton manufacture, but a dispersed industrial structure which created opportunities for the direct producers to reap some of the gains from increasing their efficiency.

The mule was only a development on the jenny, and it too was initially used at home and in small factories. The improvement made was simply the addition of roller drafting to the spinning jenny. This could have been applied earlier and equally successfully to the jenny, but the jenny was not developed in its own right.[8] The mule was also used initially on a putting-

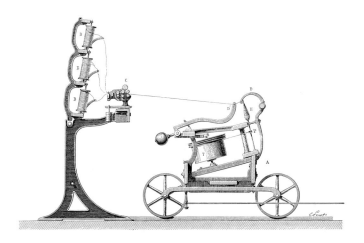

Plate 11 'Modern' spinning mule (Mary Evans Picture Library)

Plate 12 Spinning mule (Mary Evans Picture Library)

out basis. It was, however, more expensive than the jenny, and, though it remained an integral part of the domestic system until the 1790s, it was also quickly moved into mule-shed factories. Still, these were small enterprises when compared with Arkwright's warp-spinning mills.[9] Until the late 1780s mules were only built on a scale up to 144 spindles, and each mule was manually operated one at a time. It was the application of water power in 1790 which substantially increased productivity, for this allowed the installation of mules in pairs, one in front of the spinner and one behind. Steam power was applied in the same way later in the 1790s.[10]

Machine spinning came much more slowly to the woollen industry than it did to either cotton or worsted, largely because of important basic differences in materials and necessary technical processes. Woollen goods were made from short-fibred wool, worsted from long; and wool was carded while worsted and cotton were combed. The object of carding was to combine all the fibres so they would interlock or 'felt', while combing was meant to lay all the fibres in the same direction. The upshot of these different materials and preparatory processes was to affect spinning technology. The object in spinning both worsted and cotton was to elongate and to stretch fibres straight, thereby continuing the combing and roving processes; in the woollen manufacture, the object was not to straighten the fibres, but to preserve their natural curl, while also laying these fibres in the direction of the length of the thread. Spinning was not to impair the felting process

240

started in the carding of the wool. The mule was eventually adapted to this task, but even in the early decades of the nineteenth century

the mule has not, till lately, been in much repute for spinning woollen yarn, and the jenny is still thought to spin better yarn; but we have no doubt that when certain modifications are made, it will become a much more perfect method than the jenny, being much less dependent on the discretion and dexterity of the spinner.[11]

We thus see that there were good technical reasons for the different receptions offered to new spinning techniques. The jenny and, later, the mule were much greater threats to woollen spinners than they were to worsted spinners. But the worsted spinners faced the much greater hiatus of Arkwright's water frame, for, after the combing process, the processes of the worsted and cotton manufacture were very similar. Arkwright's water frame, developed for the cotton manufacture, was quickly adapted to worsteds.

Roller or water-frame spinning, invented by Wyatt in 1738 and brought into use by Arkwright, had a revolutionary impact on all three processes of carding, roving and spinning. The water frame could carry out all these processes. It was, furthermore, driven by power long before the mule was used with anything but handpower. The frame could also produce the necessary twist for warps of superior strength and wiry smoothness; it was used to make water twist of low counts cheaper than mule twist. This was a big advantage for power-loom weaving, and so the technique, in spite of other defects, was further developed to become the efficient and widely-practised process of throstle spinning.

Arkwright's water frame has been virtually identified with the origins of the factory system. It has been assumed that this was a machine which required a large capital outlay, a source of power and centralized production. But in fact it was originally designed as a small machine turned by hand and capable of being used in the home. It was Arkwright's patent which enclosed the machine within a factory, had it built only to large-scale specifications, and henceforth refused the use of it to anyone without a thousand-spindle mill. A model of the original water frame is in the Science Museum of London. It

spins beautifully and shows that the water frame could have been built in small units, placed in cottages and turned by hand. In other words, it could have been used like the jenny as a domestic spinning machine. One member of the Arkwright's partnership, I suspect it was Arkwright himself, for it seems in character, must have realized that if this had happened they would have lost control of the patent, for everyone would have copied it and built their own machine in the privacy of their own homes. By restricting the licences to units of a thousand spindles, it became economic only when they were erected in a water-powered mill. This was a vital decision in the development of the textile industry and of the Industrial Revolution which never seems to have been recognized before.[12]

But Arkwright's 100 per cent rate of profit led all to believe that the machinery and the factory system were as one. The jenny and the mule were still popular, however, and continued to be developed in their own right, for the water frame could not spin high-quality yarn or the fine weft; and machinery was soon developed which could take over the hand preparatory processes for jenny and mule spinning. Combing machinery for the worsted industry and the billy which carded cotton into rovings gave renewed advantage to the mule and the jenny.[13] And the mule, easily adapted to power, soon posed a threat to large country warp-spinning mills.

In spite of the association generally assumed between the development of motive power and the primary innovations of the textile industry, it was actually the case that steam power had a very belated effect. As Von Tunzelmann has argued, even in the precocious cotton industry all the technological breakthroughs in cotton spinning were originally developed for other forms of power – hand, horse and water. The application of steam power on any sizeable scale can be charted only from the last years of the eighteenth century. By 1800 at the most 1,500–2,000 horsepower in the form of steam engines was used to turn textile machinery and accounted for up to one-quarter of the cotton processed in that year.[14] Hand-operated machinery was still common in carding and spinning until well after 1815. The mule was hand-worked until the 1790s, and the handloom dominated weaving until after 1815. No power was applied in bleaching and printing until the later 1790s.[15]

The spinning of silk, unlike that of other textiles, was mechanized and centralized from the beginning of the eighteenth century. Some of the stages for making the organzine used for the silk warp were amenable to mechanization. The various stages involved winding the silk from the skeins upon bobbins in winding machines; sorting it into different qualities; spinning and twisting each individual thread in a mill; bringing together on fresh bobbins two or more threads already spun or twisted; twisting two or more threads together by means of the mill; and sorting the skein of twist or organzine according to fineness. The winding and twisting stages were both mechanized. The first was done on a bevelled wheel and attended to by children. 'The constant attendance of children upon this winding machine is requisite, in order to join the ends of any threads which may be broken in winding, and when the skeins are exhausted, to place new ones upon the swifts.'[16] The twisting was done on the throwing mill. Large twisting mills on Thomas Lombe's design contained machines in a circular frame about 15 feet in diameter. But the machine was basically a large version of a hand technique.

The great mills for twisting silk, originally introduced by Messrs. Lombe, though very complicated, are simple in their operations, because the complexity arises from the great number of spindles which are actuated by the same movement, every one of which produces its effect independent of the other.

A similar small version of the machine was used with only thirteen spindles as opposed to the multiples of eighty-four in the large silk mills. The small-scale machine was

> intended to be turned by hand, a method which is too expensive for this country, but is common in the south of France, where many artisans purchase their silk in the raw state, and employ their wives or children to prepare it by these machines.[17]

This chronology of the early development and diffusion of the new spinning technology shows us a much closer integration with rural manufacture and artisan or domestic industry than we generally perceive. In the face of resistance to new technology and the pull of the older methods, the obvious question is why the new machines spread in the first place. When we turn to the standard economic cost-benefit analysis, it seems unlikely that there was much push to the new technology from wage rates, for spinners were notoriously ill-paid. Fixed capital costs were also unlikely to provide any incentive. But labour costs, rather than wage rates, and capital costs, including circulating capital, probably were a factor, for labour costs were increased by embezzlement and poor quality; circulating capital costs by delays, costs of intermediaries and the uncertainties of supply. But the much more positive inducement was increases in labour productivity. The gains to be had by simply incorporating a relatively inexpensive machine with x number of spindles into a household which formerly had only one or two one-spindle wheels were obvious.

But it is also clear that the opportunities for such gains in productivity within the old framework of domestic industry were not really exploited beyond a very short period. Their potential for large-scale production was obvious, and factors, merchants and substantial manufacturers soon adapted their warehouses and workshops to take the new machines. Productivity gains in cotton became increasingly associated with scale and factory organization, and the pull of such productivity gains provided the prime mover of innovation; the prospect of windfall gains, not the spectre of falling profit margins, lured cotton manufacturers into changing their methods.

The effect of the new spinning techniques on employment and on the division of labour varied enormously among regions and branches of the textile industry. We shall look at these effects in comparison with those of other processes later in the chapter. Now we turn to innovation in the weaving and finishing processes.

WEAVING

Few improvements were made in weaving, apart from the flying shuttle, until the introduction of the power loom. The power loom was used to a certain extent in cotton at the end of the eighteenth century, but did not spread to wool and worsteds until the early to mid-nineteenth. The flying shuttle, however, had an important impact on the productivity of existing looms. By the 1770s there existed a broad and a narrow loom. The broad loom made cloth up to a hundred inches wide and needed two operators, while the narrow loom made up to half that width. The flying shuttle both increased productivity and in broad-cloth manufacture did away with one of the operators. Its other major contribution was to make it common to weave woollen cloth with a design.[18] Though introduced in 1733, the improvement was not widely used until the 1760s and 1770s, and in fact met resistance in East Anglia and Lancashire. It was, however, well received in Yorkshire where it eased the weaving of broad cloth.[19]

The really important weaving innovations of the eighteenth and early nineteenth centuries affected the silk manufacture first. Even here, weaving was not mechanized until well into the nineteenth century for largely technical reasons, for applying power to silk weaving would not save a great deal of labour. The weaver could not attend several looms at once and under any conditions would have to spend a great deal of time on 'picking the porry', that is, removing the roughness and inequalities in the warp threads. Handweaving, however, involved varying degrees of skill depending on the fineness and design of the product.

> Plain weaving is thus seen to be a very simple operation. A certain degree of proficiency in the art may doubtless be quickly and easily attained, but much practice and attention are nevertheless required, in order to form a dexterous weaver, so as to enable him to produce well woven fabrics, and to accomplish within a given time such a portion of work as will earn for him a competent subsistence.[20]

Improvements were made in figured weaving in the early nineteenth century with the introduction of the 'drawboy' in 1807 to replace one of the weavers on the complicated drawloom. And by the 1820s the Jacquard loom had been introduced from France. The Jacquard, however, was initially popular only in the Spitalfields silk industry, and the woollen industry was slow to recognize the attributes of the new machine. The Jacquard spread first into the Scottish carpet manufacture and thence by 1822 into the Coventry ribbon-weaving industry. It became part of the West Riding woollen industry only in 1827.[21]

Ribbon weaving was first done on a single handloom making one ribbon at a time; the Dutch loom, which wove several ribbons at once, was introduced in 1770, but was widely used only from the early nineteenth century. The Dutch engine loom, in spite of its name, was worked by the hands with treadles for the feet like a common loom, but each weft occupied a separate shuttle, and the shuttles were impelled by an instrument called a ladder. Male and female journeyhands who had completed a five- to seven-year apprenticeship were traditionally employed on the single handlooms, but the new Dutch looms were generally worked by skilled men.[22] The only strike heard of before the end of the Napoleonic Wars in the Coventry trade was occasioned by a journeyhand who wished his wife to be employed on a Dutch loom. The strike against employing the woman was successful, and over this period no woman was allowed to use the Dutch loom. In the period after 1815, when the hold of the larger manufacturers was challenged by small capitalists employing cheap labour, women were put on to the machines. The larger manufacturers only survived by increasing mechanization, introducing silk throwing on their premises and putting up handloom factories containing improved engine looms.[23] But in the Spitalfields silk industry and the West Country woollen industry, women did use the Dutch or engine loom. Attempts were made to exclude them from the use of this more advanced technology, but always at times of high unemployment and crisis in the industries.

Powered weaving was slow to come, not only to silk and wool, but even to cotton and linen. For the power loom took a long time to perfect. Patented in 1789, it was not until 1813 that it assumed its traditional form, and it was still defective by 1833.[24] Its development depended upon some general considerations such as the nature and property of the raw materials from which the yarns were manufactured, the qualities of yarn to be woven, the system of preparation of warp and weft for the yarn, and the organization of industry and attitudes of operatives to the consequences of the new techniques.[25] But basic mechanical imperfections still plagued the machine. The necessity of dressing the webs from time to time after they were put into the looms made it impossible for one person to do more than attend to one loom. By 1813, however, Horrocks's improved power loom was combined with Radcliffe's dressing frame. Subsequently, some enthusiastic contemporaries estimated that a boy or girl could attend to two looms and produce three times as much as the best handweaver.

The slow introduction of the power loom was to a large extent a problem of fitting this technology to other processes mechanized earlier. The power loom produced for only low-quality markets. The handloom continued to dominate the fine muslin trade, but was also a formidable rival for plain and coarse goods because of the early technical difficulties of the power loom.

In 1813 there were not more than 100 dressing machines and 2,400 power looms in use, and there were approximately 240,000 handlooms.[26] Productivity differentials were difficult to assess. In 1819 there was one weaver to one or two looms, but the average ratio of power to hand output ranged between two to one and three to one. By 1829 the number of handlooms had fallen to 225,000,[27] and power looms had increased to 55,000. But output per handloom had increased by 25–30 per cent. This was probably the result of a combination of two factors, the application of more labour to each handloom and technical improvements. The dandy loom, one such technical improvement, was a species of handloom operated by a combination of mechanical and hand movements; it was alleged to keep pace with the power loom.[28] Between 1819 and 1842, however, the average speed of the power loom had increased from 60 to 140 picks per minute. In 1820 a good handweaver could weave 172,000 picks per week, and a power-loom weaver with two looms could weave as much as 604,800 picks per week. In 1825 a power weaver with two looms and no assistance could weave 1,000,000 picks per week. By 1835 a weaver could attend four looms with the assistance of a tenter and weave 1,759,000 picks per week.[29]

FINISHING TECHNIQUES

Perhaps the most celebrated improvements in the eighteenth-century textile industries were in the finishing processes – cropping and shearing in the woollen manufacture. For it was the artisans from these trades who, along with some handloom weavers, framework knitters and worsted combers, led the celebrated Luddite machine-breaking episodes of the early years of the nineteenth century.

The mechanization of finishing processes was conducted against a background of urban skilled workers with similar characteristics. The shearman worked not at home, but in finishing shops, generally owned by independent master dressers. The gig mill mechanized the process of raising the nap but with poor results until improvements spread in the eighteenth century. Where it formerly took one man 88–100 hours to raise one piece by hand, with a machine one man and two boys could do the same job in 12 hours. Once the nap on the cloth was raised, all the surface wool had then to be removed by a process called shearing or cropping. The original shears were two large, flat, steel blades bent into a circular bow. These were worked by two shearmen whose skill consisted in operating them in a regular and parallel motion so that every part of the surface was equally cropped. Towards the end of the century a shearing frame was introduced, which simply fitted the shears into a frame moved by means of a carriage over the cloth. The machine was not very effective and in fact still required 'great care and attention to make the different cuttings join, in order to cut equally over the whole surface'.[30] The frame was used, however, and was improved by the early nineteenth century into a perpetual shearing machine, and then into a rotary machine.

A similar spirit of artisan skill and militancy existed among the cotton calico printers. But their struggle with mechanization was deflected by geographical division. The skilled calico printers centred in London, who refused to use the new cylinder printing processes, were bypassed by manufacturers such as Peel who established new centres of calico printing in Lancashire. But skilled calico printers there, too, soon grew proud and militant, and calico printing was moved to the countryside where new techniques were invented to tap a largely female labour force.

THE IMPACT OF TEXTILE MACHINERY

This exposition of the course of technical change in textiles opens up a series of issues only infrequently raised by economic historians. The main issue concerns the effect which the new technologies had on employment, skills and the division of labour. Secondly one needs to ask how closely-linked changes in work organization were with these new technologies.

We have no means of quantifying the effects of spinning innovations on employment. To some extent we can gauge the effects through the regions and industries which experienced high levels of resistance to the new machinery. But this is not enough by itself, for resistance was a political act requiring consciousness and hope. Technological unemployment could also entail a sense of hopelessness and passive acceptance. There was, in the early days of the jenny at least, less distress among the cotton spinners than the woollen spinners. Cotton was more localized, and the spinners had other

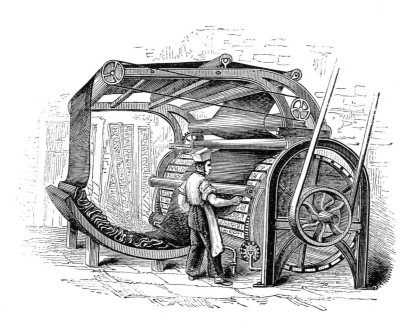

Plate 13 Gig mill (Ann Ronan Picture Library)

Plate 14 Broad perpetual shearing frame (Ann Ronan Picture Library)

branches of the manufacture to turn to in a region of rapidly growing trade. Wool, on the other hand, was diffused throughout the country, and the lot of spinners in declining agricultural districts was much more difficult.[31]

The economic theory of technological change and the economic historians who write within its framework rarely have any explanation to offer for the waves of resistance to machinery which swept through the textile industries in the eighteenth century and in the early nineteenth. The orthodox economist usually assumes, if he or she cannot prove, that technological change creates more, not less, employment; hence the actions of Luddites and anti-machinery protests of workers are seen to be irrational, or at least mistaken, or are taken to be a means of expressing other demands.

Economists certainly recognize 'factor bias' in innovation, that is, that innovations could be more or less labour-intensive; but most agree to a favourable overall economic impact. Few, apart from J. R. Hicks, accede to the possibility and even the likelihood, first discussed by Ricardo, that rapid technical change in the first part of the nineteenth century may well have called for the transfer of resources from circulating capital (or wage goods) to fixed capital, and so may simultaneously have reduced overall employment while raising profits.[32] Did this happen in the Industrial Revolution? Economic historians only reply with very tentative empirical estimates of aggregative economic categories – contributions of capital, labour and the

248

'residual' (the catch-all that includes technological change). The more careful among them at least concede the dubiety of conclusions drawn from such aggregate data, and counsel the study of individual innovations.

But on individual innovations they also prefer economic orthodoxy. Von Tunzelmann, summing up his survey of a number of innovations, plumps for long-term considerations of profitability rather than short-term cost-cutting as the inducement to most eighteenth-century innovation. Where labour appeared to be adversely affected by technical change, he argues, it was largely in those industries which had been bypassed by new technology. The Yorkshire cloth dressers, he concedes, did have a quarrel with machinery, but they were a small minority.[33]

Conclusions like this are all, however, based on the cotton industry, not the woollen, on the experience of the North, and not of the South. They give a misleading picture of the impact of technological change, one which consigns to a netherworld all the spinners, weavers and cloth finishers of the much larger eighteenth-century woollen industry. And large declining industrial regions of the South and the Midlands, and even agricultural regions where women's spinning, knitting and lacemaking formed a substantial part of the local economy, have no part in our current optimistic histories of technological change. In the textile industry alone, the spinners in the eighteenth century and the handweavers in the nineteenth were the majority. Spinning and weaving machinery did substitute directly for their labour, and, though we may well argue that hand processes continued, they did so in competition with machinery, and so at lower wages and more intensive work.

It is fashionable now for economic historians and even social historians to argue that most technology was really labour-using, not labour-saving. Indeed, this book too stresses the labour intensity of many processes. But the upshot of the argument should *not* lie with dismissing the existence of a machinery question either in the eighteenth century or in the nineteenth. For the high levels of resistance to new technology in older or declining industries, and even in the new cotton industry with its meteoric growth path, indicate that many were losing jobs or suffering wage reductions in the major manufacturing industry in Britain at the time.

Some might point to inconsistency in such diverse claims. But they are those who prefer aggregative unilinear analysis. The historian with some sensitivity to the differences over industries, regions, the economic cycle and the labour force finds no such inconsistency. Many did lose their jobs with the coming of technological innovation, but the labour of many others also became more intensive. The fixed capital of textile entrepreneurs may have increased only slowly, but the 'capital' of skilled workers – their traditional crafts and skills – was being undermined by dilution.

It is not enough, as Habakkuk himself argued, to point to the labour intensity of British industry. What is equally at issue is the skill intensity of this industry. And any effect of new spinning or weaving technology must depend on *whose* employment was reduced and whose increased; it must depend on the impact on the division of labour.

NEW TECHNIQUES, SKILLS, DIVISION OF LABOUR

Though much of the new textile technology was established in continuity with handworking and domestic production, it did change the sexual division of labour. The original jenny was best suited to being worked by children. The small country jennies of about twelve spindles had a horizontal wheel and a treadle 'which required an awkward and constrained posture'.

> The awkward posture required to spin on them was discouraging to grown up people, while they saw with a degree of surprise, children from nine to twelve years of age, manage them with dexterity, which brought plenty into families that were before overburthened with children.[34]

But a vertical wheel was substituted for the horizontal, and the treadle was replaced by a simple contrivance managed by the hand. This improved jenny, generally equipped with sixty to eighty spindles, spread widely in the eighteenth century, and was mainly operated by women. The water frame, similarly, was run by children and girls. Larger jennies of up to 120 spindles and large handmules were built in the 1790s, but these needed male operatives, and, as men cost more than half as much again as women to employ, this was not a popular alternative. 'Thus so long as low wage female labour could easily be found there was not much temptation to search for other sources of power.'[35]

Many spinners took readily to the new jennies, for these were small enough to use at home and helped enormously to increase the output of yarn. For others, who could not acquire the new jennies, there were lower wages, but also the alternative of more employment in carding and preparing wool. The high or at least decent wages of some early jenny spinners soon attracted more workers, and wages fell. By 1780 there were complaints that 'women who had been earning 8s to 9s a week on jennies of 24 spindles' could now earn only from 4s to 6s a week. And bigger jennies with more than eighty spindles proved a much more substantial threat. Larger jennies took away women's jobs and were furthermore located outside the home in the new jenny factories. The early jennies were a part of the domestic system, the machines of the poor; the large ones were monopolized by capitalists. As a contemporary petition put it, 'that the Jenneys are in the Hands of the Poor, and the Patent Machines are generally in the Hands of the Rich; and that the work is better manufactured by small Jenneys than by large ones'.[36]

It was during its domestic industry phase that mule spinning too became a male occupation and acquired craft status. When the mule was still manually operated considerable strength was needed for pushing the carriage back and forth. After power was applied women could be used, but substantial physical stamina was still required in order to maintain a given pace of work with co-ordination and attentiveness for twelve to thirteen hours a day. The mule also required considerably more skill than the jenny. 'To one accustomed to operating the jenny as Crompton was, the spinning on his new machine would be a work of art, a display of skill and judgement.'[37] The application of power to the mule did not mean automatic working: it only turned the rollers and drove the carriage and spindles during the spinning action. The operative still had to revolve the spindles and guide the spun yarn on the spindles in the form of a cop by the use of his hands as the carriage made its inward run. The spinner had to co-ordinate three operations simultaneously. First he had to push the carriage towards the roller beam. Second, by means of a faller shaft and wire he had to control the winding of yarn on to a cop chase so as to form a correctly shaped cop. Third, he had to turn the spindles by means of the fly so as to wind up the yarn being released by the inward motion of the spindles. He must avoid breaking the yarn, yet never permit it to go slack. After forty years of rigorous development along a number of different avenues, the spinning mule still required the continued attendance of a skilled operative.[38] Other factors which, from its early domestic phase, helped to restrict the machine to a predominantly male workforce were the substantial amounts of capital required to buy or build it, and the skill to maintain it. Still, women could and did learn the skills and were quite widely used even into the 1830s on the smaller mules.[39]

The possible threat posed by the more widespread introduction of women in mule spinning was reinforced by manufacturers' search for a self-acting mule. The spinners after 1824 formed a close-knit union. But an earlier existence of the union manifested itself in 1810 and 1818 in strikes over piece rates and women workers. The membership of the union in Glasgow alone was estimated at 800, 'enough to exercise direct control over several thousand dependent kin in factories'.[40] The control exercised by these spinners was what prompted a consortium of mill owners to seek the invention of a self-acting mule, finally achieved in 1830 by Richard Roberts. Roberts's improvement was a new design of headstock which incorporated a system of closed-loop feedback control. But in spite of manufacturers' hopes of using cheaper labour, the spinner still retained his tradesman status. His workload was lighter, but it was usual for him to continue to make manual adjustments throughout the course of each set of cops spun. He also had important social attributes (to be explored below) which still made it advantageous for employers to continue with their additional staffing arrangements. The self-actors could, however, be made with more spindles, and unions were prepared to accept these along with speed-up as the price of retaining the spinners' tradesman status.[41]

At the end of the eighteenth century spinning and weaving employed both skilled male tradesmen and women. As spinning passed out of the hands of female domestic workers, those in the linen trade turned increasingly to handweaving.[42] In the cotton industry, the warp-spinning mills also generated their own demand for less skilled weavers – the aged, women and children, and Irish migrants who wove the coarser grades of cloth. It was their employment which was threatened initially by the introduction of the power loom. The weaving of fine goods still primarily remained the preserve of the male craftworker. The skill of the Scottish linen weavers was turned to the production of fine muslins – several thousand looms in the Glasgow area which had formerly produced linen, silks, cambrics and lawns were changed over in the last decades of the eighteenth century to fine cottons, and the power loom was slow to spread in the area thanks to its unsuitability to the finer counts of yarn.[43] Such fine weaving was in some cases incorporated into the factory, but as skilled work on specially-developed hand machines. Oldknow, for example, introduced the manufacture of figured muslins, but these were made on newly-invented costly looms called drawing engines, worked by men assisted by boys.[44]

Specialization among products in weaving implied in effect a choice between factory production and domestic production. Until the mid-nineteenth century, production of fine muslins meant handlooms. This is borne out in a statement made by Kirkman Finlay before the Select Committee on Manufactures, Commerce and Shipping in 1833.

> A grand mistake exists in supposing that the power loom supplants the hand loom universally: the power loom used in Scotland manufactures a kind of goods in general, which the hand loom weaver of Scotland was not in the practice of working at all . . . Before power loom weaving was introduced at all in Scotland about the year 1814–15, the kind of goods generally manufactured by them were not manufactured at all in Scotland . . . I would also say that the hand loom weaver can work a great many things which it would not be the interest of any power loom manufacturer to make, especially all the finest goods, fancy goods of all kinds . . . it can never be the interest of any power loom manufacturer to make a kind of goods of which he cannot regularly and constantly dispose of a large quantity of the same kind.[45]

Baines, too, in the context of explaining wage differences, emphasized:

> There is . . . a distinction to be made among hand loom weavers according to the kind of goods on which they are employed. Those employed in weaving fancy articles, which require skill and care . . .

obtain much better wages than the weaver of plain goods . . . which require very little strength or care.[46]

Defects in the power loom as late as 1828 affecting the quality of the cloth mainly arose from a need for regular motion to draw the cloth forward as it was woven and for a simple means of varying the rate of take-up for the different qualities of fabric.[47]

TEXTILE TECHNOLOGY AND LABOUR RESISTANCE

Not only were technologies associated with specific gender categories, but there were widespread differences in their reception in workplace and community. Resistance to the introduction of new technologies was not confined to the factory age; it was also endemic to the early stages of industrialization. We have seen in Chapter 5 that such resistance was part of the story of industrial decline. But the textile industries experienced widespread differences in their patterns of technological diffusion and labour resistance. Power sources, product choice, employment structure and community relations all affected the extent to which a region took up, resisted or ignored any particular technical change. In some areas such as Essex the reaction to technical change was variable. The weavers there revolted against the factory system, but accepted the flying shuttle.[48] In Yorkshire the jenny and carding engine were introduced by domestic spinners in times of expanding employment, but combing machinery was resisted in the early nineteenth century. Spinning machinery was widely resisted in the West Country; in spite of this jennies were introduced over a wide area by the 1790s. And as noted before, Wiltshire and Somerset mounted fiercer resistance to finishing machinery than did Gloucestershire.[49] The prospect of such machinery arising in Wiltshire in fact lay behind the Wiltshire Outrages of 1802, and the shearmen received widespread public support from weavers who feared that they themselves would soon be resisting factory weaving, from small master dressers who feared the competition of large machine owners, and from some large clothiers who had other reasons for disliking the innovators.[50] The flying shuttle met a good reception in Yorkshire, but was widely resisted in East Anglia, Lancashire and the West Country. Even as late as 1822, an attempt to enforce the use of the flying shuttle along with a reduction in weaving wage rates led to widespread riots.[51]

The regional differences in the reception of new technology, at least in the woollen and worsted industries, have been attributed to the extent of social polarization. It is argued that the sharp polarity of master and man in the South contrasted with the socially more uniform small weaver communities of the North. This seems to have manifested itself in more forceful workers' resistance to machinery, instances of which we have noted already. In

Bradford-on-Avon in 1791 the mob destroyed an advanced scribbling machine. In Trowbridge in 1785 and between 1810 and 1813 workpeople rioted against the flying shuttle, as they did in West Wiltshire, postponing its introduction until 1816. Somerset clothiers who wanted their cloth dressed by the gig mill had to send it as far away as ninety miles.[52] Yet it is also true that protest against machinery was particularly strong in Lancashire, Yorkshire and the Midlands. Hargreaves's first spinning jenny was destroyed by a mob in 1767. A number of weavers were involved in these and later disturbances, and a contemporary wrote that the output of weft from jennies 'gave uneasiness to the country people, and the weavers were afraid lest the manufacturers should demand finer weft woven at the former prices, which occasioned some risings, and the jennies were opposed.' And in 1779 there were the celebrated jenny riots around Blackburn.[53] Hargreaves's move to the Midlands was not inspired by the prospect of a more docile labour force, for Nottingham in the second half of the eighteenth century had a well-known reputation for popular protest, riot and attacks on machinery,[54] all of which probably stemmed from the marked social divisions within the hosiery industry. Cloth-finishing machinery, stocking frames and power looms became the targets of disciplined Luddite attacks in 1811–12 across the West Riding, Nottinghamshire and Lancashire.

The Luddite movement was by and large based on the small local community and not on urban social structures. The personal, kinship and other social connections within a workshop culture or small quasi-peasant community created close bonds around the saboteurs. They were the necessary cover of secrecy for the highly disciplined 'guerrilla bands' moving from village to village at night that characterized Luddism in Nottinghamshire, Derbyshire and Leicestershire. Thompson in fact describes this Luddism as 'the nearest thing to a peasants' revolt of industrial workers'. The Luddites 'knew no national leadership or policy they could trust or identify with', and Luddism was always strongest in 'the local community and most coherent when engaged in limited industrial actions'.[55]

The act of machine-breaking, as we have seen, had a long history and was bound up in various degrees with the preservation of domestic industry, employment, and, especially in the case of the framework knitters, with the preservation of the customs, standards of quality and skill levels of the trade. In the case of framework knitting it was not the machine as such which provoked hostility, but the new malpractices of employers over apprenticeship and quality. This resistance to machinery, manifested in the form of machine-breaking and violent disputes, continued in the textile industries right through the 1830s, with particularly explosive episodes in Lancashire and Yorkshire in 1826 and 1829, and further bitter disputes in Scotland over self-acting mules throughout the following decade.

12

THE METAL AND
HARDWARE TRADES

The textile industries over the course of the eighteenth century developed a great diversity of structures of work organization, with which they incorporated a suitable variety of types of technical change. They form the historical archetype of the transition to factory production and steam-powered mechanical techniques. But this archetype or model of industrialization applied in the main period of the Industrial Revolution to only one part of the textile industry, namely cotton, and even here the transition was complicated and many-sided. There was much forward, backward and sideways motion as techniques were developed and manufacturing organization chosen. Textiles, moreover, provide the archetype for 'proto-industrialization', and in more ways than one. For cotton textiles made one transition from rural domestic manufacture to the factory system; while framework knitting made another transition from domestic manufacture to industrial involution or sweating.

The model of proto-industrialization has always concentrated by and large on textile production. But if we take the other great prototype of early industrial organization – Marx's model of manufactures – the industries appealed to were those containing workshops of skilled artisans, especially in the metal manufactures. As has already been said, Marx drew attention to the engineering workshop of the late eighteenth century and the early nineteenth for all the key features of 'manufactures'. He endorsed Andrew Ure's praise of the 'machine-factory' which displayed the division of labour in manifold gradations – the file, the drill, the lathe having each its different workmen in the order of skill. There was also the special prophetic feature that 'this workshop, the product of the division of labour in manufacture, produced in its turn – machines'.[1] We have argued that, in spite of his allusions to rural industry and centralized production, Marx conceived of manufactures in terms of a large workshop in the hands of a capitalist and organized on the basis of wage labour, with the rhythm of the production process still, however, dictated by the craft skill of the workers.

The correspondence between the metal trades and Marx's phase of manu-factures was limited in much the same way as was that between textiles and proto-industrialization. But the metal manufactures pose a different range of problems concerning work organization and technological change. In the first place the development of a technology dependent on manual skills was not, in the metal manufactures, in contradiction to the division of labour. For certainly manufacture was 'divided', but this did not necessarily make the labour on component parts any less skilful labour. The skill lay increasingly in the accuracy and precision manufacture of parts of an object which were then 'fitted' with others into the whole. However, the metal manufactures also transcend any simple connection with the large-scale handicraft workshop Marx imagined. Of course, these existed, but the size of units ranged from the outset from the very small domestic or garret manufacture through to the large factory, and so too did their forms of work organization.

The Birmingham hardware trades, Sheffield cutlery, the brass trades and engineering all conjure up images of a workshop culture, a high degree of skill, a large predominance of urban manufacture and the endurance of small-scale production.[2] The metal manufactures pose their own multifarious forms of specialization and development. These industries really were the locus of Nathan Rosenberg's 'continuum of small improvements', or anonymous technical change. They locked into and benefited from that innovative capital goods sector which Rosenberg credits with the saving of capital over the whole economy, and with providing the prime mechanism for technological diffusion. Here we will explore the origins, organization, technologies and labour forces of some of them.

What we will discover in delving into the metal manufactures in this period is the development of technologies based on skill, the division of labour and artisan independence on the one hand, and on the rise of the medium- and large-scale workshop or factory on the other. I will look at the significance of the metal manufactures to Britain's industrialization and explore some of the characteristics of skill, work organization and technology in the engineering trades. I shall then look at the role of the artisan and the development of various work settings in the trades. I will go on in the following chapter to discuss these issues in depth in the case of some of the Birmingham hardware trades, notably the 'toy' manufactures which established Birmingham's reputation as the 'other face' of Britain's Industrial Revolution.

METALS AND MANUFACTURE

One of the key technological principles assigned by Landes to the Industrial Revolution was the substitution of mineral for vegetable or animal raw materials, that is, the shift from a wood to a coal fuel technology, and with this the shift from the use of wood to iron and steel in machinery, tools, implements and other manufactures. The development of an iron- and coal-based technology, one of the vital characteristics of the transformation of British industry in the eighteenth century, was particularly noted by foreigners. F. and A. de la Rochefoucault-Liancourt in their *Voyages aux Montagnes* in 1786 admired the British for

> their skill in working iron – the great advantage it gives them as regards the motion, lastingness and accuracy of machinery. All driving wheels and in fact almost all things are made of cast iron, of such a fine and hard quality that when rubbed up it polishes just like steel. There is no doubt but that the working of iron is one of the most essential of trades and the one in which we are most deficient.[3]

With the effective processing of iron and widespread adaptation to its use in Britain went a great facility in the use of tools and mechanical contrivances.

J. R. Harris and Peter Mathias have stressed the empirical characteristics and the adaptive innovative content of eighteenth-century technologies which relied above all on the skilled worker.[4] This was especially so in powered and mechanized processes using coal. The foundation of the Industrial Revolution in coal, iron, steam and machinery relied at its heart on a core of practical skill which was very difficult to transmit outside the mind of the skilled workman himself. Manuals, patents, scientific observation and journalistic description were useless without the skilled worker who actually applied and adapted the technology. It is what P. Courtheoux, writing about iron puddling, has called the separation between knowledge of a process and ignorance of a craft. Methods might be described, but so much of the skilled worker's real knowledge was 'breathed in the atmosphere where he lived' rather than ever consciously formulated. As a French inspector of industry wrote in the 1820s after visiting the Sheffield region:

> These [simple workmen] are truly the metallurgists of Yorkshire and it is among them that one can gather the elements of steel making. But there, as elsewhere, there is barely a common language between the workman and the savant; it is, for example, extremely difficult to determine in many cases what qualities a workman means when he says that iron has 'body', is 'sound', 'strong', 'tough', etc.; all of these, however, are expressions which have a very precise meaning.

In the case of the iron puddlers, their skill was essential to the transformation of pig iron into wrought iron. The process consisted of stirring the molten pig iron on the bed of a reverberatory furnace. The puddler turned and stirred the molten mass until through the decarburization of air, circulating through the furnace, it became converted into malleable iron. Puddlers, underhands, rollers, and all the other iron tradesmen were tough, rough and uneducated. 'But if uneducated, [they] were not ignorant . . . A new man in the trade started to learn in earnest, the hard way, by doing, not talking, and he developed a taciturnity which lasted all his life.'[5]

Richard Cobden in the nineteenth century hailed the metal industries and the skilled workers of the eighteenth: 'Our strength, wealth and commerce grew out of the skilled labour of the men working in metals. They are at the foundation of our manufacturing greatness.'[6] These special skills applied not just to the processing of metals, but also to working in them. It is to the latter that we shall largely refer. For the large scale of the processing works, their use of mechanical and powered techniques, their centralization of processes, and the capitalist organization of their workforces form a separate problem and story in themselves. It is, furthermore, a story which has often been told in the standard histories of the Industrial Revolution. For metal processing or heavy industry forms the other side of the coin of factory production. But the metal-processing works also spawned a whole series of relatively small-scale metalworking industries using iron, steel, brass, copper and various alloys. These relied on skilled workers, diversity of output, innovative practices, and handtools, and were organized within artisan and putting-out systems. Many of these industries remained organized on a workshop or family production principle throughout the Industrial Revolution, simply adapting steam power and factory premises to the dictates of small-scale production. Metalworking spawned a distinctive form of specialization and artisan skill within elaborate networks of small-scale production side by side with large-scale works.

Engineering

An early close relationship grew up between the heavy industries and the infant engineering industry. The first great ironworks – Coalbrookdale, Carron and Bersham – were also the first builders and users of machine tools.[7] And the pinnacle of the skill and independence of the worker in metals was the early engineer, especially his forebear, the millwright. William Fairbairn, one such millwright, argued that in England before the eighteenth century the most important articles of machinery such as windmills and watermills were brought over from the continent. And as such contrivances became more used, a special class of native artificers sprang up to attend them. These were called millwrights, and they designed and erected windmills, watermills, pumping apparatus and various kinds of rough machinery. They were the first who devoted themselves exclusively to engineering work.[8] Where the staple material of the millwright had once been wood, after the mid-eighteenth century he adapted to the increasing use of iron in machinery.

The origins of engineering in the millwright's craft were often restated. A journeyman smith reporting to the Committee on Apprentices in 1813 said he was called a machinist and engineer, that the business was a new one, that the millwrights had set up in it, employed smiths and made steam engines, lathes etc.[9] As Jennifer Tann has written, the millwright of the early

Industrial Revolution worked in wood. He was concerned with the application of power to an industrial process and the transmission of that power to machinery, in other words, the linking of the prime mover via a system of shafts and gears to machines. The millwright was frequently called on to assess the power requirements of particular machines, and not infrequently to advise on the plan of a mill and its layout of machinery.[10] And Fairbairn described the millwright of former days as the 'sole representative of mechanical art', 'a kind of jack of all trades, who could with equal facility work at the lathe, the anvil or the carpenter's bench'.

> Thus the millwright of the last century was an itinerant engineer and mechanic of high reputation. He could handle the axe, the hammer, and the plane with equal skill and precision; he could turn, bore, or forge with the ease and despatch of one brought up to these trades, as he could set out and cut in the furrows of a millstone with an accuracy equal or superior to that of a miller himself.[11]

The millwrights who turned their hands to the mechanical and power needs of the woollen and cotton industry soon turned to the manufacture of machinery itself. The progress of the eighteenth-century woollen industry, premised on increasing quantities of a limited range of machinery, brought some country millwrights into the manufacture of textile machinery on a small scale. And in the early stages of the transfer of the cotton manufacture to the factory system, the traditional country millwright, such as Thomas Lowe, was used. The types of millwrighting needs thrown up by the various branches of the textile industry in turn affected the subsequent regional development of the engineering industry. The demand for millwrights was greater in Lancashire than elsewhere. In Yorkshire the smaller, less specialized millwright continued to cater to country mills, and in the West of England the limitations of the country millwright and small machine-maker, who formerly satisfied most needs, were made clear only when the cloth manufacturers began to investigate possibilities of adopting steam power.[12]

Where the early practice of the machine-maker had involved carrying his tools, including lathe, drill and grindstone, from mill to mill in order to build the machinery on the spot, now textile-machine shops grew up around the textile areas. This led to a new differentiation in workers' trades. Pattern-makers, iron and brass founders, smiths, hammermen and firemen, vicemen and filers, turners and planers came to take the place of millwrights, carpenters and blacksmiths.[13]

In fact, many of the first engineering workers owed their origins not to the millwrighting, but to the smithing trades. The smith's trade was already subdivided by the eighteenth century into the forgework of the fireman, the filing and finishing work of the viceman, and the work of the hammerman. It was the viceman who was the ancestor of the fitter, and the largest department of most nineteenth-century engineering shops remained the smithy.[14]

Alongside the smithing trades, there were metal trades established in making tools by the seventeenth century, in London, the Midlands and notably in South-West Lancashire. Peasant toolmakers to the west and south of St Helens produced chisels, pliers, vices, gauges, small lathes and files to be used by clock- and watchmakers, whitesmiths, and later machine-makers and cotton spinners. The area was also well known for its other rural metal trades, the manufacture of watch parts, locks and hinges, nails, pins and wire. A long-established force of skilled craftsmen trained to work in metal to a high degree of accuracy contributed to the machine-making and engine-building industry which soon arrived to service the textile mills.[15]

If millwrights formed one primary source of skilled engineering labour and smithing another, these were not sufficient, for the specialization and training up of workmen were also a major source of labour. This was so, in particular, in the manufacture of steam engines. Early steam engines were erected on the site they were to be used on, and this involved a great deal of fitting and local manufacture of simpler components. Boulton and Watt only supplied a man to supervise the erection of the engine. The first engine shop at Soho was on a very small scale, with only two smiths' hearths, a fitting bench and a single lathe. But the new Soho Foundry of 1795 was the first heavy-engineering shop; it concentrated on the design of patterns for castings and the manufacture of parts calling for accuracy in machining and skill in fitting, such as valves, valve chests and parts of the valve gear.[16] Watt constantly complained about the clumsiness and incompetence of his workmen, and so systematically set about training up a body of them. He tried to keep certain groups to special classes of work and encouraged them to bring up their sons to it.[17] Fairbairn reported that at Soho it was not unusual for some precise line of work to be followed by members of the same family for three generations. This, along with the improvement in tools, meant that 'the facilities thus afforded led to constant progressive improvement in the character of the work done, at the same time constantly diminishing the dependence on mere manual skill.'[18] Some of these Soho workmen eventually made their way to Manchester where they took employment as enginemen, thus providing a pool of skilled labour.[19] Later engineering workshops such as that of Maudslay in London, on a small scale in 1798 and a larger scale in 1810, formed a nursery of engineering talent for the nineteenth century.[20]

The creation of this skilled engineering labour force involved, therefore, the division of labour and specialization of function. Nor was this a recent development. The early metal trades of the St Helens region and Warrington were already highly subdivided by the seventeenth and eighteenth centuries. The manufacture of watch movements and tools was 'put out' as early as the seventeenth century to rural workers in South-West Lancashire by all the big watch firms in London, Coventry and Liverpool. The files produced in Warrington in the eighteenth century were sometimes made from start to finish by the same outworkers, but more often some workers confined themselves to forging and others to cutting, and then sent the files elsewhere to be hardened.[21] By the mid-eighteenth century most British watchmakers ordered the rough movements of the watch from specialist firms or outworkers in Lancashire. These worked from paper measurements using their own Lancashire gauge. 'Pinion wire was made at the mill; springs, by artisans who did nothing else; chains, by chainmakers (often women); cases by casemakers.'[22] In eighteenth-century engineering there was the division between fitters and turners. The fitter was acknowledged as a highly skilled craftsman, but at Soho fitting was subdivided in such a way that to each group of fitters only one article or group of articles was assigned. Similarly, turners were long known as general workmen of whom a high degree of skill was expected, and they did most of their boring on ordinary lathes. But at Soho a number of different classes of boring were separated out. By 1824, Galloway, a London engineer, had between 75 and 115 employees, and these were all divided into a number of different trades – pattern-makers, iron and brass founders, smiths, firemen, hammermen, vicemen, filers, brass, iron and wood turners. There was, in addition, in areas like Manchester, a further division of the engineering trades based on product. Rollermaking and spindlemaking, for example, became separate industries.[23]

The point of much of this specialization was greater accuracy and precision, qualities which became more and more valuable with mechanization. It was a 'transition from the workmanship of chance to the workmanship of precision'. 'The craftsman in gold and silver could compensate for differences in the quality of his metals: the constant motion of a machine required constant materials.' But the transition was a slow one, for when William Fairbairn went to Manchester in 1814, 'the whole of the machinery was executed by hand. There were neither planing, slotting nor shaping machines; and with the exception of very imperfect lathes and a few drills, the preparatory operations of construction were effected entirely by the hands of the workmen.'[24] Chipping and filing were the major craft processes behind much of engineering, and with this the chisel and file comprised the major part of the workmen's 'fixed capital'. Until Maudslay perfected a screw-cutting lathe at the beginning of the nineteenth century,

> the tools used for making screws were of the most rude and inexact kind. The screws were for the most part cut by hand: the small by filing, the larger by chipping and filing . . . and each manufacturing establishment made them after their own fashion. There was an utter want of uniformity.

These tools were owned by the workmen, 'the men were Masters', and there were large numbers of them. In 1825 there were 400 to 500 engineering masters in the London area, employing no more than 10,000 men.[25]

HARDWARE AND CUTLERY

The continued importance of skill in spite of specialization in the engineering trades was echoed in the Black Country and Birmingham hardware trades and in the Sheffield cutlery trades. Regional differentiation in terms of levels of skill appeared very early. By the end of the seventeenth century, Birmingham was tending to produce articles requiring a great deal of skilled labour, requiring few or low-cost raw materials and little transport, while cruder manufactures migrated to the rest of South Staffordshire. The cutlery trades too were divided between the high-class trade of Sheffield and the inferior common trades of the countryside.

Skill became differentiated, but the characteristic unit of production remained relatively small in scale. 'The variety in the design of the metal articles is so great, the opportunities for standardized production so few, and the importance of skill so evident, that the small unit is naturally to be preferred.'

In gunmaking, for instance, an extensive division of labour was elaborated within a structure of small-scale units of production. The gunmaker owned a warehouse in the gun quarter, acquired semi-finished parts and gave these out to specialized craftsmen who undertook the assembly and finishing of the gun. These in turn bought their parts from a whole range of independent manufacturers – barrelmakers, lockmakers, sight stampers, triggermakers, ramrod forgers, gun furniture makers and bayonet forgers. The combination of small-scale production with a high degree of fairly flexible skill meant both that manufacturers could throw the burden of depression on to the workers themselves, and that workers could turn their skills in the use of the file and the lathe to some other trade.[26]

Skill, in a similar fashion, determined the location not just of the various hardware trades, but also that of the brass and copper trades. These skills were, however, evidently spread more widely, for by the early eighteenth century many towns carried on the manufacture of brass, with no other special advantage than a resident class of artisans already skilled in working in metals. There were by that time large numbers of braziers and coppersmiths throughout the country, since more brass and copper was produced than could be economically consumed by the integrated brass founding and working establishments.[27]

Many of the metal trades, like textiles, were carried on in combination with some form of pastoral agriculture. A division of labour between the agricultural and industrial pursuits of workers developed more or less rapidly, depending on the fertility of the soil. Metalworkers in the Birmingham area kept less capital invested in agriculture than did Sheffield craftsmen in the better farmland of South Yorkshire and North Derbyshire.[28] But even these trades became more and more divorced from agriculture over the course of the seventeenth to the late eighteenth century, and craftsmen became increasingly dependent on the cash incomes derived from their forges.[29] By 1801, for instance, the towns and villages of eleven Black Country parishes contained 80,000 people, or one-third of Staffordshire's population. The area contained very large numbers of nailers (40,000 were employed in the trade in the Midlands by 1800), as well as a great range of trades from bucklemakers, chainmakers, buttonmakers, tinners and platers, japanners and pinmakers. The population of these industrial villages was by this time 'anonymous'; it was also 'very mobile, as the rapid expansion of the area attracted much casual labour, and technical change attracted populations with particular skills'.[30]

Just as the division of labour proceeded in engineering along the lines of process and product, so too in the cutlery manufacture which developed rapidly in Sheffield and its hinterland from the seventeenth century onwards. In that century forging, grinding and halfting had all been kept in the hands of the master workman. But by its latter half, the industry had divided into three trades: those producing knives were separated from the scissormakers, and these in turn from those making shears and sickles. Grinding was separated out very early in the scythe trade, that is, by 1630–50, but in most of the other trades this did not occur until the mid-eighteenth century.[31]

The skills of forging and grinding, which were gradually separated out for many of the cutlery trades from the latter half of the eighteenth century, were also generally divided into different premises. The first process, forging, was performed, depending on the product, by one or two workers. Heavier articles, such as table blades, files, tools and larger instruments, required the assistance of a striker or butty who manipulated a heavy double-headed hammer. The second process, grinding, was performed in separate departments of larger works or in separate establishments called 'wheels'. In earlier 'wheels' handpower was frequently used, with a boy turning a large fly wheel, or the 'wheels' were scattered along the banks of streams, using water power. The first steam 'wheel' was set up in 1786 and soon yielded up cases of grinders' disease, for, unlike the old methods of powering the grindstone, steam power compelled uninterrupted work day after day. This was reinforced by the continued use of drystone grinding for the lighter implements until 1840.[32]

Grinding was followed by further refinements of the blade with hammer, whitening stone, emery and buffing wheels. The final process of building up or halfting the knife was the true cutler's art; it relied only on handskill and basic tools – drills for boring, files, vices, a glazer and buffs.

The building up of a pocket knife is a task of greater complexity and one for which it is not easy to substitute mechanical process owing to the infinite variety in which these goods must be produced in order

Plate 15 Sheffield cutler finishing a knife (Ann Ronan Picture Library)

to meet the whim of the purchaser: a single firm may supply such knives in thousands of different patterns.

File cutting was a particularly skilled process, yet divided between forger, grinder and cutter. The forger moulded the steel into the right shape, the grinder ground it on a wet stone, and the cutter cut the teeth into it with hammer and chisel. 'By a succession of smart blows parallel ridges of astonishing conformity and exactness are produced, the blows following one another with wonderful rapidity.'[33]

This retention of high degrees of skill in spite of the division of labour between process and product entailed conditions of semi-independence among artisans and complex systems of industrial organization in the metal trades. But before the advance of steam power and the special dependencies created within piecework systems, the proverbial independence of the skilled metalworker was by the nineteenth century becoming more and more illusory.

BIRMINGHAM TRADES

The toy trades cover a range of new products which became identified with the Birmingham metal industries in the eighteenth century. A recent definition of the eighteenth-century toy, given in the *Victoria History of the Counties of England*, describes it as a comprehensive term

> for an assemblage of numerous kinds of more or less useful wares, of small dimensions, and varying from a few pence to many guineas in value. It included much of what is now termed jewelry, small articles of plate, sword hilts, guns, pistols, and dagger furniture, buttons, buckles, bracelets, rings, necklaces, seals, chains, chatelains, charms, mounts of various kinds, étuis, snuff boxes, and patch boxes.

It was also considered to cover any article with the common characteristic that its patterns changed with great frequency. This definition breaks the toy trades down into heavy (wares of polished iron) and lighter (steel). The heavy trades produced the 'tools and instruments used by carpenters, coopers, gardeners, butchers, glaziers, upholsterers, farriers, masons, plumbers, coachmakers, millwrights, saddlers, harnessmakers, tinmen, shoemakers, weavers, wire drawers and wheelers'. The light steel toy trades, said to have occupied half of Birmingham before the French Revolution, produced 'buckles, purse mounts, brooches, bracelets, watch chains, key rings and swivels'. The toy departments peculiar to Matthew Boulton's large hardware factory included clocks with ornamental cases, fine art bronzes, filigree work, buttons, buckles and clasps, lamps, bracelets, candlesticks, and tea irons.[34]

The toy trades were a new industry, based on international and especially the new colonial markets, making Birmingham in some senses 'proto-industrial'. But much more striking is the way in which these new industries were based on a special form of technical change integrated with a complicated structure of small-, medium- and large-scale enterprises. Their rise formed a part of the wider development of the metal industries on the one hand, and of Birmingham on the other in the eighteenth century. Aside from the rising domestic demand for all kinds of metalwares, there was also a rapid rise in exports. Metal goods made up 7 per cent of manufactured goods exported in 1722–4, and this had increased to 14 per cent by 1772–4. The Midlands was already exporting large quantities of fashion goods early in the century, for there is evidence from 1712 of exports of watches, locks, clocks, buckles, buttons, and other brass toys from the region to France.[35] Birmingham's place in the development of these industries is variously attributed to its geography, its unincorporated political status, and its role as a haven from religious persecution. Transport problems put a premium on articles where skilled labour was an important element, and this is supposed partly to have accounted for the predominance of the manufacture of small articles showing the hand of the skilled worker. The lack of incorporation of this relatively new town attracted both labour and capital which faced barriers to entry and other restrictions in many areas. Birmingham's early reputation for religious toleration formed yet another attraction for them. It was for this reason that the buckle industry was introduced from Staffordshire, for craftsmen driven from Walsall by religious persecution started making buckles in brass and copper in Birmingham.[36] The decline of the buckle manufacture owing to changes in fashion in the 1790s made room for a new expansion of the button manufacture which took over the same skills, labour force and raw materials. By 1759 there were about 20,000 employed in the toy trades in Birmingham and the surrounding district, and the value of the ornamental part of the trade was estimated at £600,000 per year, £500,000 of the total value being derived from exports.[37]

In addition to the widespread production of buttons and buckles there appeared other new toy branches distinctive to Birmingham. Japanning, a form of enamelling with a material made of a mixture of turpentine, balsam, oils, pitch, resin and wax, was started in Monmouthshire and spread to Staffordshire in the early eighteenth century. Initially executed in tin plate by hand, it was only with the introduction of papier mâché that it became a cheap, mechanical and profitable trade.[38] The stamped brass foundry trade, using sheet metal, die and hammer, was introduced by the London toymaker John Pickering and spread so rapidly in Birmingham that by 1770 the town housed stampers, die sinkers, stamp and press makers, and button stampers. Plating silver over copper also became popular in the button and buckle trades, the manufacture of snuff boxes and other products.[39]

Though most manufacturers in the town had a capital of less than £100, by the latter half of the eighteenth century there were a number with great wealth. By 1783 ninety-four manufacturers in the town had a capital greater than £5,000, eighty more than £10,000, and seventeen £20,000.[40] The large scale of enterprises in these new trades derived encouragement notably from the variety and expense of raw materials, and from the specialization of artists and finishers. Many of the processes were not suited to the family enterprise, and expensive skilled labour was most efficiently used where there was some degree of division of labour.[41]

The large size and extensive division of labour in some of the toymaking firms very likely also derived from older traditions in the integrated foundry and metalworking firms. Crowley's ironworks, which employed very large numbers of ironworkers, nailmakers and other hardware manufacturers, was a case in point. The rolling and slitting processes of ironworks were for the most part separated out early from ironmongery. The rolling and slitting mills were highly centralized and capitalist firms. Ironmongery and particularly nailmaking were organized within a domestic system; but coexisting with this were centralized works of various sizes. Work was organized in the nailmaking industry, on the one hand, through a direct merchant–employer relationship, and, on the other, through an indirect system using agents.[42]

The brass manufacture, which was very important to the emergence of the Birmingham toy trades, had a similar heritage of large-scale integrated works. The two stages of the brass and copper industries – first, the mining and smelting of copper and making of brass, and second, the working up of copper and brass into finished articles – were organized before and during the eighteenth century in large monopolistic firms such as the Mines Royal. Though brassworking and coppersmithing were largely organized on a domestic basis, they were controlled through company agents and factors. One such company, the Warmley Company, in 1767 employed 800 at one site in Warmley and another 2,000 outworkers making copper and brass spelter and utensils in copper and brass. The Anglesey Company employed 1,200 miners in Anglesey, it had smelting works at Amluck, St Helens and Swansea, and rolling mills and manufacturing works at Greenfield and Great Marlow. Brass founding was established in Birmingham in the early eighteenth century, and by 1797 there were seventy-one brass founders in the city. By the end of the century all branches of the brass and copper industry were to be found there.[43]

The evidence for large-scale workshops and factories is balanced by other evidence that most firms were very small in scale – part of a workshop-dominated economy. Large-scale processing units might be integrated into this workshop economy via the kind of co-operative organization discovered by the brass manufacturers. It is the small scale of enterprise which supports the theory of upward social mobility from artisan to small master, and which accounts for the community of interest between workmen and employers generally attributed to eighteenth- and nineteenth-century Birmingham.[44] In fact, what seems to have been most common in the Birmingham toy trades was the medium-sized firm. Handtools could constitute a fairly substantial investment. The number of tools left by bankrupt or deceased firms as advertised by *Aris's Gazette* in the 1780s indicates firms of an order greater than the individual artisan. Evidence gathered from the wills and insurance policies of several hundred metalworkers indicates levels of wealth for approximately one-third of these which place them within a medium-scale category of approximately £100 to £500. Many of these were multiple property-holders.[45]

This range in the size of firms, with a special significance for the medium-sized or fairly substantial business, corroborates the quite extensive division of labour to be found in the toy trades, which appear often to be a very good example of that division of labour, both technical and social. Lord Shelbourne's description of 1766 bears repeating:

> There a button passes through fifty hands, and each hand passes perhaps a thousand in a day – likewise, by this means, the work becomes so simple that five times in six, children of 6 or 8 years old do it as well as men, and earn from 10 pence to 8 shillings a week.[46]

For many smaller and medium-scale firms, however, production and the division of labour were decentralized. The common pattern was a fine specialization centred on the production of particular groups of articles, or alternatively on parts of articles. Firms which did final assembly and decorative work might be distinct from those which did the 'stamping, piercing, spinning, brazing, plating and annealing'. The result was a production process decentralized into separate shops in adjacent or nearby houses or in 'courts' at the backs of houses. Centralized or decentralized, the division of labour was highly developed, but so too was flexibility across a range of materials and products. This created many external economies of knowledge, credit, marketing and labour. Alfred Marshall called this combination of decentralized production processes and industrial neighbourhood in Birmingham the 'industrial district'. Many years later Sargant Florence looked to the same town for a similar phenomenon, 'industrial swarming'.[47]

It was not the toy trades, however, but two other Birmingham industries which provided the classic examples of the division of labour analysed in the *Encyclopédie*, Smith's *Wealth of Nations* and Marx's *Capital*. The needle and pin manufactures, though centred in other areas of the country, were carried out also in Birmingham from the late eighteenth century. The manufacture of needles was divided into eight main operations: pointing, stamping, eyeing, filing, hardening, strengthening, scouring and polishing. A pinworks in Birmingham in 1810 divided the production process into thirteen different operations: the wire was drawn out to a proper size by a simple engine; it was straightened by another machine; it was cut into lengths; the ends of these lengths were pointed by means of a wheel; these were cut again, each wire forming several pins; the wire was twisted by means of a wheel; the twisted wire was cut into heads; the heads were softened in a fire; the heads were put on by hand; the pins were washed; they were then boiled in a liquor of tartar and tin, dried and finally they were papered by children.[48]

Another early Birmingham industry, the nail manufacture, displayed the characteristics of the division of labour in the proto-industrial model. The iron was prepared by rolling heavy bars into sheets; the thin sheets were slit into rods which in turn were rolled into rods of the gauge required for the particular nail. The rods were then cut, headed and pointed by the nailer at his domestic forge. It was an industry carried out in the small-scale family production unit, often in some combination with agriculture, but even as early as the seventeenth century it was one of the poorest and most despised of all trades.

Nailmaking, in spite of its dispersed and very small production units and the simplicity of the basic processes, was also extremely specialized, but specialized according to product and region. By the early nineteenth century there were twenty nailmaking districts in the West Midlands, each making a different kind of nail or spike. By 1770 there were 10,000 employed in the trade in the Midlands; by 1798 35–40,000. The nailers were exploited by the ironmongers who held them in debt and controlled their sales. As early as 1655 there was a call for the nailers to co-operate in a strike against the 'Egyptian Taskmasters', that is, the ironmongers. And the trade was said to be in a state of decay in 1737, 1765 and again in 1776. Young reported in 1776 that the road from Soho was one long village of nailers who complained that their trade was failing because of disputes with America. When hands were idle they took to other branches, and their children went to Birmingham.[49]

INVENTION

Prosser regarded Birmingham as a famous centre for inventors until 1850, pointing out that many more patents were issued there than anywhere else outside London. This he supposed was due to the many skilled smiths, founders and engineers in the town. Most of the patents were granted for small improvements in the manufacture of trinkets and buttons, in machine tools, and in metal compositions and scientific instruments. Many such improvements were never patented, but rather just adopted by the small masters.[50] In spite of this widespread practice of secrecy, Birmingham acquired ninety patents between 1750 and 1800, far more than Sheffield's respectable showing of twenty-seven.[51]

Hawkes Smith described the type of invention famous in the town as that which affected 'that alone which requires more force than the arm and tools of the workman could yield, still leaving his skill and experience of head, hand and eye in full exercise'. Because of this, Birmingham had supposedly suffered less from the introduction of machinery than places where it had been a substitute for human labour. The goods produced by the Birmingham and Midland smithies in the seventeenth century were wrought or cast out of solid metal, so that the earliest working equipment was anvil, hammer, file and grindstone. The lathe succeeded these as the variety of manufacture and the trade in light and fancy articles increased in the later seventeenth century. With the addition of copper, brass and other materials, the rolling mill, stamp, press and drawbench were introduced over the course of the eighteenth century.[52]

Though most of these innovations were tools or mechanical aids to artisan skills, it was also quite likely that scientific knowledge in some form played its part. For it was 'not possible to dismiss the accuracy of the Birmingham pattern maker, moulder or polisher in 1750 as simply the product of experience'. The development of the stamp and press in the 1760s, for example, required a 'high degree of accuracy in the finish of the machine tool, calculations as to stress set up in the metal formed and the degree of leverage required to minimize the operator's effort'.[53]

The type of technology in use was not that adapted to continuous process or mass-production. Its hallmark was flexibility and application according to the dictates of artisan skill to the production of a wide range of different articles. While Soho, for example, was employing 800 to 1,000 workers in 1770 along with a wide range of sophisticated machinery, its object was not

Plate 16 Turning (Ann Ronan Picture Library)

mass-production. New patterns were constantly brought into use, new products devised, and many valuable pieces individually constructed. This was hand-operated machinery, supplemented in some cases by limited horse or water power. Steam power, though perhaps the most famous product of the town, was hardly ever used there before 1800. By 1815 there were still only forty engines in the town, but a minor proliferation of small steam engines occurred in the 1830s.[54]

Workshop industries in engineering, cutlery and hardware, and in the consumer toy trades underwent rapid expansion and technological change over the course of the eighteenth century. This expansion took place within a range of large, medium-scale and small-scale firms. The result was not a homogeneous and mutual artisan 'workshop' economy, but an economy of many social and economic divisions. We can look at some of these divisions in the recruitment of labour, apprenticeship and skills.

ARTISAN INDEPENDENCE AND SKILL

The independence of the early millwrights was proverbial; it went with an autodidact tradition and strictly enforced trade-society rules. Fairbairn reported that the millwrights of the turn of the nineteenth century formed their own 'Millwrights' Institutes' in each shop.

> On the more peaceful occasions, however, it was curious to trace the influence of these discussions on the young aspirants around, and the interest excited by the illustrations and chalk diagrams by which each side supported their arguments, covering the tables and floors of the room in which they were assembled.[55]

They formed their own benefit and trade societies which dictated the hours of work – light till dark in winter, and six till six in summer – as well as the rate of wages, with no member allowed to work for less than 7s a day.[56] Watt bemoaned the millwrights' solidarity when they went on strike in 1795:

> At some places they have left work, tho' the proprietors would give them their own terms, but they will not work till every master accedes to their proposals; they are already better paid than any other class of workmen, having a guinea per week and an allowance of 6d per day for beer, and they always make 7 days a week.[57]

The trade in some places was virtually a patrimony, and Fairbairn found it extremely difficult to gain entry himself to any of the trade societies in London which between them controlled admission to employment. But once entry was gained, the way was open to independence and eventually to individual proprietorship for those who could amass a small capital. After employment as a journeyman for several years in Manchester, Fairbairn in

271

1817 set up on his own with James Lillie. Taking on a number of small jobs sufficed to enable them to make a lathe capable of turning shafts three to six inches in diameter, and by 1824 they had acquired a sixteen-horsepower steam engine.[58]

Maudslay's rise to the proprietorship of a London engineering workshop was similar. He worked nine years for Bramah and first set up on his own in 1798 to make ships' blocks. Over the next ten years he gradually branched out to the manufacture of calico-printing machinery, small engines, and power-driven lathes. He went into partnership with Joshua Field, making improvements in the lathe and expanding his business into marine engineering. His works soon acquired a reputation for the skills of the engineers trained there; they turned out Richard Roberts, David Napier and Joseph Whitworth among others.[59]

The strict entry qualifications of the millwright and engineering trades contrasted sharply with the general lack of formal restriction in the hardware and cutlery trades, yet a form of independence still prevailed among artisans. In cutlery, the rapid expansion of the industry in the early eighteenth century undermined the power of the Cutlers' Company to impose restrictions. An attempt was made in 1791 to incorporate all those currently practising the trade into the Company, and to impose strict entry qualifications subsequently. But this, too, broke down, and in 1814 apprenticeship restrictions were abolished. Apprenticeship regulations were similarly difficult to impose in many of the hardware trades. There were guilds among the metalworkers in some parts of the West Midlands. But the wide scattering of raw materials, the simplicity of early processes, and the part-time characteristics of the occupation made any attempt on the part of the towns to monopolize the industries very difficult. The absence of formal apprenticeship restriction did not, however, imply the sway of free market forces, for it was here that workshop custom imposed its own structures. The notorious 'rattenings' of the Sheffield trade unionists, that is, the removal of the tools and wheel bands of recalcitrant members of the trade, had its origins in the legal right of the guilds to enforce their rules by the removal of the property of offenders.[60]

This artisan independence in the metal trades was reflected in the forms of industrial organization which developed through the eighteenth century and part of the nineteenth. The line dividing outworker and pieceworker, manufacturer and artisan was ill-defined. Clapham long ago pointed out the extent of semi-independence in the metal trades. The journeyman in the Sheffield trades might be an outworker or a pieceworker, but he had his own tools and forge. The small master in the Birmingham trades was independent though he might be working pretty regularly for a particular factor, and masters worked regularly on the employers' premises, as at Crowley's works in Winlaton, County Durham. 'Masters got tools and materials from a works iron keeper, then employed their own hammermen and prentices, and were credited with the selling price of their goods less cost of material and some overhead to Crowley.'[61]

Customary trade practice, particularly over apprenticeship regulation, was vital to artisan independence. Friendly and trade societies enforced customary demarcation lines on wages, prices and employment policy, exerting some degree of workplace control. And in addition, 'independence' was written into the structure of work organization, so that every skilled artisan was conceived of as a small master.[62]

The conditions of this semi-independence, however, varied with economic fluctuations, and became more constrained with the development and increasing control of intermediaries. A vital aspect of this control came through indebtedness. In the words of one historian, 'Putting out was necessarily a form of credit, though historians have often treated it loosely as a kind of wage labour.'[63] Outworkers who had the nominal independence to seek out alternative suppliers of raw materials were frequently bound in debt to one employer. Among regular workers as well as more casual workers, debt to an employer or supplier was not temporary but long-lasting. Stubs, the Warrington filemaker, spoke of one workman tied by debt to another firm of toolmakers, and so anxious was he to work for Stubs that he was willing to transfer to him his rights to the labour of his sons who were apprenticed to their father. In the pin trade, parents borrowed on the security of their young children. As T. S. Ashton put it:

> In other industries payment in truck or the new discipline must be given first place among the ills afflicting the wage earner, in the metal working trades indebtedness to the employer would seem to have been by far the most serious barrier to the attainment of economic liberty.

Courts existed for the recovery of small debts. Stubs used the Warrington Court Baron for the Recovery of Small Debts to obtain repayment of loans, and in addition for redress against workmen returning poor or insufficient work. The Birmingham small debts court, the Court of Requests, met from 1752 and dealt with 80 to 100 cases a week.[64]

Neither was the existence of a proliferation of small men a sign of 'independence'. The 'little masters' of Sheffield, for instance, multiplied not in times of prosperity, but in those of commercial stagnation and distress. These little masters might be merely factors using the labour of outworkers, or they might employ a small team and rent a room in a factory.[65] And though the Sheffield artisan might define his independence by his ownership of his own tools, it was also increasingly apparent by the nineteenth century that a local group of merchant capitalists controlled the circulating capital of the trade and the distribution of the finished product, and furthermore that industrial sites were in the hands of various rentier groups.[66] In the hardware trades the 'independence' of the artisan lay open to the abuse of the discount system, whereby manufacturers demanded a discount on goods 'sold' them by their artisans – a form of wage-cut. The small master was, furthermore, placed at a greater disadvantage in buying raw materials and selling his product. He increasingly became an outworker, to whom the larger manufacturer had no commitment in terms of capital or marketing networks.[67]

The reliance of the metal trades on the skill and semi-independent status of their workforce entailed complex systems of industrial organization based on the small-scale unit of production and interlocking networks of intermediaries. Capitalist expansion and industrialization in the metal trades found their context not in the factory but in the garret master and various forms of sweating. On the one hand, the system of outwork prevailed because of its superior advantage for the production of specialities on a small scale.[68] On the other hand, this advantage was one which could allow the garret master and the 'slaughterhouse men' to undermine the substantial workshop. In lockmaking, for instance, most employers were small masters with one to four apprentices and one or no journeyman. When apprentices had served their time, they generally had no alternative but to set up as small masters. There were many small masters and many apprentices in the trade. This was not just a feature of lockmaking, for in the latter half of the eighteenth century the custom in the metal trades in most parts of England had grown up for workmen as well as employers to take apprentices.[69] In the Birmingham trades the small garret master became more significant in the early nineteenth century, whereas earlier a large number of substantial workshops had thrived. In fact, industrialization brought a form of dualism whereby both large-scale and extremely small-scale firms probably grew at the expense of substantial artisans and medium-sized manufacturers. The appearance of more and more small garret masters was encouraged by the proliferation of various intermediaries and agents; it took its worst form in nailmaking where the 'fogging system' came into prevalence in the nineteenth century. The role of the factor ranged from the one concerned only with the distribution of the product and with financing the little masters, to the type who exercised an intimate control over raw materials and the co-ordination of labour. His major role was in finance where he formed virtually the only link between the small masters and the banks.[70]

The independence of small masters was in many cases mythical by the nineteenth century. Their working days and practices were constrained at every point by the factors, whose power was now if anything increased by the availability of steam power. For steam power in the metal trades could be hired out with room or bench space, and the worker now had to come to the place where the steam engine was housed and work the hours that the steam engine was run. Just as his markets, his raw materials and his capital were out of his own control, so too now were his place and his hours of work.[71]

If anything, factory production in the metal trades entailed just as much if not more of the traditions of independence of the domestic worker. In many cases the manufacturer grew out of a factor and remained at heart in this capacity. He did not become deeply involved in the details of manufacturing processes, and his employees carried on the traditions of domestic manufacture by providing their own tools and paying for their workspace. Deductions were frequently charged in factories against the wage for shop room, gas and power, and in foundries head casters customarily paid for the use of the sand mill.[72] Indeed, subcontracting was very common in the centralized units of the heavier metal industries, just as it was in the decentralized light industries. In the brass manufacture, the head caster paid and supervised his own moulders and labourers; journeymen were employed on a payment by results system, and underhands were employed by journeymen at daywork rates. In a brass-finishing shop of a larger works, the journeyman was expert in his branch of the trade. He organized the work of the shop and got it done efficiently; he forged, ground and hardened his own tools and kept his lathe or spindles in good order. He was designer, supervisor, toolmaker, tool setter and all-round workman.[73] In the centralized units of the light industries, too, piecework prevailed. Women subcontractors ran groups of workers in buttonmaking, papier mâché and lacquering shops of larger 'toy' factories.

In the famous engineering works of the day much the same combination of artisan independence and factory production prevailed. Eric Roll described the shop structure at Soho as a transition between handicraft production and modern mass-production, for only one basic operation was performed within each shop, and, though they were located according to a systematic order, they were still semi-independent units. This was combined with elaborate systems of piece wages. At the Soho Foundry men were engaged at a certain weekly wage. Another agreement was then made with the foreman to perform a job at a set rate or faster.[74] Maudslay's shop was actually organized by Samuel Bentham, a specialist in production organization who is often credited with the origins of the assembly line. Maudslay's example was closely followed by his student James Nasmyth in the nineteenth century, who demanded that his building be built 'all in a line'. 'In this way we will be able to keep in good order.'[75]

Factory production, the proliferation of tools and the application of steam power were regarded by some over-optimistic industrial pundits of the day as the means of overcoming the special needs for skill and independent status of workers in the metal trades. But as David Landes has pointed out much more recently, even after the invention of power tools 'each craftsman remained judge of his own performance', his specifications were approximate, and he filed down each part to fit the whole.[76]

Notwithstanding these complicated patterns of artisan independence, it is true that important and far-reaching changes took place in both work organization and in technology in the engineering trades and the hardware trades in the 1820s to 1840s. In engineering, there was a drastic reduction in the number of engineering employers after 1825, and the diffusion of machine tools from 1830 led to larger and more heavily-capitalized engineering firms. Along with this, the main locus of the industry shifted from London to South Lancashire. 'In the period 1830–50 the British engineering industry was transformed from a labour- to a capital-intensive one.'[77] There were similar developments in the Birmingham hardware trades, where in the first half of the nineteenth century larger establishments were introduced into most of the town's staple trades. As their activities expanded, this served to increase the tempo of the competitive relationship at all levels of industry. Along with such large firms there was a proliferation of small garret masters and sweated labour, with the numbers of small producers being swollen from the ranks of the unemployed workmen trying to avoid resorting to parish relief.[78]

APPRENTICESHIP AND SEXUAL DIVISION OF LABOUR

Strict entry qualifications existed in the millwrighting and some of the engineering trades; in Sheffield the Cutlers' Company had declined by the eighteenth century, but by convention formal apprenticeships still prevailed. In Birmingham there were no guild and apprenticeship regulations. How then was labour recruited and trained for its burgeoning trades? Apprenticeship even in the new trades of the town certainly existed, but took on a very different form from that found in more conventional boroughs such as Coventry.

Apprenticeship in Birmingham seems to have been a good deal more flexible than elsewhere – in the length of terms, types of training, and opportunities available. Formal apprenticeships might be only one year or much longer, and might require some premium according to the trade and employer. Matthew Boulton avoided taking on premium apprentices, preferring to take on pauper apprentices from Bedford and the South-West, or local poor children. Where they showed any aptitude, however, he did train them in drawing and other design skills.[79] There was widespread use of women's and children's labour. In Taylor's button factory women were supposed to have preponderated, and the coining staff at Soho employed 13 men, 27 women, and 16 boys.[80]

It is particularly difficult to gain any clear idea of the sexual division of labour in trades which displayed such varied industrial structures. It is said, however, that the adoption of machines for stamping and piercing extended the range of female employment, especially for young girls.[81] And it was recognized that women's work was widespread in the japanning and the stamping and piercing trades. Girls were specifically requested in advertisements for button piercers, annealers, and stoving and polishing work in the japanning trades. Another advertisement for button burnishers in 1788 also sought 'a woman that has been used to looking over and carding plain, plated and gilted buttons, also a few women that have been used to grind steels, either at foot lathes or mill'.[82] In the nineteenth century the tools were fitted into the press by male toolworkers who also attended to the condition of the tools in cutting the larger stamped work. But women worked even with the large presses, though girls were left to cut out smaller examples of the work. When women were employed in piercing and cutting-out work, they received only 8s to 12s a week and girls got 6s to 8s, while the toolmaker who superintended the work claimed 30s to 40s.

The delicacy of the work in buttonmaking and piercing, as well as in the handpainting of designs, was regarded as the special province of women and girls with their smaller hands and the deftness and concentration already acquired at household needlework. The lacquering and japanning trades required stove management and even in the nineteenth century it was women who worked in the trade. The small lacquering rooms in the brass trades, only 12 by 15 feet and 11 feet high, characteristically contained a couple of iron-plate stoves and five to six women workers.

In the nineteenth century women were still employed over a wide range of processes in the Birmingham trades, but these were by and large concentrated in the newer, lighter or more unskilled branches. In the Black Country trades there was no lighter alternative work open to women, and they worked beside the men in heavy industry – on the pitbank, in the nail manufacture, and in the manufacture of chains, saddlery, harness and hollow ware.[83] But in many of these trades, and in particular in nailmaking, they had long been degraded workers.

The most celebrated women workers of the West Midlands trades were the nailers. Their subservience in this degraded and poverty-stricken trade

Plate 17 Emailleur à la lampe, perles fausses (Mary Evans Picture Library)

reflected the wider subservience of their sex. William Hutton, on his travels in 1741, provided an exemplary male image of this workforce.

> In some of these shops I observed one, or more females, stript of their upper garment, and not overcharged with their lower, wielding the hammer with all the grace of the sex. The beauties of their face were rather eclipsed by the smut of the anvil; or in poetical phrase, the tincture of the forge had taken possession of those lips, which might have been taken by the kiss. Struck with the novelty, I enquired, 'whether the ladies of this country shod horses?' but was answered, with a smile, 'they are nailers.'
>
> A fire without heat, a nailer of a fair complexion, or one who despises the tankard, are equally rare among them.[84]

Yet women appeared to have a knowledge of a wide range of trades, if widowed tradeswomen can be used as evidence. Many women carried on with their husbands' businesses after their death, and though they may have employed some journeymen they would themselves have had to have a great deal of practical experience and knowledge to make a success of running what were in the main small artisan businesses. These women ran the businesses where one might have expected women's work – as in toy-, button- and bucklemaking, and japanning. But widows and daughters also appeared in strength in the iron business, in plumbing and glazing, in the brassfounding and pewtering trades, and among the hammer-, anvil- and edgetool-making trades.

Women occupied an important place in the Birmingham toy trades, as workers and employers. Though the evidence available does not indicate the extent to which there was a 'sexual division of labour' between individual trades and processes, it does indicate an economic and social subservience to men, for their wages were much lower, and they appear as tradeswomen and owners of businesses in their own right in effect only where they were continuing the business of a deceased husband or father. But we cannot deny the knowledge and expertise possessed by such women in these trades, for their businesses were mainly small-scale or at most medium-scale enterprises. And success for women as much as for men in these Birmingham trades was dependent on skill and on knowledge.

The general reliance on skilled labour was accompanied by an endemic labour shortage in the newer metal trades. This was reflected in the high premiums offered in the luxury japanning trades. James Bisset's family, for example, paid forty guineas for his five-year apprenticeship. When he had his own business he was able to ask premiums of two hundred guineas. Wages too were high. Arthur Young reported that labour in the surrounding countryside was paid at about £15 a year. At the same time no adult labourer in Birmingham was earning less than 7s a week and some were gaining £3. The average rate for women workers was 7s per week, and for children 1s 6d to 4s 6d. Male workers in the button trade could often gain 25s or 30s per week.[85] These wage rates cannot, however, be taken entirely at face value, for apart from the wage there were customary rights and fringe benefits on the one hand, and outpayments to apprentices, rent for bench space and 'discounts' on piece prices on the other.

The metal trades may well have been a stronghold of handicraft skill and artisanship, but these ideals of the 'manufacturing mode of production' were never static.[86] They underwent enormous change in the early nineteenth century, but they did so too in the middle of the eighteenth. Some parts of the engineering trades, the cutlery manufacture and the Birmingham trades did indeed make a transition to the factory during the nineteenth century. But all of these trades were still heavily populated by smaller producers well into the nineteenth century. In some cases such as Birmingham and Sheffield this became a divide between a few large producers and garret-type or sweated labour.

When steam power was adopted in many branches of the trades in the nineteenth century, it did not transform the labour processes, but was simply incorporated into existing technologies. The use of steam power in Birmingham did not necessarily entail large factories and capitalist control or supervision. Such power was frequently rented out in large buildings full of small workrooms sublet to individual artisans. A working man could continue to use the same basic tools developed in the eighteenth century and rent room and power to pursue his trade at greater speed and efficiency. Steam power imposed a much greater regularity on the working day, and even the self-employed artisan could no longer organize his working day around his other familial, cultural and community commitments.[87]

CONCLUSION

The age of manufactures in Britain was a complex web of improvement and decline, large- and small-scale production, machine and hand processes. This book has attempted to present some of the richness and variety of early industrial Britain. It has explicitly redressed the balance of recent teleological accounts of the process of industrialization. It has abandoned the perspective which probes back to the eighteenth century for examples of the 'modern', for instances of striking increases in productivity, and for some clearly defined path into nineteenth-century industrial greatness. It has challenged the applicability of the economists' growth models and stage theories, which have narrowed our account of historical processes to aggregate and macro-economic analysis. Such purely economic history has contributed little to understanding the wider historical framework, especially social history. In many ways, purely economic history has presented a misleading picture of the eighteenth-century economy itself: focusing on but one path into indus-trialization, it has cut us off from understanding alternative paths, and the whole experience of traditional and declining sectors.

My book has drawn on a variety of sources and forms of argument from economic, social and cultural history in order to present a more historical and less instrumental picture of eighteenth-century and early-nineteenth-century industry. The picture is incomplete: I have been able to give little space to several industries – building, mining, leatherworking, food process-ing – which deserve more prominence. Here, as in more conventionally economic histories, the focus has been on the two industries which domi-nated the foreground: textiles and metals. It is precisely through detailed focus on these two best-known cases, however, that I have sought to deepen the conventional perspective, amplifying the presentation of the economic, social and cultural experiences which lay behind the industries.

I have recounted recent debates on the status of the Industrial Revolution. Themes of slow growth and continuity were contrasted with regional change, new technologies, and women's work. I discussed the structure of industrial growth and its relation to the wider economy and society. Successive chapters examined theories of industrial change, the relations of industry to the agricultural sector and the experiences of regional industrial decline. Labour forces in manufacturing, especially women's and children's labour, were analysed, as were trade and consumption of manufactured commodities. Later chapters investigated recent theories and debates over technology and the rise of the factory system, pointing out the variety of forms of industrial structures and technologies, and their very different outcomes. Through a combination of extended narrative and socioeconomic analysis the experiences of the textile and metal industries were examined afresh.

This new edition of my book confronts the now orthodox accounts of slow growth and continuity over the eighteenth and early nineteenth centuries. The Industrial Revolution may not have been the brief dramatic event it was once held to be. But macroeconomic indicators play down the extent of change by obscuring the transformation of production processes and regions. A return to a focus on industry, though a broader range of industries than once conceived, and a return to technologies and production processes would reveal the extent of transformation and restructuring of industry over the course of the eighteenth and early nineteenth centuries. The conclusions of my first edition remain valid.

My picture of the age of manufactures has, I believe, highlighted the following points. First, industrial growth took place over the whole of the eighteenth century, not just in the last quarter of it. There was substantial growth in a whole range of traditional industries as well as in the most obviously exciting cases of cotton and iron. Second, technical change started early and spread extensively through industry. Innovation was not necessarily mechanization. It was also the development of hand and intermediate techniques, and the wider use of and division of cheap labour. It was above all a conjuncture of old and new processes, and that conjuncture affected performance and work experience. Thus, third, industrialization was about work organization; decentralization, extended workshops, and sweating were equally new departures in the organization of production. There was no necessary progression from one to another; their relative efficiency depended on the economic context, and almost any combination of them was possible. These industrial forms, furthermore, had their origins in the differences in work organization to be found in industries like metals and textiles from the very early industrial or proto-industrial phases. Marked differences in production arrangements existed from the beginning of the eighteenth century among the wool, worsted, knitting, silk, linen and cotton industries. In turn, these differences were rooted in socioeconomic structures: historically established levels of industrial concentration and social inequality, legal and customary regulations, and regional cultural traditions.

Fourth and finally, but not least, my book has demonstrated the variable impact of technical and industrial change on the division of labour, skills, employment and regions. It has shown that such change did not always and everywhere entail growth. On the contrary, regional industrial decline affected large numbers of workers, and the traditional industries practised in areas of decline, especially the South, were among the most important employers of labour in the eighteenth century. The eighteenth century was no 'golden age' for the labourer, and though decentralized processes in cottage or workshop manufacture predominated, much of this manufacture was marked by poverty and insecurity. Growth itself, moreover, need not benefit labour. The expansion of the eighteenth-century textile and metal industries depended on the recruitment of huge quantities of cheap female and child labour. This book has shown how some technologies and processes were adapted to the use of large quantities of cheap labour. But this was often the same labour which subsequently suffered the first widespread dislocation from technological change, and mounted the first great waves of resistance to machinery.

These four conclusions seem to me to point towards two directions for future research. I would suggest first that, in moving away from our current narrow vision of industrialization, we take research beyond the conventional territory of cotton, iron and steam power. Fewer people and less wealth were tied up in those technological leaders than in the traditional textile industries and metal manufactures, and this book has sought to give due attention to the range of woollen, linen, silk, cutlery and hardware trades. But large numbers were also to be found in mining, building and the food, drink and leather trades; and there were also the luxury and service trades of town and village. Existing research on these is limited, and analysis in the broad socioeconomic terms here outlined has been virtually non-existent. Accordingly, they have yet to be given their historical due. This book itself has continued the conventional focus on the textile and metal industries, but it has sought to give more weight to their range. We need now to move further out, to discover the processes, organization and labour forces of many more eighteenth-century industries.

Second, there is an urgent need for enquiry into the social realities behind 'increases in productivity'. It is beyond doubt that the technical, organizational and structural changes behind increases in labour productivity involved the dislocation of labour and communities. Hand in hand with industrialization went acute divisions in social experience. One of the most pervasive divisions was that between regions; another was the division of labour, especially by gender. Our curiosity must surely be whetted by the very different responses of workers to technological change in the eighteenth century. Some were enthusiastic or at least passive, others entirely negative. And the reasons for this seem to lie to a large extent in the regional pattern of industrial growth and decline. For the reception accorded technological change in regions where industry had ceased to grow, or where social inequality was marked, was much more negative than in regions of economic opportunity and more egalitarian social structures. The new textile machinery was fiercely resisted in the South, and especially in the West Country, while there seem to be no major instances of resistance to the introduction of machinery in Birmingham. There was more to it than simply differences in regional economic opportunity and social structures, however. Resistance to textile machinery was found in the developing North, even in the cotton districts; and almost certainly this has to be explained in terms of community and cultural traditions along with the emergence of new social divisions. This book has drawn attention to the potential role of artisan organization and especially the solidarity of the outworker communities in the reception of technical change: both of these need to be explored in further comparative research.

Still more in need of investigation is the division between male and female labour markets. In the nineteenth century the great public debates on machinery allowed the voices of artisans and sweated handloom weavers, many of them urban male workers, to be heard. But the much earlier, eighteenth-century voices of protest against the machine, voices from the countryside and especially from women, were drowned out at the time by the proclamations of the 'improvers', and have since been largely ignored by historians. My book has revealed something of the reception which women domestic workers gave to machinery, and of the complexity of their responses, both favourable and hostile. But we need to know much more about the extent to which there were 'women's technologies', and the extent to which there was a 'gender bias' in technological development. We need to know too about the behaviour of women workers in family and community work settings. What part did their work patterns and social networks play in determining the structure of work organization and the reception of new technologies?

Above all else this book indicates the need for a reconciliation of social and economic history. For too long their divorce has entailed a major gap in our understanding of the deep social divisions which accompanied industrialization, and which are still so evidently present at the heart of the current decline and restructuring of the British economy.

NOTES

INTRODUCTION

1 Lodge, *Nice Work*, 33.
2 Colley, *Britons*, 6.
3 Richards, 'Margins of the Industrial Revolution', 203–29.
4 Crafts, *British Economic Growth*.
5 Crafts, 'Industrial Revolution in Britain and France'; 'British Economic Growth, 1700–1831'; Harley, 'British Industrialization before 1841'.
6 Wrigley, *Continuity, Chance and Change*.
7 Wrigley, 'Urban Growth', 178.
8 Wrigley, *Continuity*, 57–60.
9 ibid., 5.
10 Levine and Wrightson, *The Making of an Industrial Society*.
11 Crafts, *British Economic Growth*, 69.
12 Davis, *The Industrial Revolution and British Overseas Trade*, 64–5.
13 Mokyr, *Lever of Riches*, 83.
14 ibid., 112.
15 'Memoirs of James Bisset', Warwick County Record Office.
16 Reilly, *Josiah Wedgwood*, 100–3.
17 'Hargreaves', *Chambers Cyclopedia*.
18 Richards, 'Margins', 212.
19 O'Brien, 'Introduction: Modern Conceptions', 11.
20 Thomson, 'British Industrialization', 91.
21 Landes, *Unbound Prometheus*, 122.

1 CURRENT PERSPECTIVES AND NEW DEPARTURES

1 Stone, *Europe Transformed*, 83.
2 Stedman Jones, 'The Changing Face', 40.
3 Ashton, *An Economic History of England*, 125.
4 Deane and Cole, *British Economic Growth*, 78, 166.
5 Crafts, *British Economic Growth*, 165.
6 ibid., 160–5.
7 Wrigley and Schofield, *Population History*, 528–9.
8 Crafts, 'British Industrialisation', 425.
9 ibid., 425.
10 See Floud, 'Slow to Grow', cited in Berg, 'Revisions and Revolutions', 47.
11 Wrigley, *People, Cities and Wealth*, 9.
12 Wrigley, *Continuity, Chance and Change*, 51.

13 ibid., 54.

14 ibid., 55.

15 ibid., 84, 86.

16 Wrigley, *People, Cities and Wealth*, 11–15.

17 Wrigley and Schofield, *Population History*, chs 10, 11; R. M. Smith, 'Fertility, Economy and Household Formation'; Wrigley, 'Growth of Population'.

18 Kussmaul, *A General View*.

19 The phrase is Gareth Stedman Jones's. 'The Changing Face', 36–40.

20 Crafts, *British Economic Growth*, 87.

21 Landes, 'Fable of the Dead Horse', 149; O'Brien, 'Introduction: Modern Conceptions', 9.

22 Lindert and Williamson, 'Revising England's Social Tables'; Lindert, 'English Occupations'.

23 O'Brien, 'Introduction: Modern Conceptions', 13.

24 Berg and Hudson, 'Rehabilitating the Industrial Revolution', 29.

25 O'Brien, 'Introduction: Modern Conceptions', 14.

26 Ashton, *Peter Stubs*, 4–5.

27 Landes, *Unbound Prometheus*.

28 Landes, 'Fable of the Dead Horse', 161.

29 Hudson, *The Industrial Revolution*, ch. 4, and 'The Regional Perspective'.

30 See Von Tunzelmann, *Steam Power*, 62–70.

31 Pollard, 'Regional Markets and National Development'.

32 Berg and Hudson, 'Rehabilitating the Industrial Revolution', 39.

33 These are explored by Hudson, *The Industrial Revolution*, 104.

34 ibid., ch. 4, and Hudson, *Regions and Industries*.

35 See Berg, *The Machinery Question*.

36 Crafts, *British Economic Growth*, 87.

37 Wrigley, cited in Berg, 'Revisions and Revolutions', 52, note 29.

38 Crafts, 'The Industrial Revolution', 58.

39 Berg and Hudson, 'Rehabilitating the Industrial Revolution', 33–34; Usher, *The Measurement of Economic Growth*, 8–19.

40 Mokyr, 'Technological Change', 41.

41 McCloskey, 'The Industrial Revolution', 127.

42 Berg, 'Revisions and Revolutions', 57; Rosenberg, *Inside the Black Box*.

43 Berg, 'Revisions and Revolutions', 57; Berg and Hudson, 'Rehabilitating the Industrial Revolution', 31.

44 Landes, 'Fable of the Dead Horse', 162.

45 Berg, 'Women's Work', 61–3.

46 Deane and Cole, *British Economic Growth*, 83.

47 Hobsbawm, *The Age of Revolution*.

48 Thomas and McCloskey, 'Overseas Trade and Empire', 100–1.

49 McCloskey, 'The Industrial Revolution', 121–3.

50 Thomas and McCloskey, 'Overseas Trade and Empire', 101; Crouzet, 'Towards an Export Economy', see Hudson, *The Industrial Revolution*, 167; Engerman, 'Mercantilism and Overseas Trade', 185.

51 Crafts, *British Economic Growth*, 142.

52 O'Brien, 'Introduction: Modern Conceptions', 12.

53 Price, *Masters, Unions and Men*; Breen, '"Baubles of Britain"'; Hudson, *The Industrial Revolution*, 184–5.

54 De Vries, 'Between Purchasing Power', 119.

55 O'Brien, 'Foundations of European Industrialisation', 39.

56 Cf. Cuenca Esteban, 'Are British Growth Rates Worth Revising?'

57 Crafts, 'British Industrialisation', 416.

2 INDUSTRIES

1 Defoe, cited in George, *England in Transition*, 29.
2 A. Anderson, *Historical and Chronological Deduction*.
3 Crafts, Leybourne and Mills, 'Trends and Cycles', 45–7.
4 Crafts, 'British Industrialisation', 425.
5 Hoppit, 'Counting the Industrial Revolution'; Hudson, *The Industrial Revolution*, 44.
6 Crafts, 'The Industrial Revolution', 7.
7 Hoppit, 'Counting the Industrial Revolution'.
8 Berg, *The Machinery Question*, ch. 4.
9 Coleman, *Courtaulds: An Economic and Social History*, ch. 2.
10 Harris, *The Copper King*; Harris and Roberts, 'Eighteenth-Century Monopoly', 69–82.
11 Landes, *Unbound Prometheus*, 42.
12 Crouzet, *The First Industrialists*, 32.
13 Hoffmann, *British Industry 1700–1950*; Harley, 'British Industrialization before 1841'; Crafts, Leybourne and Mills, 'Trends and Cycles'.
14 Cuenca Esteban, 'Are British Growth Rates Worth Revising?'
15 Chapman, *The Cotton Industry*, 56.
16 Hudson, *Genesis*, ch. 2.
17 Darby, *A New Historical Geography*, 56–7.
18 Hudson, *The Industrial Revolution*, 119.
19 Crafts, *British Economic Growth*, 23.
20 Whyte, 'Proto-industrialisation in Scotland', 232.
21 Mitchell and Deane, *Abstract of British Statistics*; Durie, 'The Linen Industry'.
22 Wrigley, *Continuity, Chance and Change*, 67, 77–9.
23 ibid., 57–60; Israel, *Dutch Primacy in World Trade*.
24 Crafts, Leybourne and Mills, 'Britain', 140.
25 Mokyr, 'Has the Industrial Revolution been Crowded out?'; Berg, 'Revisions and Revolutions', 52.
26 Berg, 'Revisions and Revolutions', 28.
27 ibid.
28 Levine and Wrightson, *The Making of an Industrial Society*, 214; Clapham, *Economic History*, 186.
29 Crafts, *British Economic Growth*, 23; Hyde, *Technological Change*.
30 Riden, 'Iron and Steel', 128.
31 Crouzet, *The First Industrialists*, 34.
32 Crafts, *British Economic Growth*, 22.
33 Riden, 'Iron and Steel', 127.
34 Mathias, *First Industrial Nation*.
35 Harris, *The Copper King*, 134; Hoppit, 'Counting the Industrial Revolution', 180.
36 Cited in Darby, *A New Historical Geography*, 69.
37 Schumpeter, *English Overseas Trade Statistics*, 64.
38 Gee, *Trade and Navigation of Great Britain*, 5, 69.
39 Schumpeter, *English Overseas Trade Statistics*, 52–9.
40 Davis, *The Industrial Revolution and British Overseas Trade*, 28.
41 Floud, *British Machine Tool Industry*, 36.
42 Crafts, Leybourne and Mills, 'Trends and Cycles', 46.
43 Bowley, *British Building Industry*, 64.
44 ibid., 59.
45 Clapham, *Economic History*, Vol. II, 119.

46 Bowley, *British Building Industry*, 48.
47 ibid., 49.
48 Wrigley, *Continuity, Chance and Change*, 84.
49 Chalklin, *The Provincial Towns of Georgian England*, 160–3; Chapman and Bartlett, 'The Contribution of Building Clubs'.
50 Crafts, *British Economic Growth*, 22.
51 Mounfield, 'Leather Footwear', 124; Clarkson, 'The Manufacture of Leather'; Church, 'The Shoe and Leather Industries'.
52 Weatherill, *The Pottery Trade*.
53 Barker and Harris, *A Merseyside Town*.
54 Schumpeter, *English Overseas Trade Statistics*, 64.
55 Mokyr, 'Demand vs. Supply in the Industrial Revolution', 107.
56 Martyn, 'Considerations on the East India Trade', 613.
57 Cary, *An Essay Towards Regulating the Trade*, 99.
58 O'Brien, *Foundations of European Industrialisation*, 23.
59 Chapman, *The Cotton Industry*, 56.

3 MODELS OF INDUSTRIAL TRANSITION

1 Wrigley, *Continuity, Chance and Change*.
2 Crafts, 'Why was England First?'; Mokyr, 'Has the Industrial Revolution been Crowded out?'.
3 Wrigley, 'Urban Growth'; De Vries, *European Urbanization*; Hohenberg and Lees, *Making of Urban Europe*.
4 Smith, *Wealth of Nations*, Vol. I, Book III, iii, 409.
5 ibid.
6 ibid., Book III, iv, 422.
7 ibid., Book III, iii, 408.
8 ibid., Book I, x, 131.
9 ibid., Book III, iv, 422.
10 Hudson, 'The Regional Perspective'.
11 Pollard, 'Regional Markets and National Development', 45.
12 De Vries, *European Urbanization*.
13 Wrigley, 'Urban Growth', 177–9.
14 Hohenberg and Lees, *Making of Urban Europe*, 13–120.
15 De Vries, 'Between Purchasing Power', 107.
16 Smith, *Wealth of Nations*, Book III, iii, 409.
17 ibid., Book IV, viii, 644.
18 Thorold Rogers, *Six Centuries of Work and Wages*, 489–90.
19 Marx, *Capital*, I, 911.
20 'The Babbage Principle', in Babbage's own words, was 'that the master manufacturer by dividing the work to be executed into different processes, each requiring different degrees of skill or of force, can purchase exactly that precise quantity of both which is necessary for each process, whereas if the whole work were executed by one workman, that person must possess sufficient skill to perform the most difficult and sufficient strength to execute the most laborious, of the operations into which the work is divided'. See Berg, *The Machinery Question*, 182–9.
21 Marx, *Capital*, 489–90.
22 See Diderot, *Encyclopédie*, Vol. 5, 'Epingle'.
23 Lord Fitzmaurice, *Life of Shelbourne*, 404.
24 Roll, *An Early Experiment*.
25 Chapman and Chassagne, *European Textile Printers*, 97.

26 Marglin, 'What Do Bosses Do?', 20; The Brighton Group, 'Capitalist Labour Process'; Berg, *Technology and Toil*.
27 Dobb, *Studies*, 143 and ch. 4.
28 Goldin and Sokoloff, 'Women, Children and Industrialization in the Early Republic'; Goldin and Sokoloff, 'The Relative Productivity Hypothesis'; Sokoloff, 'Transition from the Artisanal Shop'.
29 Mendels, 'Proto-industrialization'; Medick, 'The Proto-industrial Family Economy'; Jones, 'Agricultural Origins'; De Vries, *Economy of Europe*, 95–6. Some of the discussion of proto-industrialization in this section of the chapter is based on Berg, Hudson, Sonenscher, 'Introduction', *Manufacture in Town and Country*, and I am indebted to my co-authors.
30 Habakkuk, 'Population Growth'; John, 'Agricultural Productivity'; Thirsk, 'Industries in the Countryside'; Chambers, 'Vale of Trent'; Chambers, 'The Rural Domestic Industries'; Jones, 'Agricultural Origins'.
31 Mendels and Deyon, 'Proto-industrialization'; Coleman, 'A Concept too Many'.
32 Jeannin, 'Développement ou Impasse?', 52–65; Kriedte, Medick, Schlumbohm, *Industrialization*, 7; Houston and Snell, 'Proto-industrialization?'.
33 Kriedte, Medick and Schlumbohm, *Industrialization*, 111.
34 Medick, 'The Proto-industrial Family Economy', 301–10.
35 Jones, 'Environment', 494.
36 Medick, 'The Proto-industrial Family Economy', 301.
37 Medick, 'Plebeian Culture', 89–92.
38 Williamson, 'The Evolution of Hierarchy', and Millward, 'The Emergence of Wage Labour'.
39 Clapham, *Economic History*, I, 145, 191; Hudson, 'From Manor to Mill'.
40 Faucher, cited in Clapham, *Economic History*, I, 175.
41 Schremmer, 'Proto-industrialization', 123.
42 DuPlessis and Howell, 'Early Modern Urban Economy', 51 and 84.
43 For a discussion of these artisan structures in an unincorporated town such as Birmingham see Chapter 10. For further discussion of these artisan systems in Britain and France see Sabel and Zeitlin, 'Historical Alternatives'. Artisan organization and customs in Britain and France are discussed in Prothero, *Artisans and Politics*; Rule, *Experience of Labour*; Sewell, *Work and Revolution*.
44 Clapham, *Economic History*, I, 156.
45 Sabel and Zeitlin, 'Historical Alternatives'.
46 These are described in Chapman, 'Industrial Capital', 124.
47 Chapman and Chassagne, *European Textile Printers*, 215, 194. Also see Freudenberger, 'Protofactories', for a discussion of the characteristics of this industrial structure and how it was developed on the landed estates of the Hapsburg Empire in the eighteenth century.
48 See Sabel and Zeitlin for the different success rates by which three artisan regions adapted to changing markets. See Thomson, 'Variations in Industrial Structure'.
49 Coleman, 'A Concept too Many', 445.

4 AGRICULTURE, RESOURCES, ENVIRONMENT

1 Mill, 'Nature, Origins, and Progress of Rent', 177.
2 Jones, *Agriculture*, ch. 3; Thirsk, *Agrarian History*, Introduction.
3 Wrigley, 'Growth of Population', 122; Deane and Cole, *British Economic Growth*, 45; Mitchell and Deane, *Abstract of British Historical Statistics*, 8.
4 Crafts, 'British Industrialisation', 418.
5 Allen, 'Agriculture' 100; Holderness, 'Agriculture 1770–1860'; Jackson, 'Growth

and Deceleration in English Agriculture'; Overton, 'Agricultural Productivity'; O'Brien, 'Introduction: Modern Conceptions', 19.

6 Allen, 'Agriculture', 100.
7 ibid., 119, 122.
8 Crafts, *British Economic Growth*, p. 84.
9 Crafts, Leybourne and Mills, 'Britain', 115.
10 Wrigley, 'A Simple Model of London's Importance'.
11 Allen, 'Agriculture', 121.
12 Jackson, 'Growth and Deceleration in English Agriculture'; O'Brien, 'Agriculture and the Home Market'; Allen, 'Agriculture', 122.
13 Smith, *Wealth of Nations*, Vol. I, Book I, i, 17.
14 Crafts, Leybourne and Mills, 'Britain', 116; Crafts, 'British Industrialization', 424–8.
15 O'Brien, 'Introduction: Modern Conceptions', 20.
16 John initially made the case for a connection between low agricultural prices and rising industrial demand. Recent work throws this into question. See Cole, 'Factors in Demand', and Beckett, 'Regional Variation'.
17 O'Brien, 'Agriculture and the Home Market', 730; Crafts, *British Economic Growth*, 133–4.
18 Gould, 'Agricultural Fluctuations'.
19 Eversley, 'The Home Market', 206–59.
20 Jones, 'Agricultural Origins', 138.
21 These arguments are made by Hohenberg, 'Toward a Model of the European Economic System'.
22 Jones, *Agriculture*, 117.
23 Hoskins, *The Midland Peasant*, 269.
24 ibid., 310.
25 Eden, *The State of the Poor*, I, 555.
26 See Westerfield, *Middlemen*, for a survey of the distinctions between the various functions of the corn middlemen. Also see Thompson, 'The Moral Economy', for a discussion of monopolies in the retailing of corn.
27 I owe this point to Jeanette Neeson. Also see Beckett, 'Regional Variation', 41–2.
28 Cole, 'Factors in Demand', 54–7.
29 Wrigley, 'Growth of Population', 97–8.
30 Jones, *Agriculture*, 102–10, produces the usual examples of landlords investing in mining and ironworking on their estates. But the motivation behind their industrial investment may have been as dubious as that behind their investment in the land itself. For a discussion of this see Cooper, 'In Search of Agrarian Capitalism'.
31 B. L. Anderson, 'The Attorney'. Also see Rowlands, 'Society and Industry in the West Midlands', who shows from local studies that credit was available to all but the lowest levels of society, and that anyone with any land at all could raise a mortgage. Smiths and husbandmen could raise £20 to £40 in this way.
32 Burley, 'An Essex Clothier'; Ashton, *Peter Stubs*.
33 Chapman, 'Industrial Capital'.
34 Berg, 'Small-Producer Capitalism'; Hudson, *Genesis*, chs 3–4.
35 Berg, 'Women's Property and the Industrial Revolution'; Davidoff and Hall, *Family Fortunes*, 205–15.
36 The classic statement of this position is Chambers, 'Enclosure and Labour Supply'.
37 Crafts, 'British Industrialisation', 420–3.

38 Hoskins, *The Midland Peasant*, 263.
39 Jones, 'Agricultural Origins', 139.
40 For a standard statement of this position see Bythell, *Handloom Weavers*.
41 I owe this point to Jeannette Neeson.
42 Snell, *Annals of the Labouring Poor*, chs 1, 4.
43 Allen, *Enclosure and the Yeoman*, chs 12, 14.
44 Thirsk, 'Industries in the Countryside'. This paragraph is based on arguments made in Berg, Hudson, Sonenscher, 'Introduction', *Manufacture in Town and Country*, 22–3.
45 ibid. Also see Hey, 'A Dual Economy'.
46 Chambers, 'The Rural Domestic Industries', 430.
47 Jones, 'Agriculture and Economic Growth', 110–11.
48 Spufford, 'Peasant Inheritance Customs and Land Distribution', 157.
49 Howell, 'Peasant Inheritance Customs in the Midlands 1280–1800'.
50 For an early statement of this see Habakkuk, 'Family Structure'.
51 Hey, *Rural Metalworkers*.
52 Thompson, 'The Grid of Inheritance'.
53 Houston and Snell, 'Proto-industrialization'.
54 Rowlands, *Masters and Men*, 39–43.
55 See Hudson, 'Proto-industrialization'.
56 Cited in Neeson, *Commoners*, ch. 1.
57 Smith, *Wealth of Nations*, Vol. I, Book I, 101.
58 ibid., 103.
59 The extent of local industrial specialization within regions is noticed by Sydney Pollard in his *Peaceful Conquest*, 32–5, but no attempt is made to link these specializations to their individual agrarian contexts.
60 Wolfe, *Europe and the People without History*, 265, 158.
61 Mathias, 'Resources and Technology', 20.
62 ibid., 20.
63 Pollard, 'Regional Markets and National Development', 35.
64 Langton, *Atlas of Industrialising Britain*, 4.
65 Flinn, *History of the British Coal Industry*, 290.
66 Levine and Wrightson, *The Making of an Industrial Society*, 1.
67 ibid., 8.
68 ibid., ix.
69 ibid., 79.
70 ibid., 79; Flinn, *Men of Iron*, 52–4.
71 Wrigley, *Continuity, Chance and Change*, 77.
72 ibid., 81.
73 Harris, 'Skills, Coal and British Industry'.
74 Mokyr, *Lever of Riches*, 84–93.
75 Ricardo, *Principles*, ch. 3, 85.
76 Von Tunzelmann, *Steam Power*, 64–9, 84–6.

5 INDUSTRIAL DECLINE

1 Thirsk, *Economic Policy*, 109. Also see Thirsk, 'Industries in the Countryside', and 'The Fantastical Folly of Fashion'.
2 Thirsk, *Economic Policy*, 168.
3 Wrightson, *English Society*, 139.
4 Pollard, 'Industrialization and the European Economy'; Pollard, *Peaceful Conquest*.
5 Richards, 'Women in the British Economy', 343.

6 Jones, 'Constraints', 423–30; Jones, 'Environment'.
7 Polanyi, *The Great Transformation*.
8 Little, *Deceleration*, 24–31.
9 Jones, 'Constraints', 423.
10 Hudson, *The Industrial Revolution*, 101, 108.
11 Pollard, 'Regional Markets and National Development', 38.
12 Hohenberg, 'Urban Manufactures', 169.
13 MacLeod, *Inventing the Industrial Revolution*.
14 Cary, *An Essay Towards Regulating the Trade*, 99.
15 Postlethwayt, *Britain's Commercial Interest*, II, 416, 420.
16 Pollard, 'Regional Markets and National Development', 39–40.
17 Langton, 'Industrial Revolution and the Regional Geography of England', 162; Turnbull, 'Canals, Coal and Regional Growth'; cf. Hudson, *The Industrial Revolution*, 103.
18 Pollard, *Peaceful Conquest*, 19; Chandler, 'Scale and Scope'.
19 Defoe, *Tour*, 464.
20 Wrightson, *English Society*, 139.
21 Hoskins, *The Midland Peasant*, 274.
22 Jones, 'Constraints', 425.
23 Pollard, *Peaceful Conquest*, 14. For a recent detailed treatment of declining marginal regions see Richards, 'Margins of the Industrial Revolution'.
24 Jones, 'Constraints', 429; Pollard, *Peaceful Conquest*, 20.
25 Pollard, 'Regional Markets and National Development', 44.
26 Jones, 'Constraints', 426.
27 Cited in Brown, *Essex*, 1.
28 ibid., 14. Also see Coleman, 'Growth and Decay'.
29 Defoe, *Plan of English Commerce*, 257, cited in George, *England in Transition*, 55.
30 Lloyd Prichard, 'The Decline of Norwich', 373, 374; Coleman, 'Growth and Decay'.
31 Wilson, 'The Supremacy of the Yorkshire Cloth Industry', 231–7.
32 Lloyd Prichard, 'The Decline of Norwich', 375.
33 Mann, *The Cloth Industry*, 159–76.
34 Wilson, 'The Supremacy of the Yorkshire Cloth Industry', 233.
35 Jones, 'Agriculture and Economic Growth', 111.
36 Brown, *Essex*, 19–25.
37 See previous chapter and Chapman, 'Industrial Capital'.
38 Jones, 'Agriculture and Economic Growth', 105.
39 Jones, 'Environment', 498.
40 Tucker, *Instructions for Travellers*, cited in Wilson, 'The Supremacy of the Yorkshire Cloth Industry', 238.
41 ibid., 238.
42 Mann, *The Cloth Industry*, 97–9, 192.
43 Wilson, 'The Supremacy of the Yorkshire Cloth Industry', 241.
44 Brown, *Essex*, 20, 25.
45 Mann, *The Cloth Industry*, 114.
46 ibid., 114, 125, 126.
47 Jones, 'Constraints'; Mann, *The Cloth Industry*, 161, 149.
48 Pinchbeck, *Women Workers*, 155–6.
49 I owe this point to Jeannette Neeson.
50 Brown, *Essex*, 113; Burley, 'An Essex Clothier', 289.
51 Pinchbeck, *Women Workers*, 206.
52 Spencely, 'The English Pillow Lace Industry', 70.

53 Pinchbeck, *Women Workers*, 222.
54 See Chapter 4, p. 89; Snell, *Annals of the Labouring Poor*, chs 1 and 4; Allen, *Enclosure and the Yeoman*, chs 12 and 14.
55 Snell, 'Agricultural Seasonal Unemployment', 434–7.
56 Clapham, *Economic History*, I, 183.
57 Pinchbeck, *Women Workers*, 225.
58 ibid., 229, and Clapham, *Economic History*, I, 183.
59 Pollard, *Peaceful Conquest*.
60 Burley, 'An Essex Clothier'; Chapman, 'Industrial Capital'.
61 Richards, 'Margins of the Industrial Revolution', 207.
62 This paragraph is based on Pollard, *Peaceful Conquest*, 14–16.
63 Honeyman, *Origins of Enterprise*, 28–9.
64 B. M. Short, 'The De-industrialisation Process', 164–160; Hudson, *The Industrial Revolution*, 128–30.
65 Dickson, 'Aspects of the Rise and Decline of the Irish Cotton Industry', 100–16.
66 Pollard, 'Regional Markets and National Development', 44.
67 Beckett, 'Regional Variation', concludes that this depression was less intense than previously supposed, and its effects on the rest of the economy much weaker. On eighteenth-century growth see Wrigley, 'Growth of Population'; Crafts, 'British Economic Growth'; and McCloskey, 'The Industrial Revolution'.
68 Cole, 'Factors in Demand', 53.
69 This paragraph is based on Little, *Deceleration*, 65–85.
70 Randall, *Before the Luddites*, 60–1.

6 TRADE, CONSUMPTION AND MANUFACTURING

1 Crouzet, 'Towards an Export Economy', 65, 69, 81.
2 Price, 'What Did Merchants Do?', 269–70.
3 Goodman and Honeyman, *Gainful Pursuits*, 24, 25.
4 ibid., 53, 56.
5 Price, 'What Did Merchants Do?', 269–70.
6 O'Brien, 'Foundations of European Industrialisation', 21.
7 Davis, 'English Foreign Trade', 93.
8 Crouzet, 'Towards an Export Economy', 87.
9 ibid., 90–2.
10 Pollard, 'Industrialisation and the European Economy', 641, 643; Pollard, *Peaceful Conquest*.
11 Davis, *The Industrial Revolution and British Overseas Trade*, 64–5.
12 This paragraph is based on Thomson, 'British Industrialization and the External World', 83–5.
13 Mokyr, 'Demand vs. Supply in the Industrial Revolution'; Crafts, *British Economic Growth*.
14 Crafts, 'The Industrial Revolution', 48.
15 Thomson, 'British Industrialization and the External World', 86–7.
16 Cuenca Esteban, 'Are British Growth Rates Worth Revising?'
17 See Hudson, *The Industrial Revolution*, 182.
18 Engerman, 'Mercantilism and Overseas Trade', 197.
19 O'Brien, *Power with Profit*, 17–20.
20 ibid.
21 O'Brien, 'Introduction: Modern Conceptions', 12.
22 Weatherill, *The Pottery Trade*.
23 Israel, *Dutch Primacy in World Trade*, 356–7, 386, 409.
24 Steensgaard, 'Growth and Composition', 102–53.

25 Devine, *Tobacco*; Price, *Capital and Credit*.
26 O'Brien, 'Foundations of European Industrialisation', 25.
27 Thomson, 'State Intervention', 57–93.
28 O'Brien, 'Foundations of European Industrialisation', 25.
29 Steensgaard, 'Growth and Composition', 151.
30 Price, 'What Did Merchants Do?', 283–4.
31 Chapman, *Merchant Enterprise in Britain*, 7–17.
32 O'Brien, 'Agriculture and the Home Market', 773–9.
33 Clifford, 'Eighteenth-Century Goldsmithing Business'.
34 De Vries, *European Urbanisation*.
35 Wrigley, 'Urban Growth'.
36 Quoted in McKendrick, Brewer and Plumb, *Birth of a Consumer Society*, 77.
37 Robinson, 'Matthew Boulton and Josiah Wedgwood'.
38 See Douglas and Isherwood, *The World of Goods*; Clifford, 'Eighteenth-Century Goldsmithing Business'; Vickery, 'Women and the World of Goods'.
39 Weatherill, *Consumer Behaviour and Material Culture*, 41; cf. Shammas, *The Pre-industrial Consumer*.
40 Shammas, *The Pre-industrial Consumer*, 185.
41 Weatherill, *Consumer Behaviour and Material Culture*, 33–42.
42 Nenadic, 'Businessmen. The Urban Middle Classes', 74–5.
43 Sabel and Zeitlin, 'Historical Alternatives to Mass Production'.
44 The above paragraphs summarize the arguments in 'Historical Alternatives to Mass Production'.
45 Styles, 'Manufacturing, Consumption and Design', 540.
46 Said, *Orientalism*.
47 Weatherill, 'A Possession of One's Own'; Vickery, 'Women and the World of Goods', 287–9.
48 Lemire, *Fashion's Favourite*, 109.
49 Pollexfen in 1681, cited in Steensgaard, 'Growth and Composition', 127.
50 De Vries, 'Between Purchasing Power', 119.

7 WOMEN, CHILDREN AND WORK

1 Lindert and Williamson, 'Revising England's Social Tables', 385–408.
2 Hill, *Women, Work and Sexual Politics*.
3 Allen, *Enclosure and the Yeoman*, ch. 1.
4 Allen, *Enclosure and the Yeoman*, ch. 12; Snell, *Annals of the Labouring Poor*; Valenze, 'The Art of Women and the Business of Men'.
5 Hill, *Women, Work and Sexual Politics*, 125–7.
6 Higgs, 'Women, Occupations and Work', 59–80, 68–9.
7 Pearson, 'Gender Matters in Development', ch. 15.
8 Humphries, '"Lurking in the Wings"', 32–44.
9 Randall, *Before the Luddites*, 54–5, 58.
10 Smith, *Wealth of Nations*, Vol. I, Book IV, VIII, 644.
11 Collins, 'Proto-industrialization and Pre-Famine Emigration', 132–4.
12 See Rothstein, 'The Silk Industry in London', ch. 2; Lown, *Women and Industrialisation*, ch. 1.
13 Freudenberger, Mather and Nardinelli, 'Early Factory Labour Force', 1085–90, 1087; Bolin-Hort, *Work, Family and the State*, 54.
14 Sharpe, 'Literally Spinsters', 46–65, 52.
15 Pinchbeck, *Women Workers*, 204; Spencely, 'The Origins of the English Pillow Lace Industry', 81–93.
16 See Martin, 'Village Traders and the Emergence of a Proletariat'; cf. Allen,

Enclosure and the Yeoman, ch. 1, who found that shoemakers made up 15 per cent of industrial employment in the South Midlands in 1831. These trades fitted well with W. A. Lewis's petty retail trades which are enormously expanded in overpopulated economies. See Lewis, 'Economic Development', 141.
17 See Chapter 12; Behagg, *Politics and Production,* 48–9.
18 Eden, *The State of the Poor,* II, 385, III, 739, 814, 876.
19 Chambers, 'The Rural Domestic Industries', 438.
20 Cited in the Hammonds, *The Skilled Labourer,* 145.
21 Eden, *The State of the Poor,* III, 821.
22 ibid.
23 Clark, *Working Life of Women,* 111.
24 Cited in Richards, 'Women in the British Economy', 341.
25 Aspin and Chapman, *James Hargreaves and the Spinning Jenny,* 57.
26 Reddy, *The Rise of Market Culture,* ch. 2.
27 Select Committee on the State of Children.
28 Hutton, *History of Derby.*
29 Vincent, *Bread, Knowledge and Freedom,* 78.
30 *Children's Employment Commission,* 1816.
31 See MacLeod, *Inventing the Industrial Revolution,* 159–71.
32 Dean Tucker, cited in Porter, *English Society,* 213–14.
33 Eversley, 'Industry and Trade 1500–1800', 110–11.
34 See advertisements in *Aris's Gazette,* 1766–96.
35 Josiah Wedgewood, *Children's Employment Commission,* vol. I, 1816.
36 E. I. Davies, 'The Handmade Nail Trade', 142.
37 See Thirsk, *Economic Policy.*
38 Cf. Sharpe, 'Literally Spinsters', 46–65.
39 Earle, 'The Female Labour Market', 328–53, 338, 340, 346; Dent, 'Ubiquitous but Invisible', 111–29, esp. 119, 125; Cunningham, 'Employment and Unemployment of Children', 115–50, esp. 131, 133, 137.
40 Pinchbeck, *Women Workers,* 155.
41 The Hammonds, *The Skilled Labourer,* 152.
42 ibid., 149.
43 Cited in Wadsworth and Mann, *The Cotton Trade.*
44 Baines, *History of the Cotton Manufacture,* 159.
45 Wadsworth and Mann, *The Cotton Trade,* 375.
46 ibid., 301.
47 Richards, 'Women in the British Economy', 343.
48 Clapham, *Economic History,* I, 183.
49 Jones, 'Constraints'.
50 Snell, 'Agricultural Seasonal Unemployment', 436.
51 Hobsbawm, *Age of Revolution,* 55.
52 Landes, *Unbound Prometheus,* 117.
53 Pollard, 'Labour in the British Economy'.
54 Pinchbeck, *Women Workers;* Alexander, 'Women and the London Trades'.
55 Chapman and Chassagne, *European Textile Printers,* 95, 96, 194.
56 Coleman, 'Growth and Decay', 120, 123–4.
57 Wadsworth and Mann, *The Cotton Trade,* 285, 325, 332, 336.
58 Boserup, *Women's Role in Economic Development.*
59 Elson and Pearson, 'Nimble Fingers'.
60 McKendrick, 'Home Demand and Economic Growth', 186.
61 Prothero, *Artisans and Politics,* 35.
62 Phillips and Taylor, 'Sex and Skill', 82–8.
63 Godelier, 'Work and its Representations'.

64 Sharpe, 'Literally Spinsters', 55; Hill, *Women, Work and Sexual Politics*, chs 12, 13.
65 Saito, 'Labour Supply Behaviour of the Poor', 633–52, esp. 636, 645–9.
66 Gibson and Smout, *Prices, Food and Wages in Scotland*; Whyte, 'Proto-industrialisation in Scotland', 228–52, esp. 242, 247.
67 Snell, *Annals of the Labouring Poor*; Neeson, *Commoners*.
68 Medick, 'The Proto-industrial Family Economy', 304, 307, 310.
69 Chaytor, 'Household and Kinship: Ryton', 30.
70 Laslett, 'Family and Household', 555.
71 B. Collins, 'Proto-industrialization and Pre-Famine Emigration', 133.
72 Levine, *Family Formation*, 48.
73 J. Anderson, *Observations on National Industry*, I, 39.
74 Cited in Hudson, 'From Manor to Mill', 130.
75 Pinchbeck, *Women Workers*, 126.
76 Chaytor, 'Household and Kinship', 48.
77 O. Harris, 'Households and their Boundaries', 8, 150.
78 Kusamitsu, 'Industrial Revolution and Design', 118.
79 Edwards and Lloyd-Jones, 'Smelser and the Cotton Factory Family', 305.
80 Radcliffe, *New System of Manufacture*.
81 The Hammonds, *The Skilled Labourer*, 162.
82 Snell, *Annals of the Labouring Poor*, ch. 6, 331.
83 Simonton, 'Apprenticeship: Training and Gender', 227–61.
84 Lown, *Women and Industrialisation*, ch. 1.
85 Reid, 'Decline of Saint Monday', 95.
86 David Sabeen has, however, suggested to me that many of the arts typically associated with housewifery only really came into being in the eighteenth and nineteenth centuries. The finer needlework required in the working of cotton and linen fabrics was not practised by most peasant and working-class households clothed in coarse woollen clothing.
87 Samuel Bamford, *Passages in the Life of a Radical*, 111.
88 Quoted in Malcolmson, *Life and Labour in England*, 118.
89 Thompson, 'The Moral Economy Reviewed', 305–22.
90 Reddy, *The Rise of Market Culture*.
91 Randall, *Before the Luddites*.
92 These points were raised by David Washbrook, 'Markets and Custom in Eighteenth-Century South India'.

8 MACHINES AND MANUAL LABOUR

1 Landes, *Unbound Prometheus*, 41, 81, 95, 99, 105, 123.
2 For a lucid, layperson's account of some of the theories of technical change see Nathan Rosenberg, 'The Direction of Technological Change'. For a good, basic survey of the economic theories and some empirical studies of technical change see Arnold Heertje, *Economics and Technical Change*. N. von Tunzelmann, 'Technical Progress', discusses the applications of some of these theories to the British experience before 1860.
3 Habakkuk, *American and British Technology*.
4 Marx, *Capital*, I, 391.
5 David, 'Labour Scarcity'.
6 Habakkuk, 'Labour Scarcity'.
7 Saul, *Technological Change*, 'Introduction'.
8 These arguments are put in Berg, 'Power Loom'.
9 Temin, 'Labour Scarcity in America'.

10 David, 'Labour Scarcity', 33.
11 ibid., 28.
12 MacLeod, *Inventing the Industrial Revolution*, ch. 9; Mokyr, *Lever of Riches*, 165.
13 Bruland, 'Industrial Conflict'; Lazonick, 'Industrial Relations and Technical Change'; Styles, 'Embezzlement, Industry and the Law'.
14 Von Tunzelmann, 'Technology in the Early Nineteenth Century', 295.
15 Von Tunzelmann, 'Technological and Organizational Change', 258.
16 Von Tunzelmann, 'Technology in the Early Nineteenth Century', 291–3.
17 See McCloskey, *Essays on a Mature Economy*.
18 Von Tunzelmann, *Steam Power*; Hyde, *Technological Change*.
19 Sandberg, *Lancashire in Decline*; David, 'The Landscape and the Machine'; Temin, 'The Relative Decline of the British Steel Industry'.
20 Von Tunzelmann, 'Technological and Organizational Change', 259.
21 David, 'The Landscape and the Machine'; Collins, 'Harvest Technology'; Roberts, 'Sickles and Scythes', 22.
22 Sandberg, *Lancashire in Decline*; Gutman, *Work Culture and Society*, 39. For a critique of this see Lazonick, 'Factor Costs and the Diffusion of Ring Spinning'.
23 Hyde, *Technological Change*.
24 Von Tunzelmann, *Steam Power*.
25 Mokyr, *Lever of Riches*, 160.
26 Von Tunzelmann, 'Technology in the Early Nineteenth Century', 286–7.
27 Mokyr, 'Technological Change', 31.
28 Nelson and Winter, *An Evolutionary Theory of Economic Change*, 9, 17, 349.
29 Nelson, 'The Roles of Firms', 169.
30 Dosi, 'Sources, Procedures', 1131.
31 ibid., 1138.
32 ibid., 1158.
33 Mokyr, *Lever of Riches*, 294–9.
34 Mokyr, 'Technological Change', 41.
35 Rosenberg, 'Machine Tool Industry'.
36 Rosenberg, 'Economic Development'; 'The Direction of Technological Change'.
37 Harris, 'Industry and Technology'; 'Skills, Coal and British Industry'; Mathias, 'Skills and the Diffusion'.
38 Mokyr, 'Technological Change', 41.
39 Von Tunzelmann, 'Technology in the Early Nineteenth Century', 277–9.
40 MacLeod, *Inventing the Industrial Revolution*.
41 Von Tunzelmann, 'Technology in the Early Nineteenth Century', 283.
42 ibid., 285.
43 Mokyr, 'Technological Inertia', 328; Randall, *Before the Luddites*, 3.
44 Landes, 'Fable of the Dead Horse', 161.
45 Mokyr, 'Technological Inertia', 336.
46 Randall, *Before the Luddites*, ch. 3.
47 Berg, 'Workers and Machinery', 57–69.
48 Marglin, 'What Do Bosses Do?'; 'The Power of Knowledge'. See Berg, 'On the Origins of Capitalist Hierarchy'.
49 Berg, *Technology and Toil*, 'Introduction'.
50 Stone, 'The Origins of Job Structures in the Steel Industry'.
51 Lazonick, *Competitive Advantage*, 27–67.
52 Samuel, 'Workshop of the World'.
53 Von Tunzelmann, *Steam Power*.
54 Bruland, 'Industrial Conflict'.
55 Lazonick, 'Industrial Relations and Technical Change'.

56 Zeitlin, 'Craft Control and the Division of Labour'.
57 Price, *Masters, Unions and Men*.
58 These are elaborated in Chapters 10 to 12 below.
59 For example, Gray, *The Labour Aristocracy*.
60 Prothero, *Artisans and Politics*, 15.
61 This perspective has been uncovered in disputes over the masculinity of the tailoring trades in early nineteenth-century London. See Taylor, *Eve and the New Jerusalem*, ch. 4.

9 THE RISE OF THE FACTORY SYSTEM

1 Von Tunzelmann, 'Technological and Organizational Change', 268.
2 Heaton, *Yorkshire Woollen and Worsted*, 352, cited in Von Tunzelmann, 'Technological and Organizational Change', 269.
3 Von Tunzelmann, 'Technological and Organizational Change', 269.
4 Crouzet, *The First Industrialists*, 32.
5 Chapman and Butt, 'The Cotton Industry', 115.
6 Marglin, 'What Do Bosses Do?', 29.
7 ibid., 81.
8 Williamson, *Economic Institutions of Capitalism*.
9 Landes, 'What Do Bosses Really Do?', 603.
10 ibid., 607.
11 ibid., 606–7.
12 Fitton and Wadsworth, *Strutts and Arkwrights*, 79.
13 Mokyr, *Lever of Riches*, 257.
14 ibid., 255.
15 Marglin, 'What Do Bosses Do?'
16 Goldin and Sokoloff, 'Women, Children and Industrialisation in the Early Republic'.
17 Landes, 'What Do Bosses Really Do?', 615.
18 Landes, 'Small is Beautiful. Small is Beautiful?', 26.
19 Sokoloff, 'Transition from the Artisanal Shop', 372; Von Tunzelmann, 'Technological and Organizational Change'.
20 Marshall, *Industry and Trade*, 237.
21 Cf. Marglin, 'What Do Bosses Do?'; Piore and Sabel, *The Second Industrial Divide*.
22 Landes, 'Small is Beautiful. Small is Beautiful?', 26.
23 Sabel and Zeitlin, 'Historical Alternatives'.
24 Marshall, *Industry and Trade*, 237.
25 ibid., 237, 225.
26 Kenney and Florida, 'Beyond Mass Production', 133–8.
27 Sonenscher, *Work and Wages*, 44, 45.
28 Behagg, *Politics and Production*, 10.
29 Sonenscher, *Work and Wages*, 135–8.
30 Behagg, *Politics and Production*, 8.
31 Crafts, *British Economic Growth*, 69; Wrigley, *Continuity, Chance and Change*, 84.
32 Sabel and Zeitlin, 'Historical Alternatives', 146–50.
33 Landes, 'What Do Bosses Really Do?', 606–7.
34 ibid., 607.
35 Landes, 'Small is Beautiful. Small is Beautiful?', 27.
36 Berg, Hudson and Sonenscher, *Manufacture in Town and Country*; Houston and Snell, 'Proto-industrialisation?'

37 Marglin, 'Understanding Capitalism', 237.
38 The Webbs, *History of Trade Unionism*, 232–5.
39 See p. 273.
40 Chapman, 'Fixed Capital in the Cotton Industry'; Gatrell, 'Labour, Power and the Size of Firms'.
41 Gatrell, 'Labour, Power and the Size of Firms', 113.
42 Clapham, *Economic History*, Vol. I, 196.
43 Crouzet, *The First Industrialists*, 30.
44 ibid., 3.
45 Hudson, *Genesis*, 42.
46 Levine and Wrightson, *The Making of an Industrial Society*, 214; Clapham, *Economic History*, 185.
47 Riden, 'Iron and Steel', 28; Crouzet, *The First Industrialists*, 34.
48 Mathias, *Brewing Industry in England*, 542–3.
49 Sokoloff, 'Transition from the Artisanal Shop', 353, 372, 375.
50 Goldin and Sokoloff, 'Women, Children and Industrialisation in the Early Republic'; Goldin and Sokoloff, 'The Relative Productivity Hypothesis'.
51 Sokoloff, 'Inventive Activity', 846; Sokoloff and Khan, 'Democratisation of Invention'.
52 Kanefsky, 'Motive Power in British Industry', 360–76, esp. 363–9.
53 Chapman, 'The Cotton Industry', 107.
54 Cited in Porter, *English Society*, 213–14.
55 Marshall, *Industry and Trade*, 285–8.
56 Florence, *The Logic of British and American Industry*, 86–92.
57 Hudson, 'From Manor to Mill'.
58 Behagg, *Politics and Production*, ch. 1.
59 Pollard, *Labour in Sheffield*, 58.
60 Landes, 'What Do Bosses Really Do?', 622.
61 Pollard, 'Regional Markets and National Development', 42–3.
62 Chandler, *Scale and Scope*.

10 THE TEXTILE INDUSTRIES: ORGANIZING WORK

1 Defoe, *Complete English Tradesman*, 393.
2 Jenkins and Ponting, *British Wool Textile Industry*, 5.
3 Eden, *The State of the Poor*.
4 Jenkins and Ponting, *British Wool Textile Industry*, 4, 7.
5 ibid., 58–9.
6 ibid., 75.
7 Heaton, *Yorkshire Woollen and Worsted*, 264–75.
8 R. G. Wilson, 'The Supremacy of the Yorkshire Cloth Industry', 233; Lloyd Prichard, 'The Decline of Norwich', 374–6; C. Wilson, *England's Apprenticeship*, 291.
9 Brown, *Essex*, 2–11, 20.
10 Jenkins and Ponting, *British Wool Textile Industry*, 71.
11 Mann, *The Cloth Industry*, 159–63.
12 Heaton, *Yorkshire Woollen and Worsted*, 78, 285.
13 ibid., 289.
14 Thirsk, 'The Fantastical Folly of Fashion', 62–3.
15 Chambers, 'The Rural Domestic Industries', 428–9.
16 Heaton, *Yorkshire Woollen and Worsted*, 235.
17 Rogers, 'Framework Knitting', 8–10; Levine, *Family Formation*, 21.
18 Clapham, *Economic History*, I, 145.

19 Timmins, *Birmingham*, 179–83; Prest, *Coventry*, 53.
20 De Vries, *Economy of Europe*, 100; Harte, 'Rise of Protection', 109.
21 Harte, 'Rise of Protection', 76.
22 ibid., 109.
23 ibid., 103.
24 Bremner, *Industries of Scotland*, 214–30.
25 B. Collins, 'Proto-industrialization and Pre-Famine Emigration', 129–30.
26 Harte, 'Rise of Protection', 112.
27 Chapman and Chassagne, *European Textile Printers*, 4.
28 Lee, *Cotton Enterprise*, 6, 24.
29 Bremner, *Industries of Scotland*, 281; Jewkes, 'Localization of Cotton'.
30 Quoted in Bremner, *Industries of Scotland*, 282.
31 Mann, *The Cloth Industry*, 97.
32 Heaton, *Yorkshire Woollen and Worsted*, 96, 203.
33 Select Committee Appointed to Consider the State of the Woollen Manufacture; Heaton, *Yorkshire Woollen and Worsted*, 293–4.
34 Defoe, *Tour*, 491–2.
35 Hudson, 'Proto-industrialization', 51.
36 Wilson, *England's Apprenticeship*, 238.
37 Jenkins, *West Riding Wool Textile Industry*.
38 Rogers, 'Framework Knitting', 8–10, 17; D. R. Mills, 'Proto-industrialization'.
39 Warner, *Silk Industry*, 499.
40 Aspin and Chapman, *James Hargreaves and the Spinning Jenny*, 30.
41 ibid., 38.
42 The Hammonds, *The Skilled Labourer*, 209; Sholl, *Short Historical Account of the Silk Manufacture*.
43 Warner, *Silk Industry*, 513.
44 Prest, *Coventry*, 45; Lane, 'Apprenticeship', 316.
45 Prest, *Coventry*, 49.
46 Timmins, *Birmingham*, 179–83.
47 Bremner, *Industries of Scotland*, 222.
48 Lee, *Cotton Enterprise*, 2.
49 Edwards, *British Cotton Trade*, 9.
50 Lee, *Cotton Enterprise*, 3.
51 Chapman and Chassagne, *European Textile Printers*, 37–52.
52 Fitton and Wadsworth, *Strutts and Arkwrights*, 82.
53 Edwards, *British Cotton Trade*, 131, 145.
54 Friedman, *Industry and Labour*, 151.
55 Jenkins and Ponting, *British Wool Textiles*.
56 Heaton, *Yorkshire Woollen and Worsted*, 351–2.
57 Hudson, 'Proto-industrialization'.
58 Aspin and Chapman, *Hargreaves*.
59 Mills, 'Proto-industrialization', 14; Levine, *Family Formation*, 19.
60 Warner, *Silk Industry*, 58, 128, 139, 154.
61 Prest, *Coventry*, 53.
62 Durie, 'Linen Industry', 91.
63 Bremner, *Industries of Scotland*, 247–8.
64 Edwards and Lloyd-Jones, 'Smelser and the Cotton Factory Family', 306.
65 Wadsworth and Mann, cited in Edwards and Lloyd-Jones, 'Smelser and the Cotton Factory Family', 307.
66 Honeyman, *Origins of Enterprise*, 240.
67 Unwin, *Samuel Oldknow*, 32.
68 Thompson, *The Making of the English Working Class*, 304.

69 ibid., 305.
70 Fitton and Wadsworth, *Strutts and Arkwrights*, 193. 'The large employer did most of the speaking before the Parliamentary Committees, but he was hardly the characteristic figure of the trade. There were actually very few "cotton lords".'
71 Unwin, *Samuel Oldknow*, 15.
72 Lee, *Cotton Enterprise*, 146; Collier, *Family Economy*, 42.
73 Chapman, *Early Factory Masters*, 128; Chapman, 'Fixed Capital in the Cotton Industry'. Drinkwater's Manchester mill in 1792 employed 500. See Chaloner, 'Owen, Drinkwater and Factory System', 88. Mills similar in size were the Pleasley Works valued at £4,195, Robertson's mill at Linby valued at £3,600, Dale's mill at New Lanark valued at £3,500. These were Arkwright licensees and appear to have been restricted to 1,000 spindles. See Chapman, *Early Factory Masters*, 128.
74 Chapman, *Early Factory Masters*, 64.
75 Fitton and Wadsworth, *Strutts and Arkwrights*, 193; Chapman, *Early Factory Masters*, 129.
76 Clapham, 'Factory Statistics', 475–7.
77 Cited in Gatrell, 'Labour, Power and the Size of Firms', 95.
78 Chapman, 'Fixed Capital in the Industrial Revolution', cited in Gatrell, 'Labour, Power and the Size of Firms', 109.
79 ibid., 113.
80 Lloyd-Jones and Le Roux, 'Size of Firms'.

11   THE TEXTILE INDUSTRIES: TECHNOLOGIES

1 Linebaugh, 'Labour History', 320.
2 Kriedte, Medick, Schlumbohm, *Industrialization before Industrialization*.
3 Lee, *Cotton Enterprise*, 4.
4 Aspin and Chapman, *James Hargreaves and the Spinning Jenny*, 57.
5 Jenkins and Ponting, *British Wool Textile Industry*, 48; Heaton, *Yorkshire Woollen and Worsted*, 340; and Mann, *The Cloth Industry*, 126.
6 Lee, *Cotton Enterprise*, 4; Smelser, *Social Change*, 89.
7 Aspin and Chapman, *James Hargreaves and the Spinning Jenny*, 37–8.
8 Catling, 'Spinning Mule', 39.
9 Edwards, *British Cotton Trade*, 5 and 8.
10 Von Tunzelmann, *Steam Power*, 176–7.
11 *Rees's Manufacturing Industry*, V, 474.
12 Hills, 'Hargreaves, Arkwright and Crompton'.
13 Unwin, *Samuel Oldknow*, 32.
14 Von Tunzelmann, *Steam Power*, 179–83.
15 Edwards, *British Cotton Trade*, 204.
16 Lardner, *Silk Manufacture*, 196–200.
17 *Rees's Manufacturing Industry*, IV, 468–9.
18 Ponting, *Woollen Industry in the South West of England*, 61.
19 Heaton, *Yorkshire Woollen and Worsted*, 340.
20 Lardner, *Silk Manufacture*, 223.
21 Kusamitsu, 'Industrial Revolution and Design', 53–4.
22 Warner, *Silk Industry*, 117.
23 Timmins, *Birmingham*, 179–89.
24 Baines, *History of the Cotton Manufacture*, 207; Wood, *History of Wages*, 141–3. In 1815 the few power looms in Stockport were capable only of weaving strong calicoes and other coarse cloth made from low counts of yarn. A greater part of the weaving was done by hand. See Giles, 'Stockport', 37.

25 Wilkinson, 'Power Loom Developments', 129.
26 Baines, *History of the Cotton Manufacture*, 229–31; McCulloch, 'Rise of Cotton Manufacture'. Also see Select Committee Appointed to Inquire into the Present State of Manufactures, Commerce and Shipping, Testimony of H. W. Sefton, 622. 'There are now hundreds of dressers, who dress the warp previous to it being woven on the power loom, those are classes who 20 or 30 years ago were scarcely known by name, compared with their present number . . . in one mill, there are about 17 to about 350 looms, that will be one to 20 in Stockport . . . there would be about 500.'
27 The evidence of Babbage quoted by Habakkuk, *American and British Technology*, 148.
28 Contrary to Habakkuk's belief stated in ibid., 148.
29 Thompson, *The Making of the English Working Class*, 315; Wood, *History of Wages*, 141–3.
30 *Rees's Manufacturing Industry*, V, 479.
31 Pinchbeck, *Women Workers*, 149.
32 See Berg, *The Machinery Question*, ch. 4.
33 Von Tunzelmann, 'Technical Progress', 155, 161.
34 Aspin and Chapman, *James Hargreaves and the Spinning Jenny*, 48.
35 Von Tunzelmann, *Steam Power*, 176.
36 Pinchbeck, *Women Workers*, 150–1.
37 Scott-Taggart, 'Crompton's Invention', 28.
38 Catling, 'Spinning Mule', 43.
39 Baines, *History of the Cotton Manufacture*, 436.
40 Smout, *History of the Scottish People*, 385–6.
41 Catling, 'Spinning Mule', 49.
42 Collins, 'Proto-industrialization and Pre-Famine Emigration'.
43 Lee, *Cotton Enterprise*, 24.
44 Unwin, *Samuel Oldknow*, 45.
45 Select Committee Appointed to Inquire into the Present State of Manufactures, Commerce and Shipping, 75.
46 Baines, *History of the Cotton Manufacture*, 485.
47 Wilkinson, 'Power Loom Developments', 130.
48 Brown, *Essex*, 20.
49 Mann, *Cloth Industry*, 126, 149.
50 Randall, 'The Shearmen and the Wiltshire Outrages', 284–5.
51 Heaton, *Yorkshire Woollen and Worsted*, 340; Mann, *Cloth Industry*, 174–92.
52 See above, pp. 109–10. Jones, 'Constraints'.
53 Aspin and Chapman, *James Hargreaves and the Spinning Jenny*, 47; Baines, *History of the Cotton Manufacture*, 159.
54 Aspin and Chapman, *James Hargreaves and the Spinning Jenny*, 31.
55 Thompson, *The Making of the English Working Class*, 604–28, 657.

12   THE METAL AND HARDWARE TRADES

1 Marx, *Capital*, I.
2 Faucher, cited in Clapham, *Economic History*, I, 175.
3 Cited in Armytage, *Social History of Engineering*, 93.
4 J. R. Harris, 'Industry and Technology'; Mathias, 'Skills and the Diffusion'.
5 This paragraph and the passages quoted are based on J. R. Harris, 'Skills, Coal and British Industry', 177–9.
6 Cited in Briggs, 'Metals and the Imagination', 665.
7 Rolt, *Tools*, 68.

8 Pole, *Fairbairn*, 26, 33.
9 Clapham, *Economic History*, I.
10 Tann, 'Textile Millwright'.
11 Fairbairn, *Mills and Millwork*, vi.
12 Tann, 'Textile Millwright', 82, 87.
13 Jeffreys, *Story of the Engineers*, 15.
14 More, *Skill and the English Working Class*.
15 Barker and Harris, *A Merseyside Town*; Bailey and Barker, 'Watchmaking in S.W. Lancashire'; Ashton, *Peter Stubs*, 2–5; Landes, *Revolution in Time*.
16 Rolt, *Tools*, 68–9.
17 Smiles, *Industrial Biography: Iron Makers and Tool Makers*, 180.
18 Pole, *Fairbairn*, 39.
19 Musson and Robinson, 'Steam Power'.
20 Armytage, *Social History of Engineering*, 118, 127.
21 Ashton, *Peter Stubs*, 19.
22 Landes, 'Watchmaking', 11.
23 Roll, *An Early Experiment*, 18; Clapham, *Economic History*, I, 154.
24 Cited in Briggs, 'Metals and the Imagination', 667–8.
25 Burgess, '1852 Lockout', 218, 221.
26 Allen, *Birmingham and the Black Country*, 17.
27 Hamilton, *Brass and Copper*, 88, 96.
28 Hey, *Rural Metalworkers*, 7, 21.
29 Frost, 'Yeomen and Metalsmiths'.
30 Hay, 'Manufacturers and the Criminal Law', 3.
31 Lloyd, *Cutlery Trades*, 273–7.
32 ibid., 37–50; Hall, 'Trades of Sheffield', 11, 17–18.
33 Lloyd, *Cutlery Trades*, 35, 60.
34 Cited in Eversley, 'Industry and Trade 1500–1800', 87, 103. See *Journals of the House of Commons*, 1759, 496; Robinson, 'Boulton and Fothergill', 61; *Victoria History of the Counties of England*, II, *Warwick*, 199, 214.
35 Rowlands, *Masters and Men*, 127.
36 Hamilton, *Brass and Copper*, 131; Lane, 'Apprenticeship', 223.
37 Rowlands, *Masters and Men*, 135. But Taylor and Garbett reported that only 6,000 were thus employed. See *Journals of the House of Commons*, 1759, 496.
38 Lane, 'Apprenticeship', 213.
39 Hamilton, *Brass and Copper*, 267.
40 ibid., 273.
41 Rowlands, *Masters and Men*, 155.
42 Court, *Midland Industries*, 218.
43 Hamilton, *Brass and Copper*, 82, 143, 162, 236, 252, 256–8, 264–6; Hutton, *History of Birmingham*, 113.
44 Behagg, 'Custom, Class and Change', 454.
45 See Berg, 'Small-producer Capitalism'.
46 Fitzmaurice, *Life of Shelbourne*, 404.
47 Marshall, *Industry and Trade*; Florence, *The Logic of British and American Industry*.
48 *Victoria History, Warwick*, 238; Eversley, 'Industry and Trade 1500–1800', 96; *Victoria History, Warwick*, 236; Hamilton, *Brass and Copper*, 255. For a more detailed discussion of the manufacturing process in pinmaking see Diderot, *Encyclopédie*.
49 Court, *Midland Industries*, 194; Eversley, 'Industry and Trade', 87; Davies, 'The Handmade Nail Trade', 265.
50 Prosser, *Birmingham Inventors*, for details of the patents, inventions and im-

provements in the Birmingham trades before 1850. Also see *Victoria History: Warwick*.

51 MacLeod, *Inventing the Industrial Revolution*.
52 Hawkes Smith, *Birmingham and its Vicinity*, 18.
53 Eversley, 'Industry and Trade 1500–1800', 93.
54 Pelham, 'Water Power Crisis', 75–90; Court, *Midland Industries*, 257; Behagg, 'Custom, Class and Change'.
55 Fairbairn, *Mills and Millwork*, viii.
56 Pole, *Fairbairn*, 92.
57 Roll, *An Early Experiment*, 225.
58 Pole, *Fairbairn*, 112–17.
59 Armytage, *Social History of Engineering*, 118–27; Lloyd, *Cutlery Trades*, 119.
60 Court, *Midland Industries*, 53, 60; Lloyd, *Cutlery Trades*, 247.
61 Clapham, *Economic History*, I, 173–7.
62 Behagg, 'Custom, Class and Change', 466.
63 Reddy, 'Textile Trade'.
64 Ashton, *Peter Stubs*, 36.
65 Lloyd, *Cutlery Trades*, 191–7.
66 Donnelly and Baxter, 'Sheffield and the English Revolutionary Tradition', 90–1.
67 Behagg, 'Custom, Class and Change', 464.
68 Lloyd, *Cutlery Trades*, 203.
69 Ashton, *Peter Stubs*, 28.
70 Court, *Midland Industries*, 218; Allen, *Birmingham and the Black Country*, 152–4.
71 Allen, *Birmingham and the Black Country*, 152; Reid, 'Decline of Saint Monday', 95–6.
72 Allen, *Birmingham and the Black Country*, 160, 164.
73 Kelley, 'Brass Trades', 43.
74 Roll, *An Early Experiment*, 186, 194, 201.
75 Armytage, *Social History of Engineering*, 126.
76 Landes, *Unbound Prometheus*.
77 Burgess, '1852 Lockout', 222; Behagg, *Politics and Production*, 40–5.
78 Behagg, *Politics and Production*, 58.
79 Dickson, 'Aspects of the Rise and Decline of the Irish Cotton Industry'; Boulton correspondence.
80 Lane, 'Apprenticeship', 223; Eversley, 'Industry and Trade', 110–11.
81 Eversley, 'Industry and Trade', 110–11.
82 *Aris's Gazette*, 1788.
83 Allen, *Birmingham and the Black Country*, 168.
84 Hutton, *History of Birmingham*.
85 Eversley, 'Industry and Trade', 110.
86 Linebaugh, *The London Hanged*, ch. 2, outlines a typology of work and modes of production, but fails to analyse any movement or dynamic in these modes.
87 Reid, 'Decline of Saint Monday'.

BIBLIOGRAPHY

Alexander, S., 'Women and the London Trades', in Mitchell, J. and Oakley, A., *The Rights and Wrongs of Women*. Harmondsworth 1978.

Allen, G. C., *The Industrial History of Birmingham and the Black Country 1860–1927*. London 1929.

Allen, R. C., *Enclosure and the Yeoman*. Oxford 1992.

Allen, R. C., 'Agriculture and the Industrial Revolution, 1700–1850', in Floud, R. and McCloskey, D., eds, *The Economic History of Britain since 1700*, Vol. I, 2nd edition. Cambridge 1994.

Anderson, A., *Historical and Chronological Deduction of the Origin of Commerce from the Earliest Accounts to the Present Times*, 2 vols. London 1764.

Anderson, B. L., 'The Attorney and the Early Capital Market in Lancashire', in Crouzet, F., ed., *Capital Formation in the Industrial Revolution*. London 1972.

Anderson, J., *Observations on the Means of Exciting a Spirit of National Industry, Chiefly Intended to Promote the Agriculture, Commerce, Manufactures and Fisheries of Scotland*, 2 vols. Dublin 1779.

Anderson, M., *Family Structure in 19th Century Lancashire*. Cambridge 1971.

Aris's Birmingham Gazette (1750–1800).

Armytage, W. H., *A Social History of Engineering*. London 1961.

Ashton, T. S., *An Eighteenth Century Industrialist, Peter Stubs of Warrington, 1756–1806*. Manchester 1939.

Ashton, T. S., *An Economic History of England: The 18th Century*. London 1955.

Aspin, C. and Chapman, S. C., *James Hargreaves and the Spinning Jenny*. Preston 1964.

Bailey, F. A. and Barker, T. C., 'The Seventeenth Century Origins of Watchmaking in S.W. Lancashire', in Harris, J. R., ed., *Liverpool and Merseyside*. London 1967.

Bailey, W. and Nie, D. A., *English Gunmakers. The Birmingham and Provincial Gun Trade in the Eighteenth and Nineteenth Centuries*. London 1978.

Baines, E., *A History of the Cotton Manufacture in Great Britain* (1835). London 1966.

Bamford, S., *Passages in the Life of a Radical* (1884). Oxford 1984.

Barker, T. C. and Harris, J. R., *A Merseyside Town in the Industrial Revolution, St Helens 1750–1900*. London 1959.

Beckett, J. V., 'Regional Variation and the Agricultural Depression 1730–50', *Economic History Review*, February 1982.

Behagg, C., 'Custom, Class and Change in the Trade Societies of Birmingham', *Social History*, IV, October 1979.

Behagg, C., *Politics and Production in Nineteenth-Century England*. London 1990.

Berg, M., 'The Introduction and Diffusion of the Power Loom 1789–1842', MA thesis, University of Sussex 1972.

Berg, M., *Technology and Toil in Nineteenth-Century Britain*. London 1979.

Berg, M., *The Machinery Question and the Making of Political Economy 1815–1848*. Cambridge 1980.

Berg, M., 'Political Economy and the Principles of Manufacture 1700–1800', in Berg, M., Hudson, P. and Sonenscher, M., *Manufacture in Town and Country before the Factory*. Cambridge 1983.

Berg, M., 'Women's Work, Mechanisation and the Early Phases of Industrialisation in England', in Joyce, P., ed., *The Historical Meanings of Work*. Cambridge 1987.

Berg, M., 'Workers and Machinery in Eighteenth-Century England', in Rule, J., ed., *British Trade Unionism 1750–1850*. London 1988.

Berg, M., 'Commerce and Creativity in Eighteenth-Century Birmingham', in Berg, M., ed., *Markets and Manufacture in Early Industrial Europe*. London 1991.

Berg, M., 'On the Origins of Capitalist Hierarchy', in Gustafsson, B., ed., *Power and Economic Institutions: Reinterpretations in Economic History*. Aldershot 1991.

Berg, M., 'Revisions and Revolutions: Technology and Productivity Change in Manufacture in Eighteenth-Century England' in Davis, J. A. and Mathias, P., eds, *Technology and Innovation from the Eighteenth Century to the Present Day*. Oxford 1991.

Berg, M., 'Small-Producer Capitalism in Eighteenth-Century England', *Business History*, 35, 1993.

Berg, M., 'What Difference did Women's Work Make to the Industrial Revolution?', *Historical Workshop*, 35, 1993.

Berg, M., 'Women's Property and the Industrial Revolution', *Journal of Interdisciplinary History*, XXIV, 1993.

Berg, M., 'Factories, Workshops and Industrial Organisation', in Floud, R. and McCloskey, D., eds, *The Economic History of Britain since 1700*, Vol. I, 2nd edition. Cambridge 1994.

Berg, M., Hudson, P. and Sonenscher, M., eds, *Manufacture in Town and Country before the Factory*. Cambridge 1983.

Berg, M., and Hudson, P., 'Rehabilitating the Industrial Revolution', *The Economic History Review*, XLV, 1992.

Bisset, James, MS Memoirs, Warwick County Record Office.

Blaug, M., 'The Productivity of Capital in the Lancashire Cotton Industry', *Economic History Review*, XIII, 1961.

Bolin-Hort, P., *Work, Family and the State. Child Labour and the Organization of Production in the British Cotton Industry, 1780–1920*. Lund, Sweden 1989.

Boserup, E., *Women's Role in Economic Development*. London 1970.

Bowley, M., *The British Building Industry: Four Studies in Response and Resistance to Change*. Cambridge 1966.

Boyson, R., *The Ashworth Cotton Enterprise*. Oxford 1970.

Braverman, H., *Labor and Monopoly Capital*. New York 1974.

Breen, T., '"Baubles of Britain": The American and Consumer Revolutions of the Eighteenth Century', *Past and Present*, 119, 1988.

Bremner, D., *The Industries of Scotland, their Rise, Progress and Present Condition* (1869). London 1969.

Brewer, J., McKendrick, N., and Plumb, J. H., *The Birth of a Consumer Society: The Commercialisation of Eighteenth-Century England*. London 1982.

Briggs, A., 'Metals and the Imagination in the Industrial Revolution', *Journal of the Royal Society of Arts*, September 1980.

The Brighton Group, 'The Capitalist Labour Process', *Capital and Class*, I, 1976.

Brown, A. F. J., *Essex at Work, 1700–1815*. Chelmsford 1969.

Bruland, T., 'Industrial Conflict as a Source of Technical Innovation: Three Cases', *Economy and Society*, XI (2), 1982.

Burgess, K., 'Technological Change and the 1852 Lockout in the British Engineering Industry', *International Review of Social History*, XIV, 1969.

Burley, K. H., 'An Essex Clothier of the Eighteenth Century', *Economic History Review*, XI, 1958.

Bythell, D., *The Handloom Weavers*. Cambridge 1969.

Bythell, D., *The Sweated Trades*. London 1978.

Cary, J., *An Essay Towards Regulating the Trade and Employing the Poor of the Kingdom*, 2nd edition. Bristol 1719.

Catling, H., 'The Development of the Spinning Mule', *Textile History*, IX, 1978.

Chalklin, C. W., *The Provincial Towns of Georgian England. A Study of the Building Process 1740–1820*. London 1974.

Chaloner, W. H., 'Robert Owen, Peter Drinkwater and the Early Factory System in Manchester, 1788–1800', *Bulletin of the John Rylands Library*, 1954.

Chambers, J. D., 'Enclosure and Labour Supply in the Industrial Revolution', *Economic History Review*, V, 1953.

Chambers, J. D., 'The Vale of Trent 1660–1800', *Economic History Review Supplement*, no. iii, 1957.

Chambers, J. D., 'The Rural Domestic Industries during the Period of Transition to the Factory System, with Special Reference to the Midland Counties of England', *Proceedings of the Second International Congress of Economic History*, Aix-en-Provence, ii, 1962.

Chandler, A. D., *Scale and Scope*. Cambridge, Mass. 1990.

Chapman, S. D., 'Fixed Capital in the Industrial Revolution in Britain', *Journal of Economic History*, XXIV, 3, 1964.

Chapman, S. D., *The Early Factory Masters*. Newton Abbot 1967.

Chapman, S. D., 'Fixed Capital in the Cotton Industry', *Economic History Review*, XXIII, 1970.

Chapman, S. D., 'Industrial Capital before the Industrial Revolution 1730–1750', in Harte, N. and Ponting, K., *Textile History and Economic History*. Manchester 1973.

Chapman, S. D., *The Cotton Industry in the Industrial Revolution*, 2nd edition. London 1987.

Chapman, S. D., *Merchant Enterprise in Britain. From the Industrial Revolution to World War I*. Cambridge 1992.

Chapman, S. D. and Bartlett, J. N., 'The Contribution of Building Clubs and Freehold Land Societies to Working-Class Housing in Birmingham', in Chapman, S. D., ed., *The History of Working Class Housing: A Symposium*. Newton Abbot 1971.

Chapman, S. D. and Chassagne, S., *European Textile Printers in the Eighteenth Century: a Study of Peel and Oberkampf*. London 1981.

Chapman, S. D. and Butt, J., 'The Cotton Industry, 1775–1856', in Feinstein, C. H. and Pollard, S., eds, *Studies in Capital Formation in the United Kingdom 1750–1920*. Oxford 1988.

Charlesworth, A., *An Atlas of Rural Protest in Britain 1548–1900*. London 1983.

Chayanov, A. V., *The Theory of Peasant Economy* (1915), ed. Thorner Kerblay and Smith. Homewood, Ill. 1966.

Chaytor, M., 'Household and Kinship: Ryton in the Late 16th and Early 17th Centuries', *History Workshop*, X, 1980.

Church, R., *Kenricks in Hardware. A Family Business 1791–1966*. Newton Abbot 1969.

Church, R. A., 'The Shoe and Leather Industries', in Church, R. A., *The Dynamics of Victorian Business. Problems and Perspectives to the 1870s*. London 1980.

Clapham, J. H., 'Some Factory Statistics of 1815–1816', *Economic Journal*, XXV, 1915.

Clapham, J. H., *An Economic History of Modern Britain*, 3 vols. Cambridge 1926–38.

Clark, A., *Working Life of Women in the Seventeenth Century* (1919). London 1982.

Clarkson, L. A., 'The Manufacture of Leather', in Mingay, G. E., ed., *The Agrarian History of England and Wales*, Vol. VI, *1750–1850*. Cambridge 1989.

Clifford, H., 'A Study of an Eighteenth-Century Goldsmithing Business with Reference to the Garrod Ledgers 1760–1776', Ph.D. thesis, London University, 1989.

Coats, W. A., 'Changing Attitudes to Labour in the Mid-Eighteenth Century', in Flinn, M. W. and Smout, T. C., eds, *Essays in Social History*. Oxford 1974.

Cole, W. A., 'Factors in Demand', in Floud, R. and McCloskey, D., eds, *The Economic History of Britain since 1700*, vol. 1: *1700–1860*. Cambridge 1981.

Coleman, D. C., *The British Paper Industry, 1495–1860: A Study in Industrial Growth*. Oxford 1958.

Coleman, D. C., 'Growth and Decay during the Industrial Revolution: The Case of East Anglia', *Scandinavian Economic History Review*, X, no. 2, 1962.

Coleman, D. C., *Courtaulds: An Economic and Social History*. Oxford 1969.

Coleman, D. C., 'Proto-industrialization: A Concept too Many', *Economic History Review*, XXXVI, 1983.

Colley, L., *Britons Forging the Nation 1707–1837*. London 1993.

Collier, F., *The Family Economy of the Working Classes in the Cotton Industry*. Manchester 1964.

Collins, B., 'Proto-industrialization and Pre-Famine Emigration', *Social History*, VII, no. 2, 1982.

Collins, E. J. T., 'Harvest Technology and Labour Supply in Britain, 1790–1870', *Economic History Review*, XXII, 1969.

Cooper, J., 'In Search of Agrarian Capitalism', *Past and Present*, LXXX, August 1978.

Court, W. H. B., *The Rise of the Midland Industries 1600–1838*. London 1953.

Crafts, N. F. R., 'British Economic Growth, 1700–1831: A Review of the Evidence', *Economic History Review*, XXXVI, 1983.

Crafts, N. F. R., *British Economic Growth during the Industrial Revolution*. Oxford 1985.

Crafts, N. F. R., 'British Economic Growth, 1700–1850: Some Difficulties of Interpretation', *Explorations in Economic History*, 24, 1987.

Crafts, N. F. R., 'British Industrialisation in an International Context', *Journal of Interdisciplinary History*, XIX, 1989.

Crafts, N. F. R., 'Industrial Revolution in Britain and France: Some Thoughts on the Question "Why was England First?"', *Economic History Review*, XXX, 1977.

Crafts, N. F. R., 'The Industrial Revolution', in Floud, R. and McCloskey, D., eds, *The Economic History of Britain since 1700*, Vol. I, 2nd edition. Cambridge 1994.

Crafts, N. F. R. and Harley, C. K., 'Output Growth and the British Industrial Revolution: A Restatement of the Crafts–Harley View', *Economic History Review*, XLV, 1992.

Crafts, N. F. R., Leybourne, S. J., and Mills, T. C., 'Trends and Cycles in British Industrial Production, 1700–1913', *Journal of the Royal Statistical Society*, 152, 1989.

Crafts, N. F. R., Leybourne, S. J., and Mills, T. C., 'Britain', in Sylla, R. and

Toniolo, G., eds, *Patterns of Industrialisation in Nineteenth-Century Europe*. London 1991.

Crouzet, F., 'Towards an Export Economy: British Exports during the Industrial Revolution', *Explorations in Economic History*, 17, 1980.

Crouzet, M., *The First Industrialists*. Cambridge 1985.

Cuenca Esteban, J., 'British Textile Prices, 1779–1827: Are British Growth Rates Worth Revising Once Again?', *Economic History Review*, 1994.

Cunningham, H., 'The Employment and Unemployment of Children in England, c. 1680–1851', *Past and Present*, 126, 1990.

Cunningham, W., *The Growth of English Industry and Commerce*. Cambridge 1882.

Daniels, G. W., 'Industrial Lancashire Prior to and Subsequent to the Invention of the Mule', *Journal of the Textile Institute*, 1927.

Darby, H. C., *A New Historical Geography of England after 1600*. Cambridge 1976.

David, P., 'The Landscape and the Machine', in McCloskey, D., ed., *Essays on a Mature Economy: Britain after 1840*. London 1971.

David, P., 'Labour Scarcity and the Problem of Technological Practice and Progress in 19th Century America', in David, P., *Technical Choice Innovations and Economic Growth: Essays on American and British Experience in the Nineteenth Century*. Cambridge 1975.

David, P. A, 'The Computer and the Dynamo. The Modern Productivity Paradox in a Not-Too-Distant Mirror', *Warwick Economic Research Papers*, 339, 1989.

Davidoff, L. and Hall, C., *Family Fortunes: Men and Women of the English Middle Classes, 1780–1850*. London 1987.

Davies, E. I., 'The Handmade Nail Trade of Birmingham and District', M.Com. thesis, Birmingham University, 1933.

Davis, R., 'English Foreign Trade, 1700–1774', *Economic History Review*, 15, 1962.

Davis, R., 'The Rise of Protection in England 1689–1786', *Economic History Review*, XIX, 1966.

Davis, R., *The Rise of the Atlantic Economies*. London 1973.

Davis, R., *The Industrial Revolution and British Overseas Trade*. Leicester 1979.

Davis, R. and, Pollard, S., 'The Iron Industry, 1780–1850', in Feinstein, C. H. and Pollard, S., eds, *Studies in Capital Formation in the United Kingdom 1750–1920*. Oxford 1988.

De Vries, J., *The Economy of Europe in the Age of Crisis*. Cambridge 1976.

De Vries, J., *European Urbanization 1500–1800*. London 1985.

De Vries, J., 'Between Purchasing Power and the World of Goods: Understanding the Household Economy in Early Modern Europe', in Brewer, J., and Porter, R., eds, *Consumption and the World of Goods*. London 1993.

Deane, P., *The First Industrial Revolution*. Cambridge 1962.

Deane, P. and Cole, W. A., *British Economic Growth 1688–1959*. Cambridge 1969.

Defoe, D., *The Complete English Tradesman*. London 1726.

Defoe, D., *A Tour through the Whole Island of Great Britain* (1720). Harmondsworth 1971.

Dent, D. A., 'Ubiquitous but Invisible: Female Domestic Servants in Mid-Eighteenth Century London', *History Workshop*, 28, 1989.

Devine, T. M., *The Tobacco Lords: A Study of the Tobacco Merchants of Glasgow and their Trading Activities 1740–90*. Edinburgh 1975.

Dickson, D., 'Aspects of the Rise and Decline of the Irish Cotton Industry', in Cullen, L. M. and Smout, T. C., eds, *Comparative Aspects of Scottish and Irish Economic and Social History 1600–1900*. Edinburgh 1977.

Diderot, M., *Encyclopédie ou Dictionnaire Raisonné des Sciences, des Arts et des Métiers*. Paris 1755.

'Die Sinking', in Timmins, S., ed., *The Resources, Products and Industrial History of Birmingham and the Midland Hardware District*. London 1866.

Disraeli, B., *Sybil or the Two Nations*. London 1845.

Dobb, M., *Studies in the Development of Capitalism*, 2nd edition. New York 1963.

Donnelly, F. K. and Baxter, J. L., 'Sheffield and the English Revolutionary Tradition 1791–1820', in Pollard, S. and Holmes, C., eds, *Essays in the Economic and Social History of South Yorkshire*. Sheffield 1976.

Dosi, G., 'Sources, Procedures and Microeconomic Effects of Innovation', *Journal of Economic Literature*, XXVI, 1988.

Douglas, M. and Isherwood, B., *The World of Goods: Towards an Anthropology of Consumption* (1978). Harmondsworth 1980.

DuPlessis, R. and Howell, M. C., 'Reconsidering the Early Modern Urban Economy: The Cases of Leiden and Lille', *Past and Present*, XCIV, 1982.

Durie, A. J., 'The Linen Industry in Scotland', in Cullen, D. and Smout, C., *Comparative Aspects of Scottish and Irish Economic and Social History 1600–1900*. Edinburgh 1977.

Earle, P., 'The Female Labour Market in London in the Late Seventeenth and Early Eighteenth Centuries', *Economic History Review*, XLII, 1989.

Eden, F., *The State of the Poor*. 5 vols (1797). London 1966.

Edwards, M. M., *The Growth of the British Cotton Trade 1780–1815*. Manchester 1967.

Edwards, M. M. and Lloyd-Jones, R., 'N. J. Smelser and the Cotton Factory Family', in Harte, N. B. and Ponting, K. G., eds, *Essays in Textile History*. Manchester 1973.

Eliot, George, *The Mill on the Floss* (1860). London 1902.

Elson, D. and Pearson, R., 'Nimble Fingers Make Cheap Workers', *Feminist Review*, VII, Spring 1981.

Engels, F., *The Condition of the Working Class in England* (1845), ed. E. J. Hobsbawm. London 1969.

Engerman, S., 'Mercantilism and Overseas Trade, 1700–1800', in Floud, R. and McCloskey, D., eds, *The Economic History of Britain since 1700*, Vol. I, 2nd edition. Cambridge 1994.

Eversley, D. C., 'Industry and Trade 1500–1800', *Victoria County History of Warwickshire*, vii, London 1965.

Eversley, D. C., 'The Home Market and Economic Growth in England 1780', in Jones, E. L. and Mingay, G., *Land, Labour and Population in the Industrial Revolution*. London 1967.

Fairbairn, W., *Treatise on Mills and Millwork*. London 1861.

Feinstein, C., 'Capital Formation', in Mathias, P. and Postan, M. M., eds, *The Cambridge Economic History of Europe*, Vol. vii, part ii. Cambridge 1978.

Feinstein, C. H., 'National Statistics, 1760–1920', in Feinstein, C. H. and Pollard, S., *Studies in Capital Formation in the United Kingdom, 1750–1920*. Oxford 1988.

Fitton, R. S. and Wadsworth, A. P., *The Strutts and the Arkwrights 1758–1830*. Manchester 1958.

Fitzmaurice, Lord Edward, *Life of William, Earl of Shelbourne*, Vol. I, *1737–1766*. London 1875.

Flinn, M. W., *Men of Iron: The Crowleys in the Early Iron Industry*. Edinburgh 1962.

Flinn, M. W., *The History of the British Coal Industry, Volume 2, 1700–1830: The Industrial Revolution*. Oxford 1984.

Florence, Phillip Sargant, *The Logic of British and American Industry*. London 1953.

Floud, R., *The British Machine Tool Industry, 1850–1914*. Cambridge 1976.

Floud, R. and McCloskey, D., eds, *The Economic History of Britain since 1700*, 2 vols. Cambridge 1981; 2nd edition, 3 vols. Cambridge 1994.

Fores, M., 'The Myth of a British Industrial Revolution', *History*, LX, 1981.

Fores, M., 'Technical Change and the Technology Myth', *Scandinavian Economic History Review*, XXX, no. 3, 1982.

Freudenberger, H., 'Proto-industrialization and Protofactories', *Eighth International Congress of Economic History*, Section A-2: Proto-industrialization. Budapest 1982.

Freudenberger, H., Mather, K. J. and Nardinelli, C., 'A New Look at the Early Factory Labour Force', *Journal of Economic History*, 44, 1984.

Friedman, A., *Industry and Labour*. London 1977.

Froebel, F., Heinrichs, J. and Kreye, O., *The New International Division of Labour*. Cambridge 1980.

Frost, P., 'Yeomen and Metalsmiths: Livestock in the Dual Economy of South Staffordshire, 1560–1720', *Agricultural History*, XXIX, 1981.

Gaskell, P., *The Manufacturing Population of England*. London 1833.

Gatrell, V. A. C., 'Labour, Power and the Size of Firms', *Economic History Review*, XXX, 1977.

Gee, J., *The Trade and Navigation of Great Britain Considered*. London 1729.

George, D., *London Life in the Eighteenth Century*. London 1925.

George, D., *England in Transition*. London 1931.

Gibson, A. and Smout, T. C., *Prices, Food and Wages in Scotland, 1550–1780*. Cambridge forthcoming.

Giles, P. M., 'The Economic and Social Development of Stockport 1815–1836', MA dissertation, Manchester University 1950.

Godelier, M., 'Work and its Representations', *History Workshop*, X, 1980.

Goldin, C., 'The Economic Status of Women in the Early Republic: Some Quantitive Evidence', *Journal of Interdisciplinary History*, 16, 1986.

Goldin, C. and Sokoloff, K., 'Women, Children and Industrialization in the Early Republic: Evidence from the Manufacturing Censuses', *Journal of Economic History*, XLII, 1982.

Goldin, C. and Sokoloff, K., 'The Relative Productivity Hypothesis and Industrialisation: The American Case, 1820–1850', *Quarterly Journal of Economics*, XCIX, 1984.

Goodman, J. and Honeyman, K., *Gainful Pursuits: The Making of Industrial Europe 1600–1914*. London 1988.

Goody, E., *From Craft to Industry. The Ethnography of Proto-industrial Cloth Production*. Cambridge 1982.

Gould, J. D., 'Agricultural Fluctuations and the English Economy in the Eighteenth Century', *Journal of Economic History*, XXII, 1962.

Gray, R. Q., *The Labour Aristocracy in Edinburgh*. London 1980.

Gregory, D., *The Transformation of Yorkshire. A Geography of the Yorkshire Woollen Industry*. London 1982.

Gutman, H. B., *Work, Culture and Society in Industrializing America* (1966). Oxford 1977.

Habakkuk, H. J., 'Family Structure and Economic Change in Nineteenth Century Europe', *Journal of Economic History*, XXV, 1955.

Habakkuk, H. J., 'Population Growth in Nineteenth Century Europe', *Journal of Economic History*, XXVII, 1957.

Habakkuk, H. J., *American and British Technology in the Nineteenth Century: The Search for Labour Saving Inventions*. Cambridge 1962.

Habakkuk, H. J., 'Labour Scarcity and Technological Change', in Saul, S. B., ed., *Technological Change: The U.S. and Britain in the 19th Century*. London 1970.

Hall, J. C., 'The Trades of Sheffield as Influencing Life and Health, More Particularly File Cutters and Grinders', *National Association for the Promotion of Social Sciences*, October 1865.

Hamilton, H., *The English Brass and Copper Industries to 1800*. London 1926.

Hammond, J. L. and Hammond, B., *The Rise of Modern Industry*. London 1925.

Hammond, J. L. and Hammond, B., *The Skilled Labourer 1760–1832* (1919). New York 1970.

Harley, C. K., 'British Industrialization before 1841: Evidence of Slower Growth during the Industrial Revolution', *Journal of Economic History*, XLII, 1982.

Harris, J. R., *The Copper King*. Liverpool 1964.

Harris, J. R., 'Industry and Technology in the Eighteenth Century: Britain and France', Inaugural Lecture, Birmingham 1971.

Harris, J. R., 'Skills, Coal and British Industry in the 18th Century', *History*, LXI, June 1976.

Harris, J. R. and Roberts, R. O., 'Eighteenth-Century Monopoly: The Cornish Metal Company Agreements of 1785', *Business History*, V (1), 1962.

Harris, O., 'Households as Natural Units', in Young, K., Wolkowitz, C. and McCullogh, R., *Of Marriage and the Market*. London 1981.

Harris, O., 'Households and their Boundaries', *History Workshop*, XIII, Spring 1982.

Harrison, M., 'Chayanov and the Economics of the Russian Peasantry', *Journal of Peasant Studies*, ii, July 1975.

Harte, N. B., 'The Rise of Protection and the English Linen Trade 1690–1790', in Harte, N. B. and Ponting, K. G., *Textile History and Economic History, Essays in Honour of Julia de Lacy Mann*. Manchester 1973.

Hawkes Smith, W., *Birmingham and its Vicinity as a Manufacturing and Commercial District*. London 1836.

Hay, D., 'War, Dearth and Theft in the Eighteenth Century: The Record of the English Courts', *Past and Present*, 95, 1982.

Hay, D., 'Manufacturers and the Criminal Law in the Later Eighteenth Century: Crime and Police in South Staffordshire'. Unpublished paper presented to the Past and Present Colloquium, Oxford 1983.

Heaton, H., *The Yorkshire Woollen and Worsted Industry*, 2nd edition. Oxford 1965.

Heertje, A., *Economics and Technical Change* (1973). London 1977.

Hey, D., 'A Dual Economy in South Yorkshire', *Agricultural History Review*, XVII, 1969.

Hey, D., *The Rural Metalworkers of the Sheffield Region*, Leicester University Department of English Local History Occasional Papers 2nd Series No. 5, Leicester 1972.

Higgs, E., 'Women, Occupations and Work in the Nineteenth-Century Censuses', *History Workshop Journal*, 23, 1987.

Hill, B., *Women, Work and Sexual Politics in Eighteenth-Century England*. Oxford 1989.

Hills, R. L., 'Hargreaves, Arkwright and Crompton, Why Three Inventors?', *Textile History*, X, 1979.

Hobsbawm, E. J., *The Age of Revolution*. London 1962.

Hoffmann, W. G., *British Industry 1700–1950*, English translation by W. O. Henderson and W. H. Chaloner. Oxford 1955.

Hohenberg, P., 'Toward a Model of the European Economic System in Proto-industrial Perspective, 1300–1800', *Eighth International Congress of Economic History*, Section A-2: Proto-industrialization. Budapest 1982.

Hohenberg, P., 'Urban Manufactures in the Proto-Industrial Economy: Culture

Versus Commerce?', in Berg, M., ed., *Markets and Manufacture in Early Industrial Europe*. London 1991.

Hohenberg, P. and Lees, L., *The Making of Urban Europe 1000–1950*. Cambridge, Mass. 1985.

Holderness, B. A., 'Agriculture, 1770–1860', in Feinstein, C. H. and Pollard, S., eds, *Studies in Capital Formation of the United Kingdom. 1750–1920*. Oxford 1988.

Honeyman, K., *Origins of Enterprise*. Manchester 1981.

Hopkins, E., 'Working Hours and Conditions during the Industrial Revolution: A Reappraisal', *Economic History Review*, XXXV, 1982.

Hoppit, J., 'Counting the Industrial Revolution', *Economic History Review*, XLIII, 1990.

Hoskins, W. G., *The Midland Peasant*. London 1965.

House of Commons, Minutes of Evidence Taken before the Committee of the Whole House to Consider Several Petitions Against the Orders in Council, Reports from Committees, *Parliamentary Papers*, III, 1812.

Houston, R. and Snell, K., 'Proto-industrialization? Cottage Industry, Social Change and the Industrial Revolution', *Historical Journal*, XXVII, 2, 1984.

Howell, C., 'Peasant Inheritance Customs in the Midlands 1280–1800', in Goody, J., Thirsk, J. and Thompson, E. P., *Family and Inheritance, Rural Society in Western Europe 1200–1800*. Cambridge 1976.

Hudson, P., 'Proto-industrialization: The Case of the West Riding', *History Workshop Journal*, no. 12, Autumn 1981.

Hudson, P., 'From Manor to Mill. The West Riding in Transition', in Berg, M., Hudson, P. and Sonenscher, M., *Manufacture in Town and Country before the Factory*. Cambridge 1983.

Hudson, P., *The Genesis of Industrial Capital: A Study of the West Riding Wool Textile Industry, c.1750–1850*. Cambridge 1986.

Hudson, P., 'Capital and Credit in the West Riding Wool Textile Industry c.1750–1850', in Hudson, P., ed., *Regions and Industries*. Cambridge 1989.

Hudson, P., 'The Regional Perspective', in Hudson, P., ed., *Regions and Industries*. Cambridge 1989.

Hudson, P., *The Industrial Revolution*. London 1992.

Hufton, O., 'Women, Work and Marriage in Eighteenth Century France', in Outhwaite, R. B., *Marriage and Society*. London 1981.

Hufton, O., 'Survey Articles. Women in History. I. Early Modern Europe', *Past and Present*, ci, 1983.

Humphries, J., '"Lurking in the Wings": Women in the Historiography of the Industrial Revolution', *Business and Economic History*, 2nd series, 20, 1991.

Hunt, E. H., 'Industrialisation and Regional Inequality: Wages in Britain, 1760–1914', *Journal of Economic History*, XLVI, 1986.

Hunt, E. H., 'Wages', in Langton, J. and Morris, R. J., eds, *Atlas of Industrialising Britain 1780–1914*. London 1986.

Hutton, W., *A History of Birmingham to the End of the Year 1780*. Birmingham 1781.

Hutton, W., *History of Derby*. London 1817.

Hyde, C. K., *Technological Change and the British Iron Industry 1700–1870*. Princeton, NJ 1977.

Israel, J. I., *Dutch Primacy in World Trade 1585–1740*. Oxford 1989.

Jackson, R. V., 'Growth and Deceleration in English Agriculture, 1660–1790', *Economic History Review*, 2nd series, XXXVIII, 1985.

Jackson, R. V., 'Government Expenditure and British Economic Growth in the Eighteenth Century: Some Problems of Measurement', *Economic History Review*, XLIII, 1990.

Jackson, R. V., 'Rates of Industrial Growth during the Industrial Revolution', *Economic History Review*, XLV, 1992.

Jeannin, P., 'La Proto-Industrialisation: Développement ou Impasse?', *Annales Economies, Sociétés, Civilisations*, 35a, 1980.

Jeffreys, J. B., *The Story of the Engineers 1800–1945*. London 1945.

Jenkins, D. T., *The West Riding Woold Textile Industry, 1770–1835: A Study of Fixed Capital Formation*. Edington 1975.

Jenkins, D. T., 'The Wool Textile Industry, 1780–1850', in Feinstein, C. H. and Pollard, S., eds, *Studies in Capital Formation in the United Kingdom 1750–1920*. Oxford 1988.

Jenkins, D. T. and Ponting, K. G., *The British Wool Textile Industry 1770–1914*. London 1982.

Jewkes, J., 'The Localization of the Cotton Industry', *Economic History*, II, no. 5, 1930.

John, A. H., 'Agricultural Productivity and Economic Growth in England 1700–1760', *Journal of Economic History*, XXV, 1965.

Jones, E. L., 'The Constraints on Economic Growth in Southern England 1650–1850', in *Proceedings of the Third International Congress of Economic History*. Munich 1965.

Jones, E. L., 'Agricultural Origins of Industry', *Past and Present*, 40, 1968.

Jones, E. L., 'Environment, Agriculture and Industrialization', *Agricultural History*, LI, 1977.

Jones, E. L., 'Agriculture and Economic Growth in England 1660–1750: Agricultural Change', in Jones, E. L., ed., *Agriculture and the Industrial Revolution*. Oxford 1978.

Jones, E. L., 'Agriculture and Economic Growth in England 1650–1815: Economic Change', in Jones, E. L., ed., *Agriculture and the Industrial Revolution*. Oxford 1978.

Jones, E. L., ed., *Agriculture and the Industrial Revolution*. Oxford 1978.

Journals of the House of Commons, XCIII, 1759.

Kadish, A., *The Oxford Economists in the Late Nineteenth Century*. Oxford 1982.

Kanefsky, J. W., 'Motive Power in British Industry and the Accuracy of the 1870 Factory Return', *Economic History Review*, XXXII.

Kelley, T., 'Wages and Labour Organization in the Brass Trades of Birmingham and District', Ph.D. thesis, Birmingham University 1930.

Kenney, M. and Florida, R., 'Beyond Mass Production: Production and the Labour Process in Japan', *Politics and Society*, 16, 1988.

Kenrick, W., *An Address to the Artists and Manufacturers of Great Britain*. London 1774.

Kriedte, P., Medick, H. and Schlumbohm, J., *Industrialization before Industrialization* (1977), English translation. Cambridge 1981.

Kusamitsu, T., 'The Industrial Revolution and Design', Ph.D. thesis, Sheffield University 1982.

Kussmaul, A., *A General View of the Rural Economy of England 1538–1840*. Cambridge 1990.

Kussmaul, A., 'The Pattern of Work as the Eighteenth Century Began', in Floud, R. and McCloskey, D., eds, *The Economic History of Britain since 1700*, Vol. I, 2nd edition. Cambridge 1994.

Kuznets, S., *Modern Economic Growth*. New Haven and London 1965.

Landes, D. S., *The Unbound Prometheus. Technological Change and Industrial Development in Western Europe from 1750 to the Present*. Cambridge 1969.

Landes, D. S., 'Watchmaking: A Case Study in Enterprise and Change', *Business History Review*, liii, Spring 1979.

Landes, D. S., *A Revolution in Time*. Cambridge, Mass. 1985.

Landes, D. S., 'What Do Bosses Really Do?', *Journal of Economic History*, 46, 1986.

Landes, D. S., 'Small is Beautiful. Small is Beautiful?', Fondazione ASSE, Instituto per la Storia dell Umbria Contemporanea, in *Piccola e grande improsa: un problema storico*. Milan 1987.

Landes, D. S., 'The Fable of the Dead Horse; or, the Industrial Revolution Revisited', in Mokyr, J., ed., *The British Industrial Revolution: An Economic Perspective*. Oxford 1993.

Lane, J., 'Apprenticeship in Warwickshire', Vol. ii, Ph.D. thesis, Birmingham University 1977.

Langton, J., 'The Industrial Revolution and the Regional Geography of England', *Trans. Inst. Brit. Geog.*, 9, 1984.

Langton, J., 'The Physical Environment', in Langton, J. and Morris, R. J., eds, *Atlas of Industrialising Britain 1780–1914*. London 1986.

Langton, J. and Morris, R. J., eds, *Atlas of Industrialising Britain 1780–1914*. London 1986.

Lardner, D., *A Treatise on the Origin, Progressive Improvement and Present State of the Silk Manufacture*. London 1831.

Laslett, P., 'Family and Household as Work Group and Kin Group: Areas of Traditional Europe Compared', in Wall, R., Robin, J. and Laslett, P., *Family Forms in Historic Europe*. Cambridge 1983.

Laxton, P., 'Wind and Water Power', in Langton, J. and Morris, R. J., eds, *Atlas of Industrialising Britain 1780–1914*. London 1986.

Lazonick, W., 'Industrial Relations and Technical Change: The Case of the Self Acting Mule', *Cambridge Journal of Economics*, iii, 1979.

Lazonick, W., 'Factor Costs and the Diffusion of Ring Spinning in Britain Prior to World War I', *Quarterly Journal of Economics*, February 1981.

Lazonick, W., *Competitive Advantage on the Shop Floor*. Cambridge, Mass. 1990.

Lee, C. H., *A Cotton Enterprise 1795–1840. A History of McConnel and Kennedy, Fine Cotton Spinners*. Manchester 1972.

Lemire, B., *Fashion's Favourite: The Cotton Trade and the Consumer in Britain, 1660–1800*. Oxford 1991.

Levine, D., *Family Formation in an Age of Nascent Capitalism*. London 1977.

Levine, D. and Wrightson, K., *The Making of an Industrial Society: Whickham, 1560–1765*. Oxford 1991.

Lewis, W. A., 'Economic Development with Unlimited Supplies of Labour', *The Manchester School*, 22, 1954.

Lindert, P. H., 'English Occupations, 1670–1811', *Journal of Economic History*, XL (4), December 1980.

Lindert, P. H. and Williamson, J. G., 'Revising England's Social Tables', *Explorations in Economic History*, 19, 1982.

Lindert, P. H. and Williamson, J. G., 'English Workers' Living Standards during the Industrial Revolution: A New Look', *Economic History Review*, XXXVI, 1983.

Linebaugh, P., 'Labour History without the Labour Process; A Note on John Gast and his Times', *Social History*, VII, no. 3, 1982.

Linebaugh, P., *The London Hanged: Crime and Civil Society in the Eighteenth Century*. London 1991.

Little, A. J., *Deceleration in the 18th Century British Economy*. London 1976.

Lloyd, G. I. H., *The Cutlery Trades*. London 1913.

Lloyd-Jones, R. and Le Roux, A. A., 'The Size of Firms in the Cotton Industry, Manchester, 1815–41', *Economic History Review*, XXXIII, 1980.

Lloyd Prichard, M. F., 'The Decline of Norwich', *Economic History Review*, 2nd series, ii, 1950.

Lodge, David, *Nice Work*. London 1988.

Lown, J., *Women and Industrialisation: Gender at Work in Nineteenth Century England*. Cambridge 1991.

McCloskey, D. N., ed., *Essays on a Mature Economy. Britain after 1840*. London 1971.

McCloskey, D. N., 'The Industrial Revolution 1780–1860. A Survey', in Floud, R. and McCloskey, D. N., eds, *The Economic History of Britain since 1700*, Vol. I. Cambridge 1981; 2nd edition, Vol. I. Cambridge 1994.

McCulloch, J. R., 'The Rise, Progress, Present State and Prospects of the British Cotton Manufacture', *Edinburgh Review*, 1827.

McCulloch, J. R., ed., *Early English Tracts on Commerce* (1856). Cambridge 1952.

MacFarlane, A., *The Origins of English Individualism*. Oxford 1978.

McKendrick, N., 'Home Demand and Economic Growth: A New View of Women and Children in the Industrial Revolution', in McKendrick, ed., *Historical Perspectives, Studies in English Thought and Society*. Cambridge 1974.

McKendrick, N., Brewer, J. and Plumb, J. H., *The Birth of a Consumer Society*. London 1983; and in Davenport-Hines, R. P. T. and Liebenau, J., *Business in the Age of Reason*. London 1987.

MacLeod, C., *Inventing the Industrial Revolution*. Cambridge 1988.

Malcolmson, R., *Life and Labour in England 1700–1800*. London 1981.

Maloney, J., 'Marshall, Cunningham and the Emerging Economics Profession', *Economic History Review*, XXIV, 1976.

Mann, J. de Lacy, *The Cloth Industry in the West of England from 1640 to 1880*. Oxford 1971.

Mantoux, P., *The Industrial Revolution in the Eighteenth Century: An Outline of the Beginnings of the Modern Factory System in England*. London 1955.

Marglin, S., 'What Do Bosses Do? The Origins and Functions of Hierarchy in Capitalist Production', *Review of Radical Political Economy*, vi, 1974. Version reprinted in Gorz, A., ed., *The Division of Labour*. London 1976.

Marglin, S., 'The Power of Knowledge', in Stephens, F., ed., *Work Organization*. London 1983.

Marglin, S., 'Understanding Capitalism: Control Versus Efficiency', in Gustafsson, B., ed., *Power and Economic Institutions: Reinterpretations in Economic History*. Aldershot 1991.

Marshall, A., *Industry and Trade*, Appendix B. London 1919.

Martin, J. M., 'Village Traders and the Emergence of a Proletariat in South Warwickshire, 1750–1851', *Agricultural History Review*, 32, 2, 1984.

Martyn, H., 'Considerations on the East India Trade' (1701), in McCulloch, J. R., ed., *Early English Tracts on Commerce*. Cambridge 1952.

Marx, K., *The Grundrisse*, trans. and ed. M. Nicholaus. Harmondsworth 1973.

Marx, K., *Capital*, I. Harmondsworth 1976.

Mathias, P., *The Brewing Industry in England, 1700–1830*. Cambridge 1959.

Mathias, P., 'Skills and the Diffusion of Innovations from Britain in the Eighteenth Century', reprinted in Mathias, P., ed., *The Transformation of England*. London 1979.

Mathias, P., *The First Industrial Nation. An Economic History of Britain 1700–1914*. London (1969) 1983.

Mathias, P., 'Resources and Technology', in Mathias, P. and Davis, J. A., eds, *Innovation and Technology in Europe from the Eighteenth Century to the Present Day*. Oxford 1991.

Medick, H., 'The Proto-industrial Family Economy', *Social History*, October 1976.

Medick, H., 'Plebeian Culture in the Transition to Capitalism', in Samuel, R. and Stedman Jones, G., *Culture, Ideology and Politics*. London 1982.

Mendels, F., 'Proto-industrialization: The First Phase of the Process of Industrialization', *Journal of Economic History*, XXXII, 1972.

Mendels, F. and Deyon, P., 'Proto-industrialization: Theory and Reality', *Eighth International Congress of Economic History*, Section A-2: Proto-industrialization. Budapest 1982.

Mill, J. S., 'The Nature, Origins, and Progress of Rent' (1828), in *Essays on Economics and Society*, in Mill, J. S., *Collected Works*, iv. Toronto 1967.

Mill, J. S., *Principles of Political Economy* (1848), in Mill, J. S., *Collected Works*, ii, iii. Toronto 1965.

Mills, D. R., 'Proto-industrialization and Social Structure: The Case of the Hosiery Industry in Leicestershire, England', *Eighth International Congress of Economic History*, Section A-2: Proto-industrialization. Budapest 1982.

Millward, R., 'The Emergence of Wage Labour in Early Modern England', *Explorations in Economic History*, 18, 1981.

Mitchell, B. R. and Deane, P., *Abstract of British Historical Statistics*. Cambridge 1962.

Mokyr, J., 'Demand vs. Supply in the Industrial Revolution', in Mokyr, J., ed., *The British Industrial Revolution. An Economic Perspective*. Totowa, NJ 1985.

Mokyr, J., 'Has the Industrial Revolution been Crowded out? Some Reflections on Crafts and Williamson', *Explorations in Economic History*, 24, 1987.

Mokyr, J., *The Lever of Riches*. Oxford 1990.

Mokyr, J., 'Technological Inertia in Economic History', *Journal of Economic History*, 52, 1992.

Mokyr, J., 'Technological Change, 1700–1830', in Floud, R. and McCloskey, D., eds, *The Economic History of Britain since 1700*, Vol. I, 2nd edition. Cambridge 1994.

More, C., *Skill and the English Working Class*. London 1982.

Mounfield, P. R., 'Leather Footwear', in Langton, J. and Morris, R. J., eds, *Atlas of Industrialising Britain 1780–1914*. London 1986.

Musson, A. E. and Robinson, E. H., 'The Early Growth of Steam Power', *Economic History Review*, XI, 1959.

Nardinelli, C., *Child Labour and the Factory Acts*. Bloomington, Ind. 1990.

Neeson, J., 'Opposition to Enclosure in Northamptonshire *c*.1760–1800', in Charlesworth, A., *An Atlas of Rural Protest in Britain 1548–1900*. London 1983.

Neeson, J., *Commoners: Common Right, Enclosure and Social Change in England, 1700–1820*. Cambridge 1993.

Nelson, R. R., 'The Roles of Firms in Technical Advance: A Perspective from Evolutionary Theory', in Dosi, G., Giannetti, R. and Toninelli, P. A., eds, *Technology and Enterprise in Historical Perspective*. Oxford 1992.

Nelson, R. R. and Winter, S. G., *An Evolutionary Theory of Economic Change*. Cambridge, Mass. 1982.

Nenadic, S., 'Businessmen. The Urban Middle Classes and the "Dominance" of Manufacturers in Nineteenth Century Britain', *Economic History Review*, XLIV, 1991.

O'Brien, P. K., 'Agriculture and the Home Market', *English Historical Review*, 1985.

O'Brien, P. K., 'The Foundations of European Industrialisation: From the Perspective of the World', *Journal of Historical Sociology*, IV, 1991.

O'Brien, P. K., *Power with Profit: The State and the Economy, 1688–1815*. Inaugural Lecture, University of London 1991.

O'Brien, P. K., 'Introduction: Modern Conceptions of the Industrial Revolution', in O'Brien, P. K., and Quinault, R., eds, *The Industrial Revolution and British Society: Essays in Honour of Max Hartwell*. Cambridge 1993.

O'Brien, P. K., 'The State and the Economy 1688–1815', in Floud, R. and McCloskey, D., eds, *The Economic History of Britain since 1700*, Vol. I, 2nd edition. Cambridge 1994.

O'Brien, P. K. and Keyder, C., *Economic Growth in Britain and France 1780–1914*. London 1976.

Overton, M., 'Agricultural Productivity in Eighteenth-Century England: Some Further Speculation', *Economic History Review*, XXXVII, 1984.

Overton, M. and Campbell, B. S., eds, *Land, Labour and Livestock: Historical Studies in European Agricultural Productivity*. Manchester 1991.

Pawson, E., *The Early Industrial Revolution. Britain in the Eighteenth Century*. New York 1979.

Pearson, R., 'Gender Matters in Development', in Allen, D. and Mamas, A., eds, *Poverty and Development in the 1990s*. Oxford 1992.

Pelham, R. A., 'The Immigrant Population of Birmingham 1686–1726', *Birmingham Archaeological Transactions*, LXI, 1937.

Pelham, R. A., 'The Water Power Crisis in Birmingham in the Eighteenth Century', *University of Birmingham Historical Journal*, IX, 1963–4.

Phillips, A. and Taylor, B., 'Sex and Skill: Notes Towards Feminist Economics', *Feminist Review*, VI, 1980.

Pinchbeck, I., *Women Workers and the Industrial Revolution* (1930). London 1981.

Piore, M. and Sabel, C., *The Second Industrial Divide*. New York 1984.

Polanyi, K., *The Great Transformation*. London 1957.

Pole, W. A., ed., *The Life of William Fairbairn*. London 1877.

Pollard, S., *A History of Labour in Sheffield*. Liverpool 1959.

Pollard, S., 'The Factory Village in the Industrial Revolution', *English Historical Review*, LXXIX, July 1964.

Pollard, S., *The Genesis of Modern Management*. Harmondsworth 1965.

Pollard, S., 'Industrialization and the European Economy', *Economic History Review*, XXVI, November 1973.

Pollard, S., 'Labour in the British Economy', *Cambridge Economic History of Europe*, VII, Part ii, Vol. 1. Cambridge 1978.

Pollard, S., *Peaceful Conquest*. Oxford 1981.

Pollard, S., 'Coal Mining, 1750–1850', in Feinstein, C. H. and Pollard, S., eds, *Studies in Capital Formation in the United Kingdom 1750–1920*. Oxford 1988.

Pollard, S., 'The Insurance Policies', in Feinstein, C. H. and Pollard, S., eds, *Studies in Capital Formation in the United Kingdom 1750–1920*. Oxford 1988.

Pollard, S., 'Regional Markets and National Development', in Berg, M., ed., *Markets and Manufacture in Early Industrial Europe*. London 1991.

Ponting, K., *The Woollen Industry in the South West of England*. Wiltshire 1971.

Porter, Roy, *English Society in the Eighteenth Century*. Harmondsworth 1982.

Postlethwayt, M., *Britain's Commercial Interests*, Vol. 2. London 1757.

Prest, J., *The Industrial Revolution in Coventry*. London 1960.

Price, J., *Capital and Credit in British Overseas Trade: The View From the Chesapeake, 1700–1776*. Cambridge, Mass. 1980.

Price, J. M., 'What Did Merchants Do? Reflections on British Overseas Trade, 1660–1790', *Journal of Economic History*, XLIX, 1989.

Price, R., *Masters, Unions and Men. Work Control in Building and the Rise of Labour 1830–1914*. Cambridge 1980.

Prosser, R. B., *Birmingham Inventors and Inventions*. Birmingham 1881.

Prothero, I., *Artisans and Politics in Early Nineteenth Century London. John Gast and his Times*. London 1979.

Radcliffe, W., *Origin of the New System of Manufacture*. Stockport 1828.

Randall, A. J., 'The Shearmen and the Wiltshire Outrages of 1802: Trade Unionism and Industrial Violence, *Social History*, VII, no. 3, 1982.

Randall, A. J., 'The Philosophy of Luddism: The Case of the West of England Woollen Workers', *Technology and Culture*, 27, 1986.

Randall, A. J., 'The Industrial Moral Economy of the Gloucestershire Weavers in the Eighteenth Century', in Rule, J., ed., *British Trade Unionism 1750–1850*. London 1988.

Randall, A. J., *Before the Luddites: Custom, Community and Machinery in the English Woollen Industry, 1776–1809*. Cambridge 1991.

Reddy, W., 'The Textile Trade and the Language of the Crowd at Rouen 1752–1791', *Past and Present*, LXXIV, February 1977.

Reddy, W., 'Skeins, Scales, Discounts, Steam and Other Objects of Crowd Justice in Early French Textile Mills', *Comparative Studies in Society and History*, XXI, 1979.

Reddy, W., *The Rise of Market Culture*. Cambridge 1985.

Rees's Manufacturing Industry 1819–20. A Selection from the Cyclopedia; or Universal Dictionary of Arts, Sciences and Literature, by Abraham Rees, edited by Neil Cossons, 5 vols. Newton Abbot 1975.

Reflections on Various Subjects Relating to Arts and Commerce, Particularly the Consequences of Admitting Foreign Artists on Easier Terms. London 1752.

Reid, D., 'The Decline of Saint Monday', *Past and Present*, LXXI, 1976.

Reilly, R., *Josiah Wedgwood*. London 1992.

Ricardo, D., *Principles of Political Economy and Taxation*, 1821, in Dobb, M. and Sraffa, P., *Works and Correspondence of David Ricardo*, Vol. I. Cambridge 1970.

Richards, E., 'Women in the British Economy', *History*, LIII, 1974.

Richards, E., 'Margins of the Industrial Revolution', in O'Brien, P. K. and Quinault, R., eds, *The Industrial Revolution and British Society*. Cambridge 1993.

Riden, P., 'Iron and Steel', in Langton, J. and Morris, R. J., eds, *Atlas of Industrialising Britain 1780–1914*. London 1986.

Roberts, M., 'Sickles and Scythes: Women's Work and Men's Work at Harvest Time', *History Workshop Journal*, VII, 1979.

Robinson, E. H., 'Boulton and Fothergill 1762–1782 and the Birmingham Export of Hardware', *University of Birmingham Historical Journal*, vii, 1959–60.

Robinson, E. H., 'Matthew Boulton and Josiah Wedgwood: Apostles of Fashion', in Davenport-Hines, R. P. T. and Liebenau, J., *Business in the Age of Reason*. London 1987.

Rogers, A., 'Rural Industrial and Social Structure: The Framework Knitting Industry of South Nottinghamshire, 1670–1840', *Textile History*, XII, 1981.

Roll, E., *An Early Experiment in Industrial Organization, Being a History of the Firm of Boulton and Watt 1775–1805*. London 1930.

Rolt, L. T. C., *Tools for the Job. A Short History of Machine Tools*. London 1965.

Rosenberg, N., 'Technological Change in the Machine Tool Industry, 1840–1910', *Journal of Economic History*, XXIII, December 1963.

Rosenberg, N., 'The Direction of Technological Change: Inducement Mechanisms and Focusing Devices', *Economic Development and Cultural Change*, XX, 1969.

Rosenberg, N., 'Economic Development and the Transfer of Technology: Some Historical Perspectives', *Technology and Culture*, XI, 1970.

Rosenberg, N., *Inside the Black Box: Technology and Economics*. Cambridge 1982.

Ross, E., 'Survival Networks: Women's Neighbourhood Sharing in London before World War One', *History Workshop Journal*, XV, Spring 1983.

Rothstein, N. K., 'The Silk Industry in London, 1702–1766', unpublished MA thesis, London University, 1961.

Rowlands, M. B., *Masters and Men in the West Midlands Metalware Trades before the Industrial Revolution*. Manchester 1975.

Rowlands, M. B., 'Society and Industry in the West Midlands at the End of the 17th Century', *Midland History*, iv, Spring 1977.

Rowlands, M. B., 'Continuity and Change in an Industrialising Society: The Case Study of the West Midlands Industries', in Hudson, P., ed., *Regions and Industries*. Cambridge 1989.

Rule, J., *The Experience of Labour in 18th Century Industry*. London 1981.

Sabel, C. and Zeitlin, J., 'Historical Alternatives to Mass Production: Politics, Markets and Technology in Nineteenth-Century Industrialisation', *Past and Present*, 108, 1985.

Said, E., *Orientalism, Western Conceptions of the Orient*. Harmondsworth 1991.

Saito, O., 'Labour Supply Behaviour of the Poor in the English Industrial Revolution', *Journal of European Economic History*, 10, 1981.

Samuel, R., 'The Workshop of the World: Steam Power and Hand Technology in mid-Victorian Britain', *History Workshop Journal*, III, Spring 1977.

Sandberg, L., *Lancashire in Decline*. Columbus, Ohio 1974.

Sandilands, D. N., 'The History of the Midlands Glass Industry', M.Com. thesis, Birmingham University 1927.

Saul, S. B., 'Editor's Introduction', in Saul, S. B., ed., *Technological Change: The U.S. and Britain in the 19th Century*. London 1970.

Schmiechen, J. A., *Sweated Industries and Sweated Labour*. London 1984.

Schmitz, H., *Manufacturing in the Backyard, Case Studies of Accumulation and Employment in Small Scale Brazilian Industry*. London 1982.

Schremmer, E., 'Proto-industrialization', *Journal of European Economic History*, 1982.

Schumpeter, E. B., *English Overseas Trade Statistics 1697–1808*. Oxford 1960.

Scott-Taggart, W., 'Crompton's Invention and Subsequent Development of the Mule', *Journal of the Textile Institute*, XVIII, 1927.

Select Committee Appointed to Consider the State of the Woollen Manufacture of England, *Parliamentary Papers*, 1806 (268) (168a) III.

Select Committee on the State of Children Employed in the Manufactories of the United Kingdom, *Parliamentary Papers*, 1816 (397) III.

Select Committee on Children in Factories, *Parliamentary Papers*, 1831.

Select Committee Appointed to Inquire into the Present State of Manufactures, Commerce and Shipping in the United Kingdom, *Parliamentary Papers*, 1833 (690) VI.

Sewell, W., *Work and Revolution in Nineteenth Century France*. Cambridge 1982.

Shammas, C., *The Pre-industrial Consumer in England and America*. Oxford 1990.

Sharpe, P., 'Literally Spinsters: A New Interpretation of Local Economy and Demography in Colyton in the Seventeenth and Eighteenth Centuries', *Economic History Review*, XLIV, 1991.

Sholl, S., *Short Historical Account of the Silk Manufacture*. London 1811.

Short, B. M., 'The De-industrialisation Process: A Case Study of the Weald, 1618–50', in Hudson, P., ed., *Regions and Industries*. Cambridge 1989.

Sider, G. M., 'Christmas Mumming and the New Year in Outport, Newfoundland', *Past and Present*, LXXI, 1976.

Simonton, D., 'Apprenticeship: Training and Gender in Eighteenth-Century England', in Berg, M., ed., *Markets and Manufacture in Early Industrial Europe*. London 1991.

Smelser, N. J., *Social Change in the Industrial Revolution: An Application of Theory to the Lancashire Cotton Industry 1770–1840*. London 1959.

Smiles, S., *Industrial Biography: Iron Makers and Tool Makers*. London 1863.

Smith, A., *An Inquiry into the Nature and Causes of the Wealth of Nations* (1776), 2 vols. Oxford 1976.

Smith, R. M., 'Fertility, Economy and Household Formation in England over Three Centuries', *Population and Development Review*, 7, 1981.

Smout, T. C., *A History of the Scottish People 1560–1830*. London 1969.

Snell, K. D. M., 'Agricultural Seasonal Unemployment, the Standard of Living and Women's Work in the South and the East 1690–1860', *Economic History Review*, XXXIV, 1983.

Snell, K. D. M., *Annals of the Labouring Poor: Social Change and Agrarian England, 1660–1900*. Cambridge 1985.

Sokoloff, K., 'Was the Transition from the Artisanal Shop to the Non-mechanised Factory Associated with Gains in Efficiency?', *Explorations in Economic History*, 21, 1984.

Sokoloff, K., 'Inventive Activity in Early Industrial America: Evidence from Patent Records, 1790–1846', *Journal of Economic History*, 48, 1988.

Sokoloff, K. and Khan, B. Z., 'The Democratisation of Invention during Early Industrialisation: Evidence from the United States, 1790–1846', *Journal of Economic History*, 50, 1990.

Sonenscher, M., *Work and Wages: Natural Law, Politics and the Eighteenth-Century French Trades*. Cambridge 1989.

Spencely, G. F. R., 'The English Pillow Lace Industry 1845–80: A Rural Industry in Competition with Machinery', *Business History*, LXX, 1970.

Spencely, G. F. R., 'The Origins of the English Pillow Lace Industry', *Agricultural History Review*, 21, 1973.

Spufford, M., 'Peasant Inheritance Customs and Land Distribution', in Goody, J., Thirsk, J. and Thompson, E. P., eds, *Family and Inheritance in Rural Society in Western Europe 1200–1800*. Cambridge 1976.

Stedman Jones, G., 'The Changing Face of 19th-Century Britain', *History Today*, October 1991.

Steensgaard, N., 'The Growth and Composition of the Long-Distance Trade of England and the Dutch Republic before 1750', in Tracy, J. D., ed., *The Rise of Merchant Empires. Long-Distance Trade in the Early Modern World, 1350–1750*. Cambridge 1990.

Stewart, D., *Lectures on Political Economy*, Vol. 1, in Hamilton, W., ed., *Collected Works of Dugald Stewart*, viii. Edinburgh 1855.

Stone, K., 'The Origins of Job Structures in the Steel Industry', *Review of Radical Political Economy*, vi, 1976.

Stone, N., *Europe Transformed 1878–1919*. London 1983.

Styles, J., 'Embezzlement, Industry and the Law in England, 1500–1800', in Berg, M., Hudson, P. and Sonenscher, M., eds, *Manufacture in Town and Country before the Factory*. Cambridge 1983.

Styles, J., 'Manufacturing, Consumption and Design in Eighteenth-Century England', in Brewer, J. and Porter, R., ed., *Consumption and the World of Goods*. London 1993.

Sullivan, R., 'England's "Age of Invention": The Acceleration of Patents and Patentable Inventions during the Industrial Revolution', *Explorations in Economic History*, 26, 1989.

Tann, J., 'The Textile Millwright in the Early Industrial Revolution', *Textile History*, v, October 1974.

Taylor, A. J., 'Concentration and Specialization in the Lancashire Cotton Industry, 1825–50', *Economic History Review*, i, 1949.

Taylor, B., 'The Men are as Bad as their Masters', in Taylor, B., *Eve and the New Jerusalem*. London 1983.

Temin, P., 'The Relative Decline of the British Steel Industry 1880–1914', in Rosovsky, H., ed., *Industrialization in Two Systems. Essays in Honour of Alexander Gershenkron*. New York 1966.

Temin, P., 'Labour Scarcity in America', *Journal of Interdisciplinary History*, I (2), Winter 1971.

Thirsk, J., 'Industries in the Countryside', in Fisher, F. J., ed., *Essays in the Economic and Social History of Tudor and Stuart England*. Cambridge 1961.

Thirsk, J., *The Agrarian History of England and Wales*, iv, *1500–1640*. Cambridge 1967.

Thirsk, J., 'The Fantastical Folly of Fashion: The English Stocking Knitting Industry 1500–1700', in Harte, N. B. and Ponting, K. G., eds, *Textile History and Economic History*. Manchester 1973.

Thirsk, J., *Economic Policy and Projects: The Development of Consumer Society in Early Modern England*. Oxford 1978.

Thomas, R. P. and McCloskey, D. N., 'Overseas Trade and Empire 1700–1860', in Floud, R. and McCloskey, D., eds, *The Economic History of Britain since 1700, Volume I: 1700–1800*. Cambridge 1981.

Thomis, M. I. and Grimmett, J., *Women in Protest 1800–1850*. London 1982.

Thompson, E. P., 'Time, Work Discipline and Industrial Capitalism', *Past and Present*, 38, 1967.

Thompson, E. P., *The Making of the English Working Class*. Harmondsworth 1968.

Thompson, E. P., 'The Moral Economy of the Crowd', *Past and Present*, i, 1972.

Thompson, E. P., 'The Grid of Inheritance', in Goody, J., Thirsk, J. and Thompson, E. P., *Family and Inheritance, Rural Society in Western Europe 1200–1800*. Cambridge 1976.

Thompson, E. P., 'The Moral Economy Reviewed', in Thompson, E.P., *Customs in Common*. London 1991.

Thomson, J. K. J., 'British Industrialization and the External World: A Unique Experience or an Archetypal Model?', in Bienefeld, M. and Godfrey, M., eds, *The Struggle for Development: National Strategies in an International Context*. London 1982.

Thomson, J. K. J., 'Variations in Industrial Structure in Pre-Industrial Languedoc', in Berg, M., Hudson, P. and Sonenscher, M., *Manufacture in Town and Country before the Factory*. Cambridge 1983.

Thomson, J. K. J., 'State Intervention in the Catalan Calico-Printing Industry in the Eighteenth Century', in Berg, M., ed., *Markets and Manufacture in Early Industrial Europe*. London 1991.

Thorold Rogers, James E., *Six Centuries of Work and Wages* (1884). London 1917.

Timmins, S., ed., *The Resources, Products and Industrial History of Birmingham and the Midland Hardware District*. London 1866.

Toynbee, A., *Lectures on the Industrial Revolution in England* (1884). London 1969.

Tucker, J., *Instructions for Travellers*. London 1757.

Turnbull, G., 'Canals, Coal and Regional Growth during the Industrial Revolution', *Economic History Review*, 2nd series, XL, 1987.

Unwin, G., *The Guilds and Companies of London*. London 1908.

Unwin, G., *Samuel Oldknow and the Arkwrights*. Manchester 1924.

Usher, A. P., *An Introduction to the Industrial History of England*. London 1921.

Usher, D., *The Measurement of Economic Growth*. Oxford 1980.

Valenze, D., 'The Art of Women and the Business of Men: Women's Work and the Dairy Industry, *c*.1740–1840', *Past and Present*, 130, 1991.

Vickery, A., 'Women and the World of Goods: A Lancashire Consumer and her Possessions, 1751–1781', in Brewer, J. and Porter, R., eds, *Consumption and the World of Goods*. London 1993.

The Victoria History of the Counties of England, ii, *The History of the County of Warwick*. London 1965.

Vincent, D., *Bread, Knowledge and Freedom. A Study of Nineteenth-Century Working-Class Autobiography*. London 1982.

Von Tunzelmann, G. N., *Steam Power and British Industrialization to 1860*. Oxford 1978.

Von Tunzelmann, G. N., 'Technical Progress', in Floud, R. and McCloskey, D., eds, *The Economic History of Britain since 1700*, Vol. 1. Cambridge 1981.

Von Tunzelmann, G. N., 'Coal and Steam Power', in Langton, J. and Morris, R. J., eds, *Atlas of Industrialising Britain 1780–1914*. London 1986.

Von Tunzelmann, G. N., 'Technological and Organizational Change in Industry during the Early Industrial Revolution', in O'Brien, P. K. and Quinault, R., eds, *The Industrial Revolution and British Society: Essays in Honour of Max Hartwell*. Cambridge 1993.

Von Tunzelmann, G. N., 'Technology in the Early Nineteenth Century', in Floud, R. and McCloskey, D., eds, *The Economic History of Britain since 1700*, Vol. I, 2nd edition. Cambridge 1994.

Wadsworth, A. P. and Mann, J. de L., *The Cotton Trade and Industrial Lancashire 1600–1780*. Manchester 1931.

Walton, J. K., 'Proto-industrialisation and the First Industrial Revolution: The Case of Lancashire', in Hudson, P., ed., *Regions and Industries*. Cambridge 1989.

Warner, F., *The Silk Industry of the U.K.* London 1921.

Washbrook, D., 'Markets and Custom in Eighteenth-Century South India', unpublished paper, 1985.

Weatherill, L., *The Pottery Trade and North Staffordshire, 1660–1760*. Manchester 1971.

Weatherill, L., 'A Possession of One's Own: Women and Consumer Behaviour in England, 1660–1740', *Journal of British Studies*, XXV, 1986.

Weatherill, L., *Consumer Behaviour and Material Culture in Britain 1660–1760*. London 1988.

Webb, S. and B., *The History of Trade Unionism*. London 1902.

Weir, R. B., 'Brewing and Distilling', in Langton, J. and Morris, R. J., eds, *Atlas of Industrialising Britain 1780–1914*. London 1986.

Westerfield, R. B., *Middlemen in English Business* (1915). London 1968.

Whipp, R., 'Potbank and Unions: A Study of Work and Trade Unionism in the British Pottery Industry', unpublished Ph.D. thesis, Warwick University 1983.

Whyte, I., 'Proto-industrialisation in Scotland', in Hudson, P., ed., *Regions and Industries*. Cambridge 1989.

Wilkinson, W., 'Power Loom Developments', *Official Record of the Annual Conference of the Textile Institute*. Bolton 1927.

Williamson, J. G., 'Why was British Economic Growth so Slow during the Industrial Revolution?', *Journal of Economic History*, 44 (3), 1984.

Williamson, J. G., 'Debating the British Industrial Revolution', *Explorations in Economic History*, 24, 1987.

Williamson, J. G., *Coping with City Growth during the British Industrial Revolution*. Cambridge 1990.

Williamson, O. E., *Economic Institutions of Capitalism: Firms, Markets, Relational Contracting*. New York 1985.

Wilson, C., *England's Apprenticeship 1603–1763*. London 1965.

Wilson, C., 'The Other Face of Mercantilism', in Coleman, D. C., ed., *Revisions in Mercantilism*. London 1969.

Wilson, C. and Parker, G., *An Introduction to the Sources of European Economic History 1500–1800*. London 1977.

Wilson, R. G., 'The Supremacy of the Yorkshire Cloth Industry in the Eighteenth Century', in Harte, N. B. and Ponting, K. G., *Textile History and Economic History*. Manchester 1973.

Wolfe, E. R., *Europe and the People without History*. Berkeley 1982.

Wood, G. H., *The History of Wages in the Cotton Trade*. London 1910.

Wrightson, K., 'Household and Kinship in Sixteenth Century England', *History Workshop Journal*, XII, Autumn 1981.

Wrightson, K., *English Society 1500–1700*. London 1982.

Wrigley, E. A., 'A Simple Model of London's Importance in Changing English Society and Economy 1650–1750', in Patten, J., ed., *Pre-Industrial England*. Folkestone 1979.

Wrigley, E. A., 'The Growth of Population in Eighteenth Century England: a Conundrum Resolved', *Past and Present*, XCVIII, 1983.

Wrigley, E. A., *People, Cities and Wealth*. Oxford 1987.

Wrigley, E. A., 'Urban Growth and Agricultural Change: England and the Continent in the Early Modern Period', in Wrigley, E. A., *Peoples, Cities and Wealth*. Oxford 1987.

Wrigley, E. A., *Continuity, Chance and Change: The Character of the Industrial Revolution in England*. Cambridge 1989.

Wrigley, E. A., 'The Great Commerce of Every Civilised Society', *Scottish Economic and Social History*, 12, 1992.

Wrigley, E. A. and Schofield, R. S., *The Population History of England, 1541–1871: A Reconstruction*. Cambridge 1981.

Zeitlin, J., 'Craft Control and the Division of Labour: Engineers and Compositors in Britain 1890–1930', *Cambridge Journal of Economics*, 3, 1979.

INDEX

329

labour 57, 64; new 110–12; proto-
industrialization 66–72, 91–2
rural living standards 84–6, 101–2
Russia 124

Sabel, C. 194, 196
'safe box' factory 219, 238
St Bartholomew's Fair 210, 216
says and bays 104, 106, 209
scale: economies 80, 101, 144, 193–4,
200, 202, 206–7, 233; small-scale and
large-scale factories 198–206
Schmoller, Gustav 67
Schofield, R.S. 20, 86
Schumpeter, Elizabeth 32, 48
scientific management 183
Scotland 6, 114, 126; agriculture 158;
carpet industry 244; coal industry
44–5; cotton industry 28, 140, 142,
214; hand knitting 140; iron industry
200; linen 41, 43–4, 61, 72, 120,
212–13, 221, 229, 252; machinery
breaking 254; rural spinning 145–6;
textiles 41, 43–4
scribbling machinery 29, 109
scythesmiths 92, 98
Select Committee on Arts and
Manufactures (1824) 73–4
Select Committee on Manufactures,
Commerce and Shipping (1833) 252
self-acting mule 155, 175, 185–6, 233,
251, 254
self-exploitation 69, 205, 206
serge exports 106
sewing machine 173
sexual division of labour 69, 111, 141,
148–9, 156, 159, 165, 169, 250; and
apprenticeships 276–9; within
technologies 154–5
Sharpe, Pamela 9, 160
shearing frame 110, 246, 248
shearing process 246, 248, 253
Sheffield 25, 58, 161, 218; cutlery 47–8,
98, 132–3, 205–6, 256, 262–3, 272–3,
276; ironworks 47, 196; steel 48, 206,
257
Shelbourne, Lord 267
shipbuilding 51, 54
shoemaking 102
Sholl, Samuel 220
Shropshire 94, 103, 112
silk industry 38, 40, 43, 74, 92, 114;
factory system 228–9; origins 211–12;

spinning 242–3; Spitalfields 219–20,
228, 231, 244–5; weaving 244–5;
women in 139–40, 147–8, 153, 162;
work organization 219–21
skills 64, 173, 179–80, 262, 263; artisans
50, 74, 269, 271–6; defined 155–6;
division of labour 63, 75, 154–5,
250–3; female/juvenile 144–9
slave trade 117, 118
small-scale economies 205–6
small-scale factories 65–6, 74–5, 189,
190, 194, 196, 198–200, 262, 268;
Britain 203–5; United States 201–3
smelting: charcoal 45, 176; coke 45, 46,
97, 113, 176; copper 48; lead 55
Smith, Adam 8, 19, 73, 76, 77, 82, 93,
139, 268; natural progress 57–9;
urban and regional growth 59–61
smithing trades 259–60
Snell, Keith 111, 162
social change 57–76
social conflict 22
social control 100
social history 21–2, 170, 280, 283; of
technical change 169–88, 249
social institutions 175, 179–80, 182, 187,
188, 215
social power 183
social status 156; consumer behaviour
by 129, 130, 131–2
social structures 24, 181, 254, 282;
impact on work organization 215,
223–4
social values 76, 89
sociolegal institutions 175, 176
Soho foundry 260–1, 269, 271, 275
Sokoloff, K. 65–6, 75, 201
Sombart, Werner 67
Somerset 105, 109, 110–11, 150, 164,
253–4
South Sea Bubble 120
specialization 20–1, 25, 28, 69, 106, 108,
203–4; flexible 74–5, 130, 189, 194–5,
205–6; international 5, 82, 122, 180
spinning 42, 92, 109; employment of
women 115, 144–7, 149–51, 154–5;
silk 242–3; technical change 25,
235–43
spinning jenny 29, 40, 144, 154, 174–5,
229, 242; resistance to 6, 109–10,
149–50, 253–4; spread of 146–7,
236–9, 250–1